CONTENTS

Shamanism Dreams Visions:
The Uncollected Writings of Stanley Krippner

Jürgen Werner Kremer, Editor
with Laura Christine O'Donnell

1 Stanley Krippner: The Liminal Psychologist
   Etzel Cardeña

3 Altering Consciousness: A Tribute to Stanley Krippner
   Glenn C. Graves and *Sidian M. S. Jones*

8 Shamanism

11 The Psychology of Shamanism

17 Shamans, Sacred Places, and the Healing Earth

23 We Still Need Rituals in the 21st Century

26 Shamans as Healers, Counselors, and Psychotherapists

33 Hypnotic-like Procedures Used by Indigenous Healing Practitioners

46 Jim Morrison: The Crisis of a Failed Shaman

51 Learning from the Spirits:
    Candomble, Umbanda, and Kardecismo in Recife, Brazil

66 Mythic Themes in Navajo Healing, Maria Sabina's *Mazatec Velada*,
    and Mapuche Dreaming

75 Spirit Sickness and Soul Loss

80 The Future of Ethnomedicine

87 The Epistemology and Technologies of Shamanic States of Consciousness

101 Carlos Castaneda and Richard deMille: Differentiation Experiences from Events,
     and Validity from Authenticity in the Anthropology of Consciousness
     with Mark Schroll

106 Anyone Who Dreams Partakes in Shamanism

110 Indigenous Dream Models in South American Shamanic Cultures

116 Research Perspectives in Parapsychology and Shamanism

125 Parapsychology and Postmodern Psychology

132 How Healing Happens

Cover: Photo Illustration by George Berticevich, Copyright 2025

Spring/Summer 2025   Volume 34 Numbers 3 & 4

What Is ReVision?

Revisioning, as the name ReVision hints, has been central to the publication's forty year historical trajectory. As our understanding of the leading edge of transformative and consciousness-changing thinking has developed, so has the focus of our mission.

From its origins in humanistic and transpersonal psychologies, ReVision has shifted toward a framework of transdisciplinary, decolonial, and indigenous paradigms. From its origins as an academic journal it has shifted toward a publication which includes art, poetry, story, and articles that translate topics for a broader audience.

With a commitment to the future of humanity and all our relations, ReVision is dedicated to the exploration of issues that assert and value the transmotional and interconnected sovereignty of people before any institutions. Sovereignty and self-determination as foundations of peace require our human imagination as part of a sustainable world of stories and cultural practices in a particular place or ecology.

ReVision welcomes submissions from a wide range of disciplines using a broad spectrum of formats to deepen the process of inquiry, dialogue, and engaged participatory knowing and conversation.

Volume 34, Numbers 3 & 4 (978-1-7362314-5-6)

ReVision (ISSN 0275-6935) is published by *The Society for Indigenous and Ancestral Wisdom and Healing.*

Copyright © 2025 ReVision Publishing. Copyright retained by author when noted. The views expressed are not necessarily those of ReVision or its editors.

ReVision provides opportunities for publishing divergent opinions, ideas, or judgments.

Manuscript Submissions

We welcome manuscript submissions. Manuscript guidelines can be found on our webpage: http://revisionpublishing.org.

POSTMASTER: Send address changes to ReVision Publishing, P.O. Box 1855, Sebastopol, CA 95473.

Photo: Gary Newman

Subscriptions

For subscriptions mail a check to above address or go to www.revisionpublishing.org.

Individual Subscriptions

Subscription for four issues: $36 online only, $36 print only (international $72), $48 print and on-line (international $84).

Subscription for eight issues: $60 online only, $60 print only (international $96), $79 print and online (international $115).

Subscription for 12 issues: $72 online only, $72 print only (international $108), $96 print and online (international $132).

Institutional Subscriptions

$98 online only (international $134), $134 print and online (international $191).

Please allow six weeks for delivery of first issue.

Editorial Board

Editor
Jürgen Werner Kremer, PhD
Santa Rosa Junior College, Santa Rosa, CA

Associate Editor
Karen Jaenke, PhD
Independent Scholar, Richmond, CA

Assistant Editors
Michelle Boyle   Beth Glick   Laura Christine O'Donnell

Editorial and Production Management Team
Cristina Kaplan, MA
Poetry Editor

Gary Newman
Design and Production

Consulting Editors

John Adams, PhD
Saybrook University, San Francisco, CA

Matthew C. Bronson, PhD
O'Reilly Scool of Technology, UC Davis, Davis, CA

Allan Combs, PhD
California Institute of Integral Studies, San Francisco, CA

Apela Colorado, PhD
Worldwide Indigenous Science Network

Jorge Ferrer, PhD
California Institute of Integral Studies, San Francisco, CA

Mary Gomes, PhD
Sonoma State University, Rohnert Park, CA

Stanislav Grof, MD
California Institute of Integral Studies, San Francisco, CA

Stanley Krippner, PhD
California Institute of Integral Studies, San Francisco, CA

Joan Marler, MA
California Institute of Integral Studies, San Francisco, CA

S. Lily Mendoza, PhD
Oakland University, Rochester, MI

Alfonso Montuori, PhD
California Institute of Integral Studies, San Francisco, CA

Glenn Aparicio Parry, PhD
Circle for Original Thinking, Albuquerque, NM

James W. Perkinson, PhD
Ecumenical Theological Seminary, Detroit, MI

Joseph Prabhu, PhD
California State University Los Angeles, CA

Donald Rothberg, PhD
Spirit Rock Meditation Center, Woodacre, CA

Elenita Strobel, EdD
Sonoma State University, Rohnert Park, CA

Stanley Krippner

Photo: George Berticevich Photographer Copyright 2025

FOREWORD

Stanley Krippner: The Liminal Psychologist[1]

Etzel Cardeña, Lund University

Stanley Krippner

Stan is the most liminal person I know, straddling along noetic, cultural, disciplinary, and personal frontiers. I met him while I was doing my Ph.D. at the University of California, Davis, in the late 80s and our paths crossed many more times in conferences on shamanism, dreaming, and parapsychology. I could see how skillful he was as a presenter, neither rushing nor dragging his presentations, and ending always precisely in time.

He was always generous with his time even when I was a mere grad student and he was already a recognized figure. We have been friends since, although in the bargain he got, for better or worse, a friend who can also be a critic and does not think that he is a holy being, as some seem to do...

Etzel Cardeña holds the Thorsen Chair in psychology including parapsychology and hypnosis. He was elected Fellow of the American Psychological Association (APA) and the Association for Psychological Science (APS), among other organizations. His research, theoretical, historical, and pedagogical contributions have received 25 awards from various academic and professional organizations. His more than 400 publications include the influential books Varieties of Anomalous Experience (now in a second edition and translated into Portuguese), the 2 volumes of Altering Consciousness: Multidisciplinary Perspectives, Parapsychology: A Handbook for the 21st Century, and Acute Reactions to Trauma and Psychotherapy.

Photo: Chris Ryan

Stan has contributed to many areas in consciousness and we have co-authored various publications, foremost *Varieties of Anomalous Experience* (Cardeña, Lynn, & Krippner, 2000, 2014), which made history by being published by the American Psychological Association in 2000.

Stan's legacy includes supporting international communities and authors interested in the study of alterations of consciousness, anomalous cognition, and shamanism. The writeup for the American Psychological Association's 2002 Award for Distinguished Contributions to the International Advancement of Psychology credited his: "...efforts to expand the frontiers of the psychological study of consciousness... service interpreting indigenous traditions of world cultures for Western audiences (Anonymous, 2002)." He published an important overview of shamanism in response to this honor (Krippner, 2002).

From his work on dreaming and anomalous cognition, I would single out the ground-breaking studies on dream telepathy at the Maimonides Center (Ullman et al.,1973) and his 10 volumes—particularly the earlier volumes—or so of *Advances in Parapsychology Research* (with various co-editors). Stan, thanks to his bohemian side and acquaintance with many artists and musicians such as The Grateful Dead, also crossed the borders between art, science, and creativity, as in his studies of use of psychedelics and creativity (1985), and a telepathy test in a concert of the Grateful Dead (Krippner et al., 1973). His mind remains generous and creative, despite the many years weighing on his body.

All students of consciousness are in debt to this singular and courageous consciousness explorer.

Endnotes
[1] Adapted from: Cardeña, E. (2024).Celebrating three consciousness trailblazers: Jeanne Achterberg, Ruth-Inge Heinze, and Stanley Krippner. *Journal of Anomalous Experience and Cognition*, 4(1), 6-12. https://doi.org/10.31156/jaex.26220

References

Anonymous (2002). Stanley C. Krippner: Award for Distinguished Contributions to the International Advancement of Psychology (2002). American Psychologist, 57(11), 960–961. https://doi.org/10.1037/0003-066X.57.11.960

Cardeña, E., Lynn, S. J., & Krippner, S. (2000). Varieties of anomalous experience: Examining the scientific evidence. American Psychological Association.

Krippner, S. (1985). Psychedelic drugs and creativity. Journal of Psychoactive Drugs, 17(4), 235–245. https://doi.org/10.1080/02791072.1985.10524328

Krippner, S. C. (2002). Conflicting perspectives on shamans and shamanism: Points and counterpoints. American Psychologist, 57(11), 962–977. https://doi.org/10.1037/0003-066X.57.11.962

Krippner, S., & Achterberg, J. (2014). Anomalous healing experiences. In E. Cardeña, S. J. Lynn, & S. Krippner (Eds.), Varieties of anomalous experience: Examining the scientific evidence (2nd ed., pp. 273–301). American Psychological Association. https://doi.org/10.1037/14258-010

Krippner, S., Honorton, C., & Ullman, M. (1973). An experiment in dream telepathy with "The Grateful Dead." Journal of the American Society of Psychosomatic Dentistry and Medicine, 20, 9 - 17.

Ullman, M., & Krippner, S., with Vaughan, A. (1973). Dream telepathy: Experiments in nocturnal extrasensory perception. Macmillan.

---

gift
jim perkinson 11/14/98

rain consecration of tree
like endorphin down the column
like anointing
like messiah
like jazz
all on the hand
round the thigh
raising toe
creating mind
pumping blood
up bone like the
millennium
each milli-second
the flash of retinal release
the eye orgasm of hope
the shrine of lip on bread
the beat of heart storm
lightening on ocean
tornado on plain
corona of enlightenment heat
a single gift
a single gift
a single gift
of hand on hand on head
on god.

your hand on godhead
your bean in the mouth of being
your tongue stammering eternity
your knee the ground-wire of deity
your foot-soul the only depth of infinity
you are the message
you are the grammar
you are the silence between
you are what could be
you
are the only gift
there ever has been
given
like wind
through the tiny void
of charged attraction
that is your own unique molecule
and do you really think
you will disappear into the vast everything
like a drop of rain dying into the sea
or will your own broken open surface now
finally fill
with the entire ocean of what is?

Altering Consciousness: A Tribute To Stanley Krippner

Glenn C. Graves and Sidian M. S. Jones

Espiritismo ceremony, Sao Paulo, 1973

Stanley Curtis Krippner has dedicated his career to the exploration of the most enigmatic aspects of human consciousness. Born on October 4, 1932, in Edgerton, Wisconsin, Krippner found his early life marked by a voracious curiosity about the world's cultures and the puzzling aspects of the human psyche, as he was fascinated by the magicians and mentalists he encountered. His academic journey began with a Bachelor of Science degree from the University of Wisconsin–Madison, followed by a Master's degree and Ph.D. from Northwestern University's School of Education.

Photo: Stanley Krippner

Expanding and defining several areas in the study of consciousness

Krippner's first major academic appointment was at Kent State University, where he directed the Child Study Center in the School of Education. For three years, he instructed graduate students in how to diagnose children with learning disabilities and prepare programs for remediation, taking a "brain-based" approach rather than attributing their problems to poor teaching or poor parenting, approaches popular at the time (e.g., Krippner, 1971). He also taught classes on counseling and guidance, which became the focus of

Sidian Morning Star Jones is an award winning author and personal mythologist, someone who works with beliefs to help others reenchant and find meaning in life. Jones has spoken to audiences around the world and starred on a hit TLC TV show. His work has been featured on The Joe Rogan Experience, Stephen King, Apple, and Techcrunch. Jones has co-authored two books about, and is the grandson of legendary shaman Rolling Thunder, basis for the Billy Jack movies, subject of Martin Scorcese's The Rolling Thunder Revue.

Glenn Graves holds a PhD in Psychology with a specialization in Creativity and Existential-Humanistic Integrative Psychotherapy. He is the Director of Counseling Perspective, a group counseling practice based in Singapore, which also supports his MindfulPathway.com programs, which include neurotechnology in assessing and training a myriad of neurodivergent issues. Dr. Graves had the privilege of traveling to many countries with Dr. Stanley Krippner, over the years.

his doctoral dissertation (e.g., Krippner, 1961).

Krippner's career took a pivotal turn when he was asked to direct the Dream Laboratory at Maimonides Medical Center in Brooklyn, New York, in the 1960s. There he conducted groundbreaking research that explored the potential for psychic connections between individuals through nighttime dreaming. His work at Maimonides cemented his lifelong quest to understand and validate phenomena on the fringes of conventional psychological studies (e.g., Krippner, 1993).

Krippner has authored or co-authored over one thousand books and articles in peer-reviewed publications, most of them focused on the study of consciousness—in particular, parapsychology, dreams, hypnosis, post-traumatic stress disorder, and psychedelic art and music. Krippner often combined his interests as in his studies on using hypnosis to help students with learning disabilities (Krippner, 1977); on existential considerations when working with disabled people (Easton & Krippner, 1966); and on the creative aspects of dream reports (Krippner, 1981).

Krippner's most original contributions in the field of consciousness studies include his creation of psychological *models*, descriptive systems that can organize various behaviors and experiences. His model of various types of dissociation has been a useful construct (Krippner, 1997). Another model was used to compare various types of folk healers (1980), and still another proposed factors involved in producing apparent "stigmata" among spiritual adepts (Krippner & Kirkwood, 2008). He also devised a descriptive model used to compare cross-cultural aspects of the origin and function of dreams (e.g., Krippner, 1994; Krippner & Thompson, 1996).

Krippner and one of his students devised a scoring system for identifying spiritual content in dream reports (Casto, Krippner, & Tartz, 1999), which was also used to advantage with first-person reports of ayahuasca experiences (Krippner & Sulla, 2000). Krippner's studies on the content and function of dreams have contributed to a deeper understanding of their role in emotional processing, problem solving, and creativity (Krippner, 1981).

His most significant books in the consciousness field include *Dream Telepathy* (with Montague Ullman, 1973), *Personal Mythology* and *The Mythic Path* (with David Feinstein, 1988, 2008), and *Varieties of Anomalous Experience* (with Etzel Cardeña and Steven Jay Lynn, 2013). Krippner edited ten volumes of *Advances in Parapsychological Research*, a widely used resource (e.g., Krippner, 1977, 1987). Krippner developed a curriculum in consciousness studies for Saybrook University (Stang, 2019), which attracted funding that facilitated his many trips abroad (e.g., Vilenskaya, 1984).

Conducting rigorous parapsychological research that has passed the test of time

Krippner's foray into the field of parapsychology was marked by a commitment to rigorously explore phenomena that lie at the fringes of mainstream psychological science. His work in this domain encompasses the study of putative extrasensory perception, psychokinesis, and other "psi" phenomena, aiming to understand these experiences within a scientific framework.

He is best known for his studies of putative telepathy and precognition in dreams, co-authoring numerous articles with Montague Ullman, who founded the Dream Laboratory at Maimonides Medical Center (e.g., Ullman & Krippner, 1969; Ullman & Krippner, 2001), and with Charles Honorton, who was a welcome addition to the team (e.g., Honorton, Krippner, & Ullman, 1971; Krippner, Honorton, & Ullman, 1983).

The basic protocol for these studies was for a research participant to arrive at the Dream Laboratory early in the evening, meet the psychologist who would be "transmitting" the contents of a vivid art print, randomly chosen from a bevy of sealed envelopes (each containing a different art print), sit quietly while an experimenter attached electrodes to his or her head, enter the soundproof room, and fall asleep. Whenever the experimenters observed rapid eye movements on the electroencephalograph, they would wait about ten minutes and then awaken the participant, asking, "What is going through your mind?"

The responses were tape-recorded, transcribed, and sent to outside "judges," who attempted to match every night of dream reports to all the available art prints. The correct matches were compared to the incorrect matches to determine whether or not the correct ones had occurred by chance. The number of nights was determined in advance, so that there could be no "optional stopping." A few studies yielded results that were not statistically significant, but Krippner insisted on publishing them as well (Foulkes et al., 1972).

Contrary to the claim that Krippner's work in dream telepathy and precognition has not been replicated, a 2017 review in the *International Journal of Dream Research* surveyed fifty years of research on the topic, discovering that the rate of successful replications was similar to those based on more conventional psychological topics (Storm et al., 2017). Scoffers often claim that, when controls are tightened, significant results in parapsychological experiments disappear.

The 2017 review found the opposite; the tighter controls actually produced results that were equal to or somewhat better than other experiments. This was especially relevant to a study Krippner designed in which the experimenters monitoring the EEG dream reports had no idea of the purpose of the study (Krippner, Honorton, & Ullman, 1972). The studies in dream telepathy and precognition by several investigators were recognized as a basic data collection in an article published in *American Psychologist*, the flagship journal of the American Psychological Association (Cardeña, 2018).

Years after the final experiments had been concluded, Krippner worked with the neuroscientist Michael Persinger to explore the possible association of the scores obtained with the ambient geomagnetic environment (such as sunspots and electoral storms), finding that low geomagnetism was significantly associated with high ESP scores (Krippner & Persinger, 1996; Persinger & Krippner, 1989). In a later set of experiments with a Brazilian psychic claimant who manifested unusual psychokinetic effects, the opposite was discovered. In that case, higher geomagnetism was associated with elevated psychokinetic behavior (Krippner et al., 1996).

Conducting cross-cultural research in dream science, psychic claimants, and the psychology of shamanism

Krippner's interest in dreams extended beyond his decade at Maimonides. He accepted invitations to present workshops on dream interpretation in several countries, asking participants to write down a recent dream and then selecting those that could be used to teach various interpretive methods. The results were published in scientific journals (e.g., Krippner & Weinhold, 2001). Krippner used a content analysis system designed by psychologists Calvin Hall and Robert Ven de Castle (1966) for these studies, and also for studying the dreams of pregnant participants (Krippner et al., 1974) and those of male to female transgender participants (Krippner, Benjamin, & Allen, 1973; Krippner, 2022).

Krippner's curiosity about psychic claimants led him to explore several dimensions of their personalities. Since his colleague Ernest Hartmann (1991) had developed a scale to explore a person's "thick" or "thin" psychological boundaries, Krippner used it in several studies, noting that psychic claimants typically manifested "thin boundaries" (Krippner, Wickramasekera, & Tartz, 2002). He and his colleagues worked with such psychic claimants as Amyr Amiden (Krippner et al., 1995), J Z Knight (Krippner et al., 1998), and Eva Hellstrom (2004), not only exploring the nature of their purported feats, but looking the possible geomagnetic correlates of those reported effects.

His work with the psychology of shamans was instigated by his interviews with the Twyla, the Seneca Indian shaman, Don José Matsua, a Huichol shaman, and María Sabina, the Mazatec shaman whose psychedelic mushroom rituals were instrumental in founding the field of ethnomycology (Krippner & Winkelman, 1983). With Alberto Villoldo, he borrowed from Evan Harris Walker's theory of consciousness (eventually published in 2000) based on quantum physics (Krippner & Villoldo, 1976) to suggest the mechanism of unusual shamanic healing.

Krippner proposed an operational definition of *shamans* as community-sanctioned practitioners who obtain information in ways not available to their peers, using this information in the service of their community. He worked with the intertribal medicine man Rolling Thunder for two decades, documenting their encounters in two books authored with his grandson Sidian M. S. Jones (Jones & Krippner, 2012, 2016).

He remained aware that shamans could, at times, be "tricksters" who enhanced their status by sleight-of-hand, distraction of attention, and attributing meaning to coincidences (Rock & Krippner, 2011). As a result of his work with shamans, Krippner has been asked to write entries on the psychology of shamanism for various yearbooks and encyclopedias (e.g., Krippner, 2004). Moreover, in 2002, the *American Psychologist* published his article, "Conflicting Perspectives of Shamans and Shamanism," the first time this prestigious journal had published an entire article on shamanism.

Working on behalf of often-marginalized groups from the perspective of consciousness

Krippner has felt a bond with marginalized groups, having endured teasing and ridicule because of a frontal lisp in his childhood. Once it was corrected, he decided to become a speech therapist, spending two years working with children in public schools dealing with similar challenges. He often had children in his classes write stories about their dreams, using those stories during their lessons in speech improvement. (Krippner, 2024)

Krippner also felt an affinity with

> Krippner has been an acute observer of trauma and its effects on people's consciousness. His work in this area has explored the mechanisms of trauma, including how traumatic experiences can alter consciousness and affect memory, identity, and emotional regulation.

gifted and creative children, another often-marginalized group. His writings on the topic reflected his interest in consciousness, as he often reported their dreams, daydreams, and imaginative forays (Krippner & Meacham, 1968).

He was an early observer of how gender stereotypes blocked creativity (e.g., Krippner, 1967), and conducted several workshops for gifted children employing "hands-on" exercises in drama, painting, and filmmaking (e.g., Krippner & Blickenstaff, 1970).

Krippner has written about the cognitive aspects of creativity, in terms of its celebrated four Ps: Person, Process, Product, and Place (e.g., Krippner & Arons, 2020). But he also posited that creativity is not merely a cognitive function or a series of mental processes, but is deeply intertwined with the emotional, spiritual, and unconscious dimensions of human experience. His writings propose that accessing non-ordinary states of consciousness can provide individuals with a wealth of symbolic material, novel associations, and alternative perspectives that can enhance creative thinking and problem-solving abilities (source missing).

schools, he helped desegregate the hearing clinic and published an account of his efforts (Krippner, 2024).

These endeavors aligned with his interest in humanistic psychology, leading to awards from the APA Society of Humanistic Psychology and other organizations. At the same time, he was an early member of the Association for Transpersonal Psychology, writing papers on how it can become a vital element of psychological science (Friedman & Krippner).

When working with marginalized groups, Krippner became aware of how their belief systems often stunted their progress. With David Feinstein, he

including how traumatic experiences can alter consciousness and affect memory, identity, and emotional regulation. Post-traumatic stress disorder (PTSD) can take place as a result of war combat, abuse, rape, natural disasters, or any number of other potentially traumatizing events.

In his writings and seminars on trauma, Krippner has drawn upon the existing literature, describing the development of therapeutic techniques that address the complex needs of trauma survivors, incorporating storytelling, art, dreams, and body-centered practices to facilitate recovery and resilience.

Krippner is a prolific author, many of whose writings have attained prominence over the years. However, the quality of his work has not been consistent. He chaired dozens of doctoral dissertations, but a reviser for an accrediting organization found that several of them lacked rigor. At the same time, some of the dissertations he chaired have met with critical acclaim (Gordon, 2xxx).

> Veterans afflicted with war trauma are another marginalized group with whom Krippner has interacted, serving as an advisor for two organizations working with men and women suffering from PTSD (Post-Traumatic Stress Disorder).

Veterans afflicted with war trauma are another marginalized group with whom Krippner has interacted, serving as an advisor for two organizations working with men and women suffering from PTSD (Post-Traumatic Stress Disorder).

Krippner's background in consciousness studies gave him a unique perspective in working in PTSD, suggesting that therapists begin treatment by focusing on their clients' nightmares, teaching them how to transform them into ordinary dreaming through image rehearsal during the day. Once ordinary dreaming occurs, it becomes a lynchpin for further behavioral changes (Krippner & Taitz).

Given that African Americans are also an often marginalized group, it is notable that one of Krippner's earliest publications was written for a book on "White racism" (Krippner, 19). When working in the Richmond, Virginia. public

authored several books and articles on *personal mythology*, a concept employing ideas instigated by his childhood fascination with mythologies. He provided an operational definition of *myths*, noting that they were imaginative narratives that explained existential issues in ways that had behavioral consequences. In addition to personal myths, there were cultural myths, family myths, religious myths, and others (Feinstein & Krippner).

Krippner has given several workshops on both personal mythology and dream interpretation. In both, he emphasizes self-discovery, providing a framework in which people can uncover their own personal myths or interpret their own dreams.

Krippner has been an acute observer of trauma and its effects on people's consciousness. His work in this area has explored the mechanisms of trauma,

It is not uncommon for writers to "run out of steam" as they grow older. Krippner realized this and stopped doing serious writing when he turned 90. Moreover, Krippner's extensive work in fields such as parapsychology, consciousness studies, and shamanism has not been without its criticisms. These critiques often stem from the inherent challenges and controversies associated with researching phenomena that lie at the edges of mainstream scientific understanding.

Despite the criticisms, Krippner's contributions to psychological science have broadened the scope of scientific inquiry into human consciousness. He has fostered a more inclusive and open-minded approach to understanding the ways in which people experience their world.

Krippner always knew there was inherent wisdom in the inhabitants of a universe that was filled with wonder. He is an example of Albert Einstein's statement that "Nature hides her secrets because she is sublime, not because she is a trickster."

References

Cardeña, E. (2018). The evidence for parapsychological phenomena: A review. *American Psychologist*, 73(5), 663-677.

Cardeña, E., Lynn, S. J., & Krippner, S. (2013). *Varieties of anomalous experience: Examining the scientific evidence* (2nd ed.). American Psychological Association.

Casto, K. L., Krippner, S., & Tartz, R. (1999). The identification of spiritual content in dream reports. *Anthropology of Consciousness*, 10(1), 43-53.

Davies, J. A., & Pitchford, D. B. (Eds.) .(2015). *Stanley Krippner: A life of dreams, myths, and visions.* University Professors Press.

Easton, H., & Krippner, S. (1966). Disability, rehabilitation, and existentialism. In C. E. Beck (Ed.), *Guidelines for guidance: Readings in the philosophy of guidance* (pp. 427-433). William C. Brown.

Feinstein, D., & Krippner, S. (1988). *Personal mythology: The psychology of your evolving self.* Tarcher.

Feinstein, D., & Krippner, S. (2008). *The Mythic Path: Discovering the guiding stories of your past – Creating a vision for your future.* Energy Psychology Press.

Foulkes, D., Belvedere, E., Masters, R. E. L., Houston, J., Krippner, S., Honorton, C., & Ullman, M. (1972). Long-distance, "sensory bombardment" ESP in dreams: A failure to replicate. *Perceptual and Motor Skills*, 35, 731-734.

Hall, C., & Van de Castle, R. L. (1966). *The content analysis of dreams.* Appleton-Century-Crofts.

Honorton, C., Krippner, S., & Ullman, M. (1971). Telepathic transmission of art prints under two conditions. In E. Malinoff (Ed.), *Proceedings, 80th Annual Convention, American Psychological Association* (pp. 319-320). American Psychological Association.

Jones, S. M. S., & Krippner, S. (2012). *The voice of Rolling Thunder: A Medicine Man's wisdom for walking the Red Road.* (Bear

Jones, S. M. S., & Krippner, S. (Eds.). (2016). *The shamanic powers of Rolling Thunder: As experienced by Alberto Villoldo, John Perry Barlow and others.* Bear.

Hartmann, E. (1991). *Boundaries of the mind: A new theory of personality.* Basic Books.

Krippner, S. (1981). Access to hidden reserves of the unconscious through dreams in creative problem solving. *Journal of Creative Behavior*, 15, 11-23.

Krippner, S. (1993). Cross-cultural perspectives on hypnotic-like procedures used by native healing practitioners. In J. W. Rhue, S. J. Lynn, & I. Kirsch (Eds.), *Handbook of clinical hypnosis* (pp. 691-717). American Psychological Association.

Krippner, S. (1980). A suggested typology of folk healing and its relevance to parapsychological investigation. *Journal of the Society for Psychical Research*, 50, 491-500.

Krippner, S. (Ed.). (1977). *Advances in parapsychological research. Vol. 1.* New York: Plenum Press. (357)

Krippner, S. (1999, Summer). Protecting indigenous knowledge from ecopiratism. *Shaman's Drum*, pp. 8, 10-11.

Krippner, S. (1971). Time, space, and dyslexia: Central nervous system factors in reading disability. *Journal of the Reading Specialist*, 10, 128-148.

Krippner, S. (1961). The vocational preferences of high-achieving and low-achieving junior high school students. *Gifted Child Quarterly*, 5, 88-90.

Krippner, S. (1970). Race, intelligence, and segregation: The misuse of scientific data. In B. N. Schwartz & R. Disch (Eds.), *White racism* (pp. 452-464). (Dell/Laurel))

Krippner, S. (1972). Marijuana and Viet Nam: Twin dilemmas for American youth. In R. S. Parker (Ed.), *The emotional stress of war, violence, and peace* (pp. 176-225). (Stanwix House)

Krippner, S. (1977). Individual hypnosis, group hypnosis, and the improvement of academic achievement. In I. A. Greenberg (Ed.), *Group hypnosis, hypnotherapy and hypnodrama* (pp. 123-135). Nelson-Hall

Krippner, S. (1997). The varieties of dissociative experience. In S. Krippner & S. Powers (Eds.), *Broken images, broken selves: Dissociative narratives in clinical practice* (pp. 336-361). New York: Brunner/Mazel.

Krippner, S. (Ed.). (1987). *Advances in parapsychological research. Vol. 5.* Jefferson, NC: McFarland.

Krippner, S. (1993). The Maimonides ESP-dream studies. *Journal of Parapsychology*, 57, 39-54.

Krippner, S. (1994). A 10-facet model of dreaming for use in cross-cultural studies. *Dream Network*, 13(1), 9-11.

Krippner, S. (1967). block creativity. *Gifted Child Quarterly*, 11, 144- The Ten Commandments that 156.

Krippner, S. (1990). Psychedelics, hypnosis, and creativity. In C. T. Tart (Ed.), *Altered states of consciousness: A book of readings* (3rd ed.), (pp. 324-349). (Harper Collins)

Krippner, S. (1999, Summer). Protecting indigenous knowledge from ecopiratism. *Shaman's Drum*, pp. 8, 10-11.

Krippner, S. (2002). Conflicting perspectives on shamans and shamanism: Points and counterpoints. *American Psychologist*, 57, 961-977.

Krippner, S. (2012). The psychedelic adventures of Alan Watts. In P. J. Columbus & D. L. Rice (Eds.), *Alan Watts—Here and now: Contributions to psychology, philosophy, and religion* (pp. 83 102). (State University of New York Press)

Krippner, S. (in press). Foreword. In M. Winkelman (Ed.), *Handbook of entheogenic healing.*

Krippner, S., & Barrett, D. (2019). Transgenerational trauma: The role of epigenetics. *Journal of Mind and Behavior*, 40(1), 53-62.

Krippner, S. (2004). The dreams and visions of Eva Hellstrom: A Swedish psychic claimant. *Journal of the Society for Psychical Research*, 68, 210-225.

Krippner, S. (2004). Psychology of shamanism. In M.N. Walter & E.J.N. Fridman (Eds.), *Shamanism: An encyclopedia of world beliefs, practices, and culture* (pp. 204-211). ABC-CLIO.

Krippner, S., & Weinhold, J. (2001). Gender differences in the content analysis of 240 dream reports from Brazilian participants in dream seminars. *Dreaming*, 11, 35-42.

Krippner, S. (2022). Thirty dreams from transgender females in retrospect. *DreamTime*, 39(1), 17-18.

Krippner, S. (2024). *A chaotic life: Memoirs of a pioneering humanistic psychologist.* (University Professors Press)

Krippner, S. (1980). A suggested typology of folk healing and its relevance to parapsychological investigation. *Journal of the Society for Psychical Research*, 50, 491-500. *Fields*, No. 10, 25-31. (216)

Krippner, S., & Arons, M. (2020). Creativity: Person, product, or process? In A.M. Bland & S. Arons (Eds.), *The new-old: Recollections, reflections, and reconnoiterings of Mike Arons* (pp. 89-100). Colorado Springs, CO: University Professors Press.

Krippner, S., Benjamin, H., & Allen, V. (1973). *Case history data from 392 male and 71 female transsexuals* (Monograph of the American Society of Psychosomatic Dentistry and Medicine.

Krippner, S., & Blickenstaff, R. (1970). The development of self-concept as part of an art workshop for the gifted. *Gifted Child Quarterly*, 14, 163-166.

Krippner, S., & Kirkwood, J. (2008). Sacred bleeding: The language of stigmata. In J. Harold Ellens (Ed.), *Miracles: God, science, and psychology in the paranormal* (Vol. 2, pp. 154-175). Westport, CT: Praeger.

Krippner, S., & Meacham, W. (1968). Consciousness and the creative process. *Gifted Child Quarterly*, 12, 141-157.

Krippner, S., Wickramasekera, I., & Tartz, R. (2002). Scoring thick and scoring thin: The boundaries of psychic claimants. *Journal of Subtle Energies*, 11(1), 43-61.

Krippner, S., & Sulla, J. (2000). Identifying spiritual content in reports from ayahuasca sessions. *International Journal of Transpersonal Studies*, 19, 59-76.

Krippner, S., Honorton, C., & Ullman, M. (1983). An experiment in dream telepathy with the Grateful Dead. In P. Grushkin (Ed.), *Grateful Dead: The official book of the Dead Heads* (p. 90). New York: Quill.

Krippner, S., Wickramasekera, I., Wickramasekera, J., & Winstead, C.W., III. (1998). The Ramtha phenomenon: Psychological, phenomenological, and geomagnetic data. *Journal of the American Society for Psychical Research*, 92, 1-24.

Krippner, S., Posner, N., Pomerance, W., & Fischer, S. (1974). An investigation of dream content during pregnancy. *Journal of the American Society for Psychosomatic Dentistry and Medicine*, 21, 111-123.

Krippner, S., & Persinger, M. (1996). Evidence for enhanced congruence between dreams and distant target material during periods of decreased geomagnetic activity. *Journal of Scientific Exploration*, 10, 487-493.

Krippner, S., & Meacham, W. (1968). Consciousness and the creative process. *Gifted Child Quarterly*, 12, 141-157.

Krippner, S., Honorton, C., & Ullman, M. (1972). A second precognitive dream study with Malcolm Bessent. *Journal of the American Society for Psychical Research*, 66, 269-279.

Krippner, S., Winkler, M., Weil, P., Amiden, A., Lal Arora, H., Kelson, R., & Crema, R. (1995). The magenta phenomena, Part II: Twenty Sessions in Brasilia, March 1994. *Exceptional Human Experience*, 13, 44-63.

Krippner, S., & Thompson, A. (1996). A 10-facet model of dreaming applied to dream practices of sixteen Native American cultural groups. *Dreaming*, 6, 71-96.

Krippner, S., & Villoldo, A. (1976). *The realms of healing.* Millbrae, CA: Celestial Arts.

Krippner, S., & Winkelman, M. (1983). Maria Sabina: Wise lady of the mushrooms. *Journal of Psychoactive Drugs*, 15, 225-228.

Krippner, S., Winkler, M., Amiden, A., Crema, R., Kelson, R., Lal Arora, H., & Weil, P. (1996). Physiological and geomagnetic correlates of apparent anomalous phenomena observed in the presence of a Brazilian "sensitive." *Journal of Scientific Exploration*, 10, 281-298.

Paulson, D., & Krippner, S. (2007). *Haunted by combat: Understanding PTSD in war veterans including women, reservists, and those coming back from Iraq.* Praeger.

Persinger, M. A., & Krippner, S. (1989). Dream ESP experiments and geomagnetic activity. *Journal of the American Society for Psychical Research*, 83, 101-116.

Rock, A., & Krippner, S. (2011). *Demystifying shamans and their world: A multidisciplinary study.* Imprint Academic.

Stang, D. (2019, April). Stanley Krippner's six decades of consciousness studies [Interview]. *The Searchlight*, 28(2), 1; 6-7.

Storm, L. et al. (1972). On the correspondence between dream reports and content of target material under laboratory conditions: A meta-analysis of dream ESP studies, 1966-2016. *International Journal of Dream Studies*, 10 (2), 140.

Ullman, M., & Krippner, S. (1969). A laboratory approach to the nocturnal dimension of paranormal experience: Report of a confirmatory study using the REM monitoring technique. *Biological Psychiatry*, 1, 259-270.

Ullman, M., & Krippner, S. (2001). A laboratory approach to the nocturnal dimension of paranormal experience: Report of a confirmatory study using the REM monitoring technique. In K.R. Rao (Ed.), *Basic research in parapsychology* (2nd ed., pp. 142-156). Jefferson, NC: McFarland.

Ullman, M., & Krippner, S., with Vaughan, A. (1973). *Dream telepathy: Experiments in nocturnal extrasensory perception.* (Macmillan)

Vilenskaya, L. (1984). Folk healing in Indonesia and around the world: Interview with Dr. Stanley Krippner. *Psi Research*, 3(3/4), 149-157. (535)

Walker, E.H. (2000). *The physics of consciousness.* Perseus.

Zingrone, N., & Leverett, D. (Eds.). (2022). Women in Parapsychology. *Journal of Anomalistics.*

Shamanism

Stanley Krippner

Stanley Krippner's drum, by Alison Berkshire and Charlie Joseph (2011)

The term *shaman* is a social construct, one that has been described, not unfairly, as "a made-up, modern, Western category" (Taussig, 1989, p. 57). This term describes a particular type of indigenous practitioner who attends to the medical, psychological, and spiritual needs of a community, one that has granted that practitioner privileged status.

Shamans claim to engage in specialized activities that enable them to access valuable information that is not ordinarily available to other members of their community. Hence, *shamanism* can be described as a body of techniques and activities that supposedly enable its practitioners to access information that is not ordinarily attainable by members of the social group that gave them privileged status. These practitioners use this information in attempts to meet the medical, psychological, and spiritual needs of this group and its members.

Contemporary shamanic practitioners exist at the band, nomadic–pastoral, horticultural–agricultural, and state levels of societies. There are many types of shamans. For example, among the Cuna Indians of Panama, the *abisua* shaman heals by singing, the *inaduledi* specializes in herbal cures, and the *nele* focuses on diagnosis. The origin of the word "shaman" is often traced to the Siberian Tungus term for "one who is excited, moved, or raised." Alternative derivations are the Tungus word for "inner heat" and a Sanskrit term for "singer of songs."

The term entered the Western lexicon in the 17th century and anthropologists began to apply the term "shaman" to practitioners they observed in various native societies whose activities were similar. However, it is more accurate to use a society's term since there is considerable variety of practice despite the commonality of activities. Responding to the assertion that use of the word "shaman" should be restricted to the indigenous cultures of Central Asia, White (2004) stated that "shamanism is a transcultural human phenomenon that may manifest differently in different cultures" (p. 14).

Echoing White's assertion, the Buryat Mongol shaman Sarangerel (2001) wrote that techniques from her tradition "can be used by shamans from any culture or nationality" and "most [techniques] have parallels in other types of shamanism" (2001, p. x).

Krippner, S. (2005). Shamanism. In J. Henry (Ed.), *Parapsychology: Research on exceptional experiences* (pp. 149-163). New York: Routledge.

Photo: Jurgen Kramer

Winkelman's (2010) seminal cross-cultural study focused on 47 societies' *magico-religious practitioners*, who claim to interact with *nonordinary dimensions* of human existence. This interaction involves special knowledge of purported *spirit entities* and how to relate to them, as well as *special powers* that supposedly allow these practitioners to influence the course of nature or human affairs.

Winkelman coded each type of practitioner separately on such characteristics as the type of magical or religious activity performed; the technology used; the consciousness-altering procedures used (if any); the practitioner's cosmology and worldview; and each practitioner's perceived power, psychological characteristics, socioeconomic status, and political role.

Winkelman's statistical analysis yielded four practitioner groups: (a) the shaman complex (shamans, shamanic healers, and healers); (b) priests and priestesses; (c) diviners, seers, and mediums; (d) malevolent practitioners (witches and sorcerers). Shamans were most often present at the band level. Priests and priestesses were most present in horticultural/agricultural communities, and diviners and malevolent practitioners were observed in state-level societies.

Most diviners report that they are conduits for a spirit's power and claim not to exercise personal volition once they have *incorporated* these spirit entities. When shamans interacted with spirits, the shamans were almost always dominant; if the shamans suspended volition, it was only temporary. For example, shamans surrender volition during some Native American ritual dances when there is an intense *perceptual flooding*. Nonetheless, shamans purportedly knew how to enter and exit this type of intense experience.

Winkelman (2010) proposed that shamans represent a *biologically derived human specialization*, and that these potentials are actualized through social adaptations. These potentials can be described as *neurognostic* because they involve neural networks that provide the biological substrate for ways of knowing. Neurognostic potentials provide the basis for those forms of perception, cognition, and affect that are structured by the organism's neurological systems. A variety of procedures, agents, and other technologies are available to evoke limbic system slow wave discharges that synchronize the frontal cortex.

In addition, shamans can be characterized as *fantasy-prone*, endowed with capacities, genetic to some degree, which facilitates their use of imaginative processes. Paradoxically, shamans are characterized both by an acute perception of their environment and by imaginative fantasy. These traits (the ability to construct categories, the potential for pretending and role-playing, and the capacity to experience the natural world vividly) gave shamans an edge over peers who had simply embraced life as it presented itself, without the filters of myth or ritual. All of these traits may be related to the evolution of the human brain, namely the development of specialized subsystems that are activated during shifts in consciousness.

> The hallmark of cortical evolution is not the ever-increasing sophistication of specialized cortical circuitry but an increasing representational flexibility that allows environmental factors to shape the human brain's structure and function.

The hallmark of cortical evolution is not the ever-increasing sophistication of specialized cortical circuitry but an increasing representational flexibility that allows environmental factors to shape the human brain's structure and function. Shamanic technologies may represent the initial institutionalized practices for this integration, both through shifts in consciousness and community bonding rituals. These practices became codified in the form of myth, ritual, and ceremony, providing for social solidarity and specialization. Shamanic practices may have impacted human evolution in general; Dennett (2006) has observed that the ailments that early humans took to shamans for treatment could have been precisely those hospitable to placebo responses

Recurrent themes in the literature emphasize the shaman's role as mediator between the human and other-than-human worlds, the shaman's proficiency in entering various types of *trance* or *alternate states of consciousness*, the shaman's claim to access special or otherwise inaccessible knowledge, and the shaman's need to derive authority and sanction from the community that he or she serves.

Shamans enter their profession in a number of ways, depending on the traditions of their community. Some shamans inherit the role. Others may display particular bodily signs, behaviors, or experiences that might constitute a *call to shamanize*. In some cases, the call arrives late in life, giving meritorious individuals opportunities to continue their civil service, or, conversely, an individual's training may begin at birth.

The training mentor may be an experienced shaman or a spirit entity. The skills to be learned vary, but usually include diagnosis and treatment of ill-

Stanley drumming

ness, contacting and working with benevolent spirit entities, appeasing or fighting malevolent spirit entities, supervising sacred rituals, interpreting dreams, assimilating herbal knowledge, predicting the weather, and mastering their self-regulation of bodily functions and attentional states.

The Western academic and scholarly discourse with shamanism took place over several centuries, and originally was hostile and derogatory. Shamans were described as "demonic" and "diabolical," later as "schizoid" or "severely neurotic." However, contemporary scholarship has gained valuable insights by studying shamanic epistemology, phenomenology, and psychophysiology (Rock and Krippner, 2011; Winkelman, 2010).

Shamans and their belief systems are repositories of herbal knowledge, mythic enactments, and ecological concerns, all of which hold relevance to existential human concerns in the 21st century.

References

Dennett, D. (2006). *Breaking the spell: Religion as a natural phenomenon.* New York: Viking.

Rock, A. J., & Krippner, S. (2011). *Demystifying shamans and their world.* Exeter, UK: Imprint Academic.

Taussig, M. (1987). *Shamanism, colonialism, and the wild man: A study in terror and healing.* Chicago, IL: University of Chicago Press.

Sarangerel. (2001). *Chosen by the spirits: Following your shamanic calling.* Rochester, VT: Destiny Books.

White, T. (2004). *Exploring the roots of shamanism.* Shaman's Drum, 66, 10-18.

Winkelman, M. (2010). *Shamanism* (2nd ed.). Santa Barbara, CA: Praeger.

---

healing dark (63)
jim perkinson 12/12/98

spray of bullet words
like broken teeth in the ear
chattering cold truth
play of marimba feet
on the street of hot pot hole
parading grins of groins on fire
and they say the light heals
as it reveals the precise place
of compromise
that the messiah is the knife thrust
cutting black in half like a stiletto
of steel on well-chained meat.
are you, god,
a white stab of bright
between the arms
holding the child of hunger?
the revelation of shadow as despair
over the severed testicle?
the plunge through the pink gate
of defiant no-ness when
the legs lock against the thrust?
are you what scours the mind of thought
rubs raw the closed lid of desire
billows hope into a fantasy rain
breaks the wall of resistance into an
archaeological dig?
are you only light
and never a wrapped blanket
of warm is-ness?
are you always vision
seeking to light up the brain
like a synaptic volcano?
are you always clear vodka burn
in the stomach of fear?
candle of smoking hardness
staring in the eye of saint?
space is night
the bang is quiet hum of quasar
being is unseen attraction
between the opposites
electron is here and there
around the navel
and nothing is the medium of all.
do you always come like comet?
do you always pry the iris?
do you always quantify?
are you a blade?
do you cry?
can you cover
me
this
once
like a
storm
after
it
is
over?

i need you, tonight, god
not as illumination, but
like a wet lick of tongue
in the dark.

The Psychology of Shamanism

Stanley Krippner

Stanley Krippner with Holger Kalweit and Mongolian shaman

Krippner, S. (2008). The psychology of shamanism. In A. Davis & B. Horrigan (Eds.), *Conference proceedings: Shamanism & shamanic practice: Society for shamanic practitioners, fourth annual conference* (pp. 39-45). Santa Fe, NM: Society for Shamanic Practitioners.

Photo: Stanley Krippner

The psychology of shamanism has been ignored for many decades because psychologists did not value the shamanic tradition, and because earlier models of science could not do justice to its complexity. Developments in psychological phenomenology, psychological anthropology, and qualitative research, however, embody both the perspective and the tools to bring rigor and imagination to an investigation of shamanic experience that will lend understanding to its contents and its structure (Krippner, 2002). For example, Walsh (2001) has provided an analysis of shamanic phenomenology, concluding that it is "clearly distinct from schizophrenic, Buddhist, and yogic states" (p. 34), especially on such important dimensions as awareness of the environment, concentration, control, sense of identity, arousal, affect, and mental imagery.

From a psychological perspective, shamans can be described as community sanctioned spiritual practitioners who claim to deliberately modify their attention in an attempt to access information not ordinarily available to members of their social group. Shamans use this information in their attempts to ameliorate the physiological, psychological, and spiritual problems faced by the group members who gave them shamanic status. Shamans appear to have been humankind's first psychotherapists, first physicians, first magicians, first performing artists, first storytellers, and first weather forecasters (Eliade, 1951/1964). They were originally active in hunting/gathering and fishing tribes and still exist there in their most unadulterated form; however, shamanic and shamanistic practitioners also exist in nomadic-pastoral, horticultural, agricultural, and even urban societies today.

Shamanic Roles

Winkelman's (1992) seminal cross-cultural study of 47 societies focused upon *magical-religious practitioners*, i.e., those individuals who occupy a socially recognized role which has as its basis an interaction with the nonordinary, non-consensual dimensions of existence. This interaction involves special knowledge of purported spirit entities and how to relate to them, as well as special powers that allow these practitioners to influence the course of nature or human affairs in ways not ordinarily possible.

Winkelman coded each type of practitioner separately on such characteristics as the type of magical or religious activities performed, the techniques employed, the procedures used to alter consciousness, the practitioner's mythological worldview, and the practitioner's psychological characteristics, perceived power, socioeconomic status, and political role. Statistical analysis provided a division into four groups: (1) the shaman complex (shamans, shaman-healers, and healers); (2) priests and priestesses; (3) diviners, seers, and mediums; (4) malevolent practitioners (witches and sorcerers).

It turned out that the shaman was most often present in hunting/gathering and fishing societies. However, the introduction of horticulture and agriculture coincided with the rise of priests and priestesses, and of organized religions. Shamans lost much of their power to priests, but retained their healing abilities. Even so, shamanic oral traditions differ from the body of sacred scripture as maintained by an organized priesthood, remaining flexible and adaptive, each situation being unique.

Political differentiation of the society led to a further division of labor into that of healers, mediums, and malevolent practitioners. Any given society may have one or more magical-religious practitioner. Among the !Kung of southwest Africa, for example, the majority of males are magical-religious practitioners as well as a sizable minority of females (Katz, 1981).

Using Winkelman's terminology, the shaman-healer specializes in healing practices, while the healer typically works without the dramatic alterations of consciousness that characterize the shaman and, to a lesser extent, the shaman-healer. Diviners (as well as seers and mediums) act on a client's request to heal or to make prophecies after they have "incorporated" spirits.

These practitioners typically report that they are conduits for the spirits' power, and claim not to exercise personal volition once they "incorporate" (or are "possessed by") the spirits. Shamans, on the other hand, frequently interact with the spirits and sometimes "incorporate" them, but remain in control of the process, only suspending volition temporarily.

For example, volition is surrendered during some Native American ritual dances when there is an intense "flooding." Nevertheless, the shamans purportedly know how to enter and exit this type of intense experience (Winkelman, 2000). Malevolent practitioners are thought to have control over some of the "lower" spirits as well as access to power through rituals. Typically, they do not see their mission as empowering a community as a whole (as do the shamans). Rather, sorcerers are employed by individual members of their community to bring harm to enemies (inside or outside the community) or to seek favor from spirit entities for specific individuals through sorcery, witchcraft, hexes, and spells.

The more complex a society, the more likely it is to have representatives of each type of practitioner, except for the prototypical shaman. It should be kept in mind, of course, that categories are never absolute; some practitioners are difficult to classify and others switch roles according to the occasion (Heinze, 1992).

Many writers reserve the word "shamanic" to refer to practitioners and practices that dearly fall within the domain of the shaman or the shaman-healer. The same writers use the word "shamanistic" to refer to practitioners and practices that are related to the shamanic realm, but which are basically adaptations of it because one or more of the critical criteria is absent (e. g, community sanction, voluntary control of shifts in attention).

Shamanic Selection and Training

Shamans enter their profession in a number of ways, depending on the traditions of their community. Some shamans inherit the role. Others may display bodily signs (e.g., an extra digit, albinism, an unusual birthmark), behaviors (e.g., bodily fits and seizures, behavior patterns culturally associated with the opposite gender), or experiences (e.g., vivid dream recall, professed out-of-body activity). Depending on the potential shaman's culture, any of these might constitute a *call to shamanize*.

In addition, future shamans might survive a nearfatal disease and interpret this phenomenon as a call. Spirit entities might call them in dreams or in daytime reveries (Heinze, 1991, pp. 146-156). These calls may come at any age, depending on a society's tradition; in some cases, the call arrives late in life, giving meritorious individuals opportunities to continue their service to the community in ways that utilize their life experiences. On the other hand, the strange and erratic behaviors of some tribal members may be interpreted by the community as a call, thereby canalizing potentially disruptive actions into behavior patterns that are perceived to be beneficial (Katz, 1981).

In some societies, there is no formal training program, while in others the training process may last for several years. The mentors may be older shamans or even spirit entities (e.g., one's ancestors, power animals, nature spirits) all of whom are said to give instructions in the neophyte's dreams. The skills to be learned vary from society to society, but usually include diagnosis and treatment of illness, contacting spirit entities from nonordinary dimensions, supervising sacred rituals, interpreting dreams, predicting the weather, herbal knowledge, prophecy, and mastering the self-regulation of bodily functions and attentional states.

So-called spirit entities need to be contacted for different purposes. If they are dissatisfied they have to be propitiated; if a person dies without leaving a will, the deceased person's spirit needs to be contacted to determine property dispersion; if a deceased person's spirit is causing trouble, he or she needs to be appeased. Magical performance of one sort or another is learned, whether it be sleight of hand, taking advantage of synchronous events, or the purported utilization of what Westerners would call "parapsychological phenomena" (e.g., "extrasensory perception,• "psy-

> Some shamans, perhaps, have been psychotic, but, nonetheless, have been honored by the community as long as they served social needs.

chokinesis"). In most shamanic societies, a variety of chants, dances, songs, epic poems, stories, and/or symbols must be learned and used when appropriate. Some tribes arrange a special feast when the initiate passes a phase of his or her training.

In many instances, a society recognized several types of shamans. Among the Gold Eskimos, only the *siurku* shaman knows how to heal, the *nyemanti* shaman performs special rituals over a deceased person's soul after his or her death, and the *kasati* shaman conveys the soul of the deceased to the spirit world (Kalweit, 1984/1988, p. 139). Among the Cuna Indians of Panama; the *abisua* shaman heals by singing, the *inaduledi* specializes in herbal cures, and the *nele* focuses on diagnosis (Krippner, 1993).

It would be erroneous to assume that shamans represent a single constellation of traits, or that there is a "shamanic personality." Some shamans, perhaps, have been psychotic, but, nonetheless, have been honored by the community as long as they served social needs. More often, shamans undoubtedly have been men and women of great talent, mastering a complex vocabulary and a treasury of knowledge concerning herbs, rituals, healing procedures, and the purported spirit world.

Shamanic Personality Traits

Some social scientists have observed the links between shamanism and changed states of consciousness, concluding that these are symptomatic of schizophrenia. Silverman (1967) postulated that shamanism is a form of acute schizophrenia because the two conditions have in common "grossly non-reality-oriented ideation, abnormal perceptual experiences, profound emotional upheavals, and bizarre mannerisms" (p. 22).

According to Silverman, the only difference between shamanic states and contemporary schizophrenia in Western industrialized societies is "the degree of cultural acceptance of the individual's psychological resolution of a life crisis" (p. 23). Silverman claimed that the social supports available to the shaman are "often completely unavailable to the schizophrenic in our culture" (p. 29).

Devereux (1961), among others, conceptualized shamans as neurotics, epileptics, and/or hysterics.

Boyer, Klopfer, Brawer, and Kawai (1964) attempted to gather data regarding this controversy by administering Rorschach inkblots to 12 male Apache shamans, 52 non-shamans, and 7 "pseudoshamans" who claimed to possess special powers but who had not been accorded shamanic status by members of their community. Rorschach analysis demonstrated that the shamans showed as high a degree of reality testing potential as did members of the non-shamanic group.

"Pseudoshamans" were more variable on this dimension and demonstrated "impoverished personalities" (p. 179). The shamanic group was equally able to approach ambiguous stimuli as were the non-shamans, but showed a higher degree of ability to "regress in the service of the ego," a keener awareness of peculiarities, more theoretical interests, and more "hysterical" tendencies.

These tendencies were in evidence when the team examined the high frequency of anatomical and sexual responses to the Rorschach inkblots, as well as the frequent use of color. Even

> Many Siberian tribes often select "soft men" as shamans, and Siberian shamans in general frequently crossdress during their rituals in order to partake of the opposite gender's power.

so, the authors stated, "In their mental approach, the shamans appear less hysterical than the other groups" (p. 176). The study concluded that the shamans were "healthier than their societal co-members .... This finding argues against [the] stand that the shaman is severely neurotic or psychotic, at least insofar as the Apaches are concerned" (p. 179).

Noll (1983) compared verbal reports regarding the phenomenology of their unusual experiences from both schizophrenics and shamans to criteria in the 3rd edition of the *Diagnostic and Statistical Manual of Mental Disorders*. He reported that important phenomenological differences exist between the two groups and that the "schizophrenic metaphor" of shamanism is untenable (p. 455). Indeed, some social scientists (e.g., Peters Et Price-Williams, 1983) claim that such altered states as spirit possession and out-of-body experience can be therapeutic in nature.

Wilson and Barber (1981) have identified fantasy-prone personalities among their hypnotic subjects. This group is highly imaginative but, for the most part, neither neurotic nor psychotic. It is likely that many shamans would fall within this category, as the shaman's visions and fantasies are thought to represent activities in the spirit world. Also, the shaman typically exhibits considerable charisma as what Jungians refer to as a *psychopomp*, a culturally validated figure who mediates between realities. Among the psychopomp's duties are transporting souls of the dead to the spirit world, as well as travelling to the spirit world to receive instructions or to petition favor from the deities.

Cross-gender behavior has been reported to characterize shamans in many societies. Williams (1986) reviewed the way in which Native American cultures dealt with sexual diversity, finding that most tribes b.elieved that someone who is "unusual" could be easily accommodated without being regarded as "abnormal." Many tribes directed what Westerners would refer to as "effeminate" males and "masculine" females into shamanic roles, recognizing their sensitivity, androgyny, and capacity for empathy.

Many Siberian tribes often select "soft men" as shamans, and Siberian shamans in general frequently crossdress during their rituals in order to partake of the opposite gender's power. These practices are also common in Polynesia and Korea where androgynous males who serve as shamans are highly regarded for their healing abilities as well as for their purported knowledge of future events.

Altered States

Some Russian anthropologists claim that the first shamans were nature healers but during a later feudal phase of social evolution, they invented spirits that necessitated the inculcation of altered states of consciousness (ASCs) to contact them and communicate with them (Hoppal, 1984). Berman (2000) suggested that "heightened awareness" may be a more accurate description than "altered states" because shamans' intense experience of the natural world is described by them in such terms as "things often seem to blaze" (p. 30).

Most other scholars, however, favor the idea that ASCs are basic to shamanism, especially spirit "incorporation" and out-of-body experience or "journeying." Bourguignon (1974) surveyed 488 societies (57o/o of those represented in an ethnographic atlas) and discovered that 437 or 890ib were reported to have one or more institutionalized, culturally patterned ASC (p. 11). She concluded that the capacity to experience ASCs was a basic psychobiological capacity of human beings, a conclusion supported by Winkelman's (2000) review of pertinent psychoneurological data.

Mithen's (1996) vivid portrayal of the mind's "prehistory" describes the emergence of what he calls the *cognitive fluidity* that caused the cultural explosion of the Middle and Upper Paleolithic Ages, and it is likely that shamans and their ASCs were manifestations of this fluidity.

Peters and Price-Williams (1980) compared 42 societies from four different cultural areas to determine commonalties among shamanic ASCs. They identified three common elements: voluntary control of entrance and duration of the ASC; post-ASC memory of the experience; the ability to communicate with others during the ASC.

Heinze (1991) has pointed out that the basic difference between shamans and mediums appears to be that "shamans are capable of going on a magical flight and remain the actors during their performances. On the other hand, mediums become possessed by spirits who use human bodies through which they are able to act" (p. 26).

In addition, shamans characteristically travel into the spirit world more often than other practitioners do. They may journey from "middle Earth" to the "upper world" to visit ancestral spirits, to the "lower world" to visit power animals, and journey to the past, the future, and remote areas of the globe (Krippner, 2000). The spirits encountered in each of these realms will differ from society to society, but shamanic journeying is typically linked to the ability to enter ASCs.

"Incorporation" is a term often used to denote the voluntary nature of spirit embodiment; it may or may not be accompanied by amnesia for the experience, depending on the practitioner, the practitioner's training, and the practitioner's cultural tradition.

In "possession," however, the individual generally embodies the spirit in an involuntary or unpredictable manner; there is usually amnesia for the experience. In "obsession," the spirit works from the "outside," purportedly influencing the individual's behavior, characteristically in a maladaptive way.

"Exorcism" is often necessary to treat involuntary "possession" and "obsession" if a malevolent spirit is involved. Sometimes the troublesome spirit is not wicked but simply "ignorant" or "underdeveloped." The exorcist, who might be a shaman, priest, priestess, or medium, often attempts to "send" the offending spirit "into the light" because the spirit needs to progress in its evolution and spiritual development.

The notion of spirit "possession" poses problems for psychologists because it is an implicit explanation as well as a description. Crapanzano (1977) defined it as "any altered state of consciousness indigenously interpreted in terms of the influence of an alien spirit" (p. 7).

Others have defined "possession" more behaviorally, noting that the "possessed" person appears to be invaded by a different personality who manifests through changes in that person's physiognomy, personality, voice, and/or motor function. A differentiation can also be made between forms of "voluntary possession" or "incorporation" (e.g., shamans, mediums) and "involuntary possession (e.g., victims of hexes and/or of malevolent spirits).

Bourguignon (1974) distinguished between *trance* (i.e., ASCs not linked to cultural concepts of "possession" but in which spirit messages can be delivered and spirits contacted, *possession trance* (i.e., ASCs in which there is radical dissociation without subsequent recall accompanied by spirit-manifested speech and other spirit-directed behavior), and *possession* (i.e., behaviors associated with spirit invasion which do not directly involve ASCs, e.g., spirit-induced illness).

Peters and Price-Williams (1980) reported that shamans in 18 out of the 42 societies they surveyed engaged in spirit ''incorporation," 10 in out-of-body experiences, 11 in both, and 3 in some different form of ASC. Peters and Price-Williams have also compared these ASCs to a rite of passage in which an episode of panic or fear yields to insight; a new integration of various elements of one's personality results from this process.

Winkelman's (1992) cross-cultural survey of 47 societies yielded data demonstrating that at least one practitioner in each populace demonstrated ASC

> Heinze has pointed out that the basic difference between shamans and mediums appears to be that "shamans are capable of going on a magical flight and remain the actors during their performances."

induction associated with role training. The specific induction procedures included mind-altering substances (e.g., alcohol, opiates, psychedelics, stimulants, tobacco), auditory stimulation (through drumming,' etc.), exposure to extreme temperatures, sexual abstinence, social isolation, sleep induction, sleep deprivation, food restrictions, induced convulsions, excessive motor behavior, and extreme relaxation.

Winkelman's analysis indicated some distinct patterns regarding "incorporation" and "magical flight." However, Winkelman found cases of profound ASCs that involved neither "incorporation" nor "magical flight." He presented a unifying psychophysiological model of these ASCs: "a parasympathetic dominant state characterized by the dominance of the frontal cortex by slow wave discharges emanating from the limbic system" (p. 198) interacting with various social variables.

Harner (1980) and others have cited additional ways in which shamans alter consciousness, for example, jumping (e.g., the 16-24 hour ut ceremonies of Korean shamans), mental imagery (e.g., the visualization practices of the Tamang shamans of Nepal who "see" their tutelary spirits prior to "incorporating" them), chanting (e.g., the repetition of monotonous incantations by Taiwanese shamans).

Often, shamans use two or more procedures simultaneously to alter consciousness. Korean shamans combine jumping with drumming and the Arapaho Indians smoke a ceremonial pipe and rub their bodies with sage in addition to using drums. Neher (1961) has demonstrated how drumming can produce brain activation by coinciding with the theta EEG frequency (about 4 to 8 cycles per second) through auditory driving.

Others have built on and extended Neher's work, finding that theta brain waves were synchronized with monotonous drumbeats of 3-6 cycles per second, a rhythm associated with many shamanic ritual themes. Still others found trends towards enhanced positive mood states and an increase in positive immune response as measured by a concentration of salivary immunogloblin A (S-lgA) during shamanic drumming, while another team reported that rhythmic drumming had a salubrious effect upon group members' immune system as measured by increased natural killer cell activity (see Krippner, 2002).

Shamans also use naturally occurring ASCs, dreams being the primary example. Some shamanic traditions deny that they alter consciousness; Navaho shamans exhibit prodigious feats of memory in recounting cultural myths, and use sand paintings, drums, and dances, but minimize the effect these procedures have in bringing about a shift in their states of consciousness. Several similar examples may make it more appropriate to speak of shamanic "shifts of attention" rather than shamanic "states of consciousness" as a universal hallmark of the practice.

Paradoxically, shamans are characterized both by an acute perception of their environment and by imaginative fantasy. These traits include the ability to construct categories, the potential for pretending and role-playing, and the capacity to experience the natural world

> Shamanism is basically an open-ended system that can be modified, altered, revised, or changed due to the demands of historical circumstances and community requirements.

vividly. During times of social stress, these traits may have given prehistoric shamans an edge over peers who had simply embraced life as it presented itself, without the filters of myth or ritual (Berman, 2000, p. 81).

Putative "parapsychological phenomena" are frequently said to accompany shamanic practices, and a few investigators have used psychological methods to study these claims. For example, Giesler (1986) conducted several studies with members of what he terms "Afro-Brazilian shamanic cults." Both "shamans" and "initiates" attempted *remote viewing* to locate hidden objects as well as a task involving distant influence on ritual objects. He concluded, "cultists did not demonstrate [anomalous effects] on the laboratory tasks" (p. 123). Indeed, members of control groups obtained the only significant results. Nevertheless, this is a provocative area of shamanic lore that deserves additional investigation.

Shamanic Healing

The shaman's healing function is a primary focus of his or her repertoire and skills. Body and mind once were seen as a unity, hence there was no sharp division between "physical" and "mental" illness. Pain and other symptoms were viewed as sources of information that could be used in diagnosis, as were the client's dreams, "aura" or "energy field," and unusual life events.

Shamans seem to know how to mobilize the expectancy of their clients. This is one of the components of effective healing described by Torrey (1986), the others being a shared worldview, the practitioner's personal qualities, and procedures that empower the client. Frank and Frank (1991) added that all effective healing practitioners resemble shamans in that they bolster their clients' sense of mastery and self-efficacy by providing them with a "myth" or conceptual scheme that explains symptoms and supplies a "ritual" or procedure for overcoming them.

Procedures used by shamanic healers vary but may include diet, exercise, herbs, relaxation, mental imagery, surgery, prayers, purifications, and various rituals. Specific treatment procedures depend upon the diagnosis and the cultural traditions.

If a community member appears to be suffering from "soul loss," a shaman needs to search for that client's soul, restoring it before he or she succumbs to a terminal condition. Diagnosis will determine whether the soul has been stolen, "spooked" away from the body, or simply "strayed" during some other ac tivity. Treatment will aim to recover the soul through "soul-catching" or similar procedures.

Each shamanic society has its own diagnostic nosology. Some causal agents that result in sickness are the breach of a taboo, "karma" for past actions (including those from a "past life"), the intrusion of a foreign object into the body (usually by sorcery), and a jealous neighbor "casting the evil eye."

In recent years, many shamans have added the germ theory of disease to their etiological schema and may refer some clients to allopathic physicians if they exist in the neighborhood. Shamanism is basically an open-ended system that can be modified, altered, revised, or changed due to the demands of historical circumstances and community requirements.

Symbolic manipulation plays a major role in shamanic healing. The drum may serve as the vehicle with which the shaman "rides" into the spirit world during his or her ASCs. The blowing of smoke toward the four directions may represent an appeal to the "guardians" of the universe's "four quarters." For shamans and their communities, any product of human imagination represents a form of "reality." As a result, mental imagery and imagination play an important role in shamanic healing (Noll, 1986).

Shamanic healing usually involves the client's family and community. Katz (1981) proposed that rituals of transformation are the essential link in introducing a *synergistic healing community*. He noted that by providing experiences of *transpersonal bonding*, these rituals enable individuals to realize their communal responsibilities and sense their deep interconnectedness. Even when a client must be isolated as part of the healing process, this drastic procedure impresses the community with the gravity of the ailment.

There are shamanic methods of healing that closely parallel contemporary behavior therapy, hypnosis, family therapy, milieu therapy, psychodrama, and dream interpretation. Torrey (1986) concluded that shamans and psychotherapists demonstrate more similarities than differences in regard to their healing practices.

Conclusion

The psychology of shamanism is a growing field, as evidenced by the acceptance of symposia on the topic at several annual conventions of the American Psychological Association, the creation of the Society for the Anthropology of Consciousness (a division of the American Anthropological Association). and the publication of a popular magazine, *Shaman's Drum*.

Articles on shamanism sometimes appear in such scholarly journals as the *American Ethnologist, Current Anthropology, Anthropology of Consciousness*, and *Ethos*. Since 1984, the Independent Scholars of Asia have sponsored annual international conferences on the study of shamanism. There is an International Society for Shamanic Research, a group that has sponsored several international conferences.

The impact of shamanism is reflected in the call for preserving the Earth's ecology, evoking positive imagery in the treatment of personal and social distress, and attending to people's spiritual "emergencies" and crises. The quest for "healing the planet" is basically a shamanic journey; its success will depend upon humankind's successful cultivation of "the shaman within" each man and woman.

References

Berman, Morris. (2000). Wandering god: A study in nomadic spirituality. Albany: State University of New York Press.
Bourguignon, Erika. (1974). Culture and the varieties of consciousness. Boston: Addison-Wesley.
Boyer, L.B., Klopfer, B., Brawer, F.B., a Kawai, H. (1964). Comparisons of the shamans and pseudoshamans of the Apaches of the Mescalero Indian reservation: A Rorschach study. Journal of Projective Techniques, 28, 173-180.
Crapanzano, Vincente. (1977). Introduction. In V. Crapanzano a V. Garrison (Eds.), Case studies in spirit possession (pp. 1-41). New York: John Wiley & Sons. Conference Proceedings 2006 Page 44.
Devereux, George. (1961). Shamans as neurotics. American Anthropologist, 63, 1088-1090.
Eliade, Mircea. (1964). Shamanism: Archaic techniques of ecstasy (W.R. Trask, trans.). Princeton, NJ: Princeton University Press. (Original work published 1951).
Frank, Jerome O., 8: Frank, Julia B. (1991). Persuasion and healing (3rd ed.). Baltimore: Johns Hopkins University Press.
Giesler, Patric V. (1986). GESP testing of shamanic cultists. Journal of Parapsychology, 50, 123-153.
Harner, Michael J. (1980). The way of the shaman: A guide to power and healing. San Francisco: Harper and Row.

Heinze, Ruth-Inge. (1991). Shamans of the 20th century. New York: Irvington Publishers.
Hoppal, Mihaly. (Ed.). (1984). Shamanism in Eurasia. Gottingen, Germany: Edition Herodot.
Kalweit, Holger. (1988). Dream time and inner space: The world of the shaman. Boston: Shambhala. (Original work published 1984).
Katz, Richard. (1981). Education as transformation: Becoming a healer among the Kung and Fijians. Harvard Educational Review, 51, 57-78.
Krippner, Stanley. (2000). The epistemology and technologies of shamanic states of consciousness. Journal of Consciousness Studies, 7, 93-118.
Krippner, Stanley. (2002). Conflicting perspectives on shamans and shamanism: Point and counterpoints. American Psychologist, 57, 962-977.
Mithen, Steven. (1996). The prehistory of the mind: The cognitive origins of art, religion and science. London: Thames and Hudson.
Neher, Andrew. (1961). Auditory driving observed with scalp electrodes in normal subjects. Electroencephalography and Neuropsychology, 13, 449-451.
Noll, Richard. (1983). Mental imagery cultivation as a cultural phenomenon: The role of visions in shamanism (with commentaries). Current Anthropology, 443-461.

Peters, Larry G., 8: Price-Williams, Douglass. (1980). Towards an experiential analysis of shamanism. American Ethnologist, 7, 397-415.
Silverman, Julian. (1 967). Shamans and acute schizophrenia. American Anthropologist, 69, 1-31.
Torrey, E. Fuller. (1986). Witch doctors and psychiatrists. San Francisco: Harper and Row.
Walsh, Roger. (2001). Shamanic experiences: A developmental analysis. Journal of Humanistic Psychology, 4 7(3), 31-52.
Williams, Walter L (1 986). The spirit and the flesh: Sexual diversity in American Indian culture. Boston: Beacon Press.
Wilson, Sheryl C., 8: Barber, Theodore X. (1981). Vivid fantasy and hallucinatory abilities in the life histories of excellent hypnotic subjects ("somnambules"): Preliminary report with female subjects. In Eric Klinger (Ed.}, Imagery: Concepts, results, and applications (pp. 133-149). New York: Plenum Press.
Winkelman, Michael. (1992). Shamans, priests and witches: A cross-cultural study of magico-religious practitioners. Tempe, AZ: University of Arizona.
Winkelman, Michael. (2000). Shamanism: A natural ecology of consciousness and healing. London: Bergin and Garvey.

Shamans, Sacred Places, and the Healing Earth

Stanley Krippner

Stanley Krippner with members of the Yanomami Tribe in Brazilia, 2019

For tribal shamans, nature was sacred; Earth was alive and special, spots were engulfed with "power," filled with "energy;" or inhabited by "spirits." Although soil, water, and air all partook of the divine, some spots were especially numinous and these sacred places were visited by shamans for renewal, communication with the "other world," or entry into altered states of consciousness.[1] Shamans, both past and present, were socially designated practitioners who voluntarily altered their consciousness to enter the "other world," bringing back knowledge that they used to serve the needs of their community. Shamans were exceptionally sensitive to what biologist Rene DuBas referred to as "the spirit of place."[2]

Many shamans regarded the Earth as their mother. There were hills that looked like breasts, crags that looked like faces, rivers that could have been life-giving milk. But the concept of Mother Earth was not universal; each indigenous culture worked out its pantheon of deities in its own way, albeit with frequent interactions with other cultures.[3] Mother Earth was given visibility in North America by the Wanapum prophet Smohalla and the Shawnee cultural leader Tecumseh, although it had much earlier roots in the Pocahontas myth. However, many Native American tribes do not have a maternal Earth deity even though they have long traditions of respect for nature and care for the land.

In Ancient Egypt, Geb was the Earth Father. All the world's vegetation sprouted from Geb's back as he was lying on his stomach, prone. The Algonquin Indians worshipped Nokomis, the Earth Mother, and believed that all living things fed from her bosom. Balkan peasants considered Earth each person's parent and spouse, dressing the corpse for a wedding before burying it. Indeed, the first people who developed skills in the healing arts held a special reverence for Earth deities, whether they were male, female, or both.

Animism was a perspective that

Krippner, S. (1996). Shamans, sacred places, and the healing earth. In J. Swan & R. Swan (Eds.), *Dialogues with the living earth* (pp. 13-21). Wheaton, IL: Quest Books.

Photo: Stanley Krippner

saw nature as alive and sacred; it was associated with hunting and gathering tribes, especially those in the Old and Middle Stone Ages (i.e., Paleolithic and Mesolithic Ages). Totemism, an evolved strand of animism, conceptualized various animal species as related to particular clans. For the mythologist Joseph Campbell, the bear skull sanctuaries of Paleolithic times provide the earliest evidence of the veneration of a divine being.[4] Shamanism was associated with both animism and totemism and has been called "applied animism."[5]

Many contemporary writers refer to the living planet Earth as "Gaia," pointing out that active feedback processes operate to keep Earth temperature, oxidation state, and acidity constant while solar energy sustains comfortable conditions for life.[6] The Gaia concept is the most recent in a long tradition of perspectives that views Earth as a living organism whose capabilities include the ability to bear, sustain, and heal human beings.

This is a far different world view than that held by the Europeans who conquered the Americas. Despite the evidence of long-established, city-based civilizations like those of the Inca, the Aztec, and the Maya, European settlers regarded Native Americans as people with no real homes. This provided justification for "civilizing" the Indians "for their own good" into unordered communities."

No other approach could save as many souls; and no other approach could further the territorial and economic interests of the conquerors. The invaders overlooked the architectural accomplishments of Native Americans, such as building their homes in concert with nature rather than in opposition to nature, placing doorways towards the east where the sun rose, and devising floor plans so that when people awoke they would feel as though they had been reborn.

The Healing Earth and Treatment Practices

Pablo Amaringo is a contemporary shaman who has made a considerable effort to preserve the Amazonian ecosystem.

Over the years, Amaringo has utilized a powerful mind-altering brew, *ayahuasca*, in his work, and painted several of his ayahuasca visions. A book containing forty-nine of these paintings presents hundreds of animals, plants, spirits, and mythological beings. Journeys to various underwater, subterranean, and outer-space worlds are graphically detailed in these paintings.

After retiring as a healer, Amaringo organized an art school in Pucallpa, Peru, dedicated to documenting the ways of Amazonian life. The school's philosophy is the education of local youths in the care and preservation of the Amazonian ecosystem.

The concept of the healing Earth has entered into treatment procedures used by indigenous shamans and other magico-religious practitioners since prehistoric times. For example, the central element in the Navajo healing ceremony is sand painting. This painting represents, simultaneously, the spiritual and physical landscape in which the patients and their transgressions exist as well as the etiology of the disease and the mythic meaning of the procedure that has been chosen for its cure. Stones, plants, and sacred objects often are placed inside the painting. Mythological relationships among the elements are represented in colored sand. The sand figures may be clouds or snakes or whatever is needed to portray the path of the disease as it proceeds through time and space.

Dangers and diseases have their place in the matrix as well; if they have been the cause of illness or misfortune, they alone can correct it. Chanting, drumming, and a vigil bring the elements together. Patients become aware of the pattern of their sickness and their life, and how both are joined in the cosmos. Usually patients are surrounded by their friends, neighbors, and relatives who sing and pray to that purpose.[9, 10]

A variation of the sand painting is the ground painting constructed by the Southern California Diegueno Indians during the puberty ritual of young tribesmen. They convey the design of their world by representing the horizon as a circle. Also included are the world's edge, various heavenly bodies, power animals (especially the crow, coyote, snake, and wolf), and the mortar and pestle used to grind up the mind-altering plants used in these ceremonies.[11]

Some psychohistorians believe that the placenta is represented in these Indian medicine wheels-both in the temporary sand and ground paintings and in the longer-lasting constructions, of which about fifty still exist in the western parts of the United States and Canada. These structures are composed of stones placed on the ground to form a small central circle, with lines of stones radiating outward; sometimes there is an outer circle around the circumference.[12]

Used for ceremonies involving renewal and rebirth, some of the medicine wheels are said to "look more like placenta than any other religious symbols derived from intra-uterine life, including the tree of life, the pagan cross, and the sacred pole."[13] Medicine lodges are built each summer by the Plains Indians for sacred ceremonies; these lodges feature a central tree or pole-often with as many rafters as the medicine wheels have lines of stones. Although these designs could also emulate the sun, anthropologist R. B. McFarland says that he favors

> ... the placenta as the origin of the sacred circle, everyone starts life dependent on their placenta for nourishment and life's blood, long before we see the sun, and the sun doesn't have a central pole. The circle and the tree of life are both symbols of the placenta, the umbilical cord, and the network of blood vessels resembling the roots and branches of a tree.[14]

I found a similar concern in the songs of Maria Sabina, the Mazatec Indian shaman I interviewed in 1980 and whose sacred mushroom ve/adas were recorded and transcribed before her death. Many of her verses reveal her close association with nature:

Living Mother ... ,
Mother of sap, Mother of the dew ... ,
Mother who gave birth to us ... ,
Green Mother, budding Mother ... ,
These are my children ... ,
These are my babies ... ,
These are my offshoots ... ,
My buds ... ,
I am only asking, examining . ... ,
About his business as well ... ,
I begin in the depth of the water ... ,
I begin where the primordial
sounds forth ... ,
When the sacred sounds forth ... ,
I am a little woman who goes

through the water ... ,
I am a little woman who goes
through the stream ... ,
I bring my light ... ,
Ah, Jesus Christ ... ,
Medicinal herbs and sacred herbs
of Christ ... ,
I'm going to thunder ... ,
I'm going to play music ... ,
I'm going to shout ... ,
I'm going to whistle ... ,
It is a matter of tenderness, a matter
of clarity ... ,
There is no resentment ... ,
There is no rancor ... ,
There is no argument ... ,
There is no anger ... ,
It is life and well-being ... ,
It is a matter of sap ... ,
It is a matter of dew ...[15]

These excerpts from several of Maria Sabina's songs reveal a woman who reveres the Mother who gives birth to us, a woman who has entered the primordial waters of oceanic consciousness but who does not stay there. The true nature of her consciousness is oriented toward service, toward healing, toward her community, and toward the children and babies to whom she strives to bring life and well-being. For her, the human being is a part of the natural world and must join its quest for life and well-being.

In general, North American Indians felt that nature-in-movement had magical power, hence the importance given the Deer Dance by the Huichols, the Buffalo Dance by the Hopis, and the Sun Dance by the Plains Indians. The Naniamo shamanic apprentices of Vancouver Island believed that their tutelaries were mythical monsters rather than the animal spirits who assisted other members of their tribe. When I visited the Cuna Indians of Panama in 1985, I observed a dance in which each tribal member moved to the spirit of his or her power animals, bringing the energy and knowledge from the "other world" into communal activity.

The Nature of Sacred Places

Some locations in what shamans call Middle Earth are held to be more sacred than others. Shamans frequently locate "power spots" and use them in their healing ceremonies. These are the areas that are said to contain more "energy" and "vital force" than surrounding geographic locations. Taking the position that "ancient peoples are still offering us their wisdom through their sacred sites and landscapes," mythologist Paul Devereux has found that they differentiated between the physical landscape as constituted by consensual agreements, i.e., the ordinary reality of the world, and the visionary landscape of the human mind.

For example, the Balinese language contains a well-developed sensibility of dual worlds (*niskala* and *sekala*). But English can only call the alternative visionary world "symbolic," at best. By whatever name it is called, Devereux suggests that a rediscovery of the human capacity to "see" as the ancients could "see," would assist residents of industrialized societies to understand that the existence of these other landscapes rests essentially on one's willingness to believe in them. Devereux does not simply dismiss the phenomenon of the symbolic reality as existing only in the imagination; he also documents the presence of naturally magnetic stones at a variety of recognized sacred spots, and presents reasonable explanations for the verified presence of strange bright lights at some "power spots." The nearby magnetic stones could have been employed both for healing work and for altering people's consciousness.

The well-preserved Neolithic landscape of Avebury in southern England is undeniably recognized as having been a ceremonial landscape for its ancient inhabitants. It follows from Devereux's argument that it was also a landscape of the mind. This is only one example of the legacy that Devereux believes native people left the world in their sacred sites and landscapes.

A contemporary example of such a site is given by Alfonso Ortiz, who as a child in his Pueblo village had a vision that was directed to the mountaintop, the place where the paths of the living and the dead were said to converge. Ortiz recalled:

A wise elder among my people, the Tewa, frequently ... smiled and said, "Whatever life's challenges you may face, remember always to look to the mountaintop; in doing so you look to greatness. Remember this, and let no problem, however great it may seem, discourage you ..." Although he knew I was too young to understand, he also knew there was not much time left to impart this message to me and, perhaps, to others like me. In accordance with our beliefs, the ancestors were waiting for him at the edge of the village the day he died, waiting to take him on a final four-day journey to the four sacred mountains of the Tewa world. A Tewa must either be a medicine man in a state of purity or he must be dead before he can safely ascend the sacred mountain.[16]

Ortiz's statement implies that the shaman can utilize sacred geographical spots such as the mountaintop. These spots are also the places where tribal "ancestors" can be found by the shaman and consulted in time of need. James Swan has reviewed more than one hundred case histories of people having unusual experiences at power spots, and he observes that the most common experiences reported were feelings of ecstasy, unification with nature, interspecies communication, waking visions, profound dreams, the ability to seemingly influence the weather, feeling unusual "energies," and hearing words, voices, music, and songs.[17]

One explanation of the nature of sacred

places can be found in the creation myth of the Hopi Indian tribe. In the beginning, it is told, Tiowa, the Creator, saw a need to assign a guardian for Earth and he gave the position to a wise old woman named Spider Grandmother. Descending to Earth, Spider Grandmother saw that she would need help with her task as a steward. She reached down, picked up two handfuls of soil and spit into each of them. From each hand sprang a handsome young man. The three sat quietly in meditation for a time, attuning their minds to that of Tiowa.

Then Spider Grandmother sent one young man clothed in shimmering silver, Poqanghoya, to the North Pole to work his magic of giving structure and form to Earth, holding the planet together.

The other, Palongwhoya, wearing an equally spectacular costume of fiery red, carried a drum with him as he was sent to the South Pole. When Palongwhoya reached the South Pole, he sat in meditation for a time, reaching his heart-mind out into the universe. When he heard the heart beat of Tiowa, he began to imitate that rhythm on his drum, creating a harmony.

Whenever two or more things come into harmony, energy is exchanged, and so Palongwhoya's drum directed energy from the heart of the Creator into the Earth through the drum beat. This stream of life-force energy coursed downward to the very center of the Earth. Striking the center, they radiated outward again, like the seeds of an dandelion. As they emerged from the Earth's crust, they were more concentrated at some places than at others. These places are the strongest sacred places, known to the Hopis as the "spots on the fawn;" places of light as on the back of a young deer. [18]

The Exploitation of the Living Earth

Some contemporary humans claim that their needs permit them to ravish nature. As former U.S. Secretary of the Interior, Manuel Lujan, Jr., stated, "I think that God gave us dominion over these creatures." Lujan also remained unconvinced that every species needs to be preserved, saying "Nobody's told me the difference between a red squirrel, a black one, or a brown one." [19]

In a San Francisco interview with several social scientists on May 8, 1992, former Soviet leader Mikhail Gorbachev took a different position, when he said:

We must continue to move ahead on this issue in the spirit of innovative thinking. The destruction of the environment is a dramatic problem. We need to work toward a single global vision. For example, the Siberian taiga and the Amazonian rainforest are the twin lungs of the planet. In our new Foundation, we have a Center for Global Problems devoted to these issues. This is a global problem and it must be solved with global approaches.[20]

This vision of the living Earth is also implicit in the work of Nobel laureate Barbara McClintock. In studying genetic transportation, she focused on corn (a sacred food to many Native American tribes), working with nature to determine how genetic structures respond to the needs of the organism. In commenting on her work, biographer E. F. Keller states that nature is on the side of scientists like McClintock-although her underlying philosophy alarmed her peers (especially the male geneticists) and regulated her to the periphery of genetic research for many decades.[21]

Mythologist Elizabeth Sahtouris observed how Earth's relatively constant temperature and chemical balance is favorable to life. For her, Earth meets the biological definition of a loving organism, as a self-producing and self renewing system.[22] Earth is the only planet in its solar system that had the right size, density, composition, fluidity of elements, and "the right distancing and balancing of energy with its sun star and satellite moon to come alive and stay so."[23] Mythologist Charlene Spretnak adds that on the smaller celestial bodies, the electromagnetic interaction overpowered gravity's pull; on the larger ones, the opposite relationship developed. Only on Earth were the two in balance.[24]

Western scientists and philosophers who agree with the shamanic conception of Earth as a living being are in a minority. But they, in consort with indigenous people, call for awareness and sensitivity on the part of human beings in regard to the balance that must be maintained. The ancient Greeks believed that in the beginning there was darkness, personified by the god Chaos. Then appeared Gaia, the Earth goddess.

Western cultures have used their technology to insulate themselves from any limitations imposed by nature. Spretnak contends that the Western stance has been that if societies let down their guard, they would again be engulfed by chaos. But this is a misreading of nature and a dysfunctional mythology; humankind's destruction is more likely if the living, healing Earth is ignored.

Endnotes

1. Paul Devereux, Shamanism and the Mystery Lines: Ley Lines, Spirit Paths, Shape-Shifting and Out-of-Body Travel (St. Paul, Minn.: Llewellyn, 1993).
2. Rene Dubas, "The Spirit of Place." *Parabola* (winter 1993, originally published 1972), 66-68.
3. S.D. Gill, *Mother Earth: An American Story* (Chicago: University of Illinois Press, 1987).
4. Joseph Campbell, *The Way of the Animal Powers* (New York: Harper and Row, 1988).
5. Neville Drury;*The Shaman and the Magician: journeys Between Worlds* (London: Routledge and Kegan Paul, 1982).
6. Elizabeth Sahtouris, *Gaia: The Human journey from Chaos to Cosmos* (New York: Pocket Books, 1989).
7. J. Bruhac, "The Families Gathered Together:' *Parabola* (winter 1992), 36.
8. Luis E. Luna and Pablo Amaringo, *Ayajuasca Visions: The Religious Iconography of a Peruvian Shaman* (Berkeley, Calif.: North Atlantic Books, 1991).
9. Richard Grossinger, *Planet Medicine: From Stone Age Sllamanism to Post Industrial Healing*, rev. ed. (Boulder, Colo.: Shambhala, 1982), 105-106.
10. Donald Sander, *Navaho Symbols of Healing* (New York: Harvest/Harcourt Brace jovanovich, 1979).
11. Joan Halifax, *Shaman: The Wounded Healer* (New York: Crossroads, 1982).
12. R. B. McFarland, "Indian Medicine Wheels and Placentas: How the Tree of Life and the Circle of Life Are Related:' *journal of Psychohistory* 20, 1993, 543-564.
13. Ibid., 456.
14. Ibid., 462.
15. Alanso Estrada, *Maria Sabina: Her Life and Chants* (Santa Barbara, Calif.: Ross-Erickson, 1981), 107, 136, 150-151, 165, 175-176.
16. Halifax, 30.
17. James A. Swan, *Sacred Places* (Santa Fe, N.M.: Bear and Co., 1990).
18. Ibid.
19. T. Gup, "The Stealth Secretary," *Time*, May 25, 1992, 57-59.
20. Personal communication, May 8, 1992.
21. E. F. Keller, *Feeling The Organism: The Life and Work of Bt rlIIlm McClimock* (New York: W.H. Freeman, 1983).
22. Elizabeth Sahtouris, "The Dance of Life," in *Gaia's Hidden Life: The Unseen Intelligence of Nature*, eds. Shirley Nicholson and Brenda Rosen (Wheaton, Ill.: Quest Books, 1992), 18.
23. Ibid., 23.
24. Charlene Spretnak, *States of Grace* (San Francisco: HarperSanFrancisco, 1991).

M.A. Programme in Indigenous Science and Peace Studies

Is it for you?

Do you want to solve today's global crises facing humanity by transforming outdated paradigms?

Are you inspired to learn how Indigenous knowledge and Western science can be employed across disciplines and professions to transform crises and conflicts, and build peace?

Do you want to spend a year studying in an academically challenging environment, at a global university with students, faculty, and Indigenous Elders drawn from around the world?

What will you learn?

Steeped in Indigenous Knowledge Systems and methodologies, the Master's degree in Indigenous Science and Peace Studies (ISPS) will train you to be an insightful and self-reflective researcher and practitioner who understands central epistemological, ontological, and ethical issues that impact diplomacy, policymaking, and community work. You will become a reflexive communicator, trained to transform the global development field in ways that align our future societies with the values and resources rooted in the earth. Through this programme, you will obtain:

- A synthesis of indigenous scientific research and theory relevant to the transformation of conflicts and current development paradigm, as well as a diversity of perspectives that impact peace, justice, security, sovereignty, and reconciliation.
- Detailed knowledge of the United Nations System and related institutions, procedures and instruments that affect decision-making regarding Indigenous peoples and traditional knowledge relevant for work in the field.
- Skills and practices for effective scholarship honoring both Indigenous ways of knowing and emergent Western sciences; profound self-reflections as part of a renewed understanding of self and identity; and policy formulation, peacebuilding and humanitarian work.
- Knowing who you are in your complex cultural and ethnic identity, understanding the place and history of where you live and work, and understanding the integrative power of holistic and transrational processes (such as dreams and visions) is part of the programme. This process provides a unique framework and educational foundation to explore and resolve some of the world's most critical problems. It enables students to become more effective policymakers, community workers, diplomats, activists, and communicators who create change to renew life on earth.

M.A. in Indigenous Science and Peace: University-wide Courses

You will receive, along with your peers from other programmes, courses on Peace and Conflict theories and practices, the UN system, the relationship of identity politics and peacebuilding, and research methods. The students of this M.A. programme will also receive practical training on working in conflict areas. For more information about these courses and the program in general, see https://isri.wisn.org.

M.A. in Indigenous Science and Peace: Programme-specific Courses

In addition to the university-wide courses, students in this programme will take programme-specific courses.

- Ethnoautobiographical Inquiry - Ancestral and Historical Research 1
- Bridging Paradigms – The Role of Dreams and Dreaming
- Indigenous Knowledge & Research Methodologies
- Colonial History, Decoloniality, & Sovereignty Indigenous Science Methods
- Ethnoautobiographical Inquiry - Ancestral and Historical Research 2
- Representing Indigenous Mind – Decolonial Representation in Publications and Media
- The Science of Archaeoastronomy & Indigenous Star Knowledge
- Interventions – Capstone Project Preparation Model UN Conference: Committee on Indigenous Rights
- Thesis/Capstone/Internship

M.A. Programme in Indigenous Science and Peace Studies

Where will you be studying?

The M.A. in Indigenous Science and Peace Studies is offered by the internationally-recognized Department of Peace and Conflict Studies of the University for Peace. As a leading center of peace and conflict research and education, the department offers various other M.A. programmes on International Peace Studies, Media and Peace and Peace Education. It caters to a diverse, global body of students. Instruction is provided by a group of leading scholars and expert practitioners in the field.

The University for Peace - established by the UN General Assembly in 1980 - has been training leaders for peace for the past four decades. It is the world's leading educational institution in the field of peace and conflict resolution in its pursuit of the mandate given to it by the General Assembly, namely *"to provide humanity with an international institution of higher education for peace and with the aim of promoting among all human beings the spirit of understanding, tolerance and peaceful coexistence, to stimulate cooperation among peoples and to help lessen obstacles and threats to world peace and progress, in keeping with the noble aspirations proclaimed in the Charter of the United Nations."*

How to Apply?

1. Go to www.upeace.org and find the programme of your choice by visiting the Programmes section. We recommend you read the "IS IT FOR YOU" cards for each programme, as they are designed to help you find the programme best suited to your professional profile.

2. Click on Requirements in the top menu bar within the programme of your choice to learn about the required documentation you'll need to have on hand when filling out your application form.

3. Read the instructions and click on Apply Now to begin the application process.

4. Please take note of your application code before you begin filling out the form. The online application will automatically save your progress as you advance through the screens, but you will need this code to return to an unfinished application.

5. At any time during the Application Process, connect with the Admissions Team for assistance at admissions@upeace.org - UPEACE admissions notifications will come via email, so check your inbox

6. Once your Application has been submitted, the Admissions Team will review it and inform you of your admissions status.

7. Once you've been accepted at UPEACE, make sure to review your Admissions Package and fill out the necessary documentation to complete your enrolment.

8. Once your first payment has been submitted, UPEACE will contact you regarding your visa application and housing options.

9. GET READY FOR A TRANSFORMATIVE YEAR AT UPEACE!

University for Peace

We Still Need Rituals in the 21st Century

Stanley Krippner

Stanley Krippner with members of the Yanomami Tribe and Stephen Spear in Brazilia, 2019

Rituals can be defined as step-by-step procedures intended to attain a specified goal. However, the "steps" in the process generally occur in a fixed order and this order can be discerned by shifts in activity, gestures, songs, words, or other behaviors. Among indigenous people, most rituals are based on a worldview in which the daily life of the community is affected by metaphysical agencies, in other words by gods, goddesses, and spirits. To enlist the aid of these agencies, or to mitigate their displeasure, shamans and other spiritual practitioners use a variety of technologies to gain access to what they conceive of as the "spirit world."

There are rituals for fighting sorcery, locating "lost souls," for mobilizing community support for the indisposed, and for dozens of other desirable outcomes. Anthropologists have identified a typology of rituals, among them healing rituals (in which one's health is restored), calendrical rituals (in which seasons or other time spans are demarcated), commemorative rituals (ranging from paying homage to mythic events or remembering important anniversaries), initiatory rituals (in which someone gains entrance into the tradition of a select group), transition rituals ("rites of passage" in which a child becomes an adult, or in which someone enters or leaves the world), ceremonial rituals (ceremonies in which a chief assumes power, a couple is joined in matrimony, or an exchange of goods is enacted), protective rituals (conducted for the purpose of warding off attacks from malevolent spirits, wild animals, an enemy tribe, etc.), celebratory rituals (honoring victory over a hostile group, success of a hunting expedition, winning an award or prize, or enjoying a simple or elaborate feast), and rituals of affliction (during which forgiveness or relief is begged from powerful "otherworldly" forces thought to have wreaked havoc on a clan or community).

Obviously, there are overlaps among these categories, some writers would expand (or contract) this list, and others would make sharper distinctions between "rituals," "rites," and "ceremonies." Nonetheless, most of these rituals involve symbols (an image that is imbued with deeper meaning) and metaphors (activities imbued with deeper meaning).

During a celebratory ritual, a laurel wreath (or a gold medal) might be given to a champion athlete. During a wedding ceremony, blankets (or rings) might be

---

Krippner, S. (2013). Foreword: We still need rituals in the twenty-first century. In D. Eulert (Ed.), *Ritual & healing: Stories of ordinary and extraordinary transformation* (pp. 13-17). Henderson, NV: Motivational Press.

Photo: Stanley Krippner

exchanged. During a transition ritual, the deceased might be placed on an elevated platform to be consumed by birds of prey (or placed in an underground vault as protection against rejoining Nature).

A commemorative ritual might recall the "Passover" that spared the first-born Jews from Pharaoh's wrath (or wildly celebrate the advent of Lent duing Carnival or Mardi Gras).

attention to clues from society and from Nature, people can cope with a chaotic, unpredictable world and yet bring order out of chaos by constantly reframing, revising, and reinventing their lives.

Rituals are essential in this type of coping, whether one casts the coins of the I Ching, reads a spread of Tarot cards, or tosses the Rune stones or the Zulu bones. The ambiguous results of the resulting configurations allow unconscious solutions to perplexing problems to emerge, demonstrating that intentionality takes place not only at a surface level, but at more subtle and complex levels of the psyche. These rituals are not so much a matter or superstition or "magical thinking" as they are a way of allowing hidden patterns (what some people call "synchronicities") to come to emerge and expand possibilities and potential choices.

Readers of this book may be told that these stories argue for "predestination," "fixed karma," or the negation of "free will." Don't believe them. The stories that Dr. Don Eulert and his crew have pulled together will help those who have lost their way to recover it, will assist those who feel a vacuum in their souls to discover fulfillment, and will provide inspiration to readers who have despaired when contemplating how their puny efforts can change their lives, much less their societies. This book and these stories can nourish the body, the mind, the spirit, or all three.

Sometimes I am called upon to throw coins for friends who want help from the I Ching in making a decision. Several years ago, a distraught college student asked me to obtain a hexagram from the I Ching to help her decide whether or not to continue her struggles with institutionalized education.

For me, the verse was very clear, indicating that she should continue taking her courses, difficult though they were. For her, the advice was also clear and she decided to withdraw from school and join an artists' colony. I said nothing about my own interpretation because her own thinking had been clarified and she made what later events indicated was the correct decision.

Quite often, I will open a workshop with a Zulu ritual I learned during my visit to South Africa. I begin by having participants breathe into a pouch containing the imitation bones I had been given. Then I toss the bones, and one of 16 possible configurations emerges. I ask group members to interpret the resulting symbol as if it were a dream. If "the glittering stones" pattern was evoked, it might refer to the gems of wisdom people hope to obtain during the workshop. If "the journey" is the traditional appellation given to the four bones, participants might say that it refers to their personal quest for greater knowledge. But sometimes something more than projection seems to be at work.

On one occasion, "the sound of the hammer" appeared; later that day, a group of carpenters started repaid work on a nearby building and we heard hammering on and off for the remainder of the weekend. One time, "the rising snake" was the result of my toss. During the afternoon break, most of our participants went to the nearby river to wade or to swim. A young boy joined them and within minutes, a small snake slithered

> Rituals are not fossilized relics of an ancient past, but are enacted wittingly or unwittingly during the 21st century.

This marvelous book provides its fortunate readers with first-person examples of many types of rituals, with an emphasis on those that lead to transformation and healing. Readers will be surprised to learn that rituals are not fossilized relics of an ancient past, but are enacted wittingly or unwittingly during the 21st century. They will also learn how to ritualize their lives, filling each day with more intention, lucidity, mindfulness, awareness, and joy. Eating a home-cooked meal can be a ritual. Watching a sunrise or sunset can be a ritual. Rituals are involved in sports events, in musical concerts, in scientific experiments, in sexual interactions, in worship services, and in visits to a physician's clinic or a psychotherapist's office. But gang wars, terrorist strikes, spousal abuse, and suicidal acts can be highly ritualized as well. Ritualization is morally and ethically neutral; it is up to the performer of the ritual to make it life-affirming or life-denying.

But life is filled with surprises. A young person on her way to medical school might attend a theatrical performance so moving that she switches college majors and becomes an actress. A successful warrior in Kenya might receive a "call" from the spirit world, give away his weapons, and apprentice himself to a shaman. A family determined to preserve its ethnic heritage may be shocked when a child elopes with a partner from another ethnicity, soon bringing home a beautiful golden-skinned baby who looks like nobody else in the family. But being mindful, by taking nothing for granted, and by paying

> It is ritual that will save the environment. It is ritual that will bring peace to our tattered world. It is ritual that will provide balance to people rent by trauma, depression, and anxiety. And we deny or overlook ritualized living at our peril.

up his arm. He stood by in wonder as the snake wound its way toward his head. His parents panicked, screaming "Kill the snake!" But our workshop participants attempted to calm them down saying that the harmless creature was part of the pattern that was the logo of our workshop.

In the meantime, the snake slid down the boy's neck and disappeared into the water. A year later, at the same location, the bones evoked "the little tree." A workshop participant left the room, returning a few minutes later with a flower pot containing a sprouting twig that she had taken, with permission, from one of the trees in the area where the Buddha reportedly had attained Enlightenment some 2,500 years earlier. I could give other examples, but those will suffice to demonstrate the limitations of the Western cause-and-effect worldview and its linear concept of time.

In 2011 I attended one of the most remarkable rituals of my life. Chief Pat Alfred of the Namgris tribe had died. His tribe is part of the Kwakwawa'wakw Nation in Eastern Canada, and for several years his relatives had prepared an elaborate ritual known as a "potlatch." This ritual involves a series of "give-aways" in honor of a fallen leader or respected tribal member.

But in 1885 the government of British Colombia, Canada, outlawed these observances, considering them to be "pagan" and "non-Canadian." Once some of the First Nation people became lawyers and community organizers, considerable effort was put forward to reinstating these practices, which included a variety of healing rituals as well. When the 1885 law was repealed, the morale of the tribal men and women was enhanced and they returned to their traditional ways with gusto.

For me, it was a moving experience to observe the dances and dramatizations, each of which paid tribute to the late, beloved chief. There were various enactments during which tribal members wore the elaborate masks and garments that have brought recognition to these unique art forms.

The director of a series of rituals portraying the "gathering of the animals" gifted me with a hand painted drum depicting the spirits of the sea. Badly abused as a child by members of the clergy who ran the school he was forced to attend, he told me how his healing took place after studying and observing his tribe's rituals – the same rituals that had been banned in the 1880s because they were considered "pagan." I remarked, "If this is paganism, let's have more of it!"

For those prospective readers who might reject a book about rituals because they are outdated relics of an irrational past, I would give the same rejoinder. The venerable story behind the ritual might not be historically or scientifically accurate, but this is not the essence of a ritual. A ritual's soul lies in its symbols, its metaphors, its meanings, and its intentions. Rituals are both process-oriented and goal-oriented.

Each of the stories in this book is a gem. And this jewel-encrusted mosaic will reveal that ritual is alive and vital in the 21st century. It is ritual that will save the environment. It is ritual that will bring peace to our tattered world. It is ritual that will provide balance to people rent by trauma, depression, and anxiety. And we deny or overlook ritualized living at our peril.

> A ritual's soul lies in its symbols, its metaphors, its meanings, and its intentions. Rituals are both process-oriented and goal-oriented.

Swift Dreaming
Jürgen W. Kremer

For Nelly Sachs

Camouflaged in a smokecloud of errors
We have created a cosmos
Using words of cheery oblivion

Selves unmoored in eerie verbosity
Celebrate
As their reflections
petrify into the ghetto fortress,
erected to protect brittle
ghosts of what is real

From the wall's cavities
Swifts hurl themselves as razor disks
to bleed delusions
Each shriek pierces what seemed reality

Practically footless,
A-pous,
They cut through blinding smoke
As our fear
Stokes incantatory flames of vanity

Every night the swifts rise starward
Above the smokecloud of errors
With hope on their wings
To capture dreams for tomorrow
As they repeat their Sisyphean sorties.

Shamans as Healers, Counselors, and Psychotherapists

Stanley Krippner

Shipibo textile (Brazil).

Shamans can be defined as socially sanctioned practitioners who purport to voluntarily regulate their attention so as to access information not ordinarily available, using it to serve the needs of members of their community and the community as a whole (Walsh, 2007). From their perspective, shamans claim to enter the "spirit world" to obtain power and knowledge that they can use for the benefit of the social group that gave them shamanic status. Among all of the shaman's roles, those of healer, counselor, and psychotherapist are the most ubiquitous. The functions of shamans may differ in various locations, but all of them have been called upon to predict and prevent illness, or to diagnose and treat it when it occurs. Like contemporary mental health practitioners, shamans typically approach healing from four vantage points: the nature of the ailment, the nature of the client, the nature of the setting, and the nature of the treatment.

The way that shamans conceptualize the nature of the ailment varies from place to place and from practitioner to practitioner. Some divide illnesses into those of natural causation (biological and/or psychological) and those of metaphysical causation. The latter category can be subdivided still further, e.g., between those due to discarnate entities and those brought about by sorcerers; between those due to an individual's misdeeds and those brought about by a family member's transgressions; and for those who believe in "reincarnation," between those misdemeanors in a past life and those resulting from activities during the client's present incarnation.

The condition of the person seeking help also varies in conceptualization. Many traditional healing systems do not differentiate between "physical" and "mental" illness, viewing the human organism as all of one piece. It is not uncommon, however, for a client's family or tribe to be considered part of the illness because the lines between individual and community are not rigidly drawn. Some systems make other differentiations, e.g., on the basis of age, gender, social position, or belief system.

The setting is an important variable as well. Some locations are considered to be places of power and the violation of these areas can bring about disease. On the other hand, a visitation to a sacred site can be included in a client's

---

An earlier version of this article appeared in *Voices*, 28(4), 12-22. Preparation of this essay was supported by the Saybrook University Chair for the Study of Consciousness.

Photo: Stanley Krippner / West Georgia archives

therapeutic regimen. The setting for the therapeutic encounter might be in the client's home, in the practitioner's office, or in a specific spot designated by the practitioner.

The nature of the treatment will vary considerably. Some traditional healing systems divide treatment into medicinal, magical, and mystical categories — the first containing herbal medicines and physical interventions, the second comprising rituals and objects (including magical plants and their derivatives) to counteract an offending "hex" or "curse," and the third requesting the aid of discarnate entities, or using the client's own capacity to encounter spirits once he or she has entered an altered phenomenological pattern.

For E. Fuller Torrey (1986), an American psychiatrist, the nature of any effective treatment, whether conducted by shamans or other practitioners, inevitably reflects one or more of four fundamental principles. These are (1) a shared worldview that provides meaning to the diagnosis or naming process; (2) those personal qualities of the practitioner that facilitate the client's recovery; (3) positive client expectations (e.g., hope, faith, "placebo effects") that assist healing; (4) a sense of mastery on the part of the client that engenders empowerment.

A Shared World View

The naming process is one of the most important components of all types of healing. Reaching a consensus on the client's condition persuades him or her that someone understands the ailment, that he or she is not the only one who has ever had the condition, and that there is a way to get well. The identification of the offending factor may activate a series of associated ideas in the client's mind, producing contemplation, absolution, and general catharsis. Rogers (1982) pointed out that much of a shaman's effectiveness as a healer "rests upon the fact that his [or her] concepts of the supernatural are the same as those of his [or her] patients" (p. 14).

If the practitioner and the client do not share the same world view, treatment might be handicapped or prevented. Cassel (1955) described the actions of a Zulu father who, after much discussion finally agreed that his daughter should be hospitalized for tuberculosis. But then the physician made a tactical mistake. He remarked that his client's condition was contagious and that other people could catch tuberculosis from her. The father then denied the diagnosis and refused to have his daughter hospitalized. To accept the notion that his daughter was a carrier of a sickness was to tacitly agree that she was a sorcerer, for in his culture only such a malevolent person was seen to have the power of contagion.

> Some traditional healing systems divide treatment into medicinal, magical, and mystical categories.

Kleinman (1980) differentiated two types of sickness: disease and illness. The word "disease" refers to a malfunctioning of biological and/or psychological processes while the term "illness" refers to the psychosocial experience and meaning of the perceived disease.

Constructing illness from disease is a central function of health care systems, and is the first stage of healing. Illness also involves the client's reaction to the disease in terms of attention, perception, cognition, evaluation, emotional reactivity, and communication with one's family and social network. Illness shapes the disease into behavior and experience in ways unique to the individual, community, and culture. The responses of a client to his or her disease provide it with a meaningful form of explanation and, in many cases, control and recovery (p. 72).

A physician can give penicillin to any client with certain kinds of infectious diseases and that client will probably recover—often before the disease can be shaped into an illness. Penicillin is not dependent on a common language or a shared world view for its effectiveness.

However, shamanic cultures often speak of illnesses that Western medicine and psychotherapy do not accept, e.g., "bad air," an imbalance between "yin" and "yang" forces, "spirit possession." The same disease might be conceptualized very differently from one culture to the next, and the treatment procedures are often highly specific to the client as well as to the culture.

As a result, the symptoms of the same basic disease might vary widely among cultures. Levi-Strauss (1963) observed that many shamans and psychotherapists attempt to bring to a conscious level the conflicts and resistances that have remained unconscious in the client. The naming process involves the use of words as symbols for what is wrong; it is effective not only because of the knowledge that the words convey but because this knowledge permits a specific experience to take place, in the course of which clients may begin to resolve their conflicts.

For example, "spirit illness" among the Pacific Northwest Indian tribes resembles neurotic depression in Western cultures. Both are characterized by insomnia, dysphoric moods with crying spells, nostalgic despondency, and psychosomatic symptoms such as pain. Western psychotherapists look for the psychodynamic causes of depression (e.g., rupture of a relationship, loss of a job) while shamans typically attribute the condition to possession. The fainting, sighing, and labored breathing that often characterize depression often is attributed in the West to psychosomatic "conversion reactions," often genetically predisposed, but some shamans see it as reflecting the lack of air around the "possessed" victim (Jilek, 1982).

A study of native healers on Taiwan, many of them *tang-kis* or shamans, found that their categorization system was linked to the models of traditional Chinese medicine. As a result, most of their clients' sicknesses were seen to be caused by disharmony in the system of correspondences that extends from the cosmos to the individual, ultimately affecting the bodily organs and the flow of *ki* or life energy.

Other causative factors include sorcery, heredity, incorrect behavior, and bad luck—but even these are ultimately linked to the issue of harmony. Kleinman (1980) found that the Taiwanese he interviewed went "to Western-style physicians for the control of potentially life-threatening diseases" and "to *tangkis* for personally and culturally meaningful treatment of illnesses" (p. 362). For example, they did not go to Western physicians for the treatment of "fright," a cultural illness, but to native practitioners who were poised to apply the culturally sanctioned treatment for that illness.

Navajo practitioners (or *hataalii*) have constructed three major diagnostic categories of mental illness. "Moth craziness," characterized by fits of uncontrolled behavior (e.g., jumping into the fire like a moth), convulsions, rage, and violence, is held to be the main type of mental disorder and is ascribed to incestual activities. "Crazy violence" has some of the same external manifestations but is due to alcoholism. "Ghost sickness," ascribed to sorcery, manifests in unpleasant dreams, loss of appetite, dizziness, confusion, panic, and extreme anxiety. When someone knowingly or accidentally breaches taboos or offends dangerous powers, the natural order of the universe is ruptured and "infection" or "contamination" occurs.

Sorcerers violate the social order by engaging in incest, robbing the dead, or using their power unwisely (Sandner, 1979). In the concept of health and illness promulgated by the Navajo *hataalii*, the universe is an interrelated whole in which powers of both good and evil exist in a balanced and orderly relationship. When this relationship is disturbed, disharmony occurs, producing illness. Its cause, therefore, is basically metaphysical; illness occurs when the individual or group is out of harmony with the natural and supernatural worlds (Topper, 1987).

In 1980, I visited Maria Sabina, a Mazatec *sabía* or shaman in Oaxaca, Mexico, who explained how she and her client would jointly ingest mind-altering mushrooms in a sacred ceremony. This was done in an attempt to identify the client's physical, psychological, or spiritual problem. It was Sabina's belief that Jesus Christ would come to them and assist in the diagnostic process. Following this divinely inspired diagnosis, provided in a radically altered phenomenological pattern, what client could possibly argue with the ensuing judgment?

The Practitioner's Personal Qualities

Rogers (1982) pointed out that "the shaman may often be a superior individual, in relation to the people of his [or her] community. He [or she] must be strong in body and dedicated in mind, possessed of self-control, and capable of mental effort beyond that of most individuals in his [or her] society" (p. 8) But

> It did not even matter that the healing water that Hindus were given to drink came from a Muslim shaman, having been "treated" by a recitation of verses from the Koran because "the brotherhood of sickness indeed seems infinitely more inclusive than that of health."

Rogers also held that some shamans may "have been mountebanks and perhaps neurotic, but close enough to reality to use the [shamanic] image for success in healing, and for the advancement of their own power and wealth in the community" (p. 8). In general, "the shaman must...convey an image of knowledge, authority, prescience, and power"; if he or she "fails to maintain the image, his [or her] healing power may be lost and his [or her] use to the community destroyed" (p. 15).

The shaman's imaginative resources have been emphasized by Achterberg (1985) who considered dreams, visions, and other imaginative processes the source of vital information on human health and sickness. Among this information is the healing power of symbols and metaphors, among them that of the "wounded healer." If a shaman or potential shaman has overcome a personal tragedy, sickness, or debilitating condition, his or her community often will bestow respect and deference for this impressive feat. At the same time, the shaman's record of success will do more than anything to impress potential clients, and provide a psychological basis for successful treatment.

The shaman's cognitive abilities are often impressive; the Siberian Yakut shamans have a poetic language of over 12,000 words (compared to the usual Yakut vocabulary of 4,000 words) (Furst, 1973-1974). A Navajo *hataalii* must learn a curing ceremony that has compared to memorizing a Wagnerian opera (Kluckhohn & Leighton, 1962, p. 309). Their ability to remember cultural myths is mandatory for them to serve as an educator who can pass traditions and tribal wisdom on to the younger generation. They usually display a highly developed dramatic sense in carrying out healing rituals that enhance their power; sometimes clever sleight of hand effects are used in these rituals that further demonstrate their abilities to the community (Rogers, 1982, p. 12).

Kakar (1982) studied shamans' clients in India, reporting that, in general, they believed that it was the person of the healer and not his or her conceptual system or particular techniques that were "of decisive importance for the healing process." After observing the interactions between shamans and their clients, Kakar concluded that the client "is busy registering whether and how well the doctor opposite him [or her] fits into his [or her] culturally determined image of the ideal healer" (p. 39). It did not even matter that the healing water that Hindus were given to drink came from a Muslim shaman, having been "treated" by a recitation of verses from the Koran because "the brotherhood of sickness indeed seems infinitely more inclusive than that of health" (p. 40).

In her study of Australian aboriginal shamans, Berndt (1964) reported that power is the basis of their reputation because it demonstrates that their actions have supernatural backing. As a result, they can draw upon a resource that is not available to other people (p. 272). The Nanaimo Indians of Vancouver Island expect their shamans to fall unconscious during a ceremony in order to incorporate the tutelary spirits necessary for healing to occur (Jilek, 1982, p. 30).

In 1989, I interviewed Aldwin Scott, a spiritistic healer in Trinidad. Claiming to work with a coterie of "spirit guides" from Western African, European, and East Asian traditions, Scott emphasized the free will of the client. These "guides" gave advice and suggestions, but it was the client's responsibility to follow their suggested regimen of prayers, herbs, and/or good works. I saw Scott work with an afflicted townsperson and it was my impression that Scott combined a high sense of drama with a gentleness and permissiveness that demonstrated care and concern for the client (Krippner & Welch, 1992).

In traditional societies, shamans were (and are) socially designated practitioners. Each culture has its image of the prototypical healer; it is likely that the closer an individual shaman comes to matching this prototype, the more effective will be the resulting treatment. If a shaman does not possess the totality of personal qualities a client, and/or a society attributes to a healing practitioner, the interaction may still yield valuable results; however, this will depend on the strength of one or more of the other factors involved in the healing process. Frank (1973) concluded, "The patient's expectations are aroused by the healer's personal attributes, by his [or her] culturally determined healing role, or, typically, by both" (p. 76).

Positive Client Expectations

There is abundant evidence from many studies that demonstrates the importance of client expectancy. What a person *expects* to happen in healing often *will* happen if the expectations are strong enough. Weil (1983) went so far as to state that "the history of medicine is actually the history of the placebo response" (p. 227).

About half of any drug's effectiveness is due to the placebo response, in other words the expectations of the physician, the client, or both. Such remedies as lizard blood and swine teeth have no known medicinal property but seem to have worked well for centuries, apparently because clients expected them to work. Frank (1973) concluded that the apparent success of healing methods based on all sorts of ideologies and methods indicates that the healing power of faith resides in the client's state of mind, not in the validity of its object.

According to Frank, the psychological condition conducive to healing lies in several factors. These include the ability to "arouse the patient's hope, bolster his [or her] self-esteem, stir him [or her] emotionally, and strengthen his [or her] ties with a supportive group" (p. 76). Hence, efforts to heighten the client's positive expectations may be as genuinely therapeutic as specific therapeutic techniques.

Torrey (1986) has identified several factors that produce client and client expectations -- hope, faith, trust, and emotional arousal. Frank and Frank (1991) have noted that most psychotherapies use emotional arousal as part of the treatment, either at the beginning of therapy, followed by systematic reinforcement of newly developed skills and attitudes, or in the latter parts of therapy, crystallizing gains of the preceding therapeutic sessions. Kiev (1964), in his survey of folk psychiatry, cited the importance of the client's faith in the effectiveness of any type of psychotherapy. According to Berndt (1964), the fundamental requirement of the Australian aborigine *margidbu* is that a client must have faith.

This point is illustrated in a popular Gunwinggu story: "Moon and Spotted Cat," travelling together, were taken seriously ill. Unable to move about or to eat, they were barely alive. Finally, Moon managed to revive himself, rising up, becoming fully alive again. Before he went into the sky, he tried to revive Spotted Cat; but he could not do so because Spotted Cat didn't trust him. (p. 272).

This mythic tale explains the origin of death. If only Spotted Cat had trusted Moon, nobody on earth would have to die. Moon is seen as a powerful *margidbu*; he appears to die but he always returns. Human beings could have done the same had their faith been stronger.

Opler (1936) studied Apache shamans, delineating the way in which they maximized client expectation. These practitioners selected the cases they wished to treat, rejecting skeptics and those whose condition seemed hopeless. They demanded payment in advance, bringing additional pressure on the client to get well. They explained to the clients and their families how shamanic status was acquired. They also investigated the lives of their clients, often giving the client information that made it seem as if the shamans were clairvoyant.

Leighton and Leighton (1941) described the efforts made by Navajo *hataalii* to enhance the anticipation of their clients. They instructed the family to make elaborate preparations for the *hataali*'s "house call." Upon arriving, they told the client that he or she would certainly improve. The most important people in the client's life joined in the singing, reaffirming the belief that the client would recover.

In 1974, I observed Nemesio Taylo,

> As the family left the sanctuary in triumph, Taylo whispered to me, "Yes, perhaps the woman was possessed. Or perhaps she just needed a little attention."

a Christian spiritistic healer, at work in Manila. His first client of the day was an elderly woman, brought into the room by her grieving relatives who moaned, "Poor granny. She's lost her mind. She can't remember our names! She's been possessed by evil spirits!"

Taylo had her lie down on a table, and proceeded to bring his large diamond chip ring to the tips of her toes and fingers, and to her forehead. As Taylo's ring approached her body, the woman would wince with pain. "Yes, it seems to be possession," Taylo muttered and the relatives nodded their heads in agreement. For several minutes, Taylo massaged various parts of the old woman's body, moving her limbs upward and downward as he proceeded. He then prayed to Jesus Christ and brought his ring to the client's body parts again. This time she demonstrated no reaction; instead, she smiled at her relatives and, as Taylo pointed to each one, called out the correct name.

Torrey (1986) pointed out the variety of interactions that may exist within the boundaries of a shaman-client relationship. In Ghana and Sierra Leone, the client may move into the practitioner's home and spend long periods of time with him or her each day. The client, as well as 5 or 10 others, may stay one year or more undergoing treatment. In Sarawak, a practitioner may visit the client in his or her longhouse for a one-short marathon healing session (p. 39). Whether the practitioner-client interaction is long-term or short-term, Frank (1973) claimed that the "heightening of the patient's sense of mastery" is a direct or indirect effect of all successful psychotherapies (p. 218).

Shamans have used a variety of methods to empower their clients, e.g., pronouncing incantations, singing sacred songs, carrying out symbolic ritual acts, appearing to remove disease-causing objects from the body, conjuring up appeasing spirits, interpreting dreams, and administering herbal remedies (Rogers, 1982, pp. 4-5).

The client's emerging sense of mastery equips him or her with knowledge about what to do in the future to cope with life's adversities. In physical illness, a client may feel better and return to work. In addition, the client may have learned self-regulation, a dietary and exercise regimen, and other disease prevention techniques to prevent a recurrence of the ailment.

Regarding psychological problems, the client may have learned the proper prayers or amulets that counteract malevolent spirits, the healthy attitudes that counteract depression and anxiety, or the dream interpretation techniques that provide personal empowerment.

Katz (1982), in his observations of the !Kung hunters and gatherers of Botswana and the fishing and farming communities in the outer Fiji islands, was struck by the importance of synergy in empowering members of the community. This empowerment was especially evident in !Kung healing ceremonies in which all-night dances produced altered phenomenology (or !*kia*) during which "boiling energy" (or *n\um*) from the skin of the healers was transferred to the bodies of other community members.

Sickness is thought to be due to spirits of the dead attempting to pull persons into their realm. But in !*kia*, the healers express the wishes of the community to remain intact. If the healers' *n\um* is strong enough, the spirits will retreat and the ailing members of the group will live. More than 50% of the men and about 10% of the women in the tribe become healers, but there is no stigma attached to those who cannot attain *kia* because they play other roles in the ceremony, such as drumming or chanting. Katz found similar forces at work in Fiji where *mana*, like *n\um*, is a healing resource to be shared with the community. In Fiji, the suitable phenonomenological pattern is obtained by the ingestion of *yagona*, the sacred plants.

Topper (1987) has described four ways in which Navajo practitioners use symbols to make contact with their clients' unconscious processes: prayers, sand paintings, purification rites, masked dancers.

For example, sacred corn pollen is sacrificed during a time of prayer. This is the most direct and intense attempt to bring the influence of the spirits to heal the client; the ritual must be performed perfectly and behind locked doors. The door to the darkened hogan is fastened to prevent the prayer from escaping. Sharpened flints are used to expel the evil from both the client and the hogan. Topper stated that these procedures reduce the client's symptoms at the same time as they stabilize the social and emotional condition of the community.

Proper medicinal remedies can also empower a client. In 1925 a Nigerian *babalawo* or "father of mysteries" was summoned to England to treat an eminent Nigerian elder who had experienced a psychotic break. The *babalawo* successfully treated his client with rauwolfia root -- better medicine than that available to any English psychiatrist. It

> Torrey observed that when the effectiveness of psychotherapy paraprofessionals has been studied, professionals have not been found to demonstrate superior therapeutic skills.

As the family left the sanctuary in triumph, Taylo whispered to me, "Yes, perhaps the woman *was* possessed. Or perhaps she just needed a little attention." In this case, the agreement as to the diagnosis and the personal qualities of the practitioner heightened the positive expectations to produce at least a temporary improvement in the client's condition.

The physiology of client expectation is just beginning. The placebo effect, after decades of neglect, is assuming importance as an important aspect of both conventional and unconventional healing. But over the centuries, shamans (both accidentally and deliberately) have found ways to maximize the expectation and hope of their clients.

A Sense of Mastery

Learning and mastery are important components of healing. In addition, they demonstrate the difference between "curing" (removing the symptoms of an ailment and restoring a client to health) and "healing" (attaining wholeness or harmony with the community, the cosmos, and one's body, mind, emotions, and/or spirit). In other words, a client might be incapable of being *cured* because his or her illness is terminal. Yet that same client could be *healed* mentally, emotionally, and spiritually as a result of being taught by the practitioner to review his or her life, find meaning in it, and become reconciled to death (Achterberg, 1985).

was not until 1950 that the herb was introduced into Western medicine as Reserpine, a tranquilizer (Frank, 1973, p. 60).

I have had an encounter with Rolling Thunder, an intertribal medicine man living in Nevada. I observed him giving instructions to a client who had come for dream interpretation. Instead of telling the client what the dream meant, Rolling Thunder asked the client to imagine himself as each of the dream characters, so that he would be able to interpret the dream himself. He has also helped clients find their "healing song," identify with their "power animal," and locate "power objects" (Krippner, 1987).

Rogers (1982) has categorized shamanic healing procedures into eight categories: nullification of sorcery (e.g., charms, dances, songs); removal of objects (e.g., sucking, brushing, shamanic "surgery"); exorcism of harmful entities (e.g., fighting the entity, sending a spirit to fight the entity, making the entity uncomfortable); retrieval of lost souls (e.g., by "soul catchers," by shamanic journeying); eliciting confession and penance (e.g., to the shaman, to the community); transfer of illness (e.g., to an object, to a "scapegoat"); suggestion and persuasion (e.g., reasoning, use of ritual); shock (e.g., sudden change of temperature, sudden physical assault) (p. 112). In all of these procedures, symbols, colors, stories, and rituals (especially those involving group participation) can play an important role.

The nature of the ailment will determine what treatment options are available. The nature of the client's condition will determine whether the ailment should be cured or healed. The nature of the environment will determine how much of a cultural and familial support system is available to assist the client's recovery, growth, or integration. The nature of the treatment will determine how many of the four fundamental healing principles can be brought to bear.

Conclusion

Torrey (1986) surveyed indigenous psychotherapists, concluding -- on the basis of anecdotal reports -- that "many of them are effective psychotherapists and produce therapeutic change in their clients" (p. 205). Torrey observed that when the effectiveness of psychotherapy paraprofessionals has been studied, professionals have not been found to demonstrate superior therapeutic skills.

The sources of their effectiveness are the four basic components of psychotherapy —a shared world view, personal qualities of the healer, client expectations, and a process that enhances the client's learning and mastery (p. 207). Strupp (1972) observed, "The modern psychotherapist...relies to a large extent on the same psychological mechanisms used by the faith healer, shaman, physician, priest, and others; and the results, as reflected by the evidence of therapeutic outcomes, appear to be substantially similar" (p. 277).

In 1980, Nigerian legislators passed a law that integrated traditional healers into the state-run medical health service; in Zimbabwe the government has encouraged the *ngangas* to set up their own 8,000 member professional association (Seligmann, 1981). In Swaziland, traditional healers have been accorded equal professional standing with Western-oriented medical practitioners. In 1977, the United Malay National Organization, Malaysia's dominant political party, decided to promote the use of *bomohs* in the treatment of drug addiction.

The professionalization of shamanic and other traditional healers demonstrates their similarity to practitioners of Western medicine (Rock & Krippner 2011). Nevertheless, the differences can not be ignored. Rogers (1982) has contrasted the Western and shamanic models of healing, noting that in Western medicine, "Healing procedures are usually private, often secretive. Social reinforcement is rare....The cause and treatment of illness are usually regarded as secular....Treatment may extend over a period of months or years."

In shamanic healing, however, "Healing procedures are often public: many relatives and friends may attend the rite. Social reinforcement is normally an important element. The shaman speaks for the spirits or the spirits speak through him [or her]. Symbolism and symbolic manipulation are vital elements. Healing is of limited duration, often lasting but a few hours, rarely more than a few days" (p. 169).

All healing practitioners operate from a model. Shamanic models generally differ from the Western allopathic model in that they involve facilitating closeness to nature, to one's body, and to one's spiritual growth (Winkelman, 2010). Moreover, they encourage people to make life decisions in a way that reflects the ideals of harmony and knowledge. Shamanic models represent a structured and thoughtful approach to healing that attempts to mend the torn fabric of a person's (or a community's) connection with the earth as well as the splits that frequently occur between body and mind, between the spiritual and the secular.

Is the shamanic model of healing "valid"? One might ask a similar question concerning such Western systems as psychoanalysis. Torrey (1986) pointed out the lack of empirical support for the basic foundations of psychoanalysis, e.g., its dream theory, its notion of fixed psychosexual stages, its emphasis on the value of insight in the resolution of one's problems. However, "The lack of a scientific basis does not mean that psychoanalytic psychotherapy is not effective....The evidence is strong that virtually all types of psychotherapy are

> Allopathic medicine, as well as Western psychotherapy, has its roots in shamanism, and needs to explore avenues of potential cooperation with a model of healing that still contains wise insights and practical applications.

effective. For the psychoanalytic type as for the other types, it is likely that the effective ingredients are the non-specific basic components"—a shared world view, personal qualities of the practitioner, client expectations, interactions that promote learning and mastery. "The psychotherapy belief system of a Greenland Eskimo or a Tanzanian tribesman has precisely the same scientific basis." (p. 76).

In Malaysia, a World Federation of Mental Health workshop suggested collaboration between the university's department of psychiatry and the traditional *bomoh* practitioners, the psychiatrists objected, claiming that such a move would only confirm the prejudice against psychiatry as being unscientific held by other departments in the medical school (Carstairs, 1973). But allopathic medicine, as well as Western psychotherapy, has its roots in shamanism, and needs to explore avenues of potential cooperation with a model of healing that still contains wise insights and practical applications.

References

Achterberg, J. (1985). *Imagery in healing: Shamanism and modern medicine*. Boston, MA: Shambhala.
Berndt, C.H. (1964). The role of native doctors in aboriginal Australia. In A. Kiev (Ed.), *Magic, faith, and healing: Studies in primitive psychiatry today* (pp. 264-282). New York, NY: The Free Press.
Cassel, J. (1955). A comprehensive health program among South African Zulus. In B. Paul (Ed.), *Health, culture and community* (pp. 34-42). New York, NY: Russell Sage Foundation.
Carstairs, G.M. (1973). Psychiatric problems in developing countries. *British Journal of Psychiatry, 123*, 271-277.
Frank, J.D. (1973). *Persuasion and healing* (rev. ed.). New York, NY: Schocken Books.
Frank, J.D., & Frank, J.B. (1991). *Persuasion and healing* (3rd ed.). Baltimore, MD: Johns Hopkins University Press.
Furst, P. (1973-1974). The roots and continuities of shamanism. *Artscanada, 184-187*, 33-60.
Janis, I.L. (1958). *Psychological stress*. New York, NY: John Wiley & Sons.
Jilek, W.G. (1982). *Indian healing: Shamanic ceremonialism in the Pacific Northwest today*. Blaine, WA: Hancock House.
Kakar, S. (1982). *Shamans, mystics and doctors: A psychological inquiry into India and its healing traditions*. New York, NY: A.A. Knopf.
Katz, R. (1982). The utilization of traditional healing systems. *American Psychologist, 27*, 715-716.
Kiev, A. (1964). The study of folk psychiatry. In A. Kiev (Ed.), *Magic, faith and healing: Studies in primitive psychiatry today* (pp. 3-35). New York, NY: Free Press.
Kleinman, A. (1980). *Patients and healers in the context of culture*. Berkeley, CA: University of California Press.
Kluckhohn, C., & Leighton, D. (1962). *The Navaho*. Garden City, NY: Anchor Books.
Krippner, S., & Welch, P. (1992). *Spiritual dimensions of healing*. New York, NY: Irvington.
Leighton, A.H., & Leighton, D.C. (1941). Elements of psychotherapy in Navaho religion. *Psychiatry, 4*, 515-523.
Levi-Strauss, C. (1963). *Structural anthropology*. New York, NY: Basic Books.
Opler, M.E. (1936). Some points of comparison and contrast between the treatment of functional disorders by Apache shamans and modern psychiatric practice. *American Journal of Psychiatry, 92*, 1371-1387.
Rock, A.J., & Krippner, S. (2011). *Demystifying shamans and their world*. Exeter, UK: Imprint Academic.
Rogers, S.L. (1982). *The shaman: His symbols and his healing power*. Springfield, IL: Charles C Thomas.
Sandner, D. (1979). *Navaho symbols of healing*. New York, NY: Harcourt Brace Jovanovich.
Seligmann, J. (1981, September 21). The new witch doctors. *Newsweek*, p. 106.
Strupp, H.H. (1972). On the technology of psychotherapy. *Archives of General Psychiatry, 26*, 270-278.
Topper, M.D. (1987). The traditional Navajo medicine man: Therapist, counselor, and community leader. *Journal of Psychoanalytic Anthropology, 10*, 217-249.
Torrey, E.F. (1986). *Witchdoctors and psychiatrists: The common roots of psychotherapy and its future*. New York, NY: Harper & Row.
Walsh, R. (2007). *The world of shamanism: New views of an ancient tradition*. Woodbury, MA: Llewellyn.
Weil, A. (1983). *Health and healing: Understanding conventional and alternative medicine*. Boston, MA: Houghton Mifflin.
Winkelman, M. (2010). *Shamanism* (2nd ed.). Santa Barbara, CA: Praeger.

An earlier version of this article appeared in *Voices, 28*(4), 12-22. Preparation of this essay was supported by the Saybrook University Chair for the Study of Consciousness.

Photo: George Berticevich Photographer Copyright 2025

Hypnotic-Like Procedures Used by Indigenous Healing Practitioners

Stanley Krippner

According to Division 30 of the American Psychological Association, "hypnosis" typically involves an introduction to the procedure during which a subject, client, or research participant is told that suggestions for imaginative experiences will be presented.

The so-called "hypnotic induction" is an extended initial suggestion for using one's imagination, and may contain further elaboration of the introduction. The subsequent "hypnotic procedure" is used to encourage and evaluate the subject's responses to suggestions. When using hypnosis, one person (the subject) is guided by another (the hypnotist) to respond to suggestions involving changes in subjective experience, as well as alterations in perception, sensation, emotion, thought or behavior. In addition, persons can also learn self-hypnosis, which is the act of administering hypnotic procedures on one's own. If the subject responds to hypnotic suggestions, it is generally inferred that hypnosis has been induced.

Many practitioners, but not all practitioners, believe that hypnotic responses and experiences are characteristic of a so-called "hypnotic state." While some practitioners think that it is not necessary to use the word "hypnosis" as part of the hypnotic induction, others view it as essential. In other words, there are agreements and disagreements concerning the

---

Krippner, S. (2004). Hypnotic-like procedures used by indigenous healing practitioners. *Svensk Tidskrift for Hypnos*, 31(3), 125-135..

Photo: Sidian Jones

definition and description of hypnosis even by researchers, theoreticians, and practitioners who have given considerable thought to this topic.

In addition, the details of hypnotic procedures and suggestions will differ depending on the goals of the practitioner and the purposes of the clinical or research endeavor. Procedures traditionally involve suggestions to relax, although relaxation is not necessary for hypnosis and a wide variety of suggestions can be used including those to become more alert.

Suggestions that permit the extent of hypnosis to be assessed by comparing responses to standardized scales can be used in both clinical and research settings. While the majority of individuals are responsive to at least some suggestions, scores on standardized scales range from high to negligible. Traditionally, scores are grouped into low, medium, and high categories. As is the case with other positively scaled measures of psychological constructs such as attention and awareness, the salience of evidence for having achieved hypnosis increases with the individual's score.

The term "hypnosis" was adopted by James Braid (1795-1860), an English physician. Braid disliked the term "mesmerism," which had been named after its originator, Franz Anton Mesmer (1734-1815), an Austrian physician. Braid concluded that Mesmer's purported cures were not due to "animal magnetism" as Mesmer had insisted, but to suggestion. He developed the eye-fixation technique (also known as "Braidism") of inducing relaxation and called the process "hypnosis" (after Hypnos, the Greek god of sleep) because he thought that hypnotic phenomena were a form of sleep. Later, realizing his error, he tried to change the name to "monoeidism" (meaning influence of a single idea) however, the original name stuck. In other words, semantics played an important role in the history of hypnosis and actually directed the way that this modality was practiced.

Consciousness and Spirituality

Like the term "hypnosis," the word "consciousness" is a social construct. It is defined and described differently by various groups and writers. When it is translated into a non-English language, the problem intensifies, as some languages have no exact counterpart to the term. For me, "consciousness" can be defined as the pattern of perception, cognition, and affect characterizing an organism at a particular period of time. However, I would prefer to use the various aspects of consciousness when I write or speak about the topic. For example, referring to "awareness," "attention," and "memory" convey more exact and understandable meanings than using the more abstract term "consciousness."

So-called "alterations" in consciousness or "alternative states" of consciousness have been of great interest both to practitioners of hypnosis and to anthropologists. Many indigenous people engage in practices that they claim facilitate encounters with "divine entities," contact with the "spirit world,"

> Many indigenous people engage in practices that they claim facilitate encounters with "divine entities," contact with the "spirit world," and insights into "spirituality."

and insights into "spirituality." I use this latter term to refer to the wider, broader, higher, and/or deeper aspects of existence which typically occur during silent contemplation, shamanic drumming, group dancing, meditation, prayer, and various conditions brought about by such plants as peyote and mind-altering cacti or mushrooms.

Many Western observers have been reminded of hypnosis by some of these conditions, especially those in which individuals have seemed highly suggestible to the practitioner's directions, and strongly motivated to engage in prescribed activities.

There is considerable research data that indicate that these behaviors and experiences reflect expectations and role-enactments on the part of the individuals or a group. The practitioner invites these individuals to attend to their own personal needs while attending to the interpersonal or situational cues that shape their responses.

Other research data emphasize the part that attention (whether it is diffuse or concentrated) plays in enhancing the salience of the suggested task or experience. However, it is an oversimplification of a very complicated set of variables to refer to the practices of shamans and other indigenous practitioners as "hypnosis." This term originated in the 19th century and it is simply not appropriate to apply it to earlier practices, no matter how similar they might seem to contemporary hypnotic inductions and suggestions.

Historical and Cross-Cultural Issues

The historical roots of hypnosis reach back to tribal rituals and the practices of native shamans. Agogino (1965) states, "The history of hypnotism may be as old as the practice of shamanism" (p. 31), and describes hypnotic-like procedures used in the court of the Pharaoh Khufu in 3766 B.C. Agogino adds that priests in the healing temples of Asclepius (commencing in the 4th century, B.C.) induced their clients into "temple sleep" by "hypnosis and auto-suggestion," while the ancient Druids chanted over their clients until the desired effect was obtained (p. 32). Vogel (1970/1990) points out that herbs were used to enhance verbal suggestion by native healers in pre-Columbian Central and South America (p. 177).

Gergen (1985) observed that the words by which the world is discussed and understood are social artifacts, "products of historically situated interchanges among people" (p. 267). Therefore, unlike Agogino (1965), I use the description "hypnotic-like procedures" because native (i.e., indigenous or traditional) practitioners and their societies have constructed an assortment of terms to describe activities that resemble what Western practitioners refer to as "hypnosis." To indiscriminately use this term to describe exorcisms, the laying-on of hands, dream incubation, and similar procedures does an injustice to the varieties of cultural experience and their historic roots.

"Hypnosis," "the hypnotic trance," and "the hypnotic state" have been reified too often, distracting the serious investigator from the ingenious uses of human imagination and motivation reported from many cultures that are worthy of study using their own terms (Krippner, 1993).

A survey of the social science literature as well as my own observations in several traditional societies indicate that there are frequent elements of native healing procedures that can be termed "hypnotic-like." This is due, in part, to the fact that alterations in consciousness (i.e., observed or experienced changes in people's patterns of perception, cognition, and/or affect at a given point in time) are not only sanctioned but are also deliberately fostered by virtually all indigenous groups. For example, Bourguignon and Evascu (1977) read ethnographic descriptions of 488 different societies, finding that 89% were characterized by socially approved alterations of consciousness.

The ubiquitous nature of hypnotic-like procedures in native healing (e.g., Bowers, 1961) is also the result of the ways in which human capacities—such as the capability to strive toward a goal and the ability to imagine a suggested experience—can be channeled and shaped, albeit differentially, by social interactions (Murphy, 1947, chap. 8).

Concepts of sickness and of healing can be socially constructed and modeled in a number of ways. The models found in traditional (e.g., native) cultures frequently identify such etiological factors in sickness as "soul loss" and spirit "possession," "intrusion," or "invasion"—all of which are diagnosed (at least in part) by observable changes in the victims' behavior as related to their mentation or mood (Frank & Frank, 1991, chap. 5).

Unlike infectious diseases and disabilities resulting from physical trauma, these conditions—including many of those with a physiological predisposition—are socially constructed, just as the changed states of consciousness identified by Bourguignon and Evascu are shaped by historical and social forces within a culture.

For example, there is no Western equivalent for *wagamama*, a Japanese emotional disorder characterized by childish behavior, emotional outbursts, apathy, and negativity. Nor is there a counterpart to *kami*, a condition common in some Japanese communities that is thought to be caused by spirit possession.

Susto is a malaise commonly referred to in Peru and several other parts of Latin America and thought to be caused by a shock or fright, often connected with breaking a spiritual taboo. It can lead to dire consequences such as the "loss," "injury," or "wounding" of one's "soul," but there is no equivalent concept in Western psychotherapy manuals.

Cross-cultural studies of native healing have only started to take seriously the importance of understanding indigenous models of sickness and treatment, perhaps because of the prevalence of behavioral, psychoanalytic, and medical models. None of these have been overly sympathetic to the explanations offered by traditional practitioners or to the proposition that Western knowledge is only one of several viable representations of nature (Gergen, 1985). Kleinman (1980) comments,

> The habitual (and frequently unproductive) way researchers try to make sense of healing, especially indigenous healing, is by speculating about psychological and physiological mechanisms of therapeutic action, which then are applied to case material in truly Procrustean fashion that fits the particular instance to putative universal principles. The latter are primarily derived from the concepts of biomedicine and individual psychology....By reducing healing to the language of biology, the human aspects (i.e., psychosocial and cultural significance) are removed, leaving behind something that can be expressed in biomedical terms, but that can hardly be called healing. Even reducing healing to the language of behavior...leaves out the language of experience, which... is a major aspect of healing. (pp. 363-364)

The value of a cross-cultural approach is to extend the range of individual and social variation in the scientific search for an understanding of human capacities (Price-Williams, 1975). Therefore, in this presentation I will concentrate on describing the use of hypnotic-like procedures for developmental and healing purposes.

Most illnesses in a society are socially constructed, at least in part and alleged changes in consciousness also reflect social construction. Because native models of healing generally assume that practitioners, to be effective, must shift their attention and awareness (e.g., "journeying to the upper world,"

> Western hypnotic models are often assumed to represent universal processes; however, this assumption is only partially correct. In the meantime, native healing procedures are worthy of appreciation from the perspective of their own social framework and need not be Westernized with the "hypnosis" label.

"traveling to the lower world," "incorporating spirit guides," "conversing with power animals," "retrieving lost souls"), the hypnosis literature can be instructive.

Western hypnotic models are often assumed to represent universal processes; however, this assumption is only partially correct. In the meantime, native healing procedures are worthy of appreciation from the perspective of their own social framework and need not be Westernized with the "hypnosis" label.

Hypnotic-Like Procedures in Shamanism

Winkelman (1984) conducted an archival study of 47 traditional societies, identifying four groups of spiritual practitioners: shamans and shamanic healers, priests and priestesses, mediums and diviners, and malevolent practitioners. With the exception of priests and priestesses, these practitioners purportedly cultivated the ability to regulate and/or shift their patterns of perception, affect, and cognition for benevolent (e.g., healing, divining) or malevolent (e.g., casting spells, hexing) purposes.

In addition, priests and priestesses presided over rituals and ceremonies that often had, as their intent, the elicitation of changes in the behavior and experiences of their supplicants for religious purposes.

Hypnotic-like procedures are often apparent in the healing practices of native shamans. Shamans can be defined as socially sanctioned practitioners who purport to voluntarily regulate their attention and awareness so as to access information not ordinarily available, using it to facilitate appropriate behavior and healthy development—as well as to alleviate stress and sickness—among members of their community and/or for the community as a whole.

Among the shaman's many roles that of healer is the most common. The functions of shamans may differ in various locations, but all of them have been called upon to predict and prevent afflictions, or to diagnose and treat them when they occur.

Shamanic healing procedures are highly scripted in a manner similar to the way that hypnotic procedures are carefully sequenced and structured. The expectations of the shaman's or hypnotist's clients can enable them to decipher task demands, interpret relevant communications appropriately, and translate the practitioner's suggestions into personalized perceptions and images.

Just as expectancy plays a major role in hypnotic responsiveness (Kirsch, 1990), it facilitates the responsiveness of shamans' clients as well as expediting shamanic "journeying." Shamans themselves display what Kirsch (1990), in discussing the hypnosis literature, calls "learned skills"; the shamans' introduction to hypnotic-like experiences during their initiation and training generalizes to later sessions, and they can ultimately engage in "journeying" virtually at will.

For this reason, it is debatable whether shamanic "journeying" is a form of dissociation; there is no shift of the shaman's personal identity, and the shaman appears to be in control of the "journeying" process and does not incorporate the "entities" encountered along the way.

Japanese shamans of the Tohoku region believe that they can contact the Buddhist goddess Kannon who assists with their diagnoses, producing visual or auditory imagery that the shaman experiences and reports. This is an example of the "translation" that characterizes both hypnotic sessions and shamanic imagination.

These shamanic "translations" have been studied by Achterberg (1985) who considers dreams, visions, and similar processes a venerable source of vital information on human health and sickness. So ubiquitous is their process of gleaning pertinent information from fantasy-based symbols and metaphors that I (Krippner, 1987) have suggested that shamans, as a group, might be considered "fantasy prone" (p. 130). Indeed, they frequently resemble the highly hypnotizable individuals who, on the basis of interviews and personality tests, have been designated "fantasy prone" (Lynn & Rhue, 1988).

However, to engage in fantasy is simply to exercise one's imagination, and this can be done without transcending one's sense of identity. Thus, most "fantasy prone" individuals do not have frequent experiences that can be labeled either "dissociative" or "transpersonal" each time they utilize their imagination. In fact, the term "dissociative" only goes back to the end of the 18th century, while "transpersonal" is a 20th century term; neither are appropriate labels for phenomena that occurred many centuries ago.

Furst (1977) has described procedures by which North American Indians once sought (and still seek) alternative states of consciousness with spiritual components: "psychoactive plants, animal secretions, fasting, thirsting, self-mutilation, exposure to the elements, sweat lodges, sleeplessness, incessant dancing, bleeding, plunging into ice-cold pools, and different kinds of rhythmic activity, self-hypnosis, meditation, chanting, and drumming" (p. 70).

Furst uses Western, non-Indian concepts (e.g., "self-hypnosis," "trance," "meditation") that may not be directly comparable to the original experiences. Nevertheless, he goes on to describe the freedom that was typically given by North American Indian shamans to their clients to use "ecstatic trance" in order to determine their own relationship with the unseen forces of the universe. The analogous hypnotic practices here would be the various non-directive, permissive procedures in which hypnotized clients utilize their own fantasy and imagery to work toward the desired goals (e.g., Kroger, 1977, chap. 14).

> The functions of shamans may differ in various locations, but all of them have been called upon to predict and prevent afflictions, or to diagnose and treat them when they occur.

Jilek (1982, p. 30) wrote that the Nanaimo Indians of Vancouver Island "fall unconscious" in order to incorporate the tutelary spirits necessary for healing to occur (Jilek, 1982, p. 30). Rogers (1982) claims that the Alaskan Eskimo shaman's use of rhythmic drumming and monophonic chanting induces "self-hypnosis" (apparently because of their goal-directed nature) as well as placing the client "in a hypnotic trance in which the suggestions of recovery and cure are given" (p. 143).

In discussing the Ammassalik Eskimos of Eastern Greenland, Kalweit (1988) observes that their "continuous rubbing of stones against each other may be seen as a simple way of inducing a trance....The monotony, loneliness, and repetitive rhythmic movement join with the desire to encounter a helping spirit. This combination is so powerful that it erases all mundane thoughts and distracting associations" (p. 100).

Again, the use of Western concepts may be flawed descriptors for what actually occurs in these instances of remarkable behavior.

Belo (1960) claimed to have observed similarities between the behavior of Balinese healers and that of hypnotized subjects. Although there was no trained observer of hypnosis on Belo's field trips, a hypnotic practitioner observed several of her films and claimed to notice similarities between "hypnotic trance" and "mediumistic trance."

In these otherwise useful descriptions, we can observe the proclivity of Western observers to use such terms as "hypnosis" and "trance" in describing shamanic procedures rather than simply making direct behavioral comparisons or utilizing the tribe's own explanations and phenomenological descriptions.

Kirsch's (1990) discussion of the role of expectancies in hypnosis and psychotherapy is relevant to each of these cases. Hypnosis, like many culturally based rituals, serves to shape and bolster relevant expectancies that reorganize consciousness and produce behavioral changes relevant to the goals of hypnotic subjects and shamanic clients. For example, the ideomotor behavior that often characterizes hypnosis (e.g., arms becoming heavier or lighter, fingers moving to denote positive or negative responses) resembles the postures, gestures, collapsing motions, and rhythmic movements that occur during many native rituals.

In both instances, the participants claim that the movements occur involuntarily. Kirsch suspects that expectancy plays a major role, but admits that these responses are experienced as occurring automatically, without volition (p. 198).

The absence of a formal "induction" does not prevent the client from becoming receptive to a suggestion and motivated to follow it, just as most, if not all, hypnotic phenomena can be evoked without hypnotic induction (Kirsch, 1990, p. 129).

Contributing to this procedure is the multi-modal approach that characterizes Navajo chants, as well as their repetitive nature and the mythic content of the words, which are easily deciphered by those clients well-versed in tribal mythology. Sandner (1979) describes how the visual images of the sand paintings and the body paintings, the audible recitation of prayers and songs, the touch of the prayer sticks and the hands of the medicine man, the taste of the ceremonial musk and herbal medicines, and the smell of the chant incense "all combine to convey the power of the chant to the patient" p. 215).

A *hataalii* (i.e., Navajo shaman) usually displays a highly developed dramatic sense in carrying out the chant but generally avoids the clever sleight of hand effects used by many other cultural healing practitioners to demonstrate their abilities to the community (p. 241).

The Navajo chants are considered by Sandner (1979) to facilitate suggestibility and shifts in attention through repetitive singing and the use of culture-specific mythic themes (p. 245). These activities prepare participants and their community for healing sessions. These healing sessions may involve symbols and metaphors acted out by performers, enacted in purification rites, or executed in "sand paintings" composed of sand, corn meal, charcoal, and flowers—but destroyed once the healing session is over.

Some paintings, such as those used in the "Blessing Way" chant are crafted

> Joseph Campbell (1990) described the colors of the typical sand painting as those "associated with each of the four directions" and a dark center—"the abysmal dark out of which all things come and back to which they go."

from ingredients that have not touched the ground, e.g., corn meal, flower petals, charcoal. Once again, the client "translates" the symbols and metaphors, but usually not with full awareness of the ongoing process.

Hypnotic-like procedures affect the mentation of both the *hataalii* and the client during the chant. Sandner (1979) pointed out that the *hataalii*'s performance empowers the client by creating a "mythic reality" through the use of chants, dances, and songs (often accompanied by drums and rattles), masked dancers, purifications (e.g., sweats, emetics, herbal infusions, ritual bathings, sexual abstinence), and sand paintings.

Joseph Campbell (1990) described the colors of the typical sand painting as those "associated with each of the four directions" and a dark center—"the abysmal dark out of which all things come and back to which they go." When appearances emerge in the painting, "they break into pairs of opposites" (p. 30).

In addition to the chants, there are other hypnotic-like healing procedures used by the Navajo *hataalii*, one of which is a prayer session. For example, sacred corn pollen may be sacrificed during a time of prayer in an attempt to foster the influence of the spirits needed to heal the client; this ritual must be performed perfectly and behind locked doors, often at the home of the client.

The door to the darkened hogan is fastened "to prevent the prayer from escaping." Sharpened flints are used to expel the evil from both the client and the hogan. Topper (1987) held that these procedures reduce the client's symptoms at the same time as they stabilize the social and emotional condition of the community.

Topper's (1987) study of Navajo *hataalii* indicates that they raise their clients' expectations through the example they set of stability and competence. Politically, they are authoritative and powerful; this embellishes their symbolic value as "transference figures" in the psychoanalytic sense, representing "a nearly omniscient and omnipotent nurturative grandparental object" (p. 221).

Frank and Frank (1991) put it more directly: "The personal qualities that predispose patients to a favorable therapeutic response are similar to those that heighten susceptibility to methods of healing in nonindustrialized societies, religious revivals, experimental manipulations of attitudes, and administration of a placebo" (p. 184).

When treating Navajo clients, suggestion and expectancy are bolstered through reinforcing the client's belief in the power of the chant and its symbols, a tight structuring of the ceremonial performance, repetition (especially in chants, songs, and prayers), physical exhaustion of the client, dramatization of a significant event in Navajo mythology, and on rare occasions the use of mind-altering herbal substances (e.g., *datura*) to evoke a physical effect that convinces the client that power is at work.

The hypnotic-like procedures strengthen the support by family and community members as well as the client's identification with figures and activities in Navajo cultural myths, both of which are powerful elements in the attempted healing.

But do these procedures deserve a description that indicates a major shift in conscious functioning? Sandner (1979) found that his informants were insulted when it was suggested that Navajo *hataalii* change their state of consciousness to such an extent that their sense of identity is lost; such a shift would distract the practitioners from the attention to detail and the precise memory needed for a successful performance.

At best, the *hataali* appear to modify their attentional states rather than to "alter" all of their subsystems of consciousness, or their consciousness as a totality. Attention determines what enters someone's awareness. When attention is selective, there is an aroused internal state that makes some stimuli more relevant than others and thus more likely to attract one's attention.

A trait that is more characteristic of shamans than an "alternative state of consciousness" might be the unique attention that shamans give to the relations among human beings, their own bodies, and the natural world—and their willingness to share the resulting knowledge with others (Krippner 2002, p. 967).

Hypnotic-Like Procedures in Bali

In contrast, on the island of Bali, Indonesia, there are many rituals and ceremonies that utilize hypnotic-like procedures. In traditional Balinese practice, the name of the main temple ceremony is *nyimpen* and the dance of *calon arang* often is performed during *nyimpen*.

The story of Calon Arang concerns an evil widow and her only daughter who were banned to the forest for allegedly practicing black magic. There are several variations of this story but all center on her revenge against the people of the ancient Hindu Javanese kingdom of Daha after its Raja insults her by retracting an offer to marry her beautiful daughter.

Calling up her demon legions, she transforms herself into a frightening figure with ponderous hanging breasts, bulging eyes, a long flaming tongue, and a mass of unruly flowing hair. Waving her magic cloth, she has become Rangda, the queen of the witches, and wreaks havoc with her powers.

Understandably, this is one of the most powerful plays in sacred Balinese drama and its performance is typically charged with energy and emotion.

When I saw this dance performed, the dancers seemed oblivious to the outside world as they enacted the great battle between the forces of the witch and those of humankind. It started with the lesser characters whom, when faced with defeat, called upon the aid of higher forces, which transformed them into more powerful beings.

Each of the succeeding transformations was met with mounting tension on the faces of the crowd and was supported by the growing crescendo of the *gamelan* orchestra. Children who were dozing suddenly woke up. The climax finally came when the Barong, a mythical creature who frequently comes to the aid of human beings, at last faces his arch-adversary, the malevolent witch Rangda, and the dancers shift from their usual sense of identity to become players in this cosmic drama.

Thong (1994), a psychiatrist who organized the first mental hospital on Bali, describes what occurred during a performance of this dance that he witnessed:

> At that very moment, one of my staff was bringing to me another glass of the thick Balinese coffee that I had been using to keep from falling asleep at that late hour. Sud-

> The climax finally came when the Barong, a mythical creature who frequently comes to the aid of human beings, at last faces his arch-adversary, the malevolent witch Rangda, and the dancers shift from their usual sense of identity to become players in this cosmic drama.

denly, without warning, he threw the glass over his shoulder, stood upright as if in anger, and quivered with wide-open eyes. Abruptly he proceeded to turn and walk to a nearby papaya tree which he pulled out of the ground. That seems to have been some sort of signal because afterwards many others in the crowd, including a member of the orchestra, experienced the same radical transformation. My first frightening impression was that utter chaos had broken out. (p. 79)

Overwhelmed by this sudden and unexpected turn of events, Thong sat confused and bewildered with no idea of where to look or what to do. Fortunately, the Balinese themselves had no such problem. Restraining the disorderly behavior of the more violent "trancers," their attention focused once more on the stage and its surroundings.

The players still were dancing, still in what seemed to be an alternative state of consciousness, but one that was less intense. The *gamelan* played on but only with the mesmerizing continuous deep rhythm of the large gongs. Thong's most striking observation was that despite all the wailing and untamed antics, nobody was hurt. He continues,

> This led me to the conclusion that this was no true chaos; instead it was a wild but nonetheless orderly form of behavior. It was only at this point that I turned around to ask my Western companion, Christopher, a question about his feelings concerning this primal scene. The result was my second shock of the night when I saw Christopher sitting upright with the same dazed look in his eyes as the dancers. At that moment...all the trancers gathered before the Barong who began to lead a procession around the temple. Dear Christopher joined in as well. (p. 80)

It took the efforts of a *pemangku* (village priest) to gently bring Christopher and the other people back to their ordinary mode of functioning. With the help of his assistants, and armed only with holy water, the *pemangku* wandered through the crowd sprinkling the entranced revelers; the sacred water quickly revived them. Could this phenomenon be categorized as "mass hypnosis"? Such a label would be less than accurate because there was no direct goal-orientation of the affected individuals.

Some of the most dramatic changes in conscious functioning among children I have seen were in Bali. One evening, I watched the *sanghyang dedari*, a form of *legong*, the "dance of revered angels" performed by two young girls after they supposedly had incorporated "benevolent spirits."

Enveloped by the smell of sweet incense and accompanied by the music of both an all-male chorus and an all-female chorus chanting sacred songs, the two girls moved rhythmically with their eyes closed, thus protecting their beloved temple from malevolent entities. The girls danced in flawless tandem, never opening their eyes but—perhaps—carefully responding to the music, to kinesthetic cues, and to memory. Once the chanting ended, the girls fell to the ground and were attended to by the *pemangku*.

I have also witnessed the *sanghyang jaran*, during which adolescent boys dance on a bamboo hobbyhorse or simply on a tree branch. Initially, they dance around a bonfire made from coconut husks, but if the spirit dictates, they dance through the fire, often stepping on the burning husks and the coals. It is claimed that neither type of dancer has had any formal dance training; the participants insist that they can not recall the dance steps once the priest brings them back to their ordinary functioning.

Another traditional performance, the Balinese *kecak* dance, tells a story from the Hindu Ramayana collection. Sita is captured by the abhorrent Rawana but is rescued by Hanuman and his indomitable monkey army.

At one point a circle of some 150 men provide incredibly coordinated movements, and their vocalizations, "Chak-Chak-Chak," are remarkable imitations of monkey chatter. The purpose of the *kecak* dance is to drive away Rawana and his "evil spirits"; in so doing, individual awareness gives way to a group awareness, aided by the orchestration

> Not only do the players benefit from expressing these emotions and breaking the taboos, but the audience attains catharsis as well.

of the *gamelan*, a traditional percussion band and the legendary story that has been enacted for centuries. *Gamelan* musicians in Bali are described as entering "trance" through "self-hypnosis" (Suryani & Jensen, 1993), but I feel this is a reductive appellation that ignores the complexity and cohesion of this unique musical group.

In Thong's (1994) opinion, the Balinese people's repressed emotions find an outlet in the dance and drama—an outlet the culture has provided for them to abreact, either vicariously or directly. Classical dance and drama in Bali, based on legends and myths, are well attended and the more contemporary dramatic presentations are even more widely attended. In both the classical and contemporary performing arts one can encounter every possible Balinese emotion—love, joy, anger, reverence.

One can observe intrigue, sexual passion, jealousy, and the violation of all the cultural taboos. Not only do the players benefit from expressing these emotions and breaking the taboos, but the audience attains catharsis as well.

From Thong's perspective, the other Balinese arts—painting, sculpture, the creation of festival offerings—help the Balinese to maintain a healthy frame of mind. They have retained their vitality; without them, and the related cultural manifestations, the uniqueness of Bali would have crumbled long ago.

In addition, I have seen *balians* (i.e., Balinese shamans) enter what might be called alternative states of consciousness during healing and exorcism ceremonies. The *balian taksu* is a healer with mediumship talent who alters consciousness to assist in the diagnosis of the ill and unfortunate. Sometimes, the diagnosis is *bebai* in which an evil spirit has been sent by a sorcerer. The victim's rival has paid the sorcerer to practice *bebainan*, or black magic, for purposes of revenge or jealousy (Belo, 1960).

Thong concluded that in the "altruistic trance states," a dancer responds to the needs of another person or a group of people. This state is usually reached during or after the performance of a ritual and, in Bali, would encompass all hypnotic-like phenomena during religious or healing ceremonies as practiced by the *balian*. The practitioners in this group rarely show signs of psychopathology.

"Egoistic trance states," on the other hand, are entered in response to an individual's personal needs. They are not preceded by a ritual and tend to occur spontaneously. In Bali, this state is believed to be brought about by the possession of an individual by a *bebai* or evil spirit. Members of this group usually have emotional problems that typically fall into the psychiatric category of "hysterical reaction." In other words, Thong's altruistic trance state is likely to be benevolent in nature while what he refers to as the egoistic trance state is not necessarily concerned with the benefit of community members.

Thong concluded that in Balinese ritualistic dancing, the "I" gives way to a loss of ego boundaries and a change in the body image. It was his hunch that some of the dances, such as the dreamy *sanghyang* dances, were states of hypoarousal, while others, such as the *calon arang*, were states of hyperarousal.

Indeed, the *barong* dance, in both its original and tourist version, ends with the dancers pressing *kris* knives against their chests as the malevolent Rangda attempts to influence the dancers to harm themselves. The Barong, however, offers them protection. Thong determined that these hypnotic-like experiences could be divided into three stages. During the first stage, dancers are consciously or unconsciously preparing themselves; they have not yet lost reflective consciousness and still retain voluntary control and decision-making capabilities.

The second stage brings intensification at which time control is lost and consciousness is altered. During the third stage, the dancer falls into a state of exhaustion but may be capable of returning to the second stage if sufficiently aroused. The change from one stage to another can usually be recognized by distinct somatic clues such as sighs, sobs, hisses, shouts, or body movements.

Incense and scents are a common means of altering consciousness, but they seem to be incidental in Bali. Mind-altering substances such as psychedelic plants, alcohol, and even betel nut and tobacco play little or no role in Bali, despite the presence of psychedelic mushrooms (*jamur tahi sapi* in Balinese) on the island. The effects of the mushrooms are referred to as *lengehin* or dizziness; they are shunned by most Balinese who have a cultural dislike of anything that disorients them and threatens their sense of balance.

In Thong's opinion, the most important factor is the charged and expectant atmosphere that surrounds altering consciousness. In other words, the social setting and expectancy seem to be more critical than any physiological maneuver. The leaders of the community play an important role because it is often the head of the village, the *sadeg*, or some other important personage who first goes into an altered state, serving as a role model for the others.

Perhaps the occurrence of hypnotic-like procedures cross-culturally is so frequent because it plays an important cultural role. In Bali, so-called "trance dancing" serves as a useful emotional outlet both for the dancer and the observer.

> Long before Western medicine recognized the fact, Africa's traditional healers took the position that ecology and interpersonal relations affected people's health.

What Thong calls "altruistic trance states" are preceded by a ritual or ceremony in which a shift is expected and accepted as an integral element. The "trancers" in these dances are usually ordinary members of the community with no more than the average number of psychological or physical problems. These ceremonies facilitate social cohesion because they are performed on behalf of the entire community.

What Thong calls "egoistic trance states" occur outside of the ordinary cultural context. They may involve malicious magical practices, in which attempts are made (or are perceived to have been made) to influence, coerce, or harm community members. These "trancers" show a tendency for attacks of hysteria, acute psychotic reactions, and schizophrenic episodes. The Balinese themselves recognize these two types of "trancers" and react differently toward each of them.

Afro-Brazilian Healing Procedures

Unusual experiences were common in early West African cultures where individuals were considered to be closely connected with nature, the community, and their communal group. Each person was expected to play his or her part in a web of kinship relations and community networks. Strained or broken social ties were held to be the major cause of sickness.

A harmonious relationship with one's community, as well as with one's ancestors, was important for health. At the same time, an ordered relationship with the forces of nature, as personified by the *orixás* or deities, was essential for maintaining the well-being of the individual, the family, and the community.

West Africans knew that disease often had natural causes, but believed that these factors were exacerbated by discordant relationships between people and their social and natural milieu. Long before Western medicine recognized the fact, Africa's traditional healers took the position that ecology and interpersonal relations affected people's health (Raboteau, 1986).

West African healing practitioners felt that they gained access to unusual powers in three ways: by making offerings to the *orixás*, by foretelling the future with the help of an *orixá*, and by incorporating an *orixá* (or even an ancestor) who then diagnosed illnesses, prescribed cures, and provided the community with warnings or blessings. The person through whom the spirits spoke and moved performed this task voluntarily, claiming that such procedures as dancing, singing, or drumming were needed to surrender their minds and bodies to the discarnate entities (Krippner, 1989, p. 188).

The slaves brought these practices to Brazil with them; despite colonial and ecclesiastical repression, the customs survived over the centuries and eventually formed the basis for a number of robust Afro-Brazilian spiritual movements.

Books by a French writer, Alan Kardec, were brought to Brazil, translated into Portuguese, and became the basis for a related movement (i.e., Kardecism). There were followers of Mesmer in this group, but Kardec proposed that spirits, rather than Mesmer's invisible fluids, were the active agent in altering consciousness, removing symptoms, and restoring equilibrium (Richeport, 1992, p. 170).

Contemporary *iyalorixás* or *mães dos santos* ("mothers of the sprits") and *babalawos* or *pais dos santos* ("fathers of the spirits") still teach apprentices how to sing, drum, and dance in order to incorporate the various deities, ancestors, and spirit guides. They also teach the *iaôs* ("children of the *orixás*") about the special herbs, teas, and lotions needed to restore health, and about the charms and rituals needed to prevent illness.

The ceremonies of the various Afro-Brazilian groups (e.g., Candomblé, Umbanda, Batuque, Quimbanda, Xango) differ, but all share three beliefs: humans have a spiritual body (that generally reincarnates after physical death); discarnate spirits are in constant contact with the physical world; humans can learn how to incorporate spirits for the purpose of healing (Krippner, 2000).

After interviewing 40 spiritistic healing practitioners in Brazil, I (Krippner, 1989) identified five methods of receiving the "call" to become a healer: (1) coming from a family having a history of "mediumship"; (2) being "called" by spirits in one's visions and dreams; (3) succumbing to a malady or "spiritual crisis" from which one recovers in order to serve others; (4) having a revelation while reading Afro-Brazilian spiritistic literature or attending spiritistic worship services; (5) working as a volunteer in a spiritistic healing center and becoming inspired by the daily examples of compassion.

If the call is rejected, severe illness or misfortune may result; as one Candomblé medium told me, "Once the *orixá* calls, there is no other path to take" (p. 193). In this case, the spiritual dimension of human existence is recognized as so sacred and inviolate that one dare not reject its summon.

Once the apprentices begin to receive instruction in mediumship, such experiences as spirit incorporation, automatic writing, "out-of-body" travel, and recall of "past lives" lose their bizarre quality and seem to occur quite naturally. Socialization processes provide role models and the support of peers. A number of cues (songs, chants, music, etc.) facilitate "spirit incorporation," and a process of social construction teaches control, appropriate role-taking, and communal support.

Richeport (1992) observes several similarities between these mediumistic behaviors and those of hypnotized subjects, e.g., motivation, the positive use of imagination, frequent amnesia for the experience.

> As the ceremony continued, a medium began to shake violently, then appeared to demonstrate equanimity as she "incorporated" the spirit of a preto velho, a black slave from Brazil's colonial past.

It should be noted that mediums resemble shamans in many ways but lack the control of their attention and awareness that characterizes shamans. For example, shamans are usually aware of everything that occurs while they converse with the spirits, even when a spirit "speaks through" them. Mediums claim to lose awareness once they incorporate a spirit, and purport to remember little about the experience once the spirit leaves.

Both shamans and mediums engage in altered states of consciousness, but the shaman's attention, memory, and awareness seem to be enhanced, not restricted. These same facets of mentation appear to be dampened or diffused in mediumship; if there is a shift toward greater focus, it is attributed to the guiding spirit rather than to the practitioner himself or herself.

The traits most admired in mediums resemble those traits that facilitate ordinary social interactions. During more than two dozen exploratory trips to Brazilian healing centers, I have observed few instances of bizarre behavior during spiritistic ceremonies. Indeed, if a spirit seems to be taking control of the medium too quickly, the other mediums may sing a song that will slow down the process of incorporation.

Leacock and Leacock (1972) observed that the Brazilian mediums in their study usually behaved in ways that were "basically rational," communicated effectively with other people, and demonstrated few symptoms of hysteria or psychosis. They engaged in intensive training and, as mediums, pursued hard work that often put them at risk with seriously ill individuals (p. 212). These are not likely to be the favorite pastimes of fragile personalities or malingerers.

In 1973, a colleague and I attended an Umbanda ceremony in Sao Paulo, Brazil. Drums were beating, candles were flickering, and the smell of incense was wafting through the room. We took our seats with the other spectators, and noticed the gargantuan altar containing dozens of statues of *orixás*, ancestors, and Christian saints—Umbanda being the Afro-American spiritistic movement that has borrowed most heavily from Christianity. A *babalawo* appeared to be in charge of the ceremony, but four other *babalawo* and five *iyalorixás* were playing prominent roles.

As the ceremony continued, a medium began to shake violently, then appeared to demonstrate equanimity as she "incorporated" the spirit of a *preto velho*, a black slave from Brazil's colonial past. Looked upon as powerful healing spirits, the *preto velhos* are incorporated at least once a month in most Afro-Brazilian spiritistic centers, rotating with such other healing entities as the *caboclos*, or Indians of mixed blood, and the *crianças*, or children who died at young ages.

Other mediums began to engage in automatisms—twitching, writhing, screaming, flailing, and falling to the floor. Once they maintained their composure, they claimed to have incorporated *preto velhos*, and were able to engage in healing through the laying-on of hands. My colleague and I entered the healing circle where mediums prayed, sang, and gave us quick massages that were pleasant and pleasurable. (Some spiritistic healers, especially the followers of Alan Kardec, only work with the spiritual body and refrain from touching the client's physical body).

It was not long before many recipients of the healing procedures began to display hypnotic-like behavior including automatisms, conversations with the spirits, and spontaneous chanting and singing.

As the ceremony ended, obeisance was paid to the *exus*, or messengers of the *orixás*; these entities can be mischievous and so must be placated before the session, after the session, or both if the maximum results are to be obtained. Songs, prayers, and offerings of food and drink are sent their way to cajole them and insure their cooperation.

Soon the mediums left the room, doffed their white robes and crucifixes, and joined us for refreshments. They alleged not to have recalled the events of the evening, claiming that as the *pretos velhos* had worked through them, they lost their awareness of the ongoing activities.

In 1991, with several colleagues, I attended a Candomblé ceremony in the Centro Espirita of Recife, finding ourselves immersed in candlelight, incense, and drumming. Pai Ely, the founder of the Center and a "father of the spirits," had invited us to witness an initiation: A "daughter of the temple" was about to become an *iaô*—a *filha dos santos* or "daughter of the spirits." This followed a three-week period of solitude in an isolated room (the *ronco*) where her only visitor had been Pai Ely who had brought food, water, and counsel. As she emerged from the *ronco*, we noticed that her head had been shaved (the *raspagem da cabeça*) by Pai Ely, except for a thin tuft of hair in the middle of her head. We were told that this represented a modification of the original ceremony where the skin on top of the head was cut so that the *orixás* could receive a blood offering.

For several hours, we observed the initiate dance around the central open space of the Centro Espirita, accompanied by other mediums who were letting various entities "inhabit" their bodies. Some of them had been initiated years earlier, and continued to venerate the *orixás* who had originally guided them. For some it had been Oxum, the *orixá* of the fresh water lakes and rivers; for others, it had been Oxossi, the *orixá* of the forests.

Having been silent for so long, the initiate's first words would be her *proclamação de nome*, the proclamation that would confirm the *orixá* who had served as her benefactor. Later that evening, the young woman gave us the name, "Oxumaré," the "rainbow *orixá*" who presided over life's transitions. The initiate was then welcomed as the temple's newest "daughter of the spirits."

Later I discovered that Oxumaré is a man for six months, a woman for six months, and links the earth to the sky. We were told that what we had witnessed was a *saida de iaô* ceremony in which the "daughter of the temple" finally "comes out" of her seclusion. It cumulates when the *orixá* whispers a special name (i.e., *dar o nome*). It was my understanding that the *iaô* we observed already knew that she was a member of the Oxumaré lineage.

However, there are many Oxumarés; old ones, young ones, female versions, male versions, Northern Brazil Oxumarés, Southern Brazil Oxumarés; in other words, Oxumarés come in all the colors of the rainbow. The particular identity of this initiate's Oxumaré was a vital part of the ceremony and of the social construction of the new *iaô*. Further, the entire process exemplifies three phrases quite common to initiation ceremonies, namely separation (the initiate's selection), immersion (her 3-week period of solitude), and her return (her public dance and the giving of her name).

In both of these ceremonies, and in dozens of others that I have witnessed or in which I have participated, a "trance" was supposedly induced by the rhythmic drumming and movement as well as by the assault on the senses produced by the music, incense, flickering candles, and—in some temples—pungent cigar smoke.

But it was apparent to me that powerful demand characteristics were also at work. The very reason for the mediums' presence was the incorporation of spirits; as Kleinman (1980) argues, "providing effective treatment for disease is *not* the chief reason why indigenous practitioners heal. To the extent that they provide culturally legitimated treatment of illness, they *must* heal" (p. 362).

In addition, the community of believers depended on the mothers, fathers, and children of the *orixás* to provide a connection to the spirit world that would ensure the well-being of the temple, prevent illness among those who were well, and bestow healing upon those who were indisposed.

When one medium incorporated an (*orixá*), *preto velho*, *caboclo*, or *criança*, an entire series of incorporations soon followed, domino-like. Just as many participants in hypnotic sessions seem eager to present themselves as "good subjects" (Spanos, 1989), the mediums in Afro-Brazilian healing sessions may be eager to present themselves as "good mediums," and to enact behaviors consistent with this interpretation. I have also noticed that the presence of visitors appears to increase both the speed and the dramatic qualities of spirit incorporation.

A fairly consistent similarity among mediums is their supposed inability to recall the events of the incorporation after the spirits have departed. However, Spanos (1989) has pointed out that this amnesic quality could just as easily be explained as an "achievement"; each failure to remember "adds legitimacy to a subject's self-presentation as 'truly unable to remember'," hence as deeply in "trance" (p. 101). In other words, the interpretation of hypnotic phenomena as goal-directed action is helpful in understanding mediumship as an activity that meets role demands, as mediums guide and report their behavior and experience in conformance with these demands. It may not be that they lose control over the behavior as they incorporate a spirit, but rather that they engage in an efficacious enactment of a role that they are eager to maintain.

An alternative point of view would hold that the mediums actually do lose control over their behavior, entering a "trance" state" that allows "hidden parts" of themselves to manifest as secondary personalities or, in the case of the Brazilian mediums, as spirits.

But some Brazilian practitioners with whom I have discussed these issues suggest that both the "role-playing" and "dissociative" paradigms merely describe the *mechanisms* by which a medium actually incorporates the *orixá*, discarnate entity, or spirit. It is the incorporation itself, and the subsequent behavior of the spirit, that represent the crux of mediumship. Because the possibility of spirit incorporation can hardly be demonstrated at the present time, one can simply acknowledge this argument (albeit skeptically) and focus on other aspects of these phenomena.

For example, Afro-Brazilian spiritistic ceremonies enable clients and mediums to arrive at a shared worldview in which an ailment can be discussed and treated (Torrey, 1986). In some spiritistic traditions, there are mediums who specialize in diagnosis, mediums who specialize in healing by a laying-on of hands, mediums who specialize in distant healing, and mediums who specialize in intercessory prayer.

Treatment may also consist of removing a "low spirit" from a client's "energy field," integrating one's "past lives" with the present "incarnation," the assignment of prayers or service-oriented projects, or referral to a homeopathic physician. All of these procedures contain the possibility of enhancing clients' sense of mastery, increasing their self-healing capacities, and replacing their demoralization with empowerment (Frank & Frank, 1991; Torrey, 1986).

The mediums are not the only ones who appear to manifest hypnotic-like effects. Their clients also demonstrate apparent shifts in consciousness, especially while undergoing crude surgeries without the benefit of anesthetics; however, Greenfield (1992) has observed that the Brazilian mediums make no direct effort to alter their clients' awareness.

Greenfield, who attributes the benefits of these sessions to the clients' alterations of consciousness, has observed that "no one is consciously aware of hypnotizing...patients..., and unlike the mediums, patients participate in no ritual during which they may be seen to enter a trance state" (p. 23).

However, there are a number of cultural procedures that Greenfield found to be hypnotic-like in nature. One of them is the relationship of client and healer, characterized by trust, and resembling "that between hypnotist and client" (p. 23) in that these clients act positively in response to what the medium tells them.

Another procedure is the provision of a context that allows the client to become totally absorbed in the intervention, a healing ritual that galvanizes the client's attention and distracts him or her from feeling pain. Greenfield added that the spiritistic aspects of Brazilian culture foster "fantasy proneness" because large numbers of people believe that supernatural entities are helping (or hindering) them in their daily lives (p. 24).

Rogers (1982) has divided native healing procedures into several categories (p. 112): nullification of sorcery (e.g., charms, dances, songs); removal of objects (e.g., sucking, brushing, shamanic "surgery"); "expulsion" of harmful entities (e.g., fighting the entity, sending a spirit to fight the entity, making the entity uncomfortable); retrieval of "lost souls" (e.g., by "soul catchers," by shamanic journeying); eliciting confession and penance (e.g., to the shaman, to the community); transfer of illness (e.g., to an object, to a "scapegoat"); suggestion and persuasion (e.g., reasoning, use of ritual, use of herbs); shock (e.g., sudden change of temperature, precipitous physical assault). There are hypnotic-like segments of these procedures that utilize symbols, metaphors, stories, and rituals—especially those involving group participation.

Discussion

In 2003, I gave a seminar at the University of Sochi in southwestern Russia during their annual "psychology week." On the final day of the program, a local folk healer presented a series of impressive demonstrations of self-regulation feats. For his final demonstration, he brought a wooden trough to the stage, one that measured about 10 feet long by 3 feet wide. He filled the trough with the contents of a large burlap bag, specifically, large pieces of broken glass bottles.

After taking off his shoes and sox, he paused for a short period of time, then proceeded to walk on the glass, pausing now and then to jump up and down on the bottle's jagged edges. When he reached the end of the trough, he lifted up his feet to demonstrate the absence of cuts or abrasions.

The folk healer told the audience that any of them could do the same thing if they first gazed into his eyes, allowing him to transmit enough "biological energy" so that they could withstand the rigors of the task. The only volunteer was one of the university's star athletes.

> In any event, a dozen students lined up to volunteer, looked into the healer's eyes, proceeded to walk barefoot on the glass, and emerged without so much as a scratch.

He removed his shoes and sox, slowly slouched toward the trough of glass, and stared into the healer's eyes. Abruptly, the athlete decided not to take the first step, picked up his shoes and sox, and left the stage. The healer asked for other volunteers but nobody accepted his invitation.

Suddenly, a student shouted, "Dr. Krippner, can you do it?" I replied, "Of course!"

I walked up on to the stage, removed my shoes and sox, and looked into the healer's eyes. I put one foot firmly upon the glass, then the other foot, and began to walk. Halfway through, I jumped up and down on the glass, just has the healer had done.

The applause was immediate and, out of courtesy, I thanked the folk healer for his many interesting demonstrations and suggested that he write about his abilities. However, I suspected that the purported "biological energy" was a metaphor for "self-confidence."

I had observed that the broken glass consisted of shattered beer bottles that I knew consisted of thick glass that was not razor-sharp. I also assumed that the same glass had been used numerous times; hence, the burlap bag would not contain small splinters of sharp glass. In any event, a dozen students lined up to volunteer, looked into the healer's eyes, proceeded to walk barefoot on the glass, and emerged without so much as a scratch.

The most common explanation of their success by onlookers was that they had been "hypnotized," but I took a less complex view of the phenomena. What seemed to be a mysterious rite of passage involving hypnosis and "biological energy" was explainable by a simple knowledge of the composition of basic materials, in this case glass and its qualities.

"Hypnosis" is a noun while "hypnotic-like" is an adjective, hence the use of the former term lends itself to abuse more easily than utilization of the latter term. This distinction is important when one reads such accounts as that by Torrey (1986) who surveyed indigenous psychotherapists, concluding—on the basis of anecdotal reports—that "many of them are effective psychotherapists and produce therapeutic change in their clients" (p. 205). Torrey observed that when the effectiveness of psychotherapy paraprofessionals has been studied, professionals have not always been found to demonstrate superior therapeutic skills.

The sources of the effectiveness of both groups are the four basic components of psychotherapy—a shared worldview, impressive personal qualities

> In any event, a dozen students lined up to volunteer, looked into the healer's eyes, proceeded to walk barefoot on the glass, and emerged without so much as a scratch.

of the healer, positive client expectations, and a process that enhances the client's learning and mastery (p. 207).

I would suggest that an adjective such as "psychotherapist-like" would be a more accurate term than Torrey's use of the noun "psychotherapist" in describing native practitioners. I am quite comfortable with Strupp's (1972) description: "The modern psychotherapist...relies to a large extent on the same psychological mechanisms used by the faith healer, shaman, physician, priest, and others, and the results, as reflected by the evidence of therapeutic outcomes, appear to be substantially similar" (p. 277).

Especially valuable are qualitative analyses of the experiences of both practitioners and their clients. I (Krippner, 1990) have used questionnaires to study perceived long-term effects following visits to Filipino and Brazilian folk healers, finding such variables as "willingness to change one's behavior" to significantly correlate with reported beneficial modifications in health.

Cooperstein (1992) interviewed 10 prominent alternative healers in the United States, finding that their procedures involved the self-regulation of their "attention, physiology, and cognition, thus inducing altered awareness and reorganizing the healer's construction of cultural and personal realities" (p. 99). Cooperstein concluded that the concept that most closely represented his data was "the shamanic capacity to transcend the personal self, to enter into multiform identifications, to access and synthesize alternative perspectives and realities, and to find solutions and acquire extraordinary abilities used to aid the community" (p. 121).

Indeed, the shaman's role and that of the alternative healer are both socially constructed, as are their operating procedures and their patients' predispositions to respond to the treatment. It is not only important to study the effects of the hypnotic-like procedures found in native healing, but to accurately describe them, and understand them within their own framework.

The professionalization of shamanic and other traditional healers demonstrates their similarity to practitioners of Western medicine (Feinstein & Krippner, 1997). Nevertheless, the differences cannot be ignored. Rogers (1982) has contrasted the Western and native models of healing, noting that in Western medicine, "Healing procedures are usually private, often secretive. Social reinforcement is rare... The cause and treatment of illness are usually regarded as secular... Treatment may extend over a period of months or years."

In native healing, however, "Healing procedures are often public: many relatives and friends may attend the rite. Social reinforcement is normally an important element. The shaman speaks for the spirits or the spirits speak through him [or her]. Symbolism and symbolic manipulation are vital elements. Healing is of limited duration, often lasting but a few hours, rarely more than a few days" (p. 169).

Rogers (1982) has also presented three basic principles that underlie the native approach to healing: The essence of power is such that it can be controlled through incantations, formulas, and rituals; the universe is controlled by a mysterious power that can be directed through the meticulous avoidance of certain acts and through the zealous observance of strict obligations toward persons, places, and objects; the affairs of humankind are influenced by spirits, ghosts, and other entities whose actions, nonetheless, can be influenced to some degree by human effort (p. 43).

This worldview—which fosters the efficacy of hypnotic-like procedures—varies from locale to locale but is remarkably consistent across indigenous cultures. The ceremonial activities produce shifts of attention for both the healer and the client. The culture's rules and regulations produce a structure in which the clients' motivation can operate to empower them and stimulate their self-healing aptitudes.

Western practitioners of hypnosis utilize the same human capacities that have been used by native practitioners in their hypnotic-like procedures. These include the capacity for imaginative suggestibility, the ability to shift attentional style, the potential for intention and motivation, and the capability for self-healing made possible by neurotransmitters, internal repair systems, and other components of mind/body interaction. These capacities often are evoked in ways that resemble Ericksonian hypnosis (Erickson, Rossi, & Rossi, 1976) because of their emphasis on narrative accounts.

Hypnosis and hypnotic-like activities are complex and interactive, and hence take different forms in different cultures. Yet, as with other forms of therapy, "the mask...crafted by the group's culture will also fit a majority of its members" (Kakar, 1982, p. 278).

It has become increasing apparent to cross-cultural psychologists that the human psyche cannot be extricated from the historically variable and diverse "intentional worlds" in which it plays a co-constituting part. Supposedly, writing makes reality accessible by representing consensual reality, but far too often it becomes a substitute for the reality it purports to represent (Krippner, 1994).

Therefore, I am dismayed when I see Western terms haphazardly applied to indigenous practices; for example, *amok* in Indonesia has been called "a trance-like state" and *latah* "a condition akin to hysteria" (Suryani & Jensen, 1993). By investigating ways in which different societies have constructed diagnostic categories and remedial procedures, therapists and physicians can explore novel and vital changes in their own procedures—hypnotic and otherwise—that have become obdurate and rigid.

Western medicine and psychotherapy have their roots in traditional practices, and need to explore avenues of potential cooperation with native practitioners of those healing methods that may still contain wise insights and practical applications.

References

Achterberg, J. (1985). *Imagery in healing: Shamanism and modern medicine*. Boston: Shambhala.th

Agogino, G.A. (1965). The use of hypnotism as an ethnologic research technique. *Plains Anthropologist, 10,* 31-36.th

Belo, J. (1960). *Trance in Bali.* New York: Columbia University Press.th

Bourguignon, E., & Evascu, T. (1977). Altered states of consciousness within a general evolutionary perspective: A holocultural analysis. *Behavior Science Research, 12,* 199-216.th

Bowers, M.K. (1961). Hypnotic aspects of Haitian voodoo. *International Journal of Clinical and Experimental Hypnosis, 9,* 269-282.th

Campbell, J. (1990). *Transformations of myth through time.* New York: Harper & Row.th

Cooperstein, M.A. (1992). The myths of healing: A summary of research into transpersonal healing experience. *Journal of the American Society for Psychical Research, 86,* 99-133.th

Erickson, M.H., Rossi, E.L., & Rossi, S.H. (1976). *Hypnotic realities: The induction of clinical hypnosis and the indirect forms of suggestion.* New York: Irvington.th

Feinstein, D., & Krippner, S. (1997). *The mythic path.* New York: Tarcher/Putnam.th

Frank, J.D., & Frank, J.B. (1991). *Persuasion and healing* (3rd ed.). Baltimore: Johns Hopkins University Press.th

Furst, P.T. (1977). "High states" in culture-historical perspective. In N.E. Zinberg (Ed.), *Alternate states of consciousness* (pp. 53-88). New York: Free Press.th

Gergen, K.J. (1985). The social constuctionist movement in modern psychology. *American Psychologist, 40,* 266-275.th

Greenfield, S.M. (1992). Hypnosis and trance induction in the surgeries of Brazilian spiritist healer-mediums. *Anthropology of Consciousness, 2*(3-4), 20-25.th

Jilek, W.G. (1982). *Indian healing: Shamanic ceremonialism in the Pacific Northwest today.* Blaine, WA: Hancock House.th

Kakar, S. (1982). *Shamans, mystics and doctors: A psychological inquiry into India and its healing traditions.* New York: A.A. Knopf. th

Kalweit, H. (1988). *Dreamtime and inner space: The world of the shaman.* Boston: Shambhala.th

Kirsch, I. (1990). *Changing expectations: A key to effective psychotherapy.* Pacific Grove, CA: Brooks/Cole.th

Kleinman, A. (1980). *Patients and healers in the context of culture.* Berkeley: University of California Press.th

Krippner, S. (1987). Dreams and shamanism. In S. Nicholson (Ed.), *Shamanism: An expanded view of reality* (pp. 125-132). Wheaton, IL: Theosophical Publishing.

Krippner, S. (1989). A call to heal: Patterns of entry in Brazilian mediumship. In C. Ward (Ed.), *Altered states of consciousness and mental health: A cross-cultural perspective* (pp. 186-206). Los Angeles: Sage.th

Krippner, S. (1990). A questionnaire study of experiential reactions to a Brazilian healer. *Journal of the Society for Psychical Research, 56,* 208-215.th

Krippner, S. (1993). Cross-cultural perspectives on hypnotic-like procedures used by native healing practitioners. In J.W. Rhue, S.J. Lynn, & I. Kirsch (Eds.), *Handbook of clinical hypnosis* (pp. 691-717). Washington, DC: American Psychological Association.th

Krippner, S. (1994). Cross-cultural treatment perspectives on dissociative disorders. In S.J. Lynn & J. W. Rhue (Eds.), *Dissociation: Clinical and theoretical perspectives* (pp. 338-361). New York: Guilford.th

Krippner, S. (2000). Cross-cultural perspectives on transpersonal hypnosis. In E. Leskowitz (Ed.), *Transpersonal hypnosis: Gateway to body, mind, and spirit* (pp. 141-162). New York: CRC Press.th

Krippner, S. (2002). Conflicting perspectives on shamans and shamanism: Points and counterpoints. *American Psychologist, 57,* 960-977.th

Kroger, W.S. (1977). *Clinical and experimental hypnosis* (2nd ed.). Philadelphia: Lippincott.th

Leacock, S., & Leacock, R. (1972). *Spirits of the deep: Drums, mediums and trance in a Brazilian city.* Garden City, NY: Doubleday.th

Lynn, S.L., & Rhue, J. (1988). Fantasy proneness: Hypnosis, developmental antecedents, and psychopathology. *American Psychologist, 43,* 5-44.th

Murphy, G. (1947). *Personality: A biosocial approach to origins and structure.* New York: Harper and Brothers.th

Price-Williams, D. (1975). *Explorations in cross-cultural psychology.* San Francisco: Chandler and Sharp.th

Raboteau, A.J. (1986). The Afro-American traditions. In R.L. Numbers & D.W. Amundsen (Eds.), *Caring and curing: Health and medicine in Western religious traditions* (pp. 539-562). New York: Macmillan.th

Richeport, M.M. (1992). The interface between multiple personality, spirit mediumship, and hypnosis. *American Journal of Clinical Hypnosis, 34,* 168-177.th

Rogers, S.L. (1982). *The shaman: His symbols and his healing power.* Springfield, IL: Charles C Thomas.th

Sandner, D. (1979). *Navaho symbols of healing.* New York: Harcourt Brace Jovanovich.th

Spanos, N.P. (1989). Hypnosis, demonic possession, and multiple personality: Strategic enactments and disavowals of responsibility for actions. In C. Ward (Ed.), *Altered states of consciousness and mental health: A cross-cultural perspective* (pp. 96-124). Los Angeles: Sage.th

Strupp, H.H. (1972). On the technology of psychotherapy. *Archives of General Psychiatry, 26,* 270-278.th

Suryani, L.K., & Jensen, G.D. (1993). *Trance and possession in Bali: A window on Western multiple personality.* New York: Oxford University Press.th

Thong, D., with Carpenter, B., & Krippner, S. (1994). *A psychiatrist in paradise: Treating mental illness in Bali.* Bangkok, Thailand: White Lotus Press.th

Topper, M.D. (1987). *The traditional Navajo medicine man: Therapist, counselor, and community leader. Journal of Psychoanalytic Anthropology, 10,* 217-249.

Torrey, E.F. (1986). *Witchdoctors and psychiatrists: The common roots of psychotherapy and its future.* New York: Harper & Row.th

Vogel, V.J. (1990). *American Indian medicine.* Norman, OK: University of Oklahoma Press. (Original work published 1970)th

Winkelman, M. (1984). A cross-cultural study of magico-religious practitioners. In R.-I. Heinze (Ed.), *Proceedings of the International Conference on Shamanism* (pp. 27-38). Berkeley: Independent Scholars of Asia.th

---

* The preparation of this paper was supported by the Chair for the Study of Consciousness, Saybrook Graduate School.th

** Alan Watts Professor of Psychology, Saybrook Graduate School, 450 Pacific Avenue, San Francisco, CA 94133.

Jim Morrison: The Crisis of a Failed Shaman

Stanley Krippner

The Doors: John Densmore, Robby Krieger, Ray Manzarek, and Jim Morrison

Where are shamans found in industrial societies? If shamanic capacities, at least in part, have a genetic basis, one would expect them to manifest in the population at large. Some people with shamanic propensities find their way into the health care professions; these individuals can develop and express their healing capacities as physicians, psychotherapists, or nurses. But I suspect that far more of these proto-shamans become performing artists—among them, actors, poets, and musicians. Like traditional shamans, these artists shift their attention and other phenomenological properties to access their creativity. For example, John Coltrane claimed to have had a "religious conversion" while playing with the jazz icon Thelonius Monk, who would sometimes leave his piano, dance, and "go into ecstasy" during a performance. After this "conversion," Coltrane dropped his years-long heroin habit, mastered his musical craft, and became a jazz icon himself.

Like traditional shamans, these artists have communities that look to them for guidance. These communities may be comprised of their fans, their audiences, or the members of virtual communities that log on to their websites, buy their albums, read their books, or wait in lines for tickets that will give them access to the same venue in which their icon makes a personal appearance.

James Douglass Morrison's father and mother were separated during the Second World War, due to Captain (later Rear Admiral) Morrison's assignment to the Pacific theater where he flew Hellcats from an aircraft carrier. After the war, the family was travelling on a highway near Albuquerque, where Captain Morrison was an instructor in one of the military's atomic weapons programs. Suddenly, according to Jim, they came upon an overturned truck and saw the bodies of several Pueblo Indians lying on the asphalt. Captain Morrison saw to it that an ambulance was called, while his son screamed, "I want to help, I want to help! They're dying, they're dying!" While his mother held Jim in her arms, his father told him that it was a dream—it really didn't happen. But Jim later described the event as "the most important moment of my life."

He believed that as his father's car pulled away, an Indian died and his soul passed into his body. Other members of the family did not recall the incident in such dramatic terms, noting that Jim tended to embellish and exaggerate.

Later, his friends reported that Jim's account of the accident changed from one account to the next. Nonetheless, there was an accident and it did involve Native Americans. Jim wove the incident into several of his songs such as "Dawn's Highway," "Peace Frog," and "Ghost Story."

As a student at UCLA, Jim would sit for hours discussing philosophy, most notably Nietzsche, poetry, most notably Rimbaud, and art, especially the auteur Artaud. One day, Jim and his friend

---

Krippner, S. (2009). Jim Morrison: Las crisis de un chamán fracasado [Jim Morrison: The crisis of a failed shaman]. In M. Almendro (Ed.), Krisis [Crisis](pp. 363-372). Vitoria-Gasteiz, Spain: Ediciones La Llave D.H. (Spanish)

Photo: Public Domain

Dennis Jakob reflected upon William Blake's line, "If the doors of perception were cleansed, everything would appear to man as it really is, infinite." They resolved to form a band with Jim as vocalist, and call it "The Doors: Open and Closed." Another student, John DeBella, joined the discussion group; he later reminisced, "We were into the shaman: the poet inspired."

Jim completed his class requirements at UCLA but refused to attend graduation, asking that his diploma be mailed

> They resolved to form a band with Jim as vocalist, and call it "The Doors: Open and Closed." Another student, John DeBella, joined the discussion group; he later reminisced, "We were into the shaman: the poet inspired."

to him. Soon after, he started his rock group, and began to write poems and songs, producing more material in less time than he ever would again. The other members of "The Doors" were drummer John Densmore, guitarist Robby Krieger, and keyboard player Ray Manzarek. Ray was a practitioner of Transcendental Meditation, as were John and Robby to some extent. However, Jim favored drugs and shamanism, which he considered not only his path to higher consciousness but also to his creation of many of the lyrics for his songs, such as:

> What have they done to the earth?
> What have they done to our fair sister?
> Ravaged and plundered and ripped her and bit her,
> Stuck her with knives in the side of the dawn,
> And tied her with fences and dragged her down.

But other lyrics were less than shamanistic, drawing upon other influences:

> We want the world and we want it now....
> So when the music's over,
> Turn out the lights.

Light My Fire

In 1967, the group's first album, "The Doors," was released, and early that year they played at San Francisco's legendary Fillmore Auditorium. Third billed, the Doors' presentation included a song, "Take It as It Comes," dedicated to the Maharishi Mahesh Yogi, the founder of Transcendental Meditation. But it was "Light My Fire" that was to become the Doors' signature song. Years later, listeners told the surviving Doors members that "Light My Fire" was playing when they first made love, when they were inspired to create a work of art, or when they smoked marijuana in Vietnam to temporarily escape the horrors of war.

> Come on baby, light my fire
> Try to set the night on fire.

Later, the Doors played at Ciro's on the Sunset Strip, where Jim did a shaman's dance onstage, whirling, leaping, and singing into the microphone. A week later, they played to 10,000 enthusiastic fans in a San Fernando Valley stadium where they opened for the Jefferson Airplane. After the Doors played their set, much of the audience walked out, thinking that nothing could match what they had just experienced.

The *Village Voice* called Jim a "sexual shaman"; *Vogue* magazine observed that his songs "are eerie, loaded with somewhat Freudian symbolism, poetic but not pretty, filled with suggestions of sex, death, transcendence"; in a *Time* magazine interview, Jim spoke of the importance of ritual in his work: "The Doors are looking for…a ritual.…We hide ourselves in the music to reveal ourselves." And to a reporter from *Newsweek* magazine, Jim referred to his music as "a purification ritual in the alchemical sense." For the *Los Angeles Free Press*, the Doors' music "speaks of madness that dwells within us all, of depravity and dreams, but it speaks of them in relatively conventional musical terms. That is its strength and beauty, a beauty that terrifies."

In a memorable *Rolling Stone* interview, Jim described "ritual" as a "human sculpture. In a way it's like art, because it gives form to energy, and in a way it's a custom or a repetition, a habitually recurring plan or pageant that has meaning. It pervades everything." Jim's references to ritual suggest that he was aware of the shamanic use of ritual as performance. The step-by-step pattern found in shamanic rituals provides a way for them to enact a community's mythology as well as to display their own virtuosity, whether it is singing a healing song, uttering a protective prayer, or giving a celebratory oration.

For many members of the audience, a Doors performance was akin to ritual, providing a safe structure in which to enjoy the community of other Doors adepts and to glory in the musicianship of the band. Jim's devotion to ritual was played out in 1971 when he and Patricia Kennely took their vows in a Wiccan ceremony by a high priestess and witch. After the ceremony, Jim fainted.

One of the songs in the Doors' 1969 album, "The Soft Parade," was titled, "Shaman's Blues," while Jim's poem, "Celebration of the Lizard," was printed inside the album's sleeve of their 1970 album, "Absolutely Live." This poem contained the lines, "I am the Lizard King; I can do anything." Jim once commented that the lizard is identified "with the unconscious mind and with the forces of evil." He also described his poem as an "invitation to dark forces." However, the Lizard King image he projected was not to be taken seriously; Jim remarked, "it's all done tongue-in-cheek....That's just an aspect you keep for show. I don't really take that seriously. That's supposed to be ironic."

Jim's identification with the lizard is reminiscent of shamanic power animals, and his reference to irony recalls the shaman's role as trickster. Once the shaman had discovered a power animal, it was given a special place in healing rituals and called upon for advice and counsel. The power animal was taken quite seriously and sometimes assisted shamans when they acted as tricksters to jolt their communities or their clients out of old, dysfunctional ways of thinking and behaving.

In addition, Jim's equation of the lizard with "evil" and "dark forces" is not consistent with shamanic traditions. One shamanic function was to guard the community against evil, especially that engendered by sorcerers from enemy communities. But the power animals of these sorcerers, or even of rival shamans, were not evil themselves, even though they might be put to evil purposes. To the contrary, many shamans saw the lizard as having special powers, since it was able to exist comfortably in the water as well as on the land, and because its protective coloring helped it to blend in with the environment.

The Road of Excess

Jim kept trying to expand his artistic frontiers, taking an interest in movies. He and some friends met with Carlos Castaneda, attempting to secure the film rights to *The Teachings of Don Juan*, only to be rebuffed. In the meantime, Jim's poetry won him wide acclaim even among some established poets. Michael McClure was one of several writers who were impressed by Jim's poetry. He pictured Jim as an androgynous half-spirit, half-man who "lived in the woods" and worshipped intellectual beauty. McClure also recalled another Blake line, "the road of excess leads to the palace of wisdom," and felt that Jim understood this path. "He perceived with his senses," wrote McClure, "and he altered them with alcohol (sacred to Dionysus, the god of drama and intoxication), with acid, and with the interior elixir of his own ebullience and exuberance....I know of no better poet of Jim's generation....Few poets have been such public figures or entertainers...and none have had as brief or so powerful a career." McClure planned to star Jim as Billy the Kid in "The Beard," one of McClure's theatrical pieces.

Jim's poems were described by his biographers, Jerry Hopkins and Daniel Sugerman, as representing "a grotesque otherworldliness" with frequent animal references—lizards, snakes, eagles, salamanders, and wild dogs."

Nor did Jim's professed appreciation for shamanic ritual reflect the discipline and structure that is an essential part of these performances. At one minute, Jim was a raconteur, telling party-goers fascinating stories, but the next minute, he could be a raging drunk, standing on a couch, destroying the expensive paintings on the wall.

Jim extolled the insights afforded him by LSD, but he also lived a life of excess and substance abuse, ingesting huge amounts of alcohol, cocaine, and other drugs. Jim's erratic behavior onstage reached a peak when he supposedly dropped his pants during a Miami gig. The stunt got the Doors blacklisted in some cities and turned the quartet into a circus act for what Ray Manzarek called a new mob of "rock and roll voyeurs" who came not to commune with Morrison but to watch him self-destruct.

However, the *Rolling Stone* commented, "It was Morrison's willingness to appear ridiculous that also made him great."

The Doors last performed as a quartet in 1970 in New Orleans. Ray recalled that he saw Jim's spirit leave him that night: "Everyone who was there saw it, man. He lost all his energy about midway through the set. He hung on the microphone and it just slipped away. You could actually see it leave him. He was

> Traditional shamans often engage in wild, chaotic behavior. But it is a performance, not a life style; shamans respect the needs of their community and conserve their energy for their roles as healers, mediators, and protectors.

drained." "Peace Frog," a song from the Doors' 1970 record, "Morrison Hotel," contains the lyrics:

> Indians scattered on a dawn's highway bleeding
> Ghosts crowd the young child's fragile eggshell mind.

> Everyone who was there saw it, man. He lost all his energy about midway through the set. He hung on the microphone and it just slipped away. You could actually see it leave him. He was drained.

Ray's description suggests that the Indian spirit purportedly incorporated by Jim on the highway to Albuquerque had finally left him.

In his conversations with friends, in his poetry, and in his music, Jim was preoccupied with death:

> Before I sink into the big sleep
> I want to hear
> The scream of the butterfly.

When the Rolling Stones guitarist Brian Jones died, Jim distributed to his audiences copies of a poetic tribute; in several interviews, Jim suggested that his life would be a short one.

Over the years, there had been dozens of differing accounts of Jim's demise so, in 1971, when news reached his friends of his death in Paris, there was widespread disbelief. In the company of Pamela Kennealy in their Paris flat, Jim indeed had died, perhaps of a heroin overdose, perhaps of contaminated cocaine, perhaps of a heart attack, perhaps of foul play. Pamela died of a heroin overdose three years later, and for several years there were people who insisted that Jim's death was a hoax and that he was still alive, waiting for the right moment, shaman-like, to be reborn.

Thirty-six years after his death, a less fanciful scenario was presented by Sam Bernett who claimed that Morrison had died of a heroin overdose on a toilet seat in a night club and that his body was taken to his apartment and dumped into his bathtub.

In any event, Greg Kot, in the *Rolling Stone*, observed that Jim saw rock music "as a theatre of chaos, an opportunity to be pursued with reckless, sometimes self-destructive zeal....In the end, he was rock and roll by refusing to live up to anyone's definition of it but his own."

Years after Jim's death, Ray told an interviewer for *Sixteen* magazine, "When the Siberian shaman gets ready to go into his trance, all the villagers get together and shake rattles and blow whistles and play whatever instruments they have to send him off. There is a constant pounding, pounding, pounding. And these sessions last for hours and hours. It was the same way with the Doors when we played in concert....It was like Jim was an electric shaman, and we were the electric shaman's band, pounding away behind him."

The Wrong Issues

Val Kilmer, who played Jim in the Hollywood film, "The Doors," commented on the musician in a 2000 television interview for "The Actors' Studio." Kilmer's appraisal was that "He chose the wrong issues." Morrison and the Doors had recorded five gold albums in a row.

The quality of their live performances was uneven, but they were certainly, as Hopkins and Sugerman (1997) state in their biography of Morrison, "the most dramatic group on the circuit. But during many of these appearances, Jim appeared stoned, drunk, or belligerent, and many of the Doors' gigs were marred by injuries, riots, and arrests.

At one time, there were over a dozen paternity suits filed against Jim. I attended the Doors' January 1969 Madison Square Garden gig. Decades later, I discovered that my friend, the Hollywood photographer Bonnie Colodzin, had also heard the Doors, recalling that Jim's music was "of another world, and he seemed to be in that other world when he was playing."

What went wrong? What were the "wrong issues" that Jim chose? Traditional shamans often engage in wild, chaotic behavior. But it is a performance, not a life style; shamans respect the needs of their community and conserve their energy for their roles as healers, mediators, and protectors.

Jim was out of control more often than he was in control. His music and his poetry reflect craft and skill, his life style does not. He chose dissipation over control, rage over compassion, death over life. His early demise indicates his lack of concern for his own well-being. Nor, unlike traditional shamans, did he manifest concern for the audiences who idolized him and were transported by his music into other worlds.

Nevertheless, the surviving members of The Doors kept performing, and Morrison's albums enjoyed brisk sales, especially among new fans, many of whom assigned him heroic status.

In 2011, a *Rolling Stone* readers' poll placed Jim in 5th place on the list of "The Best Lead Singers of All Time." Earlier, the editors of *Rolling Stone* ranked him as 47th among the 100 "Greatest Singers of All Time," and *Classic Rock Magazine* placed him as number 22 among the "Greatest Singers of Rock."

On a trip to Paris, a friend of mine and I visited Jim's grave at the P`ere Lachaise Cemetery, not far from such other poets as Guillaume Apollinaire and Alfred de Musset as well as other performers including Sarah Bernhardt and Isadora Duncan. The usual procedure is for space to be given a 30-year limit, with remains being disinterred if fees are not paid at the end of that time. However, Jim's parents, who he once disowned, arranged for his body to rest there "in perpetuity."

References

Achterberg, J. (1985). *Imagery in healing: Sha-manDensmore, J. (2002, December 26). Should the Doors sell out? *Rolling Stone*, pp. 44-45.

Doors Music Company. When the Music's Over © 1967; Light My Fire © 1967; Peace Frog © 1970.

Hopkins, J., & Sugerman, D. (1997). *No one gets out alive*. New York: Barnes & Nobel. (Original work published 1980)

Kot, G. (2001, February 1). Reopening the Doors. *Rolling Stone*, p. 54.

Walt, V. (2007, July 30). Postcard, Paris. *Time*, p. 6.

change of season: for us?
jim perkinson 10/17/98

dark "v' drift of
geese over the river
like tamed smoke
softening the solitary stacks
the slant of light
opalescent with smell
of wet summons
to places we can no longer
hear like a leaf of gold
in drama-dance of
arabesque flight
never to be repeated
that way again
and the sky
and the blue
and the hair of skin
and the eye
and the brisk of tongue
and the bark of time
and the wine
and the loss
and the droop of green
and the flutter
and the brown carcass of desire

and the yellow iris of vision
and the bite of knowledge
and the sadness
and the sadness
and the sadness . . .

do we think we know
what this is?
do we write verse
muse heart
and croon old memory
like drunk like high
like head opened to the ancestor
like ancient rock
over ancient sea shimmering?
do we really think
this is scarlet time
for us? god in
carnival dress for us?
the metaphysics of
meta-conscious-color
of world going cold again
for us?
for us—spirit

like haitian marti gras
like bahian orixa-parade
like mantra of tantric skull of heat
like cemetery laughter
for us?
do we think
it is a show
for us?

do not love this time
do not love this earth-change
do not love this calliope play
of struck brown-red-yellow-green
ganga breath of juju change
do not!
do not love this . . .
unless you can love
the breaking of your own stem
like an old buddha
losing his last two teeth
suddenly grinning infant gums
at the ghost he alone can see
coming to fetch him
for the last time

christmas
jim perkinson 12/1/98

what births
in the space between breaths
like a prophecy in the throat
like a word under the tongue
like a groan in a world
gone cold and yellow with despair
what hovers there
in that milli-second womb
in that unprepared place
between hurt and anger
between flight and fist
between your lip and the
apocalypse?
what if you are
the fecund possibility
the incubating pulse
the hope
of the entire world?
what if the way you draw
your next breath
determines the course of history

like a bellows transfiguring
gold into fire
a gulp of air
giving room to a moan
becoming mind
birthing the slight sound
of a beat of wild and free
round and real
the revelation of anticipation
in spite of yourself?
what if your next move
is the only muscle
the messiah will ever have
this time through the night
and the chain of that causation
from your choice of concentration
from what lives under your rib cage
is inescapable?
what grins in your teeth?
what reflects like spangled neon
at the edge of your eye?

what if that thin something
that little release of
unrecognized
unrationalized
unrealized
unbeckoned
unreckoned
joy
is the very archimedian lever of god
moving the world just outside your
foot
to a parallel universe of destiny
as "delivered"
will you still disbelieve
and refuse to give birth
    to yourself?

Learning from the Spirits: Candomble, Umbanda, and Kardecismo in Recife, Brazil

Stanley Krippner

Cultural Background

In Brazil, mediumship is a central component within the ritual practice of what can be termed its "spiritistic religions." Mediumship involves the belief in the bodily incorporation of spiritual agents and/or the channeling of information from the "divine world" to the "material world," often for therapeutic purposes.

In the United States, "mediums" are conceptualized somewhat differently from "channelers"; the former group focuses on communication with the dead and the latter with a broader scope of "entities" or purported "sources" of information. Mediums and channelers both purport to be able to receive information that supposedly does not originate from consensual reality (e.g., from living persons, media, their own memory).

Some writers in the United States (e.g., Hastings, 1991; Klimo, 1998) use the term "medium" to refer to practitioners who purportedly obtain this information from deceased persons, and "channelers" to practitioners who claim

---

Krippner, S. (2008). Learning from the spirits: Candomblé, Umbanda, and Kardecismo in Recife, Brazil. *Anthropology of Consciousness*, 19, 1-32.

Photo: George Berticevich Photographer
Copyright 2025

---

to obtain information from other "spiritual entities" (e.g., deities, "nature spirits," inhabitants of "other dimensions") as well.

Mediumship is typically induced during so-called altered states of consciousness (perhaps better described as "patterns of phenomenological properties," Rock & Krippner, 2007). These "states" (or "patterns") play an important role in the rituals of spiritistic religions, i.e., those African-Brazilian religions in which "spirits" (most of whom "accompanied" slaves to Brazil during the Diaspora) occupy a central role, e.g., Batuque, Caboclo, Candomblé, Kardecismo, Macumba, Tambor de Minas, Umbanda, Xango.

Permeating these religions' mythologies are stories about a "Sky God" and his intermediaries, the *orixás* (also spelled *orishas*), who symbolize the primordial forces of nature. These *orixás* are believed to be powerful and terrifying, but also similar to humans in that they can be talked to and pleaded with, as well as cajoled through special offerings. The *orixás* and less powerful entities (e.g., *exus* and *pombajiras* who are "lower" spirits, *caboclos* or Brazilians of mixed Indian, European, and African heritage, *crianças* or spirits of babies or young children, *pretos velhos* or spirits of elderly slaves, or even of one's ancestors or former "incarnations") can take hold of the mind and body of a human through acts of voluntary "spirit incorporation," which were central features in African ritual practice.

African religious practitioners gained access to the "divine world" in three ways: by making offerings to the *orixás*; by "divining," or foretelling the future with the help of an *orixá*; and by incorporating an *orixá*, ancestral spirit, or other entity who—when benevolent—would warn the community about possible calamities, diagnose illnesses, and prescribe cures. The "medium" through whom these spirits spoke and moved, typically performed this task voluntarily.

The "trance," or pattern of phenomenological properties (such as the medium's dissociative capacities and his or her capacity to become absorbed in the task) required for the voluntary gift of the medium's mind and body to the *orixá* or spirit, was brought about by such practices as dancing, singing, and drumming. Allowing the *orixá* to "inhabit" one's body not only survived the transition from Africa to Brazil, but occasionally made use of new world indigenous techniques of mind-alteration, such as the use of strong tobacco or other psychotropic plants (Villoldo & Krippner, 1987).

Of all the Brazilian spiritist movements, Candomblé (or, more accurately, the Candomblés, given the variety of forms it has taken in different parts of the country) is the one that most closely resembles the original religions of Africa, retaining the original names and worship of many West African *orixás* (Bastide, 1960, 1971). In Candomblé, devotion is typically reserved for only the *orixás* and *exús*, which reflects its African heritage. The name "Candomblé" seems to have derived from *candombe* or *gandombe*, a community dance held by the slaves who worked on coffee and sugar cane plantations.

Among the other most prominent spiritistic movements are Umbanda and Kardecismo. Kardecismo or Kardecism is also called *Espiritismo* or Spiritism, owes more to the teachings of Allen Kardec, a French pedagogue than to the African traditions. Umbanda gives a greater emphasis to Brazil's Christian heritage than to the African *orixás*. In some parts of Brazil, Santo Daime, a religious movement using a psychoactive tea, ayahuasca, as a sacrament, has added elements of Umbanda to its services, demonstrating the syncretization that has characterized most post-colonization religious movements in Brazil (Giesler, 1985).

In fact, the Roman Catholic Church has spawned the *Culto aos Santos,* the Cult of the Saints, which is suffused with healing rituals reminiscent of African-Brazilian practices. Pentecostal Protestantism (e.g., Wood, Williams, & Chijiwa, 2007) has little use for the African-Brazilian religions, but encourages its adherents to become "seized by the Holy Spirit" as an alternative to African-based spirit incorporation. All of these religious movements can be classified as "ecstatic religions" (Lewis, 1971) because they deliberately foster shifts in their adepts' patterns of phenomenological properties. As a result, these shifts provide opportunities for direct contact with the divine world, albeit it a cosmology that varies from group to group.

Candomblé, Kardecismo, and Umbanda, as the three major spiritistic groupings (Hess, 1994), can be differentiated along an *ethnic/class*-oriented continuum of Brazilian spiritism. Umbanda is situated at the center of this continuum--with *cultos de nação* (cults of African nations, like Candomblé) at one extreme and the "more European" Kardecism on the other. *Umbandistas* typically draw from a broad range of beliefs and practices associated with either the "magical" African-Brazilian pole or the "faux scientific" European-Brazilian pole.

The ethnic make-up of these religious groups have historically reflected this continuum; with Candomblé appealing mainly to African-Brazilians of poorer segments of society, Kardecismo appealing to middle class European-Brazilians, and Umbanda appealing to a more varied mixture of ethnicities primarily from Brazil's lower socio-economic classes. However, descriptions of ongoing changes in ethnic and class demography in each religious group (Brown, 1994) defy any rigid categorization along these lines and testify to the fluid religious landscape in Brazil.

Along a spiritual continuum, however, the three groupings represent a commonality of belief in the spirit realm, the power and efficacy of spirit agents, and the ability of human clients to interact with and embody these agents through the ritualized methods of spirit incorporation.

The Pathologizing of Spiritistic Practices

In the late 19th century, and well into the 20th century, the practice of mediumship by members of these three groups and several smaller sects were identified with psychopathology by the psychiatric establishment in Brazil. Nina Rodrigues (1896/1935) conducted extensive research on various types of African-Brazilian mediumistic practices. He considered them all the outcome of "hysterical phenomena," allowed by the "extreme neuropathic or hysterical" and "profoundly superstitious" personality of the Negro.

Xavier de Oliveira (1931) claimed that in a period of 12 years, 9.4% of a total of 18,281 patients hospitalized in the Psychiatric Clinic of the University of Rio de Janeiro "suffered psychosis caused only and exclusively by Spiritism." Pacheco e Silva (1936) maintained that Spiritism "acts predominantly from proneness, aggravating an already existing psychosis or stimulating latent mental disturbances in an individual of psychopathic constitution."

Two elements played a role in the psychiatrists' viewpoint. First, the intellectuals of Brazil were attempting to create a modern Eurocentric nation, suppressing or pathologizing all "primitive" creeds and practices. Secondly, the psychiatrists were either Roman Catholic or secular materialists; for both groups, Spiritism was an enemy to be overcome (Moreira-Almeida, Silva de Almeida, & Neto, 2005, p. 14)

The seminal work of Roger Bastide (1978) took a different perspective. Bastide concluded that mental pathology explained some cases, but that "possession trance is sociological before pathological." Psychiatric theory henceforth started developing cultural sensibility, also influenced by the development of transcultural psychiatry and ethnopsychiatry (Lewis-Fernandez & Kleinman, 1995).

Within this rubric, research data have been collected that supports the position that mediumship is a skill, one that can empower its practitioners (especially if they are women in a patriarchal culture) and provide support for members of the community who are suffering from anxiety, depression, and other afflictions (Krippner, 1997).

Possession and Dissociation

The term "incorporation" is used by the spiritistic groups in Brazil to describe situations in which practitioners allow themselves to be "taken over" by a "spirit entity," exemplified by mediums who voluntarily allow the incorporation of an *orixá*. On the other hand, the term "possession" is used to define the experience of an involuntary takeover, one that is usually distressful, unwelcome, and that may be long-lasting (Negro, Palladino-Negro, & Louza, 2002, p. 65). The later type typically requires the intervention of a religious specialist who can "exorcise" or "depossess" the offending agency.

However, there have been difficulties in clarifying the relationship of "possession" to concepts like "trance," "altered states," and "dissociation." In their study of the Batuque, an African-Brazilian possession tradition, Leacock and Leacock (1972) conceive of "possession" as "the presence in the human body of a supernatural being" and trance as "an altered psychological state" (p. 217).

Although they also employ the expression "trance-possession", it would be mistaken to assume that the terms are synonymous. Distinctions must be made in regard to "possession" as belief and "possession" as experience. That is, "possession" can refer to the *belief* in the potential for voluntary or spontaneous interaction with or incorporation of a benevolent and malevolent spirit. The culturally or individually construed belief, in turn, can have consequences for individual behavior as well as social interaction. Possession can also occur without the physiological alterations of consciousness associated with "dissociative trance." The Ethiopian *zâr* cult, for example, blames the origins of many types of diseases and maladies on possession, but then induce trance *after* one is said to have been possessed in order to communicate with the spirit (Walker, 1972). This is also common in Umbanda and contemporary Brazilian Pentecostalism.

Finally, possession can be understood in terms of "trance-possession" (i.e., "possession trance") in which the incorporation of a spirit is experienced concurrently with psychophysiological changes and modifications in the conscious state that are characteristic of "dissociative trance."

The anthropologist Erika Bourguignon (1976, 1977), an investigator of "spirit possession," has differentiated between "possession" (in which a "spirit" produces changes in someone's behavior, health, or disposition without an accompanying loss of awareness); "possession trance" (in which someone loses conscious awareness, while the invading spirit's own behavior, speech patterns, and body movements "take over" that person evoking changes that can be observed by outsiders), and "trance" (a so-called "altered state of consciousness" including the loss of conscious awareness but without the presence of a spirit or other outside entity).

"Possession trance" can be voluntary or involuntary, helpful or harmful. In "possession trance," the intrusive spirit may be quite benevolent, bringing new insights to the "possessed" individual by means of "automatic writing," "channeling," or "mediumship."

Sometimes the spirit plays the role of a trickster, teaching the individual life lessons through embarrassment, playful activities, or humor. These results are quite different from those cases of "possession" in which an invading entity takes over a victim's body as the result of a malevolent sorcerer's curse or simply to gratify the spirit entity's "earthbound" impulses and desires. These types of "trance" are extremely dissociative; the client manifests experiences and behaviors that seem to exist apart from, or appear to have been disconnected from, the mainstream (or flow) of his or her conscious awareness, behavioral repertoire, and/or self-identity (Krippner, 1997, p. 8).

Psychophysiology and Dissociation

From a psychophysiological perspective "dissociation" involves the disengaging of the cognitive processes from their executive, higher-order, volitional faculties (Winkelman, 2000). Generalized psychophysiological correlates of what might be described as trance with dissociative aspects involve hemispheric lateralization that favors (in right-handed people) the right hemisphere (more closely associated with intuitive, emotive, non-logical, spatial, imaginative thought and perception) over the ordinarily dominant left hemisphere (more closely associated with linguistic and logical-type processing). This can eventually shift toward cortical synchronization (Schumaker, 1995).

Winkelman (1986) suggested that a wide range of culturally-patterned induction techniques leads to generalized *parasympathetic dominance* in which the frontal cortex exhibits high-voltage, slow-wave, synchronous EEG patterns (e.g., theta rhythms) that originate in the limbic system (hippocampal-septal region and the amygdala) and proceed to frontal regions via limbic-frontal innervations. Some alterations in consciousness, such as some forms of meditation and hypnosis, do exhibit small variances in EEG patterning, and similar differences are also noticed between voluntarily and spontaneously induced states. Winkelman (1986) also indicated that the involvement of the limbic system is an important part of the neural architecture of dissociative trance. For instance, it has been implicated in the modulation of a variety of functions including basic survival drives and hypothalamic/pituitary release of neurotransmitter and endogenous opiates.

The hypothalamic action, in turn, influences, among other things, dissociation trance-related hallucinations, analgesia, and amnesia. The hypothalamus also controls the sympathetic (excitatory) and parasympathetic (inhibitory) nervous systems, the latter being associated with decreased cortical excitation and increased hemispheric synchronization. Evidence also shows that parasympathetic dominance can be induced through excessive *sympathetic activation*; such as through drumming, dancing, and chanting, all of which are common features of ritual practice and in which the homeostatic reciprocal action of the autonomic nervous system collapses.

Lex (1979) suggested that the "*raison d'être* for rituals is the readjustment of dysphasic biological and social rhythms by manipulation of neurophysiological action under controlled conditions" (p.144). Rituals, such as those associated with possession and mediumship, therefore, not only provide psychological relief from social and environmental stressors, they are mechanisms that employ driving techniques which "tune" the nervous system through hemispheric lateralization, parasympathetic dominance, and cortical synchronization.

In a field study conducted by Don and Moura (2000), topographic brain mapping at midline scalp locations of what they referred to as "healer-mediums" revealed increased brain activity when the healer-mediums reported being incorporated by a spirit, compared to resting baseline conditions at midline scalp locations. These results suggest the presence of a hyper-aroused brain state associated with the possession trance behaviors of the mediums. In contrast, a small sample of patients monitored during possession trance revealed no high frequency brain activity.

A Call to Heal

Between 1973 and 1987, I visited Brazil six times, meeting over one hundred spiritistic mediums and attending some three dozen sessions in which they allegedly incorporated spirits and attempted various types of healing and counseling. Often with the help of an interpreter, I interviewed two Candomblé, 15 Umbanda, 14 Kardecismo, and eight "eclectic" mediums, asking them how they had become adept at incorporating spirits for the purpose of alleviating physical and/or emotional distress of their clients. There were 22 women and 18 men in this group, and they represented a dozen cities or towns in six different Brazilian states. Various methods of socialization appeared to have operated, which I was able to categorize into five pathways that allowed the practitioners to receive their "call."

The most common pathway was through dreams, visions, or similar revelatory experiences in which they were "called" by *orixás*, spirit entities, or deceased relatives. Some of them reported imagery from "past lives" that motivated them to begin a training program, usually one organized by one of the spiritistic religions. Some of the research participants reported the spontaneous incorporation of a spirit guide during a religious service. A few respondents claimed to have received personal instruction from the spirit guide, rather than from a *babalao* or *pai-de-santo* ("father of the spirits") or *iyalorixa* or *mae-de-santo* ("mother of the spirits) in a local Candomblé or Umbanda *terreiro* (temple) or Kardec healing center. This pathway was especially common among eclectic mediums, many of whom combined spiritistic doctrine with Eastern philosophy or Western psychology.

The second most common way in which some research participants received the "call" was their membership in a family that had a legacy of mediumship. From childhood, these practitioners had observed their relatives incorporating spirits, and eagerly attempted to follow the family tradition. One medium, whose mother was a celebrated Kardec medium, recalled incorporating spirits when she was seven years of age. On the other hand, I interviewed several mediums who were distressed that none of their children seemed interested in becoming mediums. They consoled themselves by claiming that the "gift" often "skips a generation" or that the "call" frequently occurs later in life.

Some practitioners began to attend spiritistic services out of curiosity or because the ceremonies were spiritually satisfying to them. They volunteered for the charitable work carried on by the *terreiro* or healing center, spending time with the aged, the infirm, the sick, the handicapped, or the orphaned. Gradually, these individuals were assimilated into the movement and requested mediumship training.

Other practitioners were identified as potential mediums when they came to a temple or center to request assistance, or when a medium came to their aid when they fell ill. As part of their treatment, they were advised to attend mediumship classes. It was not uncommon for a person who had been diagnosed with "schizophrenia" or given some other psychiatric label to be told to avoid medication and hospitalization because it would misdirect their mediumistic "gift."

A final pathway to the "call" was through attending lectures or reading books on spiritistic topics. Kardecismo and the African-Brazilian religions place a strong emphasis on charitable services and altruistic attitudes, a stance that appealed to some men and women who

> Although her father objected, she followed the "call"; as she told me, "Once the orixá calls, there is no other path to take." If one spurns the "call," disaster, sickness, or mental illness might follow.

had been successful in their career but whose life lacked meaning. Involvement in mediumship filled this existential void and provided a new avenue for the expression of their talents and capacities.

In several cases, there was an overlap of categories. In 1983, when I was in Salvador de Bahia, I interviewed Mae Menininha de Gantois (Little Girl Mother of Gantois) who lived with her family at the Casa Branca (the White Temple), one of the oldest Candomblé *terreiros* in Brazil.

She had just celebrated her 83rd birthday and took pleasure in telling me that her grandfather had been a slave from Dahomey, Africa, and that her grandmother, Maria Julia Nazare, was a *mae-do-santo* who had helped found the first Candomblé temple in 1830. Mae Menininha had a series of visions and dreams that she interpreted as a "call" to mediumship. Although her father objected, she followed the "call"; as she told me, "Once the *orixá* calls, there is no other path to take." If one spurns the "call," disaster, sickness, or mental illness might follow.

A Pai do Santo in Recife

In 1989, the results of this survey were published, and in 1990 I met Pai Ely (Father Eli), born in 1932 as Manoel Rabelo Pereira, a *pai-de-santo* in Recife, Brazil. I visited his *terreiro* or temple, the Lar de Ita, several times between 1990 and 2006, making observations and conducting interviews with him and members of his congregation.

I was especially interested in Pai Ely because he conducts both Candomblé and Umbanda services in the Center, and is well versed in both traditions. I published a case study describing his "call" and his practice, noting that his temple was one of the first to eliminate the practice of animal sacrifice, which had been a holdover from colonial times (Krippner, 1998/1999).

Formerly, Pai Ely had been a bank executive. When he was in his early 40s, he began to see and hear spirits and *orixás*. He was uncomfortable with these phenomena and fought the presence of the entities, especially when they told him that he was being "called" to become a healer. As a result of this incident and those like it, Pai Ely began to transform his social identity from a bank executive to a *pai-de-santo*.

Pai Ely told us that his teacher, Master Oascati, a man in his 70s at the time of our visit, lives in Benin, Africa. Master Oascati once told Pai Ely that he must constantly work on himself, trying to obtain clearer and purer information from the *orixás*. Master Oascati explained that it is extremely easy for one's own biases, experiences, and fantasies to contaminate the spiritual message.

In Pai Ely's words, "The *orixá* paints only one small part of the picture; the medium must paint the rest." As a result, the client receives no "pure" information; according to Pai Ely it is unusual for more than 25% of the *orixá's* message to get through. Furthermore, many of the messages are from *exús*, *pombajiras*, or "lower" ancestral spirits, not *orixás*; these entities are not "illuminated beings" and may unknowingly distort information or deliberately play tricks on the mediums and their clients. To prepare to receive the *orixás* and "higher" spirits, Pai Ely will usually engage in meditation or group prayer (Krippner, 1998/1999).

Invitation to Research

In 2000, we accepted an invitation to initiate a research study with two Brazilian spiritistic practitioners, the first a leader of rituals in both the Candomblé and the Umbanda religions, and the second a practitioner of Kardecismo Spiritism. Both were regarded as "mediums" by their communities; i.e., they were thought to be able to convey messages from the dead and from other non-corporeal entities to the living.

Our arrangements were made by Valter da Rosa Borges, a well-known Brazilian parapsychologist and author (e.g., Borges, 1992). The purpose of our study was not to evaluate the purported mediumistic abilities of these two practitioners but to initiate psychological and psychophysiological studies that, perhaps, could be emulated with other practitioners from similar cultural backgrounds.

Our theoretical framework was the "high risk model," as described by Ian Wickramasekera I (1991, 1998), that can identify individuals who are likely to have incongruence in their mind/body relationship which puts them at risk for the development of psychosomatic and psychophysiological illnesses.

The Psychophysiology of Two Mediums

In 1999, my colleagues and I enlisted Pai Ely's cooperation for a psychophysiological study of his mediumship (he is labeled 'priest' in the figures). Another well-known Recife medium, Jose' Jacques Andrade, agreed to participate (he is labeled 'artist' in the figures), and we utilized the services of a local tour guide and translator (E.O.S.), who was not associated with any of the local spiritistic movements, as an age-matched control because when one works with individuals with special abilities, it is useful to make intra-cultural comparisons (Murphy, 1969) (E.O.S. is labeled 'control' in the figures).

All three research participants signed informed consent forms (designed by the Saybrook University Institutional Review Board), and both practitioners encouraged us to use their actual names. Each of the mediums also received permission from their spirit guides to participate in the investigation, and we dubbed the spirits our "co-researchers."

Jose' Jacques Andrade, born in 1945, is a medium who is active in the Kardecismo movement. During a 1998 visit to his center, the Leonardo da Vinci Salon of Mediumistic Art, Krippner observed a Kardec ceremony, one which culminated in Andrade's "incorporation" of several famous artists (e.g., Monet, da Vinci) and a few who were unknown to anyone including Andrade himself. In preparation for this occurrence, Andrade and his group sang several hymns and prayed. Andrade, nearly deaf, did little singing as he was preparing himself, through prayer, for the incorporation of his colleagues in the divine world.

Once the aid of the spirits had been evoked, Andrade dipped both of his hands into jars of paint and, with two canvasses in front of him, swiftly began to execute remarkably attractive landscapes, still life paintings, and portraits, two at a time. For example, with one hand, he produced a landscape signed "Monet," while with the other, a still life signed "Cezanne." The other artists represented that evening included Van Gogh, Manet, Picasso, da Vinci, Degas, Portinari, and Toulouse-Lautrec.

Andrade produced these works at an

extraordinary speed, each work taking no more than ten minutes. Each painting bore at least a passing resemblance to the style of the artist being incorporated, some more than others. The artists whose style was the most delicate were the first to be incorporated, while those whose brush strokes were coarser were incorporated last, when Andrade's fingers were coated with several layers of paint. In other words, Monet and Degas would arrive on the scene before Picasso and Van Gogh.

Lima (1998) collected 107 of paintings executed by Andrade between 8 September 1994 and 7 November 1995, looking for similarities in the process itself, in the product, and in the signatures of the purported artists. Nearly 300 different artists were represented in this collection; the most frequent being Miro (3.7% of the total), Van Gogh (3.2%), and Dali (2.3%). The paintings attributed to Miro were thought to resemble the artists' later works rather than his earlier works. Lima reported that before beginning to paint, Andrade hesitated for about 20 or 30 seconds; the average time spent on a painting was 6 minutes, 28 seconds.

Andrade showed a preference for using his right hand, although he would frequently use both hands, producing two paintings at the same time, sometimes employing his palms as well as his fingertips. He would initiate the paintings from the center of the canvas, often with a circle, then branching into its other sections, whether painting a landscape, a person's head, or a still life. Andrade inscribed the letter "H" in a truncated manner, independently of the artist he was "channeling."

The amount of light during the session appeared to be linked with the choices of colors; dim lighting was associated with such dark colors as black and brown, bright lighting with white and yellow, and intermediate lighting with the major colors of the spectrum. Finally, there were many fences in the paintings, interpreted as representing Andrade's auditory challenges.

Lins (1999) reviewed the literature on "paranormal painting," noting that in a few cases, correspondences between the medium's productions and those of the deceased artist were established by judges said to have been knowledgeable concerning art history. Lins created a scale for evaluating the artist merits of these paintings; level of artistic production, diversification, length of time, peculiarities of the work, and the artist's signature. The artistic production receives a score of 0, 1, or 2 for each item on this scale; if the total is smaller than 4, Lins would not consider it a "paranormal painting."

Our third research participant, E.O.S., was born in 1945. He is a tour guide and schoolteacher. He had assisted one of us (Krippner) as a translator in 1993 and 1995, and was familiar with the spiritist religions of the area. We felt that the inclusion of a control participant was essential to determine if there were cultural constraints or environmental demand characteristics that could account, at least in part, for the results obtained from the two mediums. All research participants denied being on any form of medication before or during the testing (Wickramasekera, I., Krippner, S., & Wickramasekera II, I.; 1997).

Instruments

Research Instruments

The Dissociative Experiences Scale (DES) (Bernstein & Putnam, 1986) is used as a screening tool for both clinical and nonclinical populations to assess the frequency and intensity of dissociation in one's daily life. The revised version of the DES (Carlson & Putnam, 1993) used in this study consists of 28 items that ask what percentage of the time (i.e., 0% to 100% in intervals of 10) the individual experiences certain dissociative events or perceptions. The higher the DES score, the more likely it is that the respondent has a dissociative identity disorder; however, only 17% of those who score above 30 on the DES are diagnosed with the disorder (Carlson & Putnam, 1993).

Absorption

The Tellegen Absorption Scale (TAS) (Tellegen, 1977; Tellegen & Atkinson, 1974) appears to measure an individual's capacity for experiences that involve both the narrowing and broadening of attentional focus. These attentional states are characterized by marked restructuring of one's phenomenal self and one's world (Tellegen & Atkinson, 1974).

Roche and McConkey (1990) call absorption a capacity to experience alterations of cognition and emotion over a broad range of situational experiences. The TAS may be a reasonably good predictor of responses to cognitive suggestions under hypnosis such as hallucinations, but a less reliable predictor of hypnotically-presented ideomotor tasks (Kirsch & Council, 1992). The TAS consists of 34 true or false response items; administration time is approximately 10 minutes. A Portuguese translation of the TAS (McIntyre, Klein, & Gonçalves, 2001) was employed in this study.

Psychophysiological Measures

I. Wickramasekera, Krippner, and J. Wickramasekera (2001) obtained psychophysiological data from all three research participants with a portable computerized polygraph when they attended a parapsychological conference in Recife in 1999. I. and J. Wickramasekera collected the polygraph data; Krippner was present at most of the test sessions, which were held in a quiet and comfortable Recife hotel room.

The psychophysiological equipment that was used in this study measures hand temperature, heart rate, bilateral skin conductance, muscle tension (electromyography or EMG), and electrical brain activity (electroencephalography or EEG). In other words, it records responses from both the peripheral nervous system (PNS) and the central nervous system (CNS).

Results: Dissociative Experiences Scale

The DES was administered by Brazilian colleagues and was scored by Krippner, once the results arrived in the United States. Andrade obtained a score of 72, and Pai Ely obtained a score of 87, both scores place them in the "highly dissociative" category; E.O.S. received a score of 54, which also places him in the "highly dissociative" category. For example, all three respondents reported that they often "have the experience of sometimes remembering a past event so vividly that [it feels] as they were reliving that event," but only the mediums reported that they often "have the experience of feeling that their body does not seem to belong to them." The fact that our control participant was "highly dissociative" suggests that this trait might be cultural in nature rather than idiosyncratic.

Results: Tellegen Absorption Scale and SUDS

The Tellegen Scale was administered by Brazilian colleagues and was scored by Krippner, once the results arrived in the United States. Pai Ely obtained a score of 28, which places him in the "high absorption" category. Both Andrade and E.O.S. received scores of 21, which place them in the "medium absorption" category. For example, all three research participants claimed to be moved by songs that they enjoyed, to get caught up in the action while watching a movie, and liked to watch clouds take various shapes in the sky.

However, only Pai Ely claimed to anticipate statements from other people when discussing allegedly supernatural experiences, to feel imaginary matters with such intensity that they seemed real, and for music to evoke colorful pictures in his imagination. He also claimed to think in visual images, to be able to imagine his body becoming so heavy it would not move, and to occasionally feel "suspended in air" while listening to a band or orchestra. Because there are no Brazilian norms for either test, the results need to be viewed with caution and not overly interpreted.

The Subjective Units of Distress/Disturbance Scale (SUDS) was administered to all three participants to measure their distress or anxiety level under the three experimental conditions. As Figure 7 shows, the graphs for all three participants are distinct, with Andrade (artist) and the control participant having the highest values under the channel condition while Pai Ely (priest) had a notably lower value.

Psychophysiological Results: Andrade (Artist)

Andrade's psychophysiology was measured under two baseline resting conditions (eyes open; eyes closed). Then, while he was imagining "incorporating" a celebrated artist from the "spirit world," and finally, during his return to baseline conditions (eyes open; eyes closed). Each condition lasted for four minutes.

During the first baseline (eyes open) condition, Andrade demonstrated about a 5 degree Fahrenheit discrepancy between mean temperature in his left hand (Mean: 80.77, Standard Deviation: .25) and his right hand (Mean: 85.55, SD: .31). When Andrade was asked to close his eyes and relax (for 4 minutes), there was a drop in temperature in both his left hand (Mean: 79.57, SD: .10) and his right hand (Mean: 83.88, SD: .19).

When Andrade was asked to imagine "incorporating" an artist, his left hand temperature dropped an additional degree (Mean: 78.79, SD: .17). However, his right hand temperature barely changed (Mean:

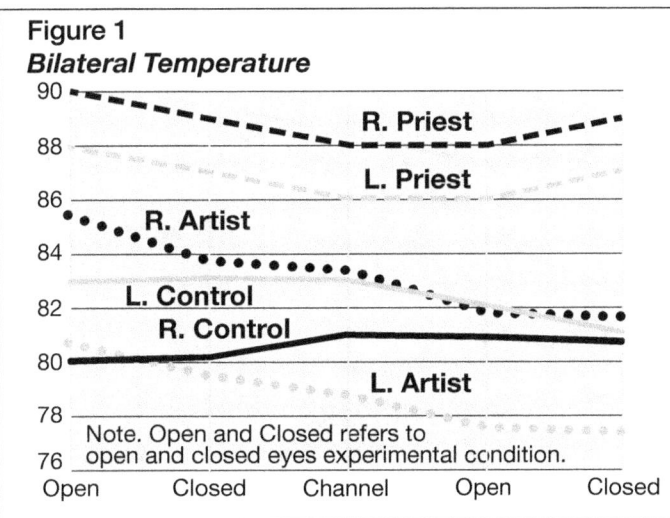

Figure 1
Bilateral Temperature
Note. Open and Closed refers to open and closed eyes experimental condition.

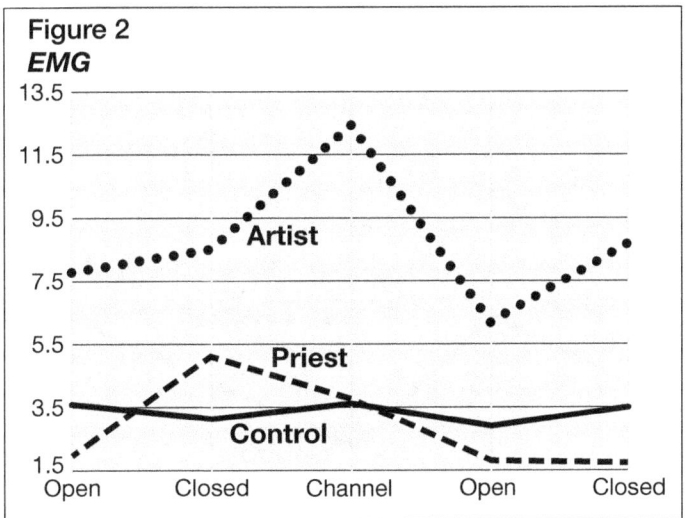

Figure 2
EMG

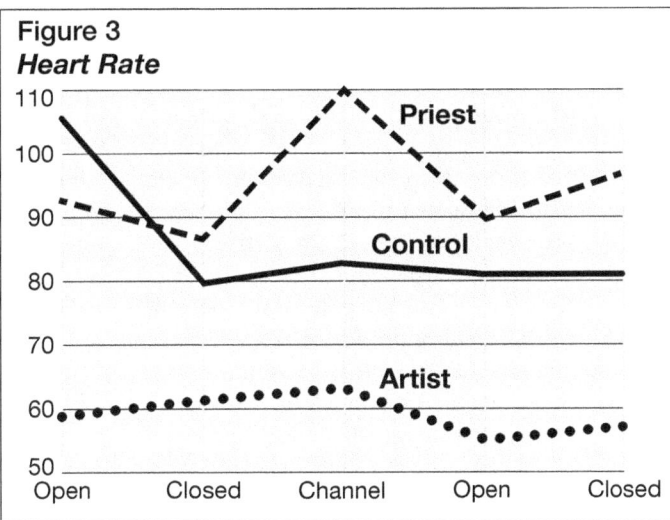

Figure 3
Heart Rate

83.46, SD: .18). When instructed to stop the imagination task and relax, first with eyes open and then with eyes closed, Andrade's temperature continued to drop in both his left hand (Mean=77.59, SD: .13) and his right hand (Mean: 81.64, SD: .15). (See Fig. 1, Artist.)

Mean frontal electromyograph (EMG) baseline readings from an eyes open condition were high (Mean: 7.8 microvolts, SD: 1.9). When instructed to close his eyes and relax, Andrade's frontal EMG actually increased (Mean: 8.5 microvolts, SD: 0.4). This result was contrary to expectations. When instructed to close his eyes and imagine "incorporating" an artist, Andrade's mean frontal EMG jumped to 12.5 microvolts (SD: 2.2). When told to stop imagining, to open his eyes, and to relax, his mean frontal EMG dropped to 6.0 microvolts (SD: 0.2). When told to close his eyes and relax, his frontal EMG increased to 8.6 microvolts (SD: 1.0). Again, this result is paradoxical. However, Andrade's increase in frontal EMG under this condition is consistent with a hypothesis of increased muscle tension in his head during the eyes closed condition, possibly driven by intrusive cognitions and/or affect. (See Fig. 2, Artist.)

Andrade's heart rate data are also consistent with the hypothesis of intrusive events occurring in the eyes closed conditions. His mean heart rate always increased modestly in the eyes closed conditions (Mean: 61.3 beats per minute, SD: 1.5 beats), and particularly during "incorporation" (Mean: 63.4 beats per minute, SD: 2.0). Andrade's mean heart rate dropped when he opened his eyes (Mean: 55.8 beats per minute, SD: 2.2). In general, Andrade's heart rate is quite low for a person of his age and increased only modestly during the imagination task. (See Fig. 3, Artist.)

Paradoxically, Andrade's mean skin conductance level (SCL) dropped across the entire session independent of any of the other conditions and instructions. Temperature was higher on the left side of Andrade's body across both baselines as well as during the imagination task. Generally, there was a greater sympathetic activation in his left hand than in his right hand. (See Fig. 4, Artist.)

The electroencephalograph (EEG) data showed an increase in the percentage of theta brain waves from the eyes open to the eyes closed baseline conditions, but a drop in alpha percentage. During the imagination task, there was an increase in the percentage of alpha comparable to the eyes open condition. Paradoxically, this increase in the percentage of alpha was also associated with a sustained increase in beta percentage, even after the imagination task was completed. (See Figs. 5 and 6.)

In general, the psychophysiological data obtained from Andrade reveals several incongruent findings: (1) There was a general reduction in SCL (skin conductance level) across conditions. Since SCL is a measure to sympathetic activation or withdrawal, it is paradoxical to find it associated with peripheral vasoconstriction and increased EMG during the imagination task which might typically be thought of as a relaxing condition. Both sets of data suggest increased sympathetic activation in these response systems. (2) The increase in muscle tension during the eyes closed imagination condition and the associated increase in the percentage of alpha activity during imagination are also paradoxical. These two measures (EMG and Alpha EEG) are typically negatively correlated, not positively correlated.

We concluded that there were markedly specific incongruences in the peripheral and central physiological response systems. In other words, there were deviations during Andrade's imagination condition that were discrepant from what is typically seen during an eyes closed imagination condition. This supports a previous finding that physiological incongruences are frequent outcomes of testing sessions with people claiming "mediumistic" abilities (Wickramasekera, 1991). Not only are there incongruences between the mediums' verbal reports and behavioral observations but between their psychophysiological response systems as well.

Psychophysiological Results: Pai Ely (Priest)

Pai Ely's psychophysiology was measured under two baseline resting conditions (eyes open; eyes closed). Then, while he was imagining "incorporating" a discarnate entity from the "spirit world," and finally, during his return to baseline conditions (eyes open; eyes closed). Each condition lasted for four minutes. Pai Ely later reported that he had imagined incorporating a "gentle" *preto velho*.

During baseline conditions before

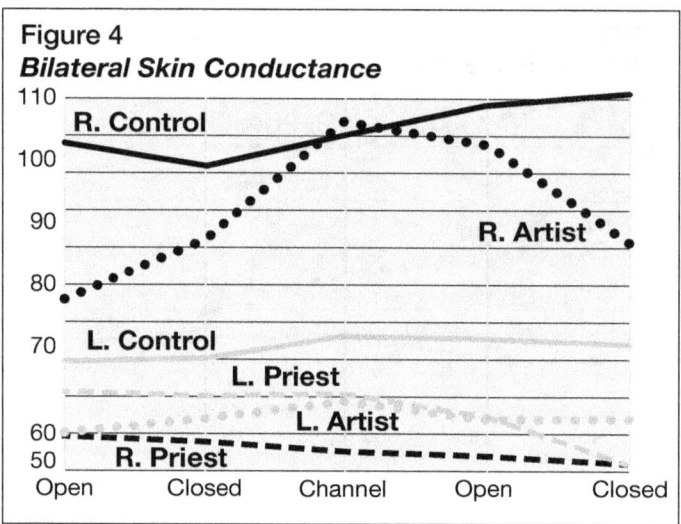

Figure 4
Bilateral Skin Conductance

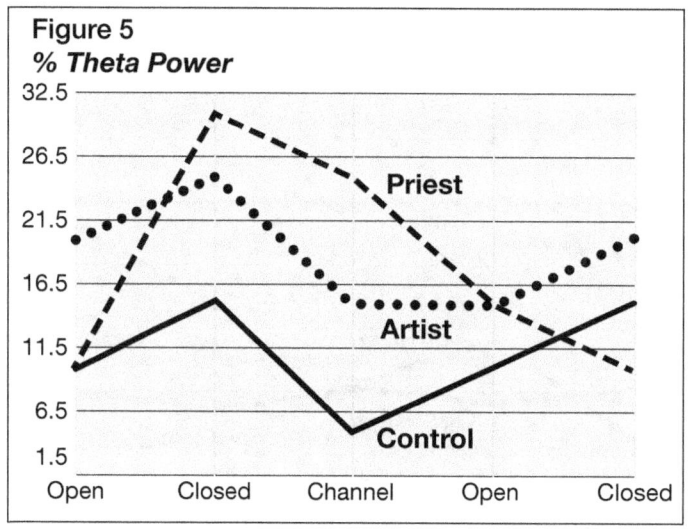

Figure 5
% Theta Power

the imagination task, Pai Ely's EMG, EEG, and SCL measures were quite normal, but his heart rate was high (Mean: 90 beats per minute). His hand temperature was discrepant when the left and right hand sides of the body were measured (left hand Mean: 90.0; right hand Mean: 88.0). (See Fig. 1, Priest.)

When Pai Ely was asked to close his eyes and relax (for four minutes), the results were similar. Hence, even before initiating the imagination task, there were notable incongruences between two of Pai Ely's psychophysiological responses (i.e., hand temperatures), and an unusual result on another measure (i.e., heart rate; see Fig. 3, Priest.). Standard deviations for each of the above mean scores were estimated as less than 1.0.

The first collection of data during the imagination condition was confounded by motor artifacts and could not be used. Pai Ely's imagination is very vivid, and he moved his hands and arms frequently, as he does when actually "incorporating" discarnate entities. This behavior is consistent with his high score (i.e., 28) on the TAS.

When Pai Ely was asked to restrain himself while imagining that he was incorporating a discarnate entity, his left hand and right hand temperature remained stable (Fig. 1, Priest.). However his percentage of theta brain waves increased in both the left and right cortical hemispheres. (Fig. 5, Priest.) In addition, his EMG, SCL, and heart rate increased during the imagination condition, and remained elevated relative to the earlier baseline data. (Figs. 2, 3, 4.)

In other words, this research participant displayed incongruences between major physiological response systems, particularly during the imagination condition. Significant sympathetic activation was observed in the autonomic nervous system (ANS), but relaxation was noted in the central nervous system (CNS). The ANS and CNS typically function in a more integrated manner. These incongru-

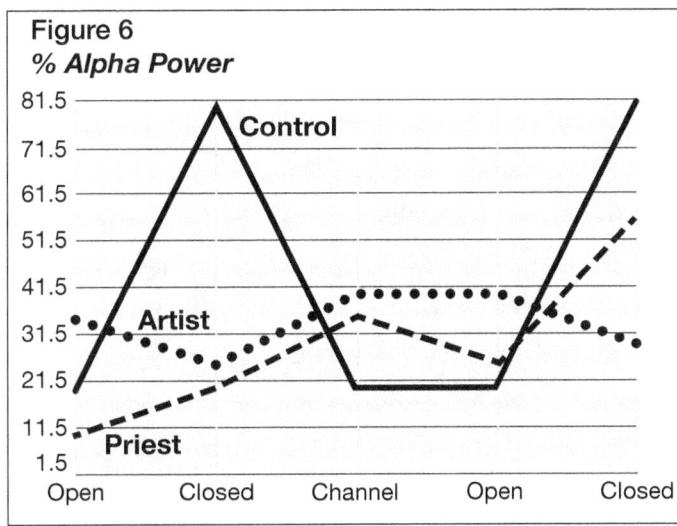

Figure 6
% Alpha Power

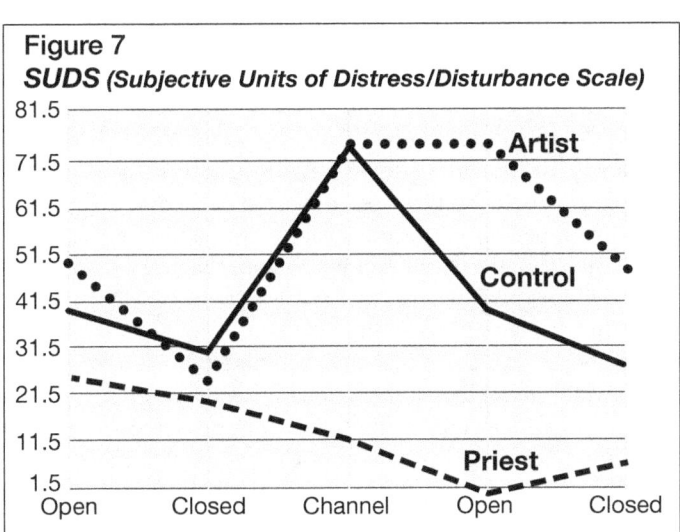

Figure 7
SUDS (Subjective Units of Distress/Disturbance Scale)

ent responses, therefore, are atypical.

Psychophysiological Results: E. O. S. (Priest)

In the case of E.O.S., there were fewer discrepancies between CNS (e.g., EEG; Figs. 5 & 6, Control) response systems. All scores were in the normal range (Figs. 2, 3, 4, Control) and were essentially congruent. However, there was a large increase in EEG alpha wave percentage in both eyes closed conditions (Fig. 6, Control). This finding is consistent with E.O.S.'s score of 21 on the TAS; although in the "medium absorption" category, it was exactly the same as that of one of the practitioners (Andrade). The EEG data are probably consistent with E.O.S.'s hypnotic ability, although this was not tested. However, studies of the association of absorption with measured response to hypnosis demonstrate only a moderate relationship (Spiegel, 1990).

Discussion: Absorption and Dissociation

Individuals who score highly on the Tellegen Absorption Scale tend to report becoming fully absorbed while they are watching a movie, television program, or theatrical performance. They also tend to be able to suspend disbelief and to become empathic (Wickramasekera II & Szlyk, 2003), especially when their companion (or, at times, a complete stranger) is undergoing stress. Those individuals scoring high on absorption have many traits in common with highly hypnotizable people, deriving meaning from body language and personal mannerisms (Fernandez, 2001).

This description is especially applicable to Pai Ely who deals daily with people under stress. There are members of his congregation, as well as many outsiders, who come to him for relief of some real or imagined misfortune, interpersonal conflict, or health problem. A frequent method of treatment involves incorporation of entities from the "spirit world," sometimes requesting that they give advice and aid, and at other times intervening to stop their purported malevolent actions against Pai Ely's clients.

Andrade did not make as high a score on the TAS as did Pai Ely, but does not have to deal as extensively or intimately with clients as does the *pai-de-santo*. In other words, the high score on the TAS might be related to the frequency with which the two practitioners engage in "spirit incorporation." When Andrade incorporates his artistic colleagues from the divine world, he often becomes so absorbed with the task that he claims not to recall the details when the discarnate entities leave the scene.

In an earlier study with seven "advanced students" at the Ramtha

School of Enlightenment in Yelm, Washington, each member of the group scored in or near the top half of the TAS distribution. Their mean score of 28.6 falls at the 85th percentile. One research participant made a score of 33, falling at the 98th percentile (Krippner, I. Wickramasekera, J. Wickramasekera, & Winstead, 1998). The TAS was part of a battery of psychological tests administered, each of them measuring the "capacity to enter altered states of consciousness" (p. 14), a capacity that was found to characterize all 7 of the students through subsequent interview data.

Hageman (2007) worked with 39 students at the same school, as part of a larger study involving 202 research participants. She reported that 67% (N: 26) fell into the "high absorption" category, 31% (N: 12) fell into the "medium absorption" category, and only 2% (N: 1) fell into the "low absorption" category. Re-tests during and after the training sessions detected an increase in absorption (as measured by the TAS) in all categorical levels. This school provides a standard curriculum for all of its students, one that emphasizes spiritual self-healing, as well as activities that involve considerable imagery training.

Hageman's (2007) group also took the Dissociative Experiences Scale (Carlson & Putnam, 1993); their scores were normally distributed at the beginning of the training sessions, but slightly over 20% received scores placing them in the "highly dissociative" category. Most of these "highly dissociative" students had also made high scores in absorption on the TAS (p. 174).

In addition, most of the seven "advanced students" studied by Krippner, Wickramasekera, Wickramasekera, and Winstead (1998) fell into the "highly dissociative" category of the Dissociative Experiences Scale. Negro, Palladino-Negro, and Louza (2002) reported that the Kardec mediums they studied in São Paulo, Brazil, attained high scores on the Dissociative Experiences Scale, and that there was a positive association between mediumship training and the control of the dissociated experiences.

The two mediums in this study also attained high scores on the Dissociative Experiences Scale and had been practicing mediumship for several decades. Their capacity for dissociative self experiences may thus play an important role in their ability to practice as a medium through differentiating and dissociating their normal identity states during their hypnotic-like procedures (Krippner, 2005).

Sociocognitive theorists of dissociation and hypnosis would probably suggest that these medium's phenomenological experiences during mediumship are created in accordance with their previous expectancies and beliefs about the role of being a medium and other contextual variables (Lynn, Pintar, & Rhue, 1997). The sociocognitive perspective on dissociation thus seems to be illustrated in Pai Ely's belief that as much as 75% of his experience during mediumship may be the result of his own biases, experiences, and fantasies. Pai Ely's description of his process of discernment of "pure" from "contaminated" information does seem to capture the sociocognitive explanation of how a person might construct a role and personal narrative about dissociative trance experiences as a kind of "believed-in imaging" (Sarbin, 1998).

We could also mention here that Neo-Dissociation theorists of hypnosis and dissociation might look at the importance of the hypnotic-like procedure (Krippner, 2005) itself in facilitating access to the self experience of the channeled cognitive subsystem or identity state (Hilgard, 1977/1986). A neo-dissociative theory or ego-state theory explanation of mediumship would probably highlight the normal polypsychic nature of human identity (Frederick, 2005) so that it probably shouldn't be too surprising that we might be able to encounter another ego state within us during a hypnotic-like procedure.

Our experience of this normally inactive ego state may thus be activated by the hypnotic-like procedures of mediumship whether or not that ego state actually represents the presence of a spirit or deity. These theorists might then speculate that a simpler explanation of mediumship could be derived through focusing on the origin of the channeled identity as stemming from ego states or cognitive subsystems that are not properly integrated within the mediums normal experience of identity. Probably everyone has some trickster-like phenomena hidden away within their self experience that they may not normally elicit but which mediums seem to develop as part of their training (Krippner, 2005).

This polypsychic aspect of human identity may significantly contribute to the difficulty Pai Ely described in discern pure from contaminated information along with sociocognitive factors. However, our data merely illustrate the sociocognitive and neodissociative perspectives on mediumship while a hoist of many other factors (including actual spirit incorporation) may actually play a role as well.

Discussion: Physiological Measures

People with incongruences between CNS and ANS responses have been described by Wickramasekera (1986a) as living episodically in two worlds, one in which they are critical, rational, and practical, and another into which their fantasy and emotional reactivity expands and deepens. As such, they are often "at risk" for somaticization, i.e., psychosomatic illnesses. Both sets of descriptors apply to Pai Ely, the *pai-de-santo* in our investigation who attained a "high absorption" score on the TAS. Not only does Pai Ely incorporate discarnate entities; he manages a large and successful enterprise, the Lar de Ita Center.

Wickramasekera's descriptors apply to some extent to the other psychic claimant, Andrade, who also displayed CNS/ANS incongruences, although receiving a TAS score in the "medium absorption" category. His duties at the Kardec temple are not as demanding as those of Pai Ely, nor does he spend the amount of time incorporating entities, as does the *pai-de-santo*. When we visited the Kardec temple, we observed a few dozen people in attendance; in contrast, Pai Ely's Candomblé/Umbanda temple was filled with several hundred people during each of our visits. In addition, we observed that Pai Ely has a team of mediums and trained assistants at his disposal at the temple.

Wickramasekera's (1991) descriptors do not particularly apply to the control research participant, E.O.S., who received a TAS score in the "medium absorption" category and displayed no noticeable CNS/ANS incongruences.

According to Wickramasekera (1986b, 1991), incongruences between CNS and ANS response systems are not unusual among spiritual practitioners. It is taken for granted that some practitioners, especially self-styled "mediums" and "channelers," will demonstrate incongruences between their behavioral observations and verbal reports. For example, they might appear calm and composed, but speak of calamitous events from their clients' "past lives," from the lives of their clients' deceased relatives, or from scenarios of their clients' purported futures. In addition, they might claim to feel relaxed, even though their physiological tests indicate that they are under tension.

Associations between TAS and incongruence are inconclusive at this point, but this is a topic deserving additional research, especially if the TAS could be administered as part of a more extensive test battery with mediumistic practitioners as the research participants. For example, it would be useful to administer the Creative Imagination Scale (Wilson & Barber, 1978) to test for fantasy-proneness, and the Hartmann Boundaries Questionnaire (Hartmann, 1991) to evaluate thinness and thickness of psychological "boundaries."

Forty Recife Mediums

In 2006 my colleagues and I collected data from 20 female and 20 male mediums who performed their services at the Lar de Ita Tempe in Recife. Each medium signed an informed consent form, was asked a number of demographic questions, and was administered the Dissociate Experiences Scale (DES), the Tellegen Absorption Scale (TAS), and Kinsey Scale (which assigns respondents to one of several sexual orientation categories). Each participant received $10.00 (U.S.) compensation (Krippner et al., 2007).

A previous study (Negro, Negro-Palladino, & Louza, 2002) obtained scores from 110 Kardec mediums on the DES and the tri-dimensional Personality Scale, indicating that high mediumship ability was associated with his DES scores, high adaptation scores, and the alleged ability to control dissociation. Those mediums who manifested pathology were younger, had less control of their dissociation, and attained lower socialization scores.

This study was the first to use the Kinsey Scale to determine sexual orientation in a sample of mediums. Kinsey and his associates (Kinsey, Pomeroy, & Martin, 1948) developed a scale to classify respondents in their historic survey of sexual behavior in the United States. Based on responses to interview questions, a score of "0" was given to those who were "exclusively heterosexual" and a score of "6" to those who were "exclusively homosexual."

Intermediate scores were given to those who were "predominantly heterosexual, only incidentally homosexual," "predominantly heterosexual, but more than incidentally homosexual," "equally heterosexual and homosexual," "predominantly homosexual, but more than incidentally heterosexual," and "predominantly homosexual, only incidentally heterosexual." A score of "X" was given to those who were "asexual."

Although the scale has been used in numerous investigations (e.g., Steiner & Norman, 1989), it is not without its critics, some of whom point out its ethnocentric bias while others have noted that its linearity might obscure subtle differences from person to person (e.g., McWhirter, Sanders, & Reinsich, 1990). The questions in the Kinsey Scale were translated by the interviewer into Portuguese for use in this study.

The mean age of the Recife mediums was 35 for females and 35 for males. The number of years of reported practice was 15 for females and 13 for males. The age of first incorporation was 21 for females and 23 for males with a range of 8 to 39. None of these differences were statistically significant.

On the Tellegen Absorption Scale, the mean female score was 25 and the mean male score was 26; these scores fall into the "moderate" range of U.S. norms. The mean female score on the DES was 56 and the mean male score was 47; the gender difference was not statistically significant and both means fall into the "high" range of the U.S. normative group.

There were no significant differences in educational level between females and males, although more of the females (45%) than males (20%) went further than grade school. Of the total group, 17% were university graduates; this group would be considered "literate" and "well educated" by Brazilian standards. More male than female mediums had post-graduate degrees and a "middle job" status. Almost all mediums held service industry jobs (e.g., homemakers, managers, nurses, secretaries, soldiers, teachers, writers).

On the Kinsey Scale, 75% of the mediums were rated as "exclusively" or "predominantly heterosexual," 22% as "exclusively" or "predominantly homosexual," and 3% as "equally heterosexual and homosexual." There were no significant gender differences. However, sexuality has been conceptualized somewhat differently in parts of Brazil; if a male's dominant mode of sexual expression involves phallic penetration, he is regarded as "macho" regardless of his partner's gender. The structure of the Kinsey Scale overlooked this traditional concept.

A significant Pearson product-moment correlation was found between then DES and the AS (especially for females), between job status and educational level, between job status and DES (females only), and (females only) between educational level and degree of heterosexuality (with the more heterosexual women having higher heterosexual scores). In reviewing these data the most striking finding was that none of the mediums scored low in absorption and almost all scored high in dissociation.

Hypnotizability tends to be modestly related to absorption (Balthazard & Woody, 1992) and one group of highly hypnotizable research participants is highly dissociative (Barber, 1999). Hence, hypnotizability may be a link that connects these two traits, at least as measured by the AS and the DES. The typical medium claims to surrender control and decision-making when incorporating spirits and *orixás*, allowing them to "speak" and "move" through the medium. This phenomenon would seem to require both the ability to dissociate and the ability to become absorbed in a task, two traits that might seem to be contradictory. The ability to reconcile these two skills demonstrates the complexity of a medium's performance and is worthy of further study.

A Kardecist Medium in Abadania

In 2005, I visited O Casa do Dom Inacio de Loyola (the House of St. Ignatius of Loyola, the founder of the Roman Catholic Jesuit Order). The Casa is located in Abadania, a small town in central Brazil. It is the site of alleged healings performed by Joao de Faria, also known as Joao de Deus (John of God). Even though he has had only a few years of formal education, de Faria performs complicated surgeries, most of them with a scalpel or forceps but none of them with anesthetics or antibiotics (Bragdon, 2002; Ravenwing, 2005).

Some of the videotapes of de Faria's "mediumistic surgery" show him inserting a surgical instrument into a client's nasal passages. The celebrated magician, James Randi (2005) has questioned the purpose of this intervention, concluding that there is no evidence that de Faria "has ever accomplished anything but revulsion by sticking forceps up a victim's nose."

The videotaped interventions also appear to show de Faria scraping the eyeball of clients with the edge of a knife. Randi has pointed out that the sclera (the white section of the eye) is relatively insensitive to touch and doubts that the knife ever reaches the cornea. Randi also noted that de Faria typically blocks the video camera with his body when it zooms in for a close-up, making a proper investigation impossible.

My visit coincided with the birthday of St. Ignatius as well as an anniversary of de Faria's first incorporation of the saint. No mediumistic surgeries were performed during the day because the

> Shortly after immersing himself in Spiritist literature, de Faria began to heal people spontaneously, often not remembering what he had done.

anniversary's festivities occupied the celebrants' time. Some 1,000 men and women, most of them dressed in white, were present for the occasion; de Faria was seated in the Casa's assembly hall, greeting and blessing visitors.

After I exchanged a few words in Portuguese with de Faria, I was taken on a tour of the premises. My tour guide told me that de Faria, as a teenager, had a vision of woman who directed him to a nearby Spiritist center where he discovered the books of Allan Kardec.

Shortly after immersing himself in Spiritist literature, de Faria began to heal people spontaneously, often not remembering what he had done. The mediums at the Kardec center told de Faria that he had incorporated King Solomon and dubbed him "Joao de Deus," a *nom de plume* that has stayed with him over the decades. Later, he began to incorporate St. Ignatius as well as a number of deceased Brazilian physicians who allegedly told de Faria that they wanted to continue their work even after bodily death.

St. Ignatius is an appropriate icon for this type of work; he selected the first Jesuits for their powers of mental imagery, among other criteria. According to St. Ignatius, learning how to develop and control their visual perception and their mental imagery prepared the supplicants to pursue novel and interesting experiences as they became exemplars of will and achievement. This approach to faith was considered unorthodox at the time, and the Jesuits underwent periods of repression and persecution, especially in Brazil. According to de Faria, St. Ignatius had retained his interest in novelty after his physical death, and was eager to continue his benevolent work through a medium (Krippner & Yanez, 2007).

A Histocytopathological Analysis

Later, I collaborated with three Brazilian physicians who had obtained permission to collect specimens of tissues for histopathological analysis (Moreira-Almedia, de Almeida, Gollman, & Krippner, 2007). I was not present when the tissues were collected but my colleagues obtained signed consent forms for all of de Faria's clients who were involved in the investigation. Each physical intervention was recorded on video and was photographed as well. All tissues were placed in a formaldehyde solution and submitted to histocytopathological analysis by the Laboratory of Pathology at the Federal University of Juiz de Fora.

Following the intervention, a clinical examination was performed, including anamnesis. A physical examination of the surgical wound was performed by my colleagues while patients were in the recovery room. Interviews with each client obtained demographic data and each client's belief system concerning mediumistic surgery. Six months later, follow-up questionnaires were sent to all clients whose tissues had been submitted for examination.

During both of our visits we observed no soliciting for donations or fees being charged for treatment. Various herbal remedies were often prescribed by de Faria (rather, by whatever saint or spirit was speaking through him). The cost of these remedies varied between one and two dollars (U.S.) and many of them contained passion flowers (so named because the bloom is shaped like a cross, reminiscent of the "Passion of Jesus Christ"). A free bowl of soup was offered to anyone who requested it; generally, several hundred bowls were consumed each day.

During both of our visits, we inspected a room filled with canes, crutches, and wheelchairs—donated by grateful recipients of the mediumistic surgeries who claimed that they no longer needed these aids. During both visits, we observed no recommendation that clients should curtail or abandon their current medical treatment.

My colleagues recovered tissues from ten clients and were able to interview six of them in the recovery room. All six declared that they were Roman Catholic and believed that they could be assisted by De Faria's interventions. No sign of infection of the surgical wound was noted despite the fact that the interventions were performed in non-sterilized conditions in an open room with dozens of spectators. All six clients reported that they had been awake and aware during the mediumistic surgeries; one woman with cancer mentioned experiencing pain during a breast incision but a man whose molar tooth was extracted claimed that the intervention was painless.

The six-month follow-up yielded completed questionnaires from all six of the clients. Four reported "significant improvement" and two reported "no improvement" (one for retinal hemorrhage and one for chronic sinusitis). One of those reporting improvement claimed that he was able to resume his sports practice, an activity that he had been forced to curtail due to disabling back pain.

Another client, suffering from a macular cyst and idiopathic abdominal pain, reported a marked improvement in her visual acuity and abdominal condition. The histocytopathological analysis for all ten clients found that their tissues and cells were compatible with their site of origin. Apart from one lipoma, the tissues were healthy, without discernable pathology.

The lack of pain reported by nine out of the ten clients could be explained, at least in part, by Chaves and Barber's (1974) model of acupuncture analgesia. They noted that there are few pain receptors in the superficial layers of skin; this is consistent with the observation by my medical colleagues that they did not observe any surgical interventions that reached a bodily cavity or internal organs. In the case of corneal scraping, that part of the eye is so sensitive that one writer (Randi, 2005) conjectured that no actual contact with the cornea takes place, although my colleagues' videotape left little room for doubt. Stressful situations, however, can promote the release of such endogenous analgesic substances as endorphins and corticotrophin-releasing factors (Latinere & Melzack, 2000; Nickell, 2007).

Greenfield (1987) suspected that hypnotic-like suggestion is responsible for the diminution of pain; one is usually awake and aware during hypnosis (Barber, 1999), and the six clients interviewed all claimed to be awake and aware during the entire procedure. Hence, suggestion may be an important element in the clients' lack of reported pain during the mediumistic surgeries.

The tissues of the two clients who reported improvement on follow-up did not display a direct match with the location of the disabling condition, suggesting that the visibility of the intervention might have produced a placebo effect. The magnitude of the placebo effect in surgeries is about the same as other placebo responses (about 35%); however, because of ethical concerns it has become difficult to evaluate the placebo effect of sham surgeries (Johnson, 1994) and the mechanism of the placebo is not fully understood (Gatzsche, 1994).

In summary, our observations indicated that de Faria performed actual physical interventions during the time my colleagues were present. Unlike a previous study of so-called Filipino "psychic surgeons" in which animal blood, human blood of a different blood type than the client's, or tissue not related to the part of the body from which they were allegedly removed (e.g., Lincoln, Wood, & Singer, 1990; Stevenson, 1976), the recovered tissues were from the client's body, hence no evidence of fraud was detected.

Because many of de Faria's clients claim to benefit from both his physical and non-physical interventions and because this and similar procedures are widely used for people around the world who have no access to Western allopathic biomedicine (or who can not afford it even when it is available), this topic deserves continued investigation (Hodges & Scofield, 1995; Ernst, 1995).

Conclusion

There are several practical implications of these data. One involves the means by which mediums access information. Another involves the health status of mediumistic practitioners. The third regards the effectiveness of their interventions.

I conjecture that mediums fall into the same general categorizes as do Barber's highly hypnotizable persons.

One group of mediums is highly motivated and uses whatever cognitive resources are at their disposal to contact the divine world and retrieve information that they believe will be helpful to their clients. Another group of mediums is highly imaginative and utilizes fantasy-prone abilities to enter the divine world, bringing back what it has to offer people in distress. A third group of mediums dissociates from the material world, yet has the capacity to control this dissociation and return when the needed information has been obtained.

The mediums we tested seem to utilize this modality frequently, given their high scores on the DES. The TAS might indicate the degree to which mediums are absorbed in their task, in part, because of their high motivation. Other measures, such as Wilson and Barber's Creative Imagination Scale (1978), could test for fantasy-proneness. Phenomenological scales and interviews could provide further information in regard to the processes mediums use to enter the divine world, communicate with spiritual entities, and return with gifts that can help their clients manage problems in living and plans for the future.

The health status of mediums has been the topic of previous studies. In their study of Kardec mediums, Negro, Palladino-Negro, and Louza (2002) found that those research participants characterized by extensive training attained favorable scores on measures of socialization and adaptation. However, pathological signs were detected among the group of younger mediums with less training; in addition, they evidenced poorer social support.

The stress that accompanies mediumship can be modified by such "buffers" as social support systems, by programs that involve voluntarily control of internal states (e.g., biofeedback, meditation), and by regimens for healthy living (see Krippner, Wickramasekera, & Tartz, 2000, pp. 59-60; Wickramasekera, 1988, 1989). There is some evidence that, at least in the United States, self-styled "mediums" and "channelers" are at greater risk than are other spiritual practitioners (e.g., "healers" and "intuitives"; see Krippner, Wickramasekera, & Tartz, 2000). If so, self-care needs to accompany the concern that these practitioners frequently demonstrate toward their students and clients.

The effectiveness of mediums is attested to by the frequency of visits by members of their community, especially in parts of the world where other methods of mental health care are virtually absent or exorbitantly expensive. Much of their performance as healers and counselors is comparable to that of a dramatic performance, one that evokes the body's self-healing mechanisms (Lynn, Pintar, & Rhue,1997).

Natural explanations suffice to explain most of the effects we observed, and it is likely that—as is the case in groups of other practitioners—fraudulent and self-serving practices are sometimes encountered. However, the interview data we elicited, the mediums' standing in their communities, and the fact that tissues removed during mediumistic surgery matched the site of their removal argue for the integrity and sincerity of this sample.

The notion that mediums could be health care resources is ignored or ridiculed by much of mainstream Western medicine and science. However, ridicule occurs at the peril of those clients who they serve and for whom mediumistic counselor, advice and even surgery is either a last resort or the only available option.

Additional research along all three of these lines could more fully demarcate the advantages and disadvantages, the limitations and delimitations, and the process of outcome of what mediums, and their contact with the divine world, have to offer. In addition, Brazilian mediums, as well as those from other cultures, represent a population that is a potential reservoir for untapped data for students of the anthropology, psychology, and sociology of consciousness.

Acknowledgements

Gratitude to the Institute of Noetic Sciences, the Saybrook Graduate School Chair for the Study of Consciousness, the Society for Scientific Exploration, the Tinker Foundation, and to Dr. Lonnie Barbach for their financial support for these investigations.

References

Barber, T.X. (1999). A comprehensive three-dimensional theory of hypnosis. In I. Kirsch, A. Capafons, E. Cardena-Buelna, & S. Amigo (Eds.), *Clinical hypnosis and self-regulation* (pp. 21-48). Washington, DC : American Psychological Association.

Bastide, R. (1960). *Les religions Africaines au Bresil* [The African religions of Brazil]. Paris: Press Universitaires de France.

Bastide, R. (1971). *African civilizations in the New World.* (P. Green, trans.). New York: Harper and Row.

Bernstein, E.M., & Putnam, F.W. (1986). Development, reliability, and validity of a dissociation scale. *Journal of Nervous and Mental Disease, 174,* 727-735.

Borges, V. da R. (1992). *Manual de parapsicologia.* [Manual of parapsychology]. Recife: Edicao Instituto Pernambucano de Pesquisas Psicobiofisicas. Bourguignon, E. (1976). *Possession.* San Francisco: Chandler & Sharp.

Bourguignon, E., & Evascu, T. (1977). Altered states of consciousness within a general evolutionary perspective: A holocultural analysis. *Behavior Science Research, 12,* 199-216.

Bragdon, E. (2002). *Spiritual alliances: Discovering the roots of health at the Casa de Dom Inacio.* Woodstock, VT: Lightening Up Press.

Brown, D. (1994). *Umbanda: Religion and politics in urban Brazil.* New York: Columbia University Press.

Carlson, E.G., & Putnam, F.W. (1993). An update on the Dissociative Experiences Scale. *Dissociation, 6,* 16-27.

Chaves, J.F., & Barber, T.X. (1974). Acupuncture analgesia: A six-factor theory. *Psychoenergetic Systems, 1,* 1-21.

Don, N.S., & Moura, G. (2000). Trance surgery in Brazil. *Alternative Therapies, 6*(4), 39-48.

Balthazard, C. G., & Woody, E. Z. (1992). The spectral analysis of hypnotic performance with respect to "Absorption". *International Journal of Clinical and Experimental Hypnosis, 40,* 21-43.

Ernst, E. (1995). Complimentary medicine: Common misperceptions. *Journal of the Royal Society of Medicine, 88,* 244-247.

Fernandez, L. (2001). The worldview of the Grade V hypnotizable person. *Hypnos, 28,* 207-208.

Frederick, C. (2005). Selected topics in ego state therapy. *International Journal of Clinical and Experimental Hypnosis, 53*(4), 339-429.

Giesler, P.V. (1985). Differential micro-PK effects among Afro-Brazilian cultists. *Journal of Parapsychology, 49,* 329-366

Gotzsche, P.C. (1994). Is there logic in the placebo? *Lancet, 344,* 925-926.

Greenfield, S.M. (1987). The return of Dr. Fritz: Spiritist healing and patronage networks in urban, industrial Brazil. Soc Sci Med, 24, 1095-1108.

Hageman, J.H. (2007). *Spirituality.* Berlin: Verlag. INCOMPLETE

Hartmann, E. (1991). *Boundaries of the mind.* New York: Basic Books.

Hastings, A. (1991). *With the tongues of men and angels: A study of channeling.* Fort Worth, TX: Holt, Rinehart and Winston.

Haviser, J. B. (Ed.). (2006). *African re-genesis: Confronting social issues in the diaspora.* Walnut Creek, CA: Left Coast Press.

Hess, D.J. (1994). *Samba in the night: Spiritism in Brazil.* New York: Columbia University Press.

Hilgard, E. R. (1977/1986). Divided consciousness. New York: John Wiley and Sons.

Hodges, R.D., & Scofield, A.M. (1995). Is spiritual healing a valid and effective therapy? *Journal of the Royal Society of Medicine, 88,* 203-207.

Johnson, A.G. (1994). Surgery as a placebo. *Lancet, 344,* 1140-1142.

Kinsey, A.C., Pomeroy, W.B., & Martin, C.E. (1948). *Sexual behavior in the human male.* Philadelphia: W.B. Saunders.

Kirsch, I., & Council, J.R. (1992). Situational and personality correlates of hypnotic responsiveness. In E. Fromm & M.R. Nash (Eds.), Contemporary hypnosis research (pp. 267-291). New York: Guilford.

Klimo, J. (1998). *Channeling: Investigations on receiving information from paranormal sources.* Berkeley, CA: North Atlantic Books.

Krippner, S. (1989). *A call to heal: Entry patterns in Brazilian mediumship.* In: C. A. Ward. (Ed), Altered states of consciousness and mental health: (pp. 186-206). Newbury Park, CA: Sage.

Krippner, S. (1997). Dissociation in many times and places. In Krippner & S.M. Powers (Eds.), *Broken images, broken selves: Dissociative narratives in clinical practice* (pp. 3-40). Washington, DC: Brunner/ Mazel.

Krippner, S. (2005). Trance and the trickster: Hypnosis as a liminal phenomenon. *International Journal of Clinical and Experimental Hypnosis. 53,* 97-118.

Krippner, S. (1998/1999). Transcultural and psychotherapeutic aspects of a Candomblé practice in Recife, Brazil. In S. Krippner & H. Kalweit (Eds.), *Yearbook of cross-cultural medicine and psychotherapy: Mythology, medicine, and healing: Transcultural perspectives* (pp. 67-86). Berlin: Verlag fur Wissenschaft und Bildung.

Krippner, S., Kasian, S. J., Hageman, J., Frankel, K., & Moriela, M. (2007). Dissociation and absorption among mediums in Recife, Brazil (in preparation).

Krippner, S., Wickramasekera, I., & Tartz, R. (2000). Scoring thick and scoring thin: The boundaries of psychic claimants. *Subtle Energies & Energy Medicine, 11,* 43-63.

Krippner, S., Wickramasekera, I., Wickramasekera, J., & Winstead, C.W. III (1998). The Ramtha phenomenon: Psychological, phenomenological, and geomagnetic data. *Journal of the American Society for Psychical Research, 92,* 2-24.

Krippner, S., & Yanez, H. (2007). Lights, sights, and Brazilian healing sites. In R.-I. Heinze (Ed.), *Proceedings of the Twenty-Third Annual International Conference on the Study of Shamanism and Alternate Modes of Healing* (pp. 233-240). Berkeley, CA: Independent Scholars of Asia.

Lariviere, W.R., & Melzack, R. (2000). The role of corticotrophin-releasing factor in pain and analgesia. *Pain, 84,* 1-12.

Leacock, S., & Leacock, R. (1972). *Spirits of the deep: A study of an Afro-Brazilian cult.* Garden City, NY: Doubleday Natural History Press.

Lewis, I.M. (1971). *Ecstatic religion: An anthropological study of spirit possession and shamanism.* New York: Penguin.

Lewis-Fernandez, R., & Kleinman, A. (1995). Cultural psychiatry: Theoretical, clinical and research issues. *Psychiatric Clinics of North America, 18,* 433-448.

Lex, B. (1979). The neurobiology of ritual trance. In E.G. d'Aquili, C.D. Laughlin Jr., & J. McManus (Eds.), *The spectrum of ritual: A biogenetic structural analysis* (pp.117-151). New York: Columbia University Press.

Lima, I.W.R. (1998). Pesquisa de atividade psicopictorafica de Jacques Andrade [Research into the psychic paintings of Jacques Andrade]. *Papels del Tercer Encuentro Psi 1998* (pp. 121-124). Curitiba, Brazil: Instituto de Psicologia Paranormal.

Lincoln, P.J., & Wood, N.J. (1979). Psychic surgery: A serological investigation. *Lancet, 239,* 1197-1198.

Lins, R.D. (1999). *Paranormal painting: A new conceptual approach and a case analysis.* Recife: Instituto Pernambucano de Pesquisas Psicobiofísicas.

Littlewood, R. (2007). *On knowing and not knowing in the anthropology of medicine.* Walnut Creek, CA: Left Coast Press.

Lynn, S.J., Pintar, J., & Rhue, J.W. (1997). Fantasy proneness, dissociation, and narrative construction. In S. Powers & S. Krippner (Eds.), Broken Selves: Dissociative narratives and phenomena (pp. 244-302). New York: Bruner/Mazel.

McIntyre, T.M., Klein, J.-M., & Gonçalves, F. (2001). *Escala de Tellegen* (Portuguese translation of the Tellegen Absorption Scale). Braga, Portugal: University of Minho.

McWhirter, D.P., Sanders, S.A., & Reinisch, J.M. (Eds.), *Homosexuality/heterosexuality: Concepts of sexual orientation.* New York: Oxford University Press.

Moreira-Almeida, A., Silva de Almeida, A. A., Gollman, A.M., & Krippner, S. (2007). A histocytopathological study of mediumistic surgery. Submitted for publication.

Moreira-Almeida, A., Silva de Almeida, A. A. & Neto, F.L. (2005). History of "spiritist madness" in Brazil. *History of Psychiatry, 16,* 5-25,

Murphy, G. (1969). The discovery of gifted sensitives. *Journal of the American Society of Psychical Research, 63,* 3-20.

Negro, P. J., Jr., Palladino-Negro, P., & Louza, M. R. (2002). Do religious mediumship dissociative experiences conform to the sociocognitive theory of dissociation? *Journal of Trauma and Dissociation, 3,* 51-73.

Nickell, J. (2007). "John of God" Healing by entities? *Skeptical Inquirer, 31* (8), 20-22.

Oliveira, X. de (1931). *Espiritismo e loucura* [Spiritism and madness]. Rio de Janeiro: A. Coelho Franco Filho.

Pacheco e Silva, A.C. (1936). Problemas de higiene mental [Problems of mental hygiene]. São Paulo: Oficinas Graficas do Juqueri.

Randi, J. (2005, February 18). The ABC Infomercial for John of God. *Swift, Online Newsletter of the James Randi Educational Foundation.* Retrieved July 1, 2006 from http://www.randi.org/jr/021805a.html#1.

Ravenwing, J. (2005). Joao de Deus, the miracle man of Brazil. *Shaman's Drum, 70,* 49-58. (Original work published 2001)

Roche, S.M., & McConkey, K.M. (1990). Absorption: Nature, assessment, and correlates. *Journal of Personality & Social Psychology, 59,* 91-101.

Rock, A. J., & Krippner, S. (in press). Shamanism and the confusion of consciousness with phenomenological content. *North American Journal of Psychology, 9,* 485-489.

Rodrigues, N. (1935). *O animismo fetichista dos negros Bahíanas* [The animistic fetish of Bahían negros]. Rio de Janeiro: Civilizacao Brasileira. (Original work published 1896)

Sarbin, T.R. (1998). Believed in imaginings: A narrative approach. In J.R. Rivera & T.R. Sarbin (Eds.), Believed-In Imaginings: The narrative construction of reality. Washington, D.C.: American Psychological Association.

Schumaker, J.F. (1995). Religion: The cultural mask of sanity. In J.F. Schumaker (Ed.) *The corruption of reality: A unified theory of religion, hypnosis, and psychopathology* (pp. 81-151). Amherst: Prometheus Books.

Singer, P. (1990). "Psychic surgery": Close observation of a popular healing practice. *Medical Anthropology Quarterly, 3,* 443-451.

Spiegel, D. (1990). Hypnosis, dissociation, and trauma: Hidden and overt observers. In J. Singer (Ed.), *Repression and dissociation: Implications for personality theory, psychopathology, and health* (pp. 232-243). Chicago: University of Chicago Press.

Steiner, D.L., & Norman, G.R. (1989). *Health measurement scales: A practical guide to their development and use.* New York: Oxford University Press.

Stevenson, I. (1976). Review of *Healing: A doctor in search of a miracle* in *Journal of the American Society for Psychical Research, 70,* 101-108.

Tellegen, A. (1977). *The Multidimensional Personality Questionnaire.* Minneapolis: National Computing Systems.

Tellegen, A., & Atkinson, G. (1974). Openness to absorbing and self-altering experience ("absorption"), a trait related to hypnotic susceptibility. *Journal of Abnormal Psychology, 83,* 268-277.

Villoldo, A., & Krippner, S. (1987). *Healing states.* New York: Fireside/Simon & Schuster.

Walker, S. (1972). *Ceremonial spirit possession in Africa and Afro-America.* Leiden: Brill.

Wickramasekera, I. (1986a). Risk factors for parapsychological verbal reports, hypnotizability and somatic complaints. In B. Shapin & L. Coly (Eds.), *Parapsychology and human nature* (pp. 19-35). New York: Parapsychology Foundation.

Wickramasekera, I. (1986b). A model of people at high risk to develop chronic stress related somatic symptoms: Some predictions. *Professional Psychology: Research and Practice, 17,* 437-447.

Wickramasekera, I. (1988). *Clinical behavioral medicine: Some concepts and procedures.* New York: Plenum Press.

Wickramasekera, I. (1989). Is hypnotic ability a risk factor for subjective (verbal report) psi, somatization, and health care costs? In L. Coly & J.D.S. McMahon (Eds.), *Psi and clinical practice* (pp. 184-191). New York: Parapsychological Foundation.

Wickramasekera, I. (1991). Model of the relationship between hypnotic ability, psi, and sexuality. *Journal of Parapsychology, 55,* 159-174.

Wickramasekera, I. (1993). Assessment and treatment of somatization disorders: The high risk model of threat perception. In J.W. Rhue, S.J. Lynn, & I. Kirsch (Eds.), *Handbook of clinical hypnosis* (pp. 587-621). Washington, DC: American Psychological Association.

Wickramasekera, I. (1995). Somatization: Concepts, data and predictions from the high risk model of threat perception, *Journal of Nervous and Mental Disorders, 183,* 15-30.

Wickramasekera, I. (1998, Spring). Out of mind is not out of body: Somatization, the high risk model, and psychophysiological psychotherapy. *Biofeedback,* pp. 8-11, 32.

Wickramasekera, I., Krippner, S., & Wickramasekera II, I. (1997). Channeling dead spirits and painters in Brazil: Psychophysiological dissociation as "incongruence" between physiological response systems in psychic claimants. Paper presented at the annual meeting of the American Psychological Association, Chicago, IL.

Wickramasekera, I., Krippner, S., & Wickramasekera, J. (2001). Case studies of "psychic sensitives": Testing predictions from a model of threat perception. Unpublished case studies. San Francisco, CA: Saybrook Graduate School and Research Center.

Wickramasekera, I. E. & Szlyk, J. (2003). Could empathy be a predictor of hypnotic ability? *International Journal of Clinical and Experimental Hypnosis. 51 (4),* 390-399.

Wilson, S.C., & Barber, T.X. (1978). The Creative Imagination Scale as a measure of hypnotic responsiveness: Applications to experimental and clinical hypnosis. *American Journal of Clinical Hypnosis, 20,* 235-249.

Winkelman, M. (1986). Trance states: A theoretical model and cross-cultural analysis. *Ethos, 14,* 174-203.

Winkelman, M. (2000). *Shamanism: The neural ecology of consciousness and healing.* Westport, CT: Bergin & Garvey.

Wood, C.H., Williams, P., Chijiwa, K. (2007). Protestantism and child mortality in Northeast Brazil, 2006. *Journal for the Scientific Study of Religion, 46,* 405-416.

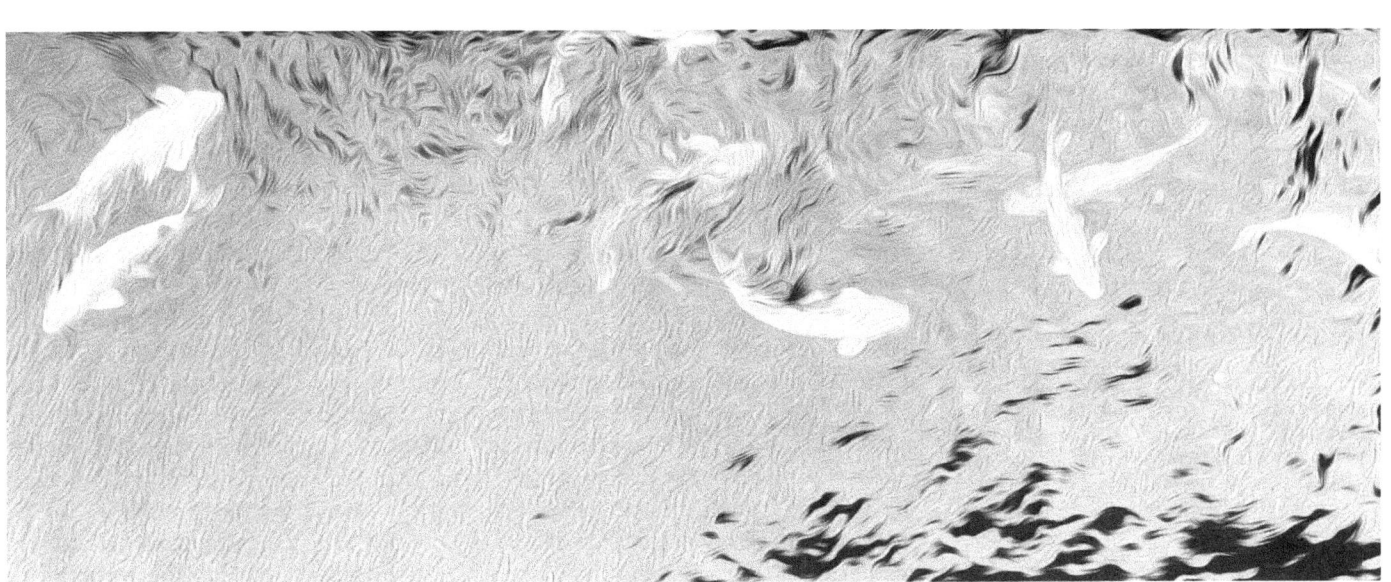

Mythic Themes in Navajo Healing, Maria Sabina's Mazatec *Velada*, and Mapuche Dreaming

Stanley Krippner

In my survey of native healing practices (e.g., Krippner,1995), I have found few storytelling projects as complex as that of the Navajo "chantway." Despite attempts at acculturation, most Navajo men and women still hold to their traditional cultural myths and participate in the corresponding rituals (Adair, Deuschle, & Barnett, 1988, p. 4). In the Navajo concept of illness, the universe is an interrelated whole in which powers of both good and evil exist in a balanced and orderly relationship. When this relationship is disturbed, disharmony occurs, producing illness, the cause of which is basically metaphysical. It is felt that illness takes place when the individual or group is out of harmony with the natural and supernatural worlds.

Navajos have constructed three major diagnostic categories of mental illness. "Moth craziness," is characterized by fits of uncontrolled behavior (e.g., jumping into the fire like a moth), rage, violence, and convulsions; it is attributed to incestual activities. "Crazy violence" has some of the same external manifestations as "moth craziness" but is due to alcoholism. "Ghost sickness," ascribed to sorcery, manifests in nightmares, loss of appetite, dizziness, confusion, panic, and extreme anxiety. When someone knowingly or accidentally breaches taboos or offends dangerous powers, the natural order of the universe is ruptured and "contamination" or "infection" occurs that must be redressed (Sandner, 1979).

Maria Sabina, Salvador Roquet, and Stanley Krippner

When the family has determined that treatment is necessary, a "hataałii" (or "singing shaman") is called in, frequently accompanied by an herbalist and/or a diagnostician (both of whom are of lower status). The herbalists gather plants and make medicines, some of which are used directly, and some of which are used ceremonially by the hataałii. The diagnosticians are usually women and "listen" to the spirits for a

---

Krippner, S. (1997). The role of mandalas in Navajo and Tibetan rituals. In J. D. Douglass (Ed.), *Proceedings of the First International Conference on the Study of Mandalas* (pp. 1J-18J). Williamsburg, VA: Association of Teachers of Mandala Assessment.

Photo | Chacruna

statement of the problem. Other diagnostic procedures include hand trembling, star gazing, candle gazing, and crystal gazing—all of which involve the inward focusing of the practitioner's attention, with the purpose of facilitating insight as to the nature of the problem.

Navajo hataałii utilize a number of therapeutic procedures, most notably one or more of the 10 basic chantways, complex patterns of activities centered around cultural myths which tell of heroes or heroines who once journeyed to spiritual realms in their quest for special knowledge. The symptoms for which a given chant is prescribed are based on connections with the specific chant myth. For example, "Hail Way" is prescribed for muscular tiredness and soreness because the hero, Rain Boy, suffered from these symptoms when he was attacked by his enemies; "Big Star Way" protects the client against the powerful influences of the stars and the dangers of the night.

It takes several years to learn a major chant, some of which consist of hundreds of songs. Hosteen Klah, a famous Navajo hataałii who died in 1937, knew more chants than any other healer of his era, one of them a chant that took 9 days to complete. The effectiveness of the chant is felt to be the result of its accurate performance because this evokes healing power from the spirits. For example, the "Night Chant" employs 24 sequences containing a total of 324 songs; its hero is Dawn Boy who enters the presence of the gods at a sacred canyon. His song, which must be sung perfectly by the hataałii to be successful, appeals to the deities for assistance.

There is an emphasis on the correctness of the procedures when a chantway is performed; as a result, the hataałii is in an extremely vigilant frame of mind. The ability to remember the chantway is mandatory if a hataałii is to serve as an educator who can pass traditions and tribal wisdom on to the younger generation. Contributing to this goal is the multi-modal approach that characterizes chants, as well as their repetitive nature and the mythic content of the words which are easily deciphered by those clients well-versed in tribal mythology.

Sandner (1979) describes how the various sensory modalities are combined: "The visual images of the sand paintings and the body painting, the audible recitation of prayers and songs, the touch of the prayer sticks and the hands of the medicine man, the taste of the ceremonial musk and herbal medicines, and the smell of the chant incense—all combine to convey the power of the chant to the patient." (p. 215). A hataałii usually displays a highly developed dramatic sense in carrying out the chantway.

The chant is considered by Sandner (1979) to facilitate suggestibility and shifts in attending through repetitive singing and the use of culture-specific mythic themes (p. 245). These activities

> It takes several years to learn a major chant, some of which consist of hundreds of songs.

prepare participants for a healing session that may involve symbols and metaphors acted out by performers, enacted in purification rites, or executed in "sand paintings" composed of sand, corn meal, charcoal, and flowers—but destroyed once the healing session is over. Some paintings, such as those used in "Blessing Way," are crafted from ingredients that have not touched the ground, e.g., corn meal, flower petals, charcoal.

There are 5 steps in the typical chantway ceremony: (1) preparation (in which the client is "purified"), (2) presentation of the client to the healing spirits, (3) evocation of these spirits to the place of the ceremony, (4) identification of the clients with a positive mythic theme, (5) transformation of the clients into a condition where ordinary and mythic time and space merge, and a release from the mythic world and return to the everyday world where past transgressions are confessed, where new learnings are assimilated, and where life changes are brought to fruition.

Sandner (1979) points out that these procedures empower the client by creating a "mythic reality" through the use of chants, dances, and songs (often accompanied by drums and rattles), masked dancers, purifications (e.g., sweats, emetics, herbal infusions, ritual bathings, sexual abstinence), and sand paintings. Joseph Campbell (1990) described the colors of the typical sand painting as those "associated with each of the four directions" and a dark center—"the abysmal dark out of which all things come and back to which they go." When appearances emerge in the painting, "they break into pairs of opposites" (p.30).

Within the context of this mythic reality, especially as made visible in the designs constructed in sand by the hataałii, the client is taken into "sacred time" and is able to bring a total attentiveness to the healing ceremony. The presence of culturally significant symbols may maximize clients' imagination and motivation, empowering their self-healing capacities through an identification with symbols held to have therapeutic consequences. The client follows a specific regimen for the next four days to protect members of the community from his or her newly acquired powers.

The role of the community is important in another way; the chants are attended by large numbers of people, many of whom might be asked to participate. This type of participation may increase clients' sense of personal power, magnify their imagination as they attend to the chants, and provide social reinforcement and increased motivation. The mentation of the practitioner, the client, and the community may all be affected by the ceremony. Not only do clients believe that they derive "energy" from the sand painting by sitting on it, the hataałii is dusted with the decorated sand, is touched with feathers and other "power objects," and clients claim to feel the power emanating from the sand painting.

In addition to the chantway, there are other narrative healing procedures used by the Navajo hataałii, one of which is a prayer session. For example, sacred corn pollen may be sacrificed during a time of prayer in an attempt to foster the influence of the spirits needed to heal the client; this ritual must be performed perfectly and behind locked doors, often at the home of the client. The door to the darkened hogan is fastened to prevent the prayer from escaping. Sharpened flints are used to expel the evil from both the client and the hogan. Topper (1987) holds that these procedures reduce the client's symptoms at the same time as they stabilize the social and emotional condition of the community.

Topper's (1987) study of Navajo hataałii indicated that they raise their clients' expectations through the example they set of stability and competence. Politically, they are authoritative and powerful; this embellishes their symbolic value as "transference figures" in the psychoanalytic sense, representing "a nearly omniscient and omnipotent nurturative grandparental object" (p. 221). Frank and Frank (1991) put it more directly: "The personal qualities that predispose patients to a favorable therapeutic response are similar to those that heighten susceptibility to methods of healing in non-industrialized societies, religious revivals, experimental manipulations of attitudes, and administration of a placebo" (p.184).

When treating clients, suggestion and expectancy are bolstered through reinforcing the client's belief in the power of the chant and its symbols, a tight structuring of the ceremonial performance, repetition (especially in chants, songs, and prayers), physical exhaustion of the client, dramatization of a significant event in Navajo mythology, and on rare occasions the use of psychotropic herbal substances (e.g., datura) to evoke a physical effect that convinces the client that power is at work.

As important as the impact of the chant and prayers on the hataalii's consciousness may be, Sandner (1979) insists that the Navajo practitioner "relies on knowledge, not trance phenomena or magical effects. The chant work is a restrained and dignified procedure, and for the most part the medicine man represents for the patient a stable, dependable leader who is a helper and guide until the work is ended" (p. 258).

In other words, two crucial factors in the client's treatment appear to be the personal qualities of the hataalii and the expectancies of the client; shifts in attending may be more useful in intensifying the abilities of the practitioner and the receptivity of the client than in providing any type of innate therapeutic effectiveness. These procedures may reinforce the support by family and community members as well as the client's identification with figures and activities in Navajo cultural myths, both of which are powerful elements in the attempted healing.

The Mazatec *Velada*

Specialists in the Nahuatl language have decoded poetry that praises psychedelic ("mind-manifesting") plants and their effects, while ethnomycologists (specialists in the role played in cultures by mind-altering mushrooms) have identified mushrooms in pre-Conquest codices, the painted picture-writing of Mesoamerica. One such codice, painted in a Mixtec scriptorium, portrays a creation myth in which the god Quetzalcōātl is carrying a woman bedecked with mushrooms on his back, in the manner of a bridegroom carrying his bride. Another scene depicts seven gods and goddesses holding mushrooms that they are about to ingest. Following the Conquest, the use of psychedelic plants was banned by Spanish military and religious authorities. Nevertheless, some Indians identified peyote with the infant Jesus as well as with St. Peter, while others decorated the walls of the churches they painted with psychedelic morning glory vines and small children said to represent the spirit of the "*hongitos*" (i.e., little mushrooms) (Wasson, 1980).

The ritual use of psychedelic substances did not disappear completely. In some remote areas it continued, escaping the Inquisition's persecution. In 1955, Wasson and his party met Doña María Sabina, a Mazatec "*sabia*" (wise one, or shaman) who, with encouragement from a town official, invited them to ingest the mushrooms (primarily Psilocybe mexicana) with her. Wasson (1981) found Sabina to be "an artist in her mastery of the techniques of her office," and an example of "the extraordinary shaman [who] is entitled to be called a virtuoso. His [or her] voice, his [or her] verses filled with tradition..., his [or her] dancing, his [or her] percussive effects—these he [or she] works up in response to his [or her] little audience and in fulfillment of his [or her] genius" (p. 225).

María Sabina was later visited by Estrada(1981) who pieced together her oral autobiography. He also translated the spontaneous poetry she sang after ingesting the *hongitos*, e.g.,

> Mother of good palms
> Mother of good hands
> Your words are medicine
> Your breath is remedial
> That is the work of our flower
>   with sap,
> Our flower of the dew
> Our budding children, our sprouting children
> Holy Father
> You are my Father
> And you Mother who art in the
>   house of heaven
> You, Christ, you my Father
> We are going to cure, we are going
>   to cure with herbs
> That is what our budding children,
> Our sprouting children are for,
> That is the work of our flower
>   with sap,
> Our flower of the dew....
> Fresh herbs
> Herbs of clarity
> Medicinal herbs
> Sacred herbs.
>   (Estrada, 1981, p. 120)

These poems characterized Doña María's "*veladas*" or nighttime mushrooms rituals in which she and her client ate the mushrooms and used the ensuing insights, imagery, and stories for therapeutic and healing purposes.

> We are going to arrive there
> We are going to prostrate ourselves
> Our woman great vibrant-winged
>   one...,
> Our little music woman
> Our drum woman

> It takes several years to learn a major chant, some of which consist of hundreds of songs.

Our little woman of the networks of light
Our little mistress of the mountains
Our little number woman beneath the water.
(Estrada, 1981, p. 186)

Rothenberg (1981) studied the poems associated with Doña María 's veladas and declared her to be a "great oral poet" (p. 10) whose work eventually found its way into films, records, and poetry readings. Rothenberg observed that when she was "called" to shamanize, Doña María visualized an open book that grew until it reached the size of a person. She claims that a divine voice told her that "this is the Book of Wisdom. It is the Book of Language. Everything that is written in it is for you. The Book is yours, take it so that you can work." In accepting this call, Doña María became a woman of language. Wasson (1981) added that her shamanic language demonstrates links with both her Siberian predecessors (where the mushrooms also "speak" through the mouth of the shaman) and the Nahuatl Wise Ones (who arrived at secret knowledge through the "*amoxtli*" or "sacred book").

Doña María's oral autobiography describes how her role as sabia gave full expression to her creative gifts. Born in 1894, Doña María 's father died when she was very young, and she originally ate the mind-altering psilocybin mushrooms to assuage hunger while working in the fields. She observed her first *velada* when she was about six. On one occasion when she ate the mushrooms, she had a mental image of death standing near her sister during an illness. Purported "spiritual beings" told the young woman how to cure her sister and soon Doña María became a well-known "*curandera*," administering medical herbs to clients in the Mexican state of Oaxaca where she lived.

From adolescence until the death of her second husband, Doña María 's use of the mushrooms was sporadic because of the prohibition against sexual activity before their ingestion. Once she achieved shamanic status in the eyes of her community, she no longer prescribed herbs, because a *sabia* is considered to have a higher calling. Doña María's great grandfather, grandfather, great aunt, and great uncle had all been "*sabios*" or *sabias*. Her call, therefore, was not unexpected by her community. The social construction of Doña María's shamanic role took place over several decades, and was reflected by the changes in her activity. As a *sabia*, she no longer ate the mushrooms to allay her hunger but as a spiritual technology to assist her clients. As a *sabia*, she monitored her dreams carefully, knowing that they might be an important source of power and knowledge for her.

In 1980, I was a member of a group that visited the hamlet of Huautla de Jiminez in Oaxaca, Mexico. In one of her two interviews with us, Doña María told us that Jesus Christ worked through the mushrooms, dispensing wisdom and treating illness. She said that the mushrooms sprout "because God wills it." From Doña María's perspective, several functions (e.g., making the diagnosis, identifying the cause of the ailment, determining the treatment) are performed when the sabia and her clients eat the mushrooms together. She stated that "higher spiritual beings," usually Jesus Christ, work through the mushrooms, revealing the origin of the client's disease as well as the remedy.

Before the arrival of the Spaniards, the mushrooms were felt to have been the gift of Quetzalcōātl, the feathered serpent deity representing the unity of sky and earth. Although Roman Catholic priests prohibited the use of the mushrooms, the Mazatecs took the practice underground, eventually replacing Quetzalcōātl with Jesus Christ. Doña María had no conflict with the local Roman Catholic church; she attended Mass faithfully and helped to found a local women's society, the Sisterhood of the Sacred Heart of Jesus. Indeed, the local priest came to her defense when federal authorities attempted to prevent her from conducting her mushroom veladas.

Doña María's ceremonial liturgy contained a variety of Roman Catholic images, but at its core were the same odes and psalms that were uttered by the high priests of Montezuma, the Aztec ruler who was captured by the Spanish invaders in 1521. The Spanish Inquisition outlawed the veladas, which then went underground for more than four centuries. Once it was discovered that the ceremonies were still being held, Huautla de Jiminez was deluged by visitors from North America and Western Europe. Doña María was sympathetic with their desire for spiritual knowledge but was also critical of them because they did not respect Mazatec traditions and ate the mushrooms without adequate preparation or the guidance of a "wise one."

During our interviews with Doña María, she demonstrated a presence that was both compassionate and regal, changing into her "*huipil*" (i.e., traditional robe), before photographs were taken, and quickly administering a cleansing and blessing to the members of our party, including one woman who began to weep uncontrollably after her exposure to Doña María's charisma, even though Doña María remarked that her body was now too frail to accommodate the power of the mushrooms. Wasson (1981) observed that the mythical origin of the *veladas* dated from the time when Piltzintecuhtli, the Noble Infant, received the sacred mushrooms as a gift from Quetzalcōātl, and that Doña María's frequent references to Jesus represent a synthesis of the Christian and pre-Conquest religions.

As Doña María approached the ninth decade of her life, she retired as an active practitioner. She remarried and lived peacefully in Huautla de Jiminez until her death in 1985. Doña María had allowed recordings and transcripts to be made of the songs and chants that accompanied her *veladas*. In one of

> In one of her two interviews with us, Doña María told us that Jesus Christ worked through the mushrooms, dispensing wisdom and treating illness.

them, she described what might be called her narrative project:

> I am the woman of the great rain,
> I am the woman of the sacred rain,
> I am the woman of the flowing water,
> I am the little whirling woman of colors beneath the water,
> I am the little whirling woman of colors beneath the sea...,
> I am a woman of good words.
> (Estrada, 1981, p. 153)

In another, she related a visionary experience:

> I go up to heaven,
> Beneath the gaze of your glory,
> There is your paper and your Book,
> I am a woman who sounds forth with divinity,
> Where the shooting stars are showering,
> Where the flocks of the Lord's eagles are, the sacred eagles.
> (Estrada, 1981, pp. 153-154)

The Mapuche Peuma

In 1993, I met Lonko Kilapan during a lecture engagement in Santiago, Chile. As president of the Araucanian Confederation, he had organized a small museum which displayed Araucanian artifacts, and wrote several books (e.g., Kilapan, 1974, 1978) about Araucanian lore. Technically, "Araucano" or "Araucanian" refers to a larger, geographically more extensive population, culturally more heterogeneous group than the contemporary Mapuche people, most of whom live on reservations (Faron, 1968). The terms "Araucano" and "Araucanian" also refer to the language spoken by the Mapuche. In an interview and subsequent letter, Kilapan provided me with considerable information about the use of "*peumas*" (i.e., dream reports) by this native group. He spoke of dream reports as "stories" that have a variety of sources but which can be used beneficially by the dreamer.

I found a more extensive treatment of Kilapan's descriptions in a doctoral dissertation by Degarrod (1989), "Dream Interpretation among the Mapuche Indians of Chile." Degarrod collected 380 dream reports and their interpretations over a period of 17 months in the field, identifying four levels of analysis in the dream: (1) the "intratextual" level, which focuses on specific dream imagery; (2) the "contextual" level, which deals with the social and personal life of the dreamer as well as the dreamer's reactions to his or her dreams; (3) the "intertextual" level, which relates a particular dream to other dream texts of the same individual or that of others; (4) the "retrospective" level where the dreamer examines the events following the dream for the purpose of understanding its meaning. By conceptualizing the Mapuche dream reports in this way, Degarrod was able to describe their utilization for purposes of personal healing and tribal cohesion.

Much to my surprise, I found these data about Mapuche dreams to fit easily into a model of dreaming outlined by Ullman and Zimmerman (1979) who asked several questions about dreams and their social uses:

1. What is the function of dreaming? A dream report (or peuma) provides the Mapuche with information about present or future actions of others on the dreamer, guides decision-making and provide a rationale for one's actions, and/or serves as a channel of communication between the dreamer and other people, and between the dreamer and the spirit world. One way that dreams can be divided is into present-oriented and future-oriented dreams.

2. What motivates people to recall their dreams? Dreams are extremely important to the Mapuche. They can validate knowledge and the assumption of traditional roles and careers. For ordinary dreamers, prestige is obtained if the meaning of a dream is presented in a way that seems effortless. They can be used to diagnose illness, especially sexual possession. Dreams are often sought by the Mapuche, especially in times of stress. Especially valuable are the dreams of "machi" (i.e., shamans) who traditionally are women), diviners, chiefs, ritual leaders, and the "official" tribal dreamers. These dreams often express the traditional codes of Mapuche society, as dictated by the spirits (i.e., the "supernaturals"). In addition, diviners are said to locate lost objects in dreams by sleeping with an object that was once in physical contact with what had been lost.

3. What is the source of dreams? Among the Mapuche, dreaming is an activity of the "pulli" (i.e., the soul) that leaves the body at night, wandering about encountering other souls. The soul's nighttime experiences are recalled at dawn when the soul reunites with the body. In the case of ordinary persons, the soul wanders without volition and is a mere receiver of its experiences. Through dreams, the soul encounters benign spirits who may give good advice, or malevolent spirits who may do it harm. Through these encounters, the dreamer learns about the present or the future, and upon recalling and interpreting the dreams takes the appropriate action.

4. How do dreams convey their meanings? Dreams can convey their meanings either literally or symbolically. A dead relative coming to take the dreamer on a journey can symbolize death. Sometimes the decision is made by default; dreams narrated to public audiences are accompanied by literal interpretations while those narrated in the privacy of the home often undergo symbolic interpretation.

5. Are the meanings of dreams universal? The Mapuche are very flexible in their interpretation process. They examine dreams in relationship to the circumstances of the people around them. The intervention of others in the interpretation process permits the dream's meaning to be modified and manipulated. The contextual waking reality is taken into account during interpretation. Mapuche dream interpretation is an open system; dreamers can modify and maneuver the meanings of the dreams according to their specific social context.

6. What is the role of one's current life situation in dreams? Dreams guide Mapuche actions and decisions because dreaming, imagining, and thinking are on the same continuum.

In imagining and thinking, the soul also leaves the body but with volition, embarking on a much shorter journey. (Death is the longest journey of them all, while visions are visits to the dreamer by spirits.) Waking reality is balanced with dreaming reality during the interpretation process.

7. What techniques are used to work with dreams? Dream interpretation among the Mapuche is flexible. Through various modes of interpretation, dreamers can relate to different levels of time, of their culture, to other members of their tribe as well as outsiders, and to the world of the spirit.

   a. For example, through intratextual analysis, the dreamer connects his or her dream imagery with common cultural and personal symbols. Contextual analysis integrates the dream with his or her social and individual life situation. Intertextual analysis integrates the dream with the dreamer's previous dreams and sometimes with the dreams of other family members. Retrospective analysis permits the full meaning of dreams to be found and new symbols to be created. Any of these types of analysis may permit conversions from a metaphoric reversal to a literal system of analysis.

   b. Dreams considered to be negative are shared as soon as possible, and the interpretation is usually communal, within the family. This allows dreamers to intervene in each other's problems, and may facilitate healing. The interpretation of positive dreams is more likely to be a private matter. The classifications are made on the basis of the predictions in the dream. If the dream is ambiguous, the dreamer may wait for future events to assist in the interpretation.

   c. There are informal gatherings at which these dream reports are narrated as part of four different types of oratory: ritualized speech, improvised emotionally-toned songs, accounts of heroic deeds, and narratives of folk tales.

8. What is the role of the dreamworker? Most Mapuche dream interpretation is conducted within the family

> A Mapuche shaman can determine the direction of his or her dreams, bringing volition to the process in order to visit the spirit realm and communicate with his or her spirit advisors.

each morning and before important events. Difficult and troublesome dreams are taken to the shaman or other knowledgeable person. Each family and individual participating in the process brings to it their own idiosyncrasies and belief system. A Mapuche shaman can determine the direction of his or her dreams, bringing volition to the process in order to visit the spirit realm and communicate with his or her spirit advisors. Shamans often use mind-altering substances to heal through dreams, to obtain specific information about the future, or to contact the spirits. Contextual analysis can determine who has the prerequisite characteristics for becoming a shaman, and legitimize shamanic initiation through dreams. However, in Mapuche society, everyone is considered to be a potentially important dreamer.

9. What role does dreaming play in the dreamer's culture? Dreams are fully intertwined with all aspects of Mapuche culture. Dream interpretation is not an isolated event; it is integrated into all aspects of the dreamer's life through the multi-level analysis. Through intertextual and contextual analysis, the dreamer establishes communication with other people. This sharing and interpretation of dreams effects different types of communication between the narrators and the participants of the event. The dreamer's social position and the nature of the dream influence the rendition of the dream report, where the dream report is discussed, and the type of interpretation used. Dreams also are used to validate various aspects of the culture such as myths, songs, and social rankings.

10. How are anomalous and visionary dreams viewed? Through the dream experience itself and various means of analysis, the Mapuche can link and integrate different people and time periods. Retrospective analysis, by providing information about the future, links the dreamer's present activity to future events. Intertextual analysis links past dreams to those of the present. Because of these intertemporal links, the interpretation system helps to shape and influence the Mapuche views of the past, the present, and the future. It is customary for dreams about the "supernaturals" to be interpreted literally. It is typical for positive dream reports to be communicated only after their prophecy has been fulfilled. This retrospective analysis permits the verification of premonitions received in dreams and perpetuates, thereby, the use of dreams as forecasting devices. It also establishes the dreamer as a competent channel of communication with the spirit world.

As an example of Mapuche dreamwork, Degarrod (1989) cites a puzzling dream that was reported by "Julio" during her fieldwork:

> They dressed me with white clothing like a
> Catholic priest. The clothing fit me very nicely.
> It wasn't loose like priests usually wear, but a
> little tighter. It felt very good on my body as
> if it belonged to me. (p. 94)

Julio was confused because to dream of clothes is a negative sign, but white is positive. However, he felt good in the dream and enjoyed its imagery, so he decided to postpone labelling the dream. Two weeks later, a ceremony was held among people from two Mapuche reservations. The Roman Catholic church was organizing the event, and planned to have both chiefs and priests lead the ceremony. To Julio's delight, he was one of the persons chosen to lead prayers. He felt proud because of his position in the ritual, being surrounded by important people. Retrospective analysis had enabled him to interpret the dream. It had announced that he would act like someone of importance in front of the community. In addition, he had found a new symbol; henceforth, for him to dream of white clothing would be a positive sign.

The Mapuche often change their dream reports over time, following the contributions of family and community members. This phenomenon is reminiscent of research between dream content and personality. When dream content analysis scores were compared with personality test scores for a sample of university students in Canada, no significant relationships were found. However, when the students filled out questionnaires which asked them about dream content, significant relationships were found in such areas as extraversion, agreeableness, conscientiousness, and openness.

The authors of this study concluded that "one's personality may tell us little about what a person actually dreams, but it can tell us a great deal about what a person thinks she/he dreams" (Bernstein, Belicki, & Gonzalez, 1995, p. 139). These research data and the Mapuche's proclivity to relate dreams in ways that reinforce their status correspond with postmodern distinctions between "fixed texts" and "fluid texts," the latter term being more descriptive of dream reports.

It is apparent that the Mapuche dream legacy is a complete model of dreaming and dreamworking, even in Western terms. In contrast to the Western dismissal of dreams, the Mapuche dreamworking project allows for the integration of dreams into every major facet of waking life. Indeed, there is no rigid division between the Mapuches' dream life and waking life (Faron, 1968).

The same can be said for many other dream models in native America, especially those practiced before the arrival of the Europeans. Among most North and South American Indian tribes, the shaman was the focal dreamworker, but it was acknowledged that "everyone who dreams has a bit of shaman" within them (Kracke,1987).

Research Data on Mythic Themes

The Navajo, Mazatec, and Mapuche use of storytelling in their chantways, veladas, and dream reports reveal the healing potential of mythic themes. Mythic stories and statements reflect existential human concerns and have behavioral consequences. There are some psychological research data that can be profitably interpreted within the framework of mythic narratives. For example, various laboratories have employed subliminal psychodynamic activation with a 4-millisecond exposure of stimuli intended to activate unconscious symbiotic-like fantasies. Usually the words "Mommy and I Are One," or some variant, are utilized. The beneficial effects of this stimulation are often dramatic and long-lasting (Silverman & Weinberger, 1985).

In one study, a group of tobacco smokers was administered behavior modification techniques for smoking cessation during 12 sessions. Half the group was given the subliminal message "Mommy and I Are One" while the others were given a neutral message.

All subjects in both groups had stopped smoking by the end of the experiment. However, at a later follow-up, 67% of those subjects who had been receiving the symbiotic subliminal exposure were still abstainers as compared to only 13% of the subjects who had received a neutral subliminal message (Palmatier & Bornstein,1980). Similar results have been reported for other groups receiving symbiotic stimuli when compared with control groups receiving neutral messages such as "People Are Walking."

These groups have included (1) adolescents with personality disorders who were receiving psychotherapy in a residential treatment center; (2) college students engaged in group therapy; (3) persons with assertiveness difficulties receiving assertiveness training; (4) alcoholics in an Alcoholics Anonymous counseling program; (5) people phobic to insects receiving systematic desensitization; and (6) obese persons receiving behavior modification techniques for reducing food intake.

Most of the subjects showing improvement in these studies were male. When it was observed that about half the females studied did not attain similar results, such messages as "Daddy and I Are One" and "My Lover and I Are One" were substituted. These messages produced significant positive results, perhaps because they stimulated fantasies involving someone other than "Mommy" who was less likely to threaten a woman's sense of self-identity. Such messages as "Mommy and I Are the Same," "Mommy and I Are Alive," and "Mommy Is Inside Me" were found to be ineffective.

It is likely that these messages did not evoke unconscious fantasies with as many mythic themes as did "Mommy and I Are One." This message may have stimulated such positive, growth-facilitating personal myths as those centering around completion, nurturance, and union. If a fantasy can connote a situation where one is constantly fed and nurtured, one can reduce the necessity to seek dependency gratification in maladaptive behavior such as alcoholism, drug abuse, and overeating. Feeling protected and comforted may reduce anxiety and mobilize positive effort for behavior change.

Activation of symbiotic-like fantasies might also enhance receptivity to psychologists and other helping persons who may be unconsciously perceived, in part, as "Mommy," the mythic helping figure. The psychotherapist usually is experienced as a caring person who conveys acceptance, empathy, and warmth (Rogers,1957). In addition, research data exist indicating that treatment outcome can be improved by matching the psychotherapist and the client on various cognitive dimensions (Frank & Frank, 1991; Parloff, Waskow, & Wolfe, 1978).

Other research data demonstrated that such messages as "Mommy Feeds Me Well" and "Mommy Holds Me Safely" did not produce positive effects (Silbert, 1982) indicating that deep-seated mythic symbiotic-like gratifications rather than general "good mothering" gratifications are involved in successful treatment programs.

O'Dowd (1987) noted that the psychoanalyst Otto Rank had observed the importance of these symbiotic-like yearnings in the 1920s. According to O'Dowd, fantasies of oneness with the mother increase receptiveness to psychotherapists and promote adaptive behaviors because they gratify dependency-related needs. A related but alternative explanation of these treatment programs has been offered by Tabin and Tabin (1987) who observed that "My Girl and I are One" was more effective for men than "Mommy and I are One." Rather than lending itself to a symbiotic interpretation, "Girl" suggests a sexual interpretation that is more obvious than when "Mommy" is used (Kaye, 1975). However, "Mommy" may involve sexual fantasies as well.

Indeed, when an authority figure subliminally reassures male subjects that their most primal sexual fantasies are permissible, the subjects may experience heightened personal adaptation because these urges are intimately connected with their early ego development.

Both "Girl" and "Mommy" carry two implicit messages: permission for sexual fantasy and simultaneous protection for masculine identity under the aegis of the authoritative experimenter. However, "Girl" may be a stronger stimulus because of its capacity to evoke among male subjects a condition that is ultimately more enhancing to their ego than "Mommy." Tabin and Tabin's hypothesis also is consistent with the greater effectiveness of "My Lover and I Are One" than "Daddy and I Are One" for female subjects.

Both the symbiotic and the sexual hypotheses are mythic in nature; in the case of some subjects, the latter may even reflect the accounts of Oedipus' and Electra's attraction to their opposite-sex parents found in Greek mythology. An alternative to this Freudian explanation would be the Jungian position that the most effective stimuli represent an "inner marriage"—the union of a man with his "anima"(repressed "female" potentials) or a woman's integration of her "animus" (repressed "male" capacities).

Additional research data that lend themselves to mythic interpretation are found in the results reported by users of the Imagery of Disease Test (Achterberg & Lawlis, 1984). For example, cancer patients are asked to imagine pictures of their tumors, their white blood cells, and their current medical treatment. They are then asked to draw the three images and to discuss these drawings in a structured interview. The interview protocol is scored on 14 dimensions, e.g., activity level, frequency of positive images, symbolism, vividness.

The total score on the Imagery of Disease Test was found to predict, at a 2-month follow-up, the status of cancer with 93% accuracy for those patients in total remission, and 100% accuracy for those who had died or had rapid deterioration (Achterberg & Lawlis, 1979). In a number of studies of cancer patients, the images have had greater predictive value than any of the medical tests utilized (Achterberg, 1985).

The images that were found to be significantly related to a change in the status of the disease were consistent across the groups of cancer patients studied. For example, patients who were to experience new tumor growth typically drew their cancer cells as large, hard, impregnable objects such as crabs, lobsters, scorpions, and submarines. Snails and slugs were associated with a better prognosis. Some of the positive symbols for the immune system's white blood cells were white knights, Vikings, and religious symbols. Those white blood cells images associated with a poor prognosis were clouds and feathers.

The mythic content of these images appears to be of use in predicting the course of a disease. Patients may harbor either adaptive or maladaptive health myths. Some may be telling themselves, "My cancer is powerful and impregnable; it lurks beneath the surface and is beyond my control." In contrast, some patients may be telling themselves, "My tumors are vulnerable; my medical treatment and immune system are capable of eliminating them." Similar unconscious beliefs have been reflected in health imagery that has allowed the correct prediction of blood glucose levels in diabetes, speech clarity among patients with laryngectomies, and degree of pain among patients undergoing back surgery (Achterberg & Lawlis, 1980).

Conclusion

Mahoney (1996) describes how storytelling brings to psychotherapy the perspective that clients are more than passive and reactive objects of manipulations. Instead, they are viewed as proactive agents who are able to participate in the reorganization of their lives. With their therapists, these clients co-create personal realities which evolve into a reciprocity, not only between their environment and themselves, but also between and within different levels of their own activities. In other words, people organize their worlds by organizing themselves. In their own way, these individuals are constructing "creation myths" that have more than a passing resemblance to the creation myths constructed and accepted by entire premodern societies (Maclagan, 1977).

Psychotherapeutic approaches with mythic components may be able to communicate with the deepest levels of one's psyche and soma, facilitating positive unconscious motivation as well as maximizing the function of the immune system. The therapeutic value of mythic statements and stories may derive, at least in part, from their symbols and metaphors, those artistic and literary devices that have been able to move people profoundly over the millennia. The mythic projects of native peoples, of necessity, have been performed through formal and informal rituals, most of which are permeated by storytelling. These stories manifest themselves in the chantways, *veladas*, and dreamworking rituals described in this chapter.

Even in today's technological world, storytelling may serve as a resource that is able to promote individual and group well-being if its messages are honored, respected, and understood. Many groups of native people have been aware of the healing power of stories, and the models implicit in their rituals are worthy of attention and study.

References

Achterberg, J. (1985). Imagery and healing: Shamanism and modern medicine. Boston: Shambhala.

Achterberg, J., & Lawlis, G.F. (1979). A canonical analysis of blood chemistry variables related to psychological measures of cancer patients. Multivariate Experimental Clinical Research, 4: 1-10, 1979.

Achterberg, J., & Lawlis, G.F. (1980). Bridges of the bodymind: Behavioral approaches to health care. Champaign, IL: Institute for Personality and Ability Testing.

Achterberg, J., & Lawlis, G.F. (1984). Imagery and disease. Champaign, IL: Institute for Personality and Ability Testing.

Adair, J., Deuschle, K.W., & Barnett, C.R. (1988). The people's health: Anthropology and medicine in a Navajo community. Albuquerque: University of New Mexico Press.

Bernstein, D.M., Belicki, K., & Gonzalez, D. (1995). Trait personality and its relationship to two different measures of dream content. Sleep Research, 24, 139.

Campbell, J. (1990). Transformations of myth through time. New York: Harper & Row.

Degarrod, L.N. (1989). Dream interpretation among the Mapuche Indians of Chile. Unpublished doctoral dissertation, University of California, Los Angeles.

Estrada, A. (1981). María Sabina: Her life and chants. Santa Barbara, CA: Ross-Erikson.

Faron, L. (1968). The Mapuche of Chile. New York: Holt, Rinehart and Winston.

Frank, J.D., & Frank, J.B. (1991). Persuasion and healing: A comparative study of psychotherapy (3rd ed.). Baltimore: Johns Hopkins University Press.

Gonoçalves, Ó.F. (1995). Hermeneutics, constructivism, and cognitive-behavioral therapies: From the object to the project. In R.A. Neimeyer & M.J. Mahoney (Eds.), Constructivism in psychotherapy (pp. 195-230). Washington, DC: American Psychological Association.

Kaye, M. (1975). The therapeutic value of three merging stimuli for male schizophrenics. Unpublished doctoral dissertation, Yeshiva University, New York.

Kilapan, L. (1974). El origen griego de los araucanos [The Greek origin of the Araucanians]. Santiago, Chile: Editorial Universitaria.

Kilapan, L. (1978). Sistema numeral araucano [Araucanian numerology]. Santiago, Chile: Editorial Universitaria.

Kracke, W.H. (1987). "Everyone who dreams has a bit of shaman": Cultural and personal meanings of dreams—evidence from the Amazon. Psychiatric Journal of the University of Ottawa, 12, 65-71.

Krippner, S. (1995). A cross-cultural comparison of four healing models. Alternative Therapies in Health and Medicine, 1, 21-29.

Maclagan, I. (1977). Creation myths: Man's introduction to the world. New York: Thames & Hudson.

Mahoney, M.J. (1996). Constructivism and the study of complex self-organization. Constructive Change, 1, 3-8.

O'Dowd, W.T. (1987). Comment on Silverman and Weinberger: Rankian hypotheses confirmed. AmericanPsychologist, 42, 955-956.

Palmatier, J.R., & Bornstein, P.H. (1980). The effects of subliminal stimulation of symbiotic merging fantasies on behavioral treatment of smokers. Journal of Nervous and Mental Disease, 168, 715-720.

Parloff, M.B., Waskow, I.E., & Wolfe, B.E. (1978). Research on therapist variables in relation to process and outcome. In S.I. Garfield & A.E. Bergin (Eds.), Handbook of psychotherapy and behavior change (pp. 232-282). New York: John Wiley and Sons.

Rogers C.R. (1957). The necessary and sufficient conditions of therapeutic personality change. Journal of Consulting Psychology, 21, 95-103.

Rothenberg, J. (1981). Preface. In A. Estrada, María Sabina: Her life and chants (pp. 7-11). Santa Barbara, CA: Ross-Erikson.

Sandner, D. (1979). Navaho symbols of healing. New York: Harcourt Brace Jovanovich.

Silbert, J. (1982). Human symbiosis, the holding environment and schizophrenia. Unpublished Doctoral Dissertation, New York University, New York.

Silverman, L.H., & Weinberger, J. (1985). Mommy and I are one: Implications for psychotherapy. American Psychologist, 40, 1296-1308.

Sullivan, L.E. (1988). Icanchu's drum. New York: Macmillan.

Tabin, J., & Tabin, C. J. (1987). An alternative interpretation of oneness. American Psychologist, 42, 954-955.

Topper, M.D. (1987). The traditional Navajo medicine man: Therapist, counselor, and community leader. Journal of Psychoanalytic Anthropology, 10, 217-249.

Ullman, M., & Zimmerman, N. (1979). Working with dreams. Los Angeles: Tarcher.

Wasson, R.G. (1980). The wondrous mushroom: Mycolotry in Mesoamerica. New York: McGraw-Hill.

Wasson, R.G. (1981). A retrospective essay. In A. Estrada, María Sabina: Her life and chants (pp. 13-20). Santa Barbara, CA: Ross-Erikson.

Ullman, M., & Zimmerman, N. (1979). Working with dreams. Los Angeles: Tarcher

---

504 pages

ReVision Publishing

Only $25.00

Includes shipping

Order from:
ReVision Publishing
https://revisionpublishing.org/books/

Spirit Sickness and Soul Loss

Stanley Krippner

I previously discussed people's needs for a social group and a moral code. I also discussed the roles each play in the human species' evolution. For a behavior to have survival value, it needs to contribute to reproductive success. That behavior would be passed on to future generations, allowing them to survive.

For example, early humans evolved to survive, not to discover truth. If they believed that eating a foul-tasting herb would cure a malady, they would give it a try. The herb might not contain medicinal properties, but many people would get well despite this. Those who responded to what are now called "placebo effects" passed on their genes to future generations. Those who did not survive had no opportunity to pass anything on. It was millenarian before researchers discovered the power and the placebo effect. The word "placebo" comes from a Latin term, "I

Adapted from: Krippner, S., Riebel, L., Ellis, D.J., & Paulson, D.S. (2021). *Understanding suicide's allure: Steps to save lives by healing psychological scars.* Santa Barbara, CA: Praeger.

Photo: George Berticevich Photographer
Copyright 2025

will please." And this is exactly what sick people did when given a remedy or asked to participate in a ritual that would prolong their live.

Survival often involved placating deities, making offerings, and conducing bloody rituals, sacrificing both human and other animals. Once language, mathematics, and measurement became available, scientific ways of thinking developed. Science, wherever it takes place, is a special story of the world. Native American science used metaphors to tell this story. Native Americans found meaning in all of Nature and used their "metaphoric minds" to fathom these connections. These metaphors could be sculpted, as with the 1,348-foot-long Serpent Mount in Ohio, the petroglyphs in the Mojave Desert, and the elaborate sand paintings that accompany the Navajo chantway ceremonies.

Popular usage of the word "myth" is derogatory. "Myth" is equated with falsehood and superstition, as well it might be given the cultural myths that engaged in human sacrifice. However, we have used the word "myth" with an anthropological perspective, and native storytellers used both metaphor and symbolism to tell stories about the creation and destruction of the universe, the beginning and end of societies, and the birth, death, and possible rebirth of individuals. We propose that myth evolved into science, just as magic evolved into technology. Evolution can be cultural as well as biological. Native scientists viewed humans as participating in the unfolding of Nature.

The French anthropologist Lucien Levy-Bruhl used the term *participation mystique* to describe how native people interact with the natural world. An anthropologist, Levy-Bruhl was influenced by the sociological work of Emile Durkheim's and used the term "group ideas" to describe such phenomena as cultural myths. In his book *How Natives Think* (1926), Levy-Bruhl proposed that is not opposed to logical thinking but combines it with group ideas that Western writers would consider irrational and superstitious. Levy-Bruhl cautioned that Westerners ignore these non-linear, "romantic" ways of thinking at their peril as they represent a resource that could be live-saving. This "metaphor mind" is itself primordial, as evidenced by ancient myths, rituals, and artwork.

The Metaphor Mind

Gregory Cajete (2000) has proposed that this type of mind evolved before early humans developed language. Once they did, the holistic perspective of the metaphoric mind got chopped up and labeled until, eventually, it receded into the unconscious. Yet, the metaphor mind continues to operate, lying in wait until the conscious, rational mind calls upon its special skills for help. And then it emerges in creative play, contemplative mediation, imaginative reverie, community rituals, and its campfire stories and nighttime dreams.

Westerners, with their emphasis on the rational mind and language, tend to ignore the metaphoric mind, yet it is the foundation of native science. Understanding native science begins with developing the creative ability to decipher layers of meaning embedded in symbols that have been used for thousands of years. They are still used artistically and linguistically to depict structures and relationship to places. The creation stories of native science are embedded in the processes of Nature from which they are drawn, or point toward human nature on which they attempt to reflect.

Native science honors the primacy of direct experience, as well as interconnectedness, relationship, holism, quality, and value. It is difficult to generalize about native science since there were over one thousand tribes in North America when the Europeans arrived. After decimation by wars and disease, there are now half that many tribes and all of them saw their cultural traditions ridiculed, even forbidden. The past few decades have seen a renaissance in Native American ceremonial practices, especially with the Sun Dance, the Gourd Dance, and rituals using peyote and other vision-evoking plants. Shamans used several methods of disciplined inquiry in their search for medicinal substances, including trial and error, self-administration of likely substances, and keen observation especially when monitoring the effects of a medicine over time.

You may remember that Durkheim (1951) identified four types of suicide, including *anomic suicide,* which results from feelings of not belonging, of losing one's personal direction. Wolfgang Jilek, a Canadian psychiatrist, has used the term *anomic depression* to describe a malaise brought associated with feelings of discouragement, defeat, a low self-image, and existential frustration. It is the latter symptom that gives the term its name, "anomic." Existentially-oriented therapists use the French term when referring to social alienation, usually resulting from social upheaval. That criterion was cited by both Durkheim and Jilek.

The tribes in the Pacific Northwest studied by Jilek (1982) referred to the condition as "spirit sickness" and other tribes have used a variety of terms including "soul loss." A person with such a diagnosis is at risk for suicide because of profound spiritual problems. To heal the spirit and to retrieve the soul, Native American practitioners have developed a variety of interventions including sweat lodges, community rituals, herbal tinctures, and "journeying." The journey is performed by the tribal shaman. The word "shaman" is used by cultural anthropologists to refer to a certain type of native healers, specifically those who share three characteristics:

1. They have been socially-sanctioned; their community has given them that title and the accompanying role. Unlike most physicians in the Western world, shamans do not make a rational decision, followed up by training. They are "called" in some way, and their community needs to verify that call and provide the means to follow it.

2. They can access information in ways that are not ordinarily available to other members of tribe (Lewis, 2003). Sometimes a tribal member will pray for a loved one who, following the prayer, makes a remarkable recovery. However, shamans claim that they can perform each of these "journeys" at will," or "on demand."

3. Shamans use the information they obtained to help or to heal members of their community. Nobody can claim the title of "shaman" (or whatever term is used by a tribe) without having a community to which he

> The tribes in the Pacific Northwest studied by Jilek referred to the condition as "spirit sickness" and other tribes have used a variety of terms including "soul loss." A person with such a diagnosis is at risk for suicide because of profound spiritual problems.

or she is responsible. It can even be by a "virtual Communism," one connected by the Internet or social media.

Different names for this type of practitioner are used by different tribes However, shamans, by whatever name they are called, differ from sorcerers who may use similar interventions as shamans but who charge for their services and do not work on behalf of their community. Diviners or mediums incorporate "spirits," as do most shamans. However, the alleged "spirit" takes control of the medium. Shamans, on the other hand, are in control of the "spirit" and does not lose the sense of personal identity, as to diviners and mediums. Priests and priestesses are religious functionaries who preside at a community's spiritual rituals; some of them engage in healing but it is typically a "laying-on of hands," not a step-by-step procedure requiring careful training and execution.

The Shamanic Journey of Fawn Journeyhawk

Spiritual sickness and soul loss may lead to suicide and shamans have a variety of interventions they can perform to prevent death. Some cultures hold that people have more than one soul; soul retrieval consists of bringing back the lost sold so that the afflicted persons can regain their balance and equilibrium. Other cultures believe that the meandered away during a dream, and that there needs to be an initial dream that will enable retrieval. There may be a variety of rituals performed to retrieve the errant soul, such as burning incense, going on a special diet, and participating in magic rituals5.

In one type of "shamanic journeying," the shaman makes a trip to the locale of the client's missing soul. The soul might have been lost due to a sickness. It might have disappeared as the result of a curse. It may have slipped away while its owner performed an act that was immoral, such as violating a tribal taboo or hurting a defenseless child. Fawn's reputation brought Fernando, a suicidal Vietnam War veteran with PTSD, to see Fawn Journeyhawk at her center in Arizona.

Fernando's sleep was marred by nightmares in which he relived the moment when he killed every member of a Vietnamese family because he believed they were carrying firearms. When he discovered that they were simply transporting groceries, it was too late. Following several days of preparation, Fawn "took a journey" to Vietnam where she begged the spirits of that family for forgiveness. Apparently, Fawn was successful because the veteran's nightmares chanted dramatically. No longer did Fernando's dreams replay the tragic instrument. Instead, they used symbols and metaphors – a collection of dollars swept to their death by a flood, a group of animals shot by overly-zealous hunters, a small house ravaged by a flamethrower. Dreams commonly use symbols and metaphors to aid the emotional processing of a disturbing experience. Within a few months, Fernando was sleeping well and had no further thoughts of suicide.

Fawn Journeyhawk, who spent most of her life in Arizona, was of Shawnee and Cree ancestry. As a child she reported vivid dreams to her parents and performed spontaneous healing ceremonies for friends and relatives when they became indisposed. Concerned about this bizarre behavior, a social worker took Fawn to a psychiatrist. The psychiatrist gave Fawn a diagnosis of "clinical depression with schizophrenic tendencies" and put her on medication. The medication inhibited Fawn's dreams but induced a drug dependency that she took years to beat.

Once she was no longer taking medication, Fawn began recalling her dreams. This time, the dreams began to serve a teaching purpose. Such Indian spirits as "Red Tomahawk Halfmoon Wahoo Kahoonehaw, and Stormy Winds taught her how to shamanize, and she soon had people from various parts of the state arrival at her "medicine lodge" for assistance. Because of her own addiction history, Fawn was especially adept in work with drug addicts, substance abusers, and alcoholics, many of them "at risk" for suicide.

Fawn was aware of the allure that both drug addiction and suicide cast on their potential victims. She described the "spirit" of cocaine as a glamorous woman dressed in black, one who is difficult to resists. The "spirit" of heroin (and other opiates) can be either male or female. This "spirit" is "strong, selfish, and demanding"; it is difficult to break lose once one has given in to the allure. Alcohol's "spirit" is "low-class and cheap." Alcohol's allure is due to his banality; people tend to think this entity is "just like me," and do not see what harm can come from imbibing it. Indeed, Fawn felt that alcohol is one of two drugs that can be used in moderation, the other being marijuana. As for nicotine, this "spirit" is the most addictive of them all. This spirit can be of either gender and is able "shift its shape" so that it resembles the user, or someone close to the user. By the time the disguise is discovered, it is too late.

In treating addiction, Fawn called upon "White Owl," an ally from the "spirit world." Fawn would ask her client to prepare for healing by fasting and praying of several days. When Fawn went on

> Some cultures hold that people have more than one soul; soul retrieval consists of bringing back the lost sold so that the afflicted persons can regain their balance and equilibrium.

her "journey," she was accompanied by White Owl. She would adopt her "warrior stance" and fight the alluring "spirit" for the possession of her client's soul. Fawn and white Owl would then take the client's soul to a "crystal cave" where more healing would take place. Following the soul retrieval, Fawn's client was given daily instructions on how to keep the sold intact because losing it again would pose an even more formidable task of getting it back.

Ricki Soaring Dove reached Fawn's

medicine lodge at a low point in her life. Suffering from a chronic sinus condition, Ricki was barely able to breathe. No physician had been able to provide even temporary relief. so miserable that she had contemplated suicide. Fawn advised her no to put all thoughts of suicide on the table. Once there, it became obvious to Ricki, as well as Fawn, that killing herself would cut short the lessons she needed to learn in this life. To start all over again, was too heavy a burden for Ricki to contemplate, and so she started to work with Fawn on her health issues. Following a week of fasting and taking herbal medicine, Ricki "journeyed" with Fawn to the "crystal cave." When they returned, Fawn gave her some actual crystals for her to contemplate between sessions. After four meeting with Fawn, Ricki's sinuses were clear. She commented, "No one who I have seen for counseling has been able to delineate and pull back the armor as effectively as Fawn was able to do."

In 2018, Fawn passed on while in a California hospice. Visitors reported seeing a double rainbow when she died. Caretakers of Fawn's Arizona medicine lodge also reported seeing a double rainbow. They had not been informed of the similar manifestation before they made their comments.

Altruistic Suicide in a Brazilian Tribe

In 2011 I attended a conference in Curitiba, the theme of which was consciousness and its dimensions (Krippner, 2006). Toward the end of the conference, a few participants were invited to make a trek into the nearby rainforest for a special ceremony arranged by Joaõ Guarani, a shaman for the Eastern Guarani tribe. He was referred to as a paje', the term for "shaman" used by most of the Brazilian tribes.

The group entered a dome made of twigs and animal hides and was seated on the ground around a fire. Several members of the tribe began to play drums and three beautiful statuesque native women performed a traditional dance. Once it was over, participants thought that this event was certainly worth their long trip.

But it was not over. Dom Joaõ pulled out a huge pipe, filling it with a smoking mixture, took a long drag, and passed it on. No group member reported an effect, but everyone enjoyed the bonding that this ritual had provided.

But it was not over. Dom (a title of respect, corresponding to the Spanish term "don") Joaõ emptied the pipe and filled it with another substance. He lit it, took a toke, and passed it on. The smell and taste were different, but also quite pleasant.

But it was still not over. Dom Joaõ again emptied the pipe and refilled it, took several puffs, and passed it around. Again, nobody felt a shift in perception or emotion, but enjoyed the camaraderie.

> Indigenous people from both continents feel that their relationship with Nature is broken when they are separated from their land. In addition to undermining their spiritual base, the seizure of their land has disrupted the social structure of the community.

But it was still not over. Dom Joaõ put the pipe aside and brought forth a gourd. He took a quaff of the contents and passed it on. Everyone drank from the gourd and passed it on, thinking that this would be a fitting ending to the ceremony.

But it was still not over. Dom Joaõ brought forth another gourd, drank some of the contents, and sent it around the circle. Again, it was pleasant and seemed to be an herbal mixture of some sort.

And the ceremony continued. Dom Joaõ took a third gourd, imbibed part of the contents, and once again passed it on. This time the six mixtures, alone or in combination had an incredible effect upon me and the other group members. My mind was clear, and I thought that I had been blessed by Oxala, the African-Brazilian god of clarity. Nothing I had every experienced had ever cleaned the doors of perception so thoroughly—not prayer, not meditation, not LSD, not ayahuasca, or other psychedelics.

The thought passed my mind, "If Dom Joaõ could patent this mixture, he would be able to raise his tribe out of poverty with the sales." Of course, I knew that this was not his way of doing things, as authentic shamans do not commercialize their magical technology.

Suddenly, Dom Joaõ asked us each to give a prayer. My limited Portuguese has never been as fluent as it was that night. I knew that ranchers and farmers had illegally stolen parts of the Guarani homeland, cutting down trees and turning the land into cattle ranches. Many young people had hanged themselves from the trees in protest. I prayed that the youth stop killing themselves and conserve their energies for more direct confrontations with the ranchers and farmers who had stolen their land. However, I knew that they had lost confidence not only in themselves but in the magical rituals and tribal myths that had given them their identity for thousands of years.

Dom Joaõ gave the final prayer, one that asked the deities to protect us on our way back to our homes. As the members of our group started to leave, the shaman turned to me and asked how I had known about the young people's self-sacrifice. I told him that I was a member of the Rainforest Action Network, a socially active group in the United States dedicated to the preservation of the rainforests of the world.

A leader of the Guarani tribe had been a guest at one of our meetings. She told us about the farmers' and ranchers' perfidy and the suicides that were mounted in protest. I told Dom Joaõ that the farmers and ranchers could not care less if a few dozen girls and boys gave their lives to stop the destruction of their homeland. Instead, I hoped they would take non-violent action to save their homeland.

If my Portuguese had been better, I would have told him how the local shaman Rolling Thunder and his spiritual warriors had stopped the destruction of the pinion nut trees in Nevada by non-violent means. These nuts were an inexpensive source of protein for the local Indians. Rolling Thunder's son, Buffalo Horse worked with him on that project. He also helped the crew of the popular television show "Sixty Minutes" produce a feature story about it. He also was an adviser for the documentary, "The Broken Treaty of Battle Mountain," that received wide attention. Buffalo Horse told me, "The ranchers wanted to clear the land and get rid of the pinion nut trees. They took two big caterpillar tractors and put chains between them and when the chains rolled along, they would tear up the land.

The trees would literally explode. They could clear 20 acres in about an hour. They would destroy so many of those trees that they lined up down the road as far as the eye could see. And nobody could pick nuts from the trees or use them as firewood. They would just burn them. This was an insult because pinion nuts are sacred to our people. And you could live on pinion nuts forever if you had nothing else to eat. A pinion nut tree is literally the 'Tree of Life.'"

RT and his spiritual warriors videotaped the destruction of the trees. A few members of his group took the videotape to Washington, DC, to get the support of important politicians. Their pleas fell on deaf ears, the notable exception being Senator Edward Kennedy from Massachusetts. He knew of President Richard Nixon's interest in Native American rights and went directly to the White House. The result was a bipartisan effort that stopped the ranchers dead in their track—at least for a while.

In the meantime, Rolling Thunder and his spiritual warriors had instituted a delaying tactic. In the dead of night, they poured sand into the fuel tanks of the tractors. The next day they couldn't run, and it took several days before the sand was extricated. Shortly afterwards, the executive order stopped the illegal activity completely.

Dom Joaõ listened intently to my story, much of which had to be translated due to my limited Portuguese vocabulary. He said that he would pass on this information to members of his tribe, especially the young people. Since that time, however, outsiders have murdered Guarani activists and tribal leaders who attempted to regain their land. The high suicide rate continues; young Guarani kill themselves twice as often as other tribal youth and six times as frequently as young people in the general population.

In 1988, a new Brazilian constitution returned land to Brazil's Indians, but farmers and ranchers disregarded it, claiming that it was holding back the country's "progress." It is this "progress," of course, that has polluted the oceans, contaminated the air, and devastated the forests.

Indigenous people from both continents feel that their relationship with Nature is broken when they are separated from their land. In addition to undermining their spiritual base, the seizure of their land has disrupted the social structure of the community. In addition to suicide, these indigenous people have a high rate of murder, spouse abuse, and alcohol and drug addiction. All too often, tribal leaders who speak out against the outrage are beaten, tortured, or murdered.

In 2014, Marcos Vernon, a Guarani leader, exclaimed, "This here is my life, my soul. If you take me away from this land, you take my life." Shortly after making this statement, Vernon was murdered as he attempted to lead his tribe back to their homeland. Survival International, in their November 2014 newsletter, observed that Guarani leaders "are being killed one by one by ranchers; gunmen as a result of their campaign for their ancestral land to be mapped and returned to them." Ironically, the territory stolen from the Guarani-Kaiowá is often used for sugar cane production. Some of the produce is used for alcohol, the substance that, in another form, has triggered its own type of slavery.

Durkheim would place the suicide of the young tribal members in his altruistic category. But they also remind us of the fifth category we proposed, that of moral wounding. The loss of these vibrant young women and men is a tragedy for the Earth, which needs commitment and wisdom to half the destruction of the planet and its inhabitants, human and non-human alike.

TAKEAWAY POINTS

- Group ideas or cultural myths play an important role in suicidality, sometimes promoting suicide and sometimes preventing it.

- Shamans are socially-designated tribal healers who can access useful information in unique ways such as "journeying."

- "Soul loss" and "spirit sickness" are terms used by shamans to describe people whose spiritual problems have put them at risk for suicide. Shamanic interventions for these maladies may have relevance for other groups of suicidal people.

References

Cajete, G. (2000). *Native science: Natural laws of interdependence.* Santa Fe, NM: Clear Light.

Durkheim, E. (1951). *Suicide: A study in sociology.* Glencoe, IL: The Free Press. (Original work published in French, 1897).

Jilek, W.G. 1982). *Indian healing: Shamanism ceremonialism in the Pacific Northwest today.* Blaine, WA: Hancock House.

Krippner, S. (2006). We know how. In S.M.S. Jones & S. Krippner (Eds.). *The shamanic powers of Rolling Thunder* (pp. 107-112). Rochester, VT: Bear.

Levy-Bruhl, L. (1926) *How natives think.* Chicago, IL: University of Chicago Press. (Original work published 1910)

Lewis, I.M. (2003). *Ecstatic Religion: A study of shamanism and spirit possession.* (2nd ed.). New York, NY: Routledge.

The Future of Ethnomedicine

Stanley Krippner

The beginning of a new century often provides an opportunity for major disciplines to take stock of themselves, their progress, or their lack of it. Bruce J. West (2006) has evaluated Western medicine, concluding that it has "gone wrong," and that ancient, traditional medical systems can help correct its path. F. David Peat (2002) also called for a revisioning of Western medicine, pointing out that Native American concepts of reality in general and the body specifically portrayed a very different perspective on health and sickness. Hence, readers who plunge into this chapter will encounter world views and paradigms that often diverge from what they have been taught by the media or what they have learned in medical school or university classes.

At a Glance

This contribution defines "ethnomedicine," describes its scope, and points out its value as Western physicians and health care professionals search for new

Traditional herbal medicnes

medical treatments, improved technologies, and diverse ways of conceptualizing prevention, diagnosis, and treatment. "Curing" is differentiated from "healing," and "illness" is contrasted to "disease." The parameters of medical models are delineated, using an Andean system as an example. Traditional treatment is not romanticized; it has a record of failures as well as successes. The role played by social construction is an essential key to an evaluation of various enthomedicines, past and present.

Objectives

After reading this article, the reader should be able to:

Krippner, S. (2009). The future of ethnomedicine. In L. Freeman, Mosby's complementary and alternative medicine: A research-based approach (3rd ed., pp. 574-580). St. Louis, MO: Mosby/Elsevier.

Photo: World Health Organization

1. Define "ethnomedicine" and related terminology,
2. Cite the basic principles of treatment that characterize both Western medicine and various enthomedicines,
3. Give examples of both endogenous and exogenous concepts that underlie enthomedicines,
4. Cite the four basic principles of all medical (and other therapeutic) treatments,
5. Give examples of how power and privilege can undercut even the most effective enthomedicines,

6. Make suggestions as to how Western allopathic biomedicine can work with indigenous models of healing, since they are utilized by eight out of ten people worldwide;
7. Gain insight into the ongoing clashes between cultural mythologies, spiritual paradigms, and medical narratives, and suggest ways to reach a compromise or a synthesis—or at least a détente.
8. Suggest research strategies involving ethnomedicine that will improve health care around the world.

Introduction

The term "ethnomedicine" refers to the comparative study of indigenous (or traditional) medical systems. Typical ethnomedical topics include causes of sickness, medical practitioners and their roles, and specific treatments utilized. The explosion of ethnomedical literature has been stimulated by an increased awareness of the consequences of the forced displacement and/or acculturation of indigenous peoples, the recognition of indigenous health concepts as a means of maintaining ethnic identities, and the search for new medical treatments and technologies. In addition, the anthropologist Arthur Kleinman (1995) found ethnographic studies to be an "appropriate means of representing pluralism...and of drawing upon those aspects of health and suffering to resist the positivism, the reductionism, and the naturalism that biomedicine and, regrettably, the wider society privilege" (p. 195).

There are two basic conceptual frameworks within traditional medical belief systems, the endogenous and the exogenous concepts. As an example of the former, sickness is caused by the loss or capture of a client's soul, or part of the soul, or one of the souls. As a result, the soul has left the client's body, has entered another realm, and the client suffers as a result. Treatment involves the practitioner's intervention to recapture the soul and restore the balance of the client's spiritual forces.

In the latter instance, sickness is caused by the intrusion of a real or symbolic object within the individual; these objects range from pebbles to small animals to chunks of plastic to toxic substances such as viruses. (Morley & Wallis, 1978).

In his exhaustive study of cross-cultural practices, Torrey (1986) concluded that effective treatment inevitably contains one or more of four fundamental principles:

9. A shared world view that makes the diagnosis or naming process possible;
10. Certain personal qualities of the practitioner that appear to facilitate the patient's recovery;
11. Positive patient expectations that assist recovery;
12. A sense of mastery that empowers the patient.

If a traditional medical system yields treatment outcomes that its society deems effective, it is worthy of consideration by biomedical investigators. This consideration is to those who are aware of the fact that less than 20 percent of the world's population is serviced by Western allopathic biomedicine. However, what is considered to be "effective" varies from society to society. Western biomedicine places its emphasis upon "curing" (removing the symptoms of an ailment and restoring a patient to health), while traditional medicine focuses upon "healing" (attaining wholeness of body, mind, emotions, and/or spirit).

Some patients might be incapable of being "cured" because their sickness is terminal. Yet those same patients could be "healed" mentally, emotionally, and/ or spiritually as a result of the practitioner's encouragement to review their life, finding meaning in it, and becoming reconciled to death. Patients who have been "cured," on the other hand, may be taught procedures that will prevent a relapse or recurrence of their symptoms. This emphasis upon prevention is a standard aspect of traditional medicine, and is becoming an important part of biomedicine as well.

A differentiation can also be made between "disease" and "illness." From either the biomedical or the ethnomedical point of view, one can conceptualize "disease" as a mechanical difficulty of the body resulting from injury or infection, or from an organism's imbalance with its environment. Orellana (1987) adds that a "disease" exists whether or not a culture recognizes it, and whether or not the patient is aware of its existence (p 27). "Illness," however, is a broader, socially contextualized term implying dysfunctional behavior, mood disorders, or inappropriate thoughts and feelings. These behaviors, moods, thoughts, and feelings can accompany an injury, infection, or imbalance – or can exist without them. These sicknesses to a large degree are "socially constructed," and the way that they are constructed varies from society to society.

Thus, English-speaking people refer to a "diseased brain" rather than an "ill brain," but of "mental illness" rather than of "mental disease." Cassell (1979) goes so far as to claim that allopathic biomedicine treats disease but not illness; "physicians are trained to practice a technological medicine in which disease is their sole concern and in which technology is their only weapon" (p. 18).

> Treatment involves an intervention to remove, kill, or neutralize the intruding objects, restoring the client to health.

Power and Traditional Practice in Bolivia

Biomedical technology often determines what is to be taken as authoritative knowledge and, in turn, establishes a particular domain of power. Western biomedicine typically extends this privileged position to economics, politics, and class relationships. J.W. Bastien (1992), who has observed this struggle in Bolivia, reported that the power of allopathic biomedicine is jealously guarded by legislation, medical schools, licensing, and medicinal terminology. It is no wonder that indigenous, traditional people frequently view biomedicine as serving powerful groups while, in the meantime, they are struggling for a vestige of power over their own lives (p.17).

For example, when I was in Bolivia, I was told that Bolivian pharmacists and physicians once successfully curtailed the influence of traditional practitioners by public humiliation, restrictive laws (and imprisonment for their violation), and denial of licenses (Krippner, 2002). Even though some traditional practitioners incorporated various aspects of allopathic biomedicine into their procedures, physicians and politicians portrayed these healers, at best, as members of an antiquated tradition and, at worst, as charlatans (Bastien, 1992, pp. 25 - 32).

However, the populace observed the success of traditional treatments, especially on the part of practitioners following the Kallawaya tradition, a practice that emphasizes diet, steam baths, and herbal remedies. The increasing surplus of allopathic physicians in Bolivia exacerbated the situation. Mounting a counterattack, many traditional healers stereotyped biomedical physicians as kharisris, mythological figures who steal fatty tissue, the source of force and energy in folk tradition (pp.17 - 18).

By the 1980s, most Bolivian physicians and nurses discontinued efforts at integrating ethnomedicine into their work because their superiors did not promote it (Bastien, 1992, p.38). At the same time, there was a resurgence of Kallawaya practice because the value of medical plants was touted by Western research. Further, Bolivian peasants could not afford biomedical treatments; in 1984 the cost of a penicillin injection was about $10.00 U.S., several days' wages for peasants (pp. 54 - 55). In the 1990s, communication between physicians and herbalists in Bolivia improved because of the worldwide interest in ethnomedicine.

The two groups collaborated on several conferences and even jointly staffed a few clinics. Walter Alvarez, a gynecologist and surgeon as well as a Kallawaya practitioner, told me that he was instrumental in helping the Kallawaya practitioners in one community create a clinic staffed by both an allopathic physician and a Kallawaya herbalist. In the meantime, I observed that biomedical techniques have found their way into Kallawaya practice without a loss of the tradition's unique identity (Krippner, 2002).

The value of ethnomedical practitioners and their incorporation into biomedical systems has become widely heralded since their advocacy by the World Health Organization (WHO) at a conference in Alma-Ata, Kazakhstan, in 1972. However, such incorporation has been hindered by the high cost of training folk healers, the reluctance of the medical bureaucracy to accept them, and the decline of ethnomedicine in many parts of the world. The World Health Organization's objective of available medical care for all people of the earth depends upon granting folk healers professional autonomy as well as to educate them in abandoning worthless (and sometimes harmful) practices, and to teach them and their communities about effective public health measures. Many ethnomedical practitioners use adaptive strategies that are living and dynamic systems, subject to change in response to the community and the environment (Ellis & Ellis, 1989). My trip to Bolivia taught me that Kallawaya, as well as other Andean medical systems, provide a myriad of adaptive strategies in some of the most variable environmental zones of the world.

When Medical Myths Clash

The saga of Kallawaya practice in Bolivia is reminiscent of what occurs when mythic systems clash, either between cultures or within an individual or family (Feinstein & Krippner, 2006). When dealing with ethnomedicine, a "myth" can be defined as a narrative statement about existential human issues (such as health issues) that impact attitudes and behaviors. Some myths can be subjected to verification (e.g., "conception on the night of a full moon will result in the birth of a male baby"; "nearly everyone would benefit from using cholesterol lowering drugs") while others are not easily verifiable (e.g., "crib death is the result of an ancestral curse"; "There will never be a better way to prevent tooth decay than to fluoridate water"). But those myths that can not be subjected to verification can be seen as functional or dysfunctional from the perspective of health care and the prevention and treatment of sickness. Kaufmann (2006) has used the term "malignant" to describe dysfunctional myths that are an intrinsic part of mainstream medicine, despite his estimate that some 200,000 people die in the United States each year from medical mistreatment.

In addition, a 2006 report observed that 1.5 million people in the United States are injured each year by medication errors, including the poor handwriting of some physicians that leads to incorrect prescriptions being filled. The cost of treating victims of these errors exceeds 3.5 billion dollars (U.S.). Moreover, some widely prescribed drugs are ineffective for more than half the patients who take them, many surgical procedures are unnecessary, and some sicknesses are "constructed" by pharmaceutical companies, business corporations, and the medical system to insure profits (Lundberg, 2000; Moynihan & Henry, 2006).

The social construction of illness accounts for what has been called "culture-specific" maladies. For example, in Mexican-American *Curanderismo*, afflictions due to *mal de ojo* ("the evil eye") or *susto* (a shock that results in "soul loss") are difficult to operationalize and verify by means of allopathic medical standards. However, they can be reframed psychologically in terms of interpersonal jealousy or intrapersonal stress disorders, allowing health care providers and *curanderas* to work jointly for a patient's benefit (Trotter & Chavira, 1997). The Denver Public Schools has prepared a high school study guide to educate students, both Latino/Latina and Anglo, on the history and practices of *Curanderismo* (Martinez, 2000).

Staunch advocates of biomedicine and biopsychiatry often view folk healing as a superstition-laden obstacle to

> Treatment involves an intervention to remove, kill, or neutralize the intruding objects, restoring the client to health.

the dissemination of Western medical care, while traditional healers view biomedicine as detrimental to the holistic, community-centered health practices they have advocated for millennia (Ellis & Ellis, 1987). When discussing a traditional medical system's confrontation with allopathic medicine, an "old myth" (in this case, traditional folk healing) is often challenged by a "counter-myth" (in this case, allopathic biomedicine). Several outcomes are possible. The counter-myth can prevail and the old myth is relegated to ignominy (as occurred when "bleeding" of patients was replaced by more effective types of treatment such as antibiotics). The old myth prevails, and the counter-myth fades away (as occurred in parts of the Amazon rainforest where biomedical practices are shunned in favor of ancient practices).

A compromise can be worked out, in which both mythic worldviews continue to operate, sometimes together and sometimes apart (as is the case in Bolivia where allopathic and Kallaway practitioners both serve their coterie of patients). Sometimes there is a synthesis, where the old myth and the counter-myth merge into a "new myth" that preserves the best of both perspectives (as occurred when Dr. Alvarez incorporated both medical traditions into his own practice and the clinic he initiated).

The future of ethnomedicine will hinge on how these mythic clashes are worked out in one part of the world or another. The World Health Organization is hopeful that a synthesis will occur, or at least a compromise whether mutual respect is given each tradition by the other.

The increased number of immigrants and displaced people in the world has brought these mythic clashes into the open. Sometimes the evidence dictates that old medical myths need to be replaced, notably in regard to prevention and treatment of AIDS in Sub-Saharan Africa. In some parts of the area, the myth that AIDS among men can be cured if the afflicted has sex with a virgin has had disastrous consequences. In other parts of Africa the alleged cure is to have sex with a post-menopausal woman, and in still others the cure is to have sex with an infant. These myths are dysfunctional, representing extremely irrational ways of removing an intruding agent, in this case the HIV virus. In the meantime, one in ten people test as HIV positive in Tanzania, South Africa, and neighboring countries.

There are more optimistic outcomes of mythic clashes. Anthony Okello, a traditional healer in Uganda, treats minor aches, pains, and fevers with local herbs; however, he has been trained to recognize symptoms of HIV and sends these patients to the local hospital for antiretroviral drug treatment. The supply of these expensive medications has increased as a result of such donors as the Bill and Melissa Gates Foundation, and Uganda has pledged that they will be supplied to any Ugandan who needs them. The major roadblock is the infrastructure; there is one allopathic physician for every 20,000 citizens. However, there is one traditional healer for every 150 citizens and so Anthony Okello and other practitioners are playing important roles. Training is being made available by the Traditional and Modern Health Practitioners Together against AIDS, a group based in the capital city of Kampala, a group representing a synthesis of the two bodies of medical practice. Another group, Prometra, is based in Senegal. A member of the group, Yahaya Sekagya, runs an outdoor school for traditional healing. He admits that Western medicine works better for bone fractures and blood transfusions, but teaches the identification and use of local plants for many ailments, accompanied by chanting, drumming, and dancing to call the spirits for consultation and assistance (Faris, 2006).

In Africa, the degree of mythic synthesis varies from country to country; Nigeria, Mali, and Equatorial Guinea, as well as Uganda, are mainstreaming traditional practitioners. South African physicians, however, balk at legislation that would formalize the *isangoma* and other traditional healers (*ibid.*). However, Canada has over 100 native treatment facilities, more than any other country in regard to its population, where dances, songs, and ceremonies are integrated into the treatment programs. In New Zealand, Maori practitioners have played an important role in preventive medicine and AIDS education for decades, and in Australia, aboriginal healers have used sand pictures and "dreamtime" to portray safe sexual practices (MacLennan, 1992).

One form of synthesis is the emergence of "narrative medicine." Just as traditional practitioners listened carefully to their patients and responded by telling a mythical story about their sickness, an experimental group of medical students from around the world was asked to write a description of a recent patient who had moved them deeply. Rita Charon (2006), the originator of the pilot program, held at an Israel medical school, gave the students five minutes to write a story, poem, or dialogue about the patient. One student told of a dying patient, with no family, who had three wishes: "Sit with me." "Bring me for a walk in the fresh air." "Listen to my autobiography." Charon concluded that her pilot experiment had been successful and that "narrative medicine" can develop skills that enable physicians to recognize, absorb, and be moved by stories of illness. They develop the ability to pay attention, and to develop rapport with those who suffer in a manner similar to that practiced by shamans, medicine men, and medicine women for millennia.

> In some parts of the area, the myth that AIDS among men can be cured if the afflicted has sex with a virgin has had disastrous consequences.

Another form of synthesis, as practiced in the United Kingdom, has been effective in caring for patients with arthritis. The group Arthritis Care has developed an "expert patient" program that provides people with the knowledge, skills, and motivation to take control of their illnesses. Patients learn how to release their pain through relaxation, meditation, massage, humor, and social support – all of which are reminiscent of procedures used by indigenous practitioners. This program was so successful that the British government decided to fund an extension through the Long-term Medical Alliance. One patient commented, "I know what is happening in my body better than my doctor does," demonstrating the empowerment provided by this program (Moore, 2000).

Such groups as the Society for Shamanic Practitioners are making active efforts to provide a synthesis between shamanic procedures and those of Western medicine and psychotherapy. The 178-member World International Property Organization is attempting to protect indigenous people from outside exploitation of their herbal remedies. The future of ethnomedicine will depend upon projects of this nature, syntheses that nurture a careful examination of existing evidence regarding the effectiveness of traditional treatments, the resolution of quality control of the substances used, and the provision for research when no data are available (e.g., Albuquerque, 2006; Orellana, 1987).

The "Tomato Effect" in Medicine

The momentum of the past few centuries has been the waning of shamanism and other traditional practices in developing countries. This may be an example of the "Tomato Effect" in medicine, a term that refers to the rejection of worthwhile traditional procedures and treatments because they clash with those that are accepted by mainstream practitioners. The tomato, brought to Europe from the Americas in the 1600s, was not seen as fit for human consumption by physicians because it was a member of the nightshade family. The fact that Native Americans had eaten tomatoes for centuries without ill effects was ignored by the members of the medical establishment. After two centuries of tomato-eating by Europeans who rejected the medical establishment's prohibitions without falling ill, physicians stopped objecting in the 1820s. In this case ingestion of the tomato represented a counter-myth that was rejected by the European physicians who championed the old myth that nightshades were poisonous.

Objections to the tomato aside, power began to gravitate away from folk healers and neighborhood doctors to highly technical allopathic biomedicine with its pills, procedures, instruments, and immunizations. Authorities in white coats replaced the friendly folk healers and bedside physicians, multiplying like sorcerer's brooms into a myriad of specialists sweeping in and out of examination rooms. Costs went up, caring went down, and patients became seen as consumers as they struggled for survival and autonomy. Lives were prolonged, but patient satisfaction and practitioner gratification plummeted.

Even so, in its 2000 report on world health, the World Health Organization estimated that 36 countries have more successful health care programs than those in the United States, even though that country ranks number one in the amount of money spent on health care. In the United States, life can be prolonged with medical technology; emergency medical treatment is excellent and the genome has been mapped. However, 120 million Americans have chronic degenerative diseases. Over 50 million more have autoimmune diseases. Nine out of ten medications suppress symptoms but do not cure these two types of diseases. Hence, many Americans seek other treatments, among them ethnic minorities whose standard of health care is decades removed from care given to the Euro-American majority (Satcher & Pamies, 2006).

> They estimated that there are over two million hospitalizations in the United States each year and more than 100,000 deaths from the "side effects" of pharmaceutical drugs.

In 1998, David Eisenberg and his colleagues published some noteworthy statistics in the *Journal of the American Medical Association*. They estimated that there are over two million hospitalizations in the United States each year and more than 100,000 deaths from the "side effects" of pharmaceutical drugs. These numbers, combined with previously documented information that takes into account the mistakes and misuses of pharmaceutical drugs, brings the number to over 5 million hospitalizations and more than 250,000 deaths annual, in other words, nearly 700 deaths per day. A 2006 study came to similar conclusions. This makes mainstream medical treatment the third leading cause of death in the United States. In addition, over one third of the 5,000 hospitals in the United States are losing money and as many as 1,000 have closed.

In the meantime, the active ingredients in prescription medications cost a fraction of the price paid by consumers; For example, a 100 tablets of Celebrex cost the consumer about $130.00 (U.S.), while the cost of the active ingredients in 100 tablets are about sixty cents, a markup price of 22,000% (Davis, personal communication, 5 June 2006).

In the meantime, over 40% of the U.S. population is estimated to be using generic drugs as well as complimentary and alternative medical procedures. Americans spend over 30 billion dollars on these services yearly, even though the costs usually are not reimbursed. Visits to complimentary and alternative practitioners exceed visits to primary care physicians by over 200 million visits per year. People who gravitate to these practitioners have been found to acknowledge the importance of treating illness within a larger context of spirituality and life meaning, one that embraces a holistic orientation to life (Jenkins & Barrett, 2004).

Many patients believe that their experiences have been marginalized because they challenge the dominant discourses of professionals. The self-statements of these patients often appear to be mocking, angry, or despairing as they find themselves reduced by allopathic physicians to "diseased brains" and reduced to biochemical reactions rather than acknowledged as the enigmatic but distressed persons they know themselves to be. Thus, they suffer from the unpleasant physical, emotional, and cognitive side effects of antipsychotic medications, the violence of electroconvulsive therapy, because the "social construction" of illness has been replaced by the "corporate construction" of illness (Jenkins & Barrett, 2004).

Caveats of Traditional and Allopathic Medicines

Some advocates of traditional medicine assume that pharmaceutical remedies manufactured in developing countries are safe and effective. However, *Bebetina*, an over-the-counter pain reliever for children manufactured in Ecuador, was found to contain high levels of lead after one user, a three-year-old child, was diagnosed as suffering from lead poisoning. As a result, Westchester Country, New York, has banned the sale of *Bebetina* in 1996. Advocates of *Bebetina* had spread news by word of mouth about its low cost and purported efficacy in Latino communities (Fax cover sheet, 2006).

However, several medicines approved by the United States Food and Drug Administration have been implicated in negative side effects as well. Use of the arthritis pain reliever *Vioxx* has been linked to 100,000 heart attacks and strokes. *Celebrex*, *Bextra*, and other pain killers have also come under scrutiny for causing similar problems (Williams, 2006).

Furthermore, a respected medical journal, the *Public Library of Science Medicine*, ran a special issue on this topic. Various observers accused pharmaceutical companies of "disease mongering," inflating the market for a drug by convincing people that they are sick and in need of medical treatment. The journal has given instances of campaigns to increase drug sales by "medicalizing" such aspects of everyday life as irritability in children, twitching legs, mood swings, and irregularities in sexual performance.

These have become "corporate constructed" illnesses, often labeled "attention deficit hyperactivity," "restless leg syndrome," "bipolar disorders," "frigidity," and "erectile dysfunction," all of them purportedly requiring immediate pharmaceutical treatment. The journal's guest editors observed, "Informal alliances of pharmaceutical corporations, public relation firms, doctors' groups, and patient advocates promote these ideas to the public and policy makers, often using mass media to push a certain view of a particular health problem" (Moynihan & Henry, 2006).

In the meantime, over 200 pharmaceutical companies are investigating plant derivatives, many of them in rain forests and jungles. Over 6,000 alkaloids have been isolated from nearly 4,000 varieties of plants. National groups such as the Foundacao Brasileira and the Comision Amazonica are monitoring the work of drug companies to be sure that indigenous people are compensated for any discoveries.

Cultural Subpopulations and Medical Care

Information about various aspects of ethnomedicine is crucial in such multicultural societies as the United States. In 2006, the National Committee on Vital Health Statistics called for the collection of data on disparities in health care (Monitor Staff, 2006). Specific suggestions included improving the quality, reliability, and completeness of information on racial, ethnic, and linguistic subpopulations; strengthening the ability to analyze, report, and share information on these subpopulations; asking private health insurance plans to collect specific information on these subpopulations; performing "cluster sample" studies on groups often missed in large surveys such as Native Americans and Pacific Islanders.

Geography can influence one's quality of health care, right down to the specific street where someone lives. For example, a neighborhood may lack a market where fresh fruit and vegetables can be bought, but might be lined with fast food restaurants. As a result of these environmental factors, people in the neighborhood could find themselves at risk for developing diabetes or obesity, and for lacking bodily resistance to communicable diseases. The same area might lack exercise centers, walking trails, or jogging paths, further increasing the possibility of diabetes and obesity.

> In the meantime, over 200 pharmaceutical companies are investigating plant derivatives, many of them in rain forests and jungles.

Health care professionals dealing with a broad range of cultural groups need to implement a three-step process:

1. Awareness of cultural differences and their impact on medical outcomes.
2. Acquisition of a knowledge base of the cultures in their service area, including rules of interaction, religious dictates about who may examine a patient (and how), whether eye contact is permitted, in what ways respect is dictated, and the person in the family or community who is expected to make final decisions about treatment.
3. Information about traditional cultural beliefs about health and sickness, etiology and prevention, and diagnosis and treatment.

Suzanne Salimbene (2005) has warned practitioners not to make assumptions about patients based on cultural stereotypes. She has itemized a number of vital questions to help practitioners determine how closely a culturally diverse patient adheres to his or her cultural group, and the degree of assimilation to the majority culture's medical belief system. Sample questions include:

1. "Why have you come in to see us today?"
2. "What do you think has caused this condition?"
3. "Before coming here, have you tried to improve this condition?"

4. "If so, what have you tried?"
5. "Have you consulted anyone else, such as a relative, an herbalist, or a spiritual healer?"
6. "If so, what did that person advise?"
7. "What do you think the outcome was of their advice?"

The sum of this body of awareness has been termed "cultural and linguistic competence," and appropriate training has been mandated by the state of New Jersey, among others. In 2000, the United States Department of Health and Human Services published a set of standards for culturally and linguistically appropriate services, and similar guidelines have been adopted by such groups as the American Medical Association and the Joint Commission on Accreditation of Healthcare Organizations.

Spirituality as Adaptive

Both the endogenous and exogenous dimensions of traditional healing include a spiritual component (Morley & Wallis, 1978). This component is an aspect of the healing system that refers to those experiences and attitudes that reflect an alleged transcendent entity or process that inspires devotion and directs behavior (Krippner, 2003).

Over one hundred articles have appeared in peer-reviewed journals on health and spirituality. They include such dimensions as intrinsic values, life meaning and purpose, community relationships and faith-based support groups, and reported occurrences that go beyond one's ordinary, everyday experiences.

These articles contain considerable data indicating that people with internalized spiritual values score higher on measures of spiritual and mental health than those without such values (p. 195). These spiritual values and attitudes can occur with or without adherence to a religious belief system or membership in a religious organization. Indeed, there are some data that link certain rigid and dogmatic religious myths and belief systems with poor mental health (e.g., Ellis & Yaeger, 1989).

The growing body of such data requires health care providers to be aware of both the spiritual and religious dimensions of personal, familial, and cultural belief systems concerning health brought to their hospital, office, or clinic by an immigrant, refugee, or displaced person.

Does the positive association of spirituality and health provide evidence for the existence of a spiritual aspect of the cosmos? Nicolas Humphrey (2006) examines this question from the perspective of evolutionary psychology.

Human beings who experienced their uniqueness and their connection with spiritual forces probably took a greater "interest in their own personal survival," as well as the survival of their family and neighbors (pp. 125-126). One's sense of self-worth became "inflated," one held greater expectations for oneself and one's children, and one was gifted with something so special that it "persisted even beyond death" (pp. 125-129). These myths may not be falsifiable, but they could well have been adaptive; natural selection favored those who held these beliefs while those who lacked them fell out of the gene pool.

In conclusion, it can be seen that the world of the 21st century, with its plethora of civil wars, external invasions, AIDS and other pandemics, ecological crises, joblessness in one's homeland, and the constant search for better opportunities is producing unparalleled challenges for health care personnel.

References

Albuquerque, U.P. (2006). Re-examining hypotheses concerning the use and knowledge of medicinal plants: A study in the Caatinga vegetation of Northeast Brazil. *Journal of Ethnology and Ethnomedicine*, 2, 30-36.

Astin, J. (1998). Why patients use alternative medicine: Results of a national survey. *Journal of the American Medical Association*, 279, 1548-1553.

Bastien, J.W. (1992). *Drum and stethoscope: Integrating ethno medicine and biomedicine in Bolivia*. Salt Lake City: University of Utah Press.

Charon, R. (2006). *Narrative medicine: Honoring the stories of illness*. New York: Pantheon.

Connecticut Department of Public Health - Fax Sheet. *Children's pain reliever seized due to high lead content*. Retrieved August 1, 2006, from http://www.dph.state.ct.us/BRS/Lead/Recalls/Bebetina%20Advisory.pdf

Davis, S.L. (2006, June 5). Personal communication. Washington, DC: Budget Analyst, Department of Commerce, sdavis@doc.gov.

Eisenberg, D.M., Davis, R.B., Ertner, S.L., Appel, S., Wilkey, S., Van Rompay, M., & Kessler, R. (1998). Trends in alternative medicine use in the United States, 1990-1997. *Journal of the American Medical Association*, 280, 1569-1575.

Ellis, A., & Yaeger, R.A. (1989). *Why some therapies don't work - the dangers of transpersonal psychology*. Buffalo, NY: Prometheus Books.

Ellis, W.N., & Ellis, M.M. (1989, March-April). Cultures in transition. *The Futurist*, pp. 22-25.

Faris, S. (2006, July 24). Calling all healers. *TIME*, pp. 42-43.

Feinstein, D., & Krippner, S. (2006). *The mythic path* (3rd ed.). Santa Rosa, CA: Elite Press.

Humphrey, N. (2006). *Seeing red: A study in consciousness*. Cambridge, MA: Harvard University Press.

Jenkins, J.H., & Barrett, R.J. (Eds.). (2004). *Schizophrenia, culture, and subjectivity: The edge of experience*. Cambridge: Cambridge University Press.

Kaufmann, J.M. (2006). *Malignant medical myths*. West Conshohocken, PA: Infinity.

Krippner, S. (2002). The Kallawaya healing system of the Andes. In C.E. Gottschalk-Batschkus & J.C. Green (Eds.), *Handbook of Ethnotherapies* (pp. 437-442). Munich: Institut fur Ethnomedizine.

Krippner, S. (2003). Spirituality and healing. In D. Moss, A. McGrady, T.C. Davies, & I. Wickramasekera (Eds.), *Handbook of mind-body medicine for primary health care* (pp. 191-201). Thousands Oaks, CA: Sage.

Lundberg, G.P. (2000). *Severed trust: Why American medicine hasn't been fixed*. New York: Basic Books.

MacLennan, A. (1992, October/November). Native healing ways now on global network. *The Journal*, p. 3.

Martinez, L.A. (2000). *Curanderismo: Holistic healing*. Denver: Denver Public Schools and the Metropolitan State College of Denver.

Monitor Staff. (April, 2006). A call for data collection to eliminate health disparities. *Monitor on Psychology*, pp. 44-45.

Moore, W. (2000, March 19). Health report: Patient power. *The Observer*, p. 71.

Morley, R., & Wallis, R. (Eds.). (1978). *Culture and curing: Anthropological perspectives on traditional medical beliefs and practices*. London: Peter Owen.

Moynihan, R., & Henry, D. (2006). The fight against disease mongering: Generating knowledge for action. *Public Library of Science Medicine*, 3(4), e191.

Orellana, S.L. (1987). *Indian medicine in highland Guatemala*. Albuquerque, NM: University of New Mexico Press.

Peat, F.D. (2002). *Blackfoot physics*. Boston: Weiser Books.

Satcher, D., & Pamies, R.J. (2006). *Multicultural medicine and health disparities*. New York: McGraw Hill.

Salimbene, S. (2005). *What language does your patient hurt in? A practical guide in culturally competent patient care*. Amherst, MA: Diversity Resources.

Trotter, R.T., & Chavira, J.A. (1997). *Curanderismo: Mexican American folk healing* (2nd ed.). Athens, GA: University of Georgia Press.

West, B.J. (2006). *Where medicine went wrong: Rediscovering the path to complexity*. London: World Scientific.

Williams, D.G. (2006). Legal drugs kill, too. *Alternatives for the Health-Conscious Individual*, 11, 66-67, 69.

The Epistemology and Technologies of Shamanic States of Consciousness

Stanley Krippner

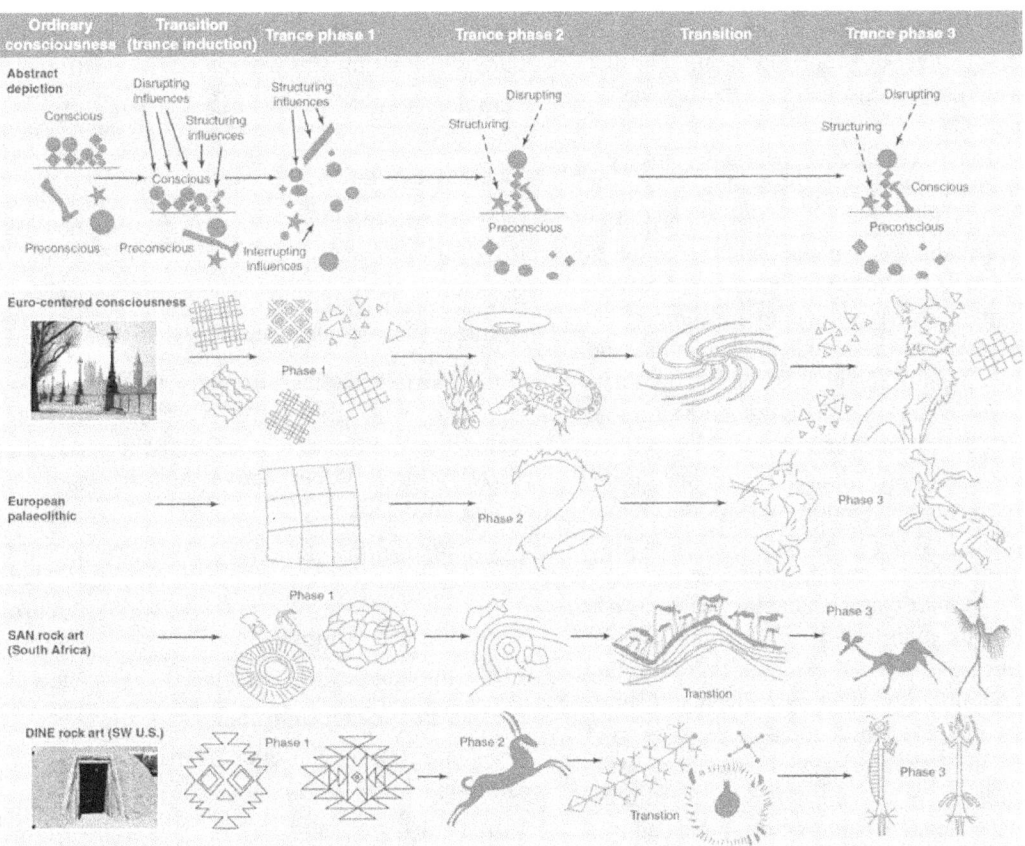

"The brain is a machine assembled not to understand itself, but to survive."
(E. O. Wilson, 1998)

Although the term "shaman" is of uncertain derivation, it is often traced to the language of the Tungus reindeer herders of Siberia where the word *šaman* translates into "one who is excited, moved, or raised" (Casanowicz, 1924; Lewis, 1990, pp. 10-12). An alternative translation for the Tungus word is "inner heat," and an alternative etymology is the Sanskrit word *saman* or "song" (Hoppal, 1987). Each of these terms applies to the activities of shamans, past and present, who enter what is often described as "an ecstatic state" in order to engage in spiritual practices that benefit their community (pp. 91-92). The adaptive character of shamanism is confirmed by its ubiquitous appearance around the world, not only in hunter-gatherer and fishing societies, but in centralized societies as well.

Much of the behavior of other animals is instinctive, and their experience modifies these complex, inborn patterns of behavior. However, drives and biological propensities, not innate behavior patterns, characterize humans. Non-human animals, especially gorillas and chimpanzees, probably compare environmental stimuli to the memory images from past interactions. Humans fall on this continuum as well, and the satisfaction of their vital needs was once highly dependent on their ability to use these images to produce the tools and procedures appropriate for drive satisfaction. Eventually, these procedures included a variety of social interactions including speech and ritual behavior (Guryev, 1990, p. 124; V. Turner, 1968).

Ritual afforded an opportunity to express the community's conceptions of reality into a social setting. Ritual, a step-by-step social performance, is the key to the structure of a group's mythology, or worldview. In shamanic

---

Krippner, S. (2000). The epistemology and technologies of shamanic states of consciousness. *Journal of Consciousness Studies*, 7, 93-118.

Shamanic states chart created by Jurgen Kremer based on Tart and other sources.

societies especially, ritual is a stylized technology, one whose symbols and metaphors may well trigger healing, relieve suffering, and provide a link between the ordinary world and those realms purportedly traversed by the shaman (Krippner, 1993; E. Turner, 1992, p. 14; V. Turner, 1968).

The *Veladas* of María Sabina

Shamanic rituals were essential to the career of the Mazatec Indian María Sabina, who lived in the state of Oaxaca, Mexico. Born about 1894, María Sabina led a life of severe hardship. Her father died when she was quite young, and her first husband abused her terribly. After his death, she married again but her second husband died when she was in her 40s.

Since childhood, María Sabina had been interested in herbs and worked for a period of time as a *curandera* or herbalist. Later, she felt that she had been called to become a *sabía* (i.e., "one who knows") and ingested psilocybin mushrooms as a way of "knowing" the condition and treatment of her clients. During my interviews with her in 1980, doña María told me that Jesus Christ and other spiritual entities came to her and her client during the *veladas* (evening mushroom ceremonies), bringing information about her client's problem and its resolution.

As a *sabía* or shamanic healer, María Sabina manifested considerable control during the *veladas*, chanting liturgies containing an overlay of Roman Catholic imagery which cloaked the odes used by the Indian priests who had been overthrown by the Spaniards in the 1520s. The Spanish Inquisition outlawed the *veladas*, but the Mazatecs took them underground for four centuries.

One night, María Sabina dreamed that it was her mission to share this sacred knowledge with the world. Soon after this dream, on June 29, 1955, a group of U.S. investigators headed by R. Gordon Wasson arrived. Eventually, doña María and the psilocybin mushrooms were featured in *Life* magazine, and the field of ethnomycology was born (Estrada, 1981; Wasson, 1981). Doña María's reported dream is unique for several reasons: it ran counter to the attempt of male elders to keep their practices secret, and its egalitarian and universal motive violated the political power of her society's male hierarchy. She paid dearly for this action; her grocery store was burned to the ground and her son was murdered.

María Sabina's worldview is expressed in her chants; in one, she apparently alludes to her shamanic journeys:

I am a woman who flies.

I am the sacred eagle woman, [the mushroom] says;

I am the Lord eagle woman;

I am the lady who swims;

Because I can swim in the immense,

Because I can swim in all forms.

I am the shooting star woman,

I am the shooting star woman beneath the water,

I am the lady doll,

I am the sacred clown,

Because I can swim,

Because I can fly.

(Estrada, 1981, abridged, pp. 93-94, 96)

Doña María's feelings of unity with nature and with the spirit world is revealed by another set of chants; the lyrics also portray her active role in attaining knowledge:

I have the heart of the Virgin,

I have the heart of Christ,

I have the heart of the Father,

I have the heart of the Old One,

It's that I have the same soul,

The same heart as the saint, as the saintess;

I am a spirit woman,

A woman of good words, good breath, good saliva,

I am the little woman of the great expanse of the waters,

I am the little woman of the expanse of the divine sea.

I am a woman who looks into the insides of things,

A woman who investigates, Holy Father,

I am a woman born, I am a child born,

I am a woman fallen into the world.

(pp. 107, 129-130)

In other words, María Sabina employed an investigatory way of knowing; she "looks into the insides of things." She, and other shamans, learn from "the spirits," "the waters," and "the divine sea." Tradition and holy writ might provide source material for the shaman, but it is his or her "heart" and "soul" that are the final arbiters of knowledge.

Shamanism as a Biologically Derived Specialization

Winkelman (1997) proposes that María Sabina and other shamans represent a "biologically derived" human specialization, and that these potentials are actualized through social adaptations. This proposition could be used to explain the worldwide appearance of shamans as well as the fundamental role of altered conscious states and/or heightened perception in shamanic healing and divination practices. An example of divination has been given by Lerche (2000). In his quest for the lost tribes of the Peruvian Chachapoya (or "cloud people"), he consulted a shaman who drew on the power of ritual objects. The shaman had a vision that some of the tombs remained unharmed and, soon after the consultation, Lerche detected a mummy bundle in a tomb high on a cliff (p. 68).

These potentials can be described as "neurognostic" because they involve neural networks that provide the biological substrate for ways of knowing (Laughlin, McManus, & d'Aquili, 1990), i.e., epistemology. I would add that these neurognostic potentials are not the exclusive domain of shamans; primordial humans performed healing and divinatory functions themselves before specialization established a hierarchy. Evidence for this position can be found in fairly egalitarian tribal societies such as the !Kung of southwestern Africa where about half the males and a sizable number of females shamanize, producing the "boiling energy" (i.e., sweat) used in their healing rituals (Katz, 1982).

Neurognostic potentials provide the basis for those forms of perception, cognition, and affect that are structured by the organism's neurological systems. They are probably reflected in what Jungians call "archetypes," which can be conceptualized as the predispositions that provide organizing principles for the basic modes of consciousness and elementary behavior patterns, including the intuitive capacity to initiate, control, and mediate everyday behavior.

Stevens (1982) suggests that "from the viewpoint of modern neurology, Jung's work stands as a brilliant vindication of...the value of intuitive knowledge" (pp. 273-274). When ritualized shamanic performance is described as "archetypal," the activity reflects biologically based modes of consciousness, a replacement of the ordinary waking state through discharge patterns that produce interhemispheric synchronization and coherence, limbic-cortex integration, and integral discharges that synthesize cognition, affect, and behavior (Winkelman, 1992).

Shweder (1979) found that Zinacanteco shamans in Mexico possess cognitive capacities that distinguish them from non-shamans such as having available a number of constructive categories, imposing these forms onto ambiguous situations; these integrative capacities may have facilitated the development of shamanic epistemologies over the millennia.

A variety of procedures, agents, and other technologies are available to evoke limbic system slow wave discharges that synchronize the frontal cortex (Mandell, 1980). In addition, shamans can be characterized as "fantasy-prone" (Wilson & Barber, 1983), endowed with capacities, genetic to some degree, that facilitate their use of imaginative processes. Fantasy-proneness exists on a continuum; most humans engage in fantasy, imagination, and play (especially "pretending" and "role-playing") periodically, but shamans draw upon this trait for their specialization.

Many of the early shamans may not have been dependent on transient consciousness alteration but manifested a heightened perceptual style that was part of their everyday state of consciousness. Berman (2000) suggests that "heightened awareness" may be a more accurate description of shamanic consciousness than "altered state" because their intense experience of the natural world is described by them in such terms as "things often seem to blaze" (p. 30).

Paradoxically, shamans are characterized both by an acute perception of their environment and by imaginative fantasy. These traits (the ability to construct categories, the potential for pretending and role-playing, and the capacity to experience the natural world vividly) gave shamans an edge over peers who had simply embraced life as it presented itself, without the filters of myth or ritual (Berman, 2000, p. 81).

All of these traits may be related to the evolution of the human brain, namely the development of specialized subsystems that are activated during shifts in consciousness. The hallmark of cortical evolution is not the ever-increasing sophistication of specialized cortical circuitry but an increasing representational flexibility that allows environmental factors to shape the human brain's structure and function (Gazzaniga, 1994; Quartz & Sejnowski, 1997).

Pinker (1997) suggests that the "mind" is made up of many modules, each honed by aeons of evolution, and shamans may have learned to integrate these modules (Winkelman, 2000, p. 7). If so, shamanic technologies represent the initial institutionalized practices for this integration, both through shifts in consciousness and community bonding rituals (Winkelman, 1997). These practices became codified in the form of myth, ritual, and ceremony, providing for social solidarity and specialization.

McClenon (1997) hypothesizes that the benefits of shamanic states of consciousness elicited an evolutionary increase in genes that would expedite this condition. However, all cultural changes in the past 90,000 to 100,000 years of *homo sapiens sapiens* (i.e., modern humans) have been environmental, not genetic (deMause, 1998).

Therefore, this essay takes the position that once *homo sapiens sapiens* arrived on the scene, and once shamanism developed as a societal specialization, the contributions of shamanism to the evolution of human consciousness took on socio-cultural roots that built upon humanity's biological (i.e., neurognostic) groundings.

The initiation and direction of thought and behavior owes as much to social construction as it does to biology (Rychlak, 1997, p. 143). Furthermore, all human societies contain inventive people but some of them provide more unusual materials and more favorable conditions for utilizing new technologies than do other environments (Diamond, 1997, p. 408). It is likely that spiritual activities originally involved the entire clan, but changing social and economic conditions brought about shamanic specialization and, later, a priesthood (Anisimov, 1963) and social inequality (Berman, 2000, p. 82).

Shamanic Technologies

The oral traditions that preserved the myths that structured a culture's identity and worldview may not have been originated by shamans, but eventually were passed down by them (Wiercinski, 1989). For example, María Sabina and her fellow shamans preserved, in their chants and rituals, Mazatec mythologies for more than four centuries, preserving their cultural identity in the face of Span-

> Shamanism comprises a group of techniques by which practitioners deliberately alter or heighten their conscious awareness to enter the so-called "spirit world," accessing material that they use to help and to heal members of the social group that has acknowledged their shamanic status.

ish oppression. To facilitate this societal function, many shamans developed techniques to assist the elicitation and movement of "inner heat," to enable their shamanic journeys, and to facilitate their contact with the "upper" and "lower" worlds. This technology allowed them to encounter spirits, ancestors, animal totems, and other resources that had found their way into mythological songs and stories.

Epistemology is concerned with the nature, characteristics, and processes of knowledge, and in this essay, I am suggesting that shamanic epistemology drew upon perceptual, cognitive, affective, and somatic ways of knowing that assisted early humans to find their way through an often unpredictable, sometimes hostile, series of environmental challenges. Not only did early humans have to become aware of potentially dangerous environmental objects and activities, they needed to have explanatory stories (enacted as mythic rituals) at their disposal to navigate through the contingencies of daily encounters and challenges. The acute perceptual abilities of shamans, in combination with their intuition and imagination, met their societies' needs.

Eliade (1972) writes of the "technologies of the sacred," and, for me, shamanism is most accurately defined as a collection of these technologies. Shamanism comprises a group of techniques by which practitioners deliberately alter or heighten their conscious awareness to enter the so-called "spirit world," accessing material that they use to help and to heal members of the social group that has acknowledged their shamanic status[11].

In psychological terms, shamans are socially designated practitioners who claim to self-regulate their psychological functions to obtain information unavailable to other members of their social group. Shamans were probably humanity's original specialists, combining the roles of healers, storytellers, weather forecasters, performing artists, ritualists, and magicians. A chief or chieftainess directed the tribe's political, civic, and military life, and the shamans were in charge of a tribe's spiritual life, but occasionally these two roles converged in a single, remarkable individual.

Mythological worldviews arise from epistemologies which, in turn, are fueled by the motives, needs, and traditions of a group in a specific time and place. Examples would be pre-classical worldviews that conceptualized people as an integral part of nature; knowledge was mediated through tribal shamans and their activities. For the ancient Greeks and other classical groups, knowledge was obtained through rationally constructed metaphysical systems; in Asia and other parts of the world, these systems were less individualistic and more communal. In medieval European societies, knowledge was scholastic and could be found in the correct interpretation of sacred scriptures.

The modern approach to knowledge involves a proper application of the empirical scientific method, taking as axiomatic that there can only be one possible answer to any question —a position shared by the metaphysical and scholastic epistemologies that were based on very different assumptions (Krippner, 1995).

Although I disagree with the anti-epistemological slant of many so-called "postmodernists," I am pleased that postmodernism points to the need for honoring multiple narratives, and becoming aware of the process by which narratives are constructed (see Berman, 2000, p. 323).

Tribal people did not necessarily insist that their mythic worldview was applicable to their neighbors; even when locked in battle, there often was a regard and respect for their opponents' courage. In postmodern writing, there is also a respect for diversity, empathy for other human beings, and concern for other life forms; all are reminiscent of shamanic worldviews.

Postmodernists hold that there can be many viable worldviews, depending on who is asking the question and the methodology used in answering it (Krippner, 1995). Therefore, the case can be made that postmodernists have returned full circle to certain premodern shamanic perspectives, regaining valuable aspects of an epistemology that was denigrated as a result of colonization and conquest.

Shamanic eclecticism and syncretization was apparent in my interviews with María Sabina, who put her epistemology into concrete terms. At the time of our interviews, doña María had

> "When someone came to me for help, we would eat the mushrooms together. Jesus Christ is in the mushrooms and he revealed to us the solution to the problem."

retired from active shamanizing, but she told me, "When someone came to me for help, we would eat the mushrooms together. Jesus Christ is in the mushrooms and he revealed to us the solution to the problem." Wasson (1981) observed that the mythical origin of doña María's *veladas* dates back to the time when Piltzintecuhtli, the "Noble Infant," received the sacred plants as a gift from Quetzalcoatl. Doña María's references to Jesus represent a synthesis of the Christian and the pre-Conquest religions (p. 17).

Categories of Spiritual Practitioners

Winkelman (1992) studied the records of religious and magical practices in 47 different societies, past and present, finding documentary evidence from these societies identifying several categories of spiritual practitioners. These practitioners claimed to have access to spiritual entities (e.g., deities, ghosts, spirits). They directed a society's spiritual activities (e.g., prayer, sacred ceremonies), employing special powers (e.g., casting spells, bestowing blessings, exorcising demons) that allowed them to influence the course of human affairs in ways not possible by other members of their social group.

Winkelman found remarkable similarities among these clusters of practitioners, especially regarding the manner in which their roles changed as societies became more complex. For example, he found shamans in those groups with no formal social classes; their presence was typical of hunting and gathering tribes and fishing societies.

The Creek, Crow, and Kiman were among the Native American tribes that awarded considerable prestige to the shamans in their midst. Each society had a different word to describe what are now called "shamans," and the specific duties expected of these practitioners differed from group to group.

Once a society became sedentary, centralized, and began to practice agriculture, social stratification took place; in addition to the division of labor, political and economic divisions occurred. Priests or priestesses emerged, taking control of a society's religious rituals while the shaman's political power and social status were reduced. According to Winkelman, the term "shaman/healer" (or "shamanic healer") is a more accurate description of this practitioner because healing became his or her major function.

The role of the shamanic healer became specialized and formal; official initiation ceremonies and training procedures became more common. Political development beyond the level of the local community was observed in almost all the societies in which priests were present.

The Jivaros in South America and the Ibo tribe in western Africa are among the few groups in which priests were assigned a healing function; priests also served healing purposes in Japanese Buddhist and Kurd Dervish groups. However, the shamanic healer typically engaged in more self-regulatory activities and the accessing of changed states of consciousness than did priests and priestesses.

Political integration became even more complex when separate judicial, military, and legislative institutions appeared. Along with this complexity, the malevolent practitioner (i.e., sorcerer or witch) appeared. Originally, shamans cast hexes and spells on tribal enemies; these functions were taken over by the sorcerer and, for a price, were often directed against members of one's own social group. Potions and charms became the province of witches and their associates. The shamanic healer's scope of action was now reduced not only by priests, but by sorcerers and/or witches as well. There were sorcerers among the Aztecs. There were witches among the Navajos. In my visit to Oaxaca to interview María Sabina, I found a society replete not only with *sabias* (shamanic healers) such as doña María, but sorcerers (*brujos*) as well as the local Roman Catholic priest.

Further political complexities and continued dependence on agriculture became associated with the development of another practitioner, the diviner or medium, such as those found among the Eurasian Kazakhs. At one time the shaman's repertoire had included divination and talking with spirits; later, mediums and diviners began to specialize in this feat, often "incorporating" the spirits and allowing them to speak and act through their voices and bodies.

At this point, the shaman's role was dispersed to the extent that the only remaining functions were specialized healing capacities as the performing of healing songs and dances, dispensing herbal medicines, and diagnosis, bonesetting, midwifery, and surgery. Winkelman refers to these practitioners as "healers" (or "shamanistic healers"). Like shamanic healers, shamanistic healers held the healing of one's spirit in high regard, but became more involved in individual work than in community work. Furthermore, changing one's state of consciousness and journeying to the spirit world no longer was a core element of their work, as was the case with shamans and shamanic healers.

This classification system was found to be quite accurate when cross-societal comparisons were made (Winkelman, 1997). With only two exceptions, shamans never were found in tribal groups that displayed an administrative political organization beyond the local level. No shamans were found in sedentary societies where the nomadic way of life was absent.

When Winkelman traced the development of these four categories (i.e., the "shaman complex," priests, diviners, malevolent practitioners), he did not assign the terms "higher" and "lower" to the states of consciousness utilized while engaging in their practices.

The shaman's ways of knowing depended on accessing information from spiritual entities in "upper worlds," "lower worlds," and in "middle earth" (i.e., ordinary reality). In contrast, the priest's epistemology was dependent on a body of revealed knowledge, often preserved in the form of sacred scripture. Diviners used their own bodies as vehicles for information that was transmitted through them, while malevolent practitioners also depended upon traditional knowledge, either written or passed down verbally.

It was not unusual for this material to resemble a "cook-book" that spelled out the technology which was to be used to inflict various hexes and spells. In contrast, shamanic ways of knowing were dynamic and active. Shamanism demanded both flexibility and strength on the part of the practitioner who would bargain, negotiate, or plead with spiritual entities for the knowledge that would save his or her community from a plague or restore a lost soul to its owner.

Shamanic States of Consciousness

The word "consciousness" is used in various ways, but I define it as the pattern of an organism's perceptual, cognitive, and affective activities and/or experiences at any given moment in time. An alteration of consciousness is a significant shift or deviation in an organism's customary pattern as experienced by that organism and/or observed by others.

Some of these shifts have been considered "states" of consciousness because they are marked by behaviors and experiences that typically cluster together; each society has its own conception of what constitutes an "ordinary" state of consciousness and what may be considered "changed" or "altered" states of consciousness. Winkelman (1992) notes that in each of the 47 societies he studied at least one type of practitioner demonstrated a shift in consciousness associated with his or her apprenticeship and role-training. Wade (1996) adds that "Virtually all shamanic experiences occur in an altered state, which cannot be regarded as a naturally-occurring developmental stage" (p. 277).

Bourguignon (1976) studied 488 societies (57% of those represented in an ethnographic atlas), reporting that 437 of them (89%) had one or more institutionalized, culturally patterned changed state of consciousness, some of which were only experienced by the society's spiritual practitioners.

What can we make of the other 11%? Berman (2000) proposes that "such beliefs and practices, even if wired into the brain in terms of capacity, get triggered only in certain cultural contexts" (p. 29). This emphasis on context is apparent in Peters and Price-Williams' (1980) comparison of 42 societies from four different cultural areas. They determined three commonalties among changed states of consciousness entered by shamans: voluntary control of entrance and duration of the altered state; ability to communicate with others during the altered state; memory of the experience at the conclusion of the altered state. Shamans in 18 of the cultures studied by Peters and Price-Williams (1980) engaged in spirit "incorporation," 10 in out-of-body experience or journeying, 11 in both, and 3 in some different altered state.

However, there are shamanic groups, such as the Navajo *hataali*, who deny entering altered states. The *hataali* rely on knowledge, not trance phenomena or magical effects. Their chant work is "a restrained and dignified procedure," and they represent, for the client, "a stable dependable leader who is a helper and guide until the work is ended" (Sandner, 1979, p. 258). To me, this seems more like a case of heightened perception than an altered state.

Those shamans who enter altered states employ various technologies. These include ingesting mind-altering plants (e.g. María Sabina), chanting (again, doña María), concentrating, dancing, drumming, jumping, fasting, running, visualizing, participating in sexual activity, refraining from sexual activity, engaging in lucid dreaming, and going without sleep. Rarely is one procedure used in isolation. For example, mind-altering plants are often ingested in the evening; sleep deprivation, restricted nighttime vision, and accompanying music often enhance the experience's profundity. Song and dance were important elements in ritual, and probably preceded it.

Naturally occurring altered states, such as dreaming and daydreaming, may also be utilized (Harner, 1988; Rogers, 1982). Whitley (1998) suggests that one of the functions of rock and cave image-making may have been to record the images elicited in shamanic states of consciousness.

The Ojibway Indians shocked Jesuits priests on their arrival in North America with their behavior during their traditional healing procedures. It was customary for Ojibway *wabeno* (shamans) to heal by means of drumming, rattling, chanting, dancing erotically (while naked), and handling live coals. The *wabeno* then rubbed their heated hands over the client while chanting the songs previously learned in their vision quests (Grim, 1983, pp. 144-145).

Among the Dieguenos and Luisenos Indians of southern California, potential shamans were selected as early as nine years of age on the basis of their dreams. It was important that a prospective shaman in these tribes also had visionary experiences that resulted from ingesting such mind-altering plants as datura or jimson weed during their ceremonials. During these altered states, the novice received a guardian spirit in the form of an animal totem as well as healing songs and other knowledge about cures and dream interpretation (Rogers, 1982, p. 21).

Symbolic manipulation is apparent in shamanic rituals, and altered states often help to access these symbols. Symbols are more than ritual markers that denote the beginning, middle, or end of the process; they serve as keys that unlock the door to a full participation in the ritual, taking participants into another order of reality where spirits come to life and healing dramas unfold (V. Turner, 1968). The drum often symbolizes the "World Tree" the shaman needs to climb so as to reach the "upper world" (or descend to the "lower world") during the altered state. What they find in these realms differs from society to society; in some, the "upper world" is the home of ancestors, but for others, they reside in the "lower world."

The ritualistic blowing of smoke in four directions symbolizes an appeal to spirits in the "four quarters" of the universe. Directionality is apparent in the elaborate Navajo sand paintings that the shamans destroy after they have served their purpose. Symbolism is also evident in the reports from those vision quests of the Plains Indians that helped future warriors contact their guardian spirits. Dobkin de Rios (1984) describes these quests as attempts at "personal ecstatic learning" in the service of eliciting biochemical changes in the body that would enhance the altered state. Hence, tribal shamans played an important role in preparing, instructing, and guiding their initiates, as well as interpreting their visions (p. 57).

The Evolving Mind

As the study of the origin, nature, and limits of knowledge, epistemology is closely associated with Western concepts of consciousness (Winkelman, 2000, p. 177). For many years, Durkheim's (1912/1995) theories were especially influential. Taking Australian totemism as the prototype for all early spiritual experience, Durkheim focused on the feelings of security gained by life in a secure group. He conjectured that early tribes projected these feelings on to whatever object they were close to at the time they experienced them. In this way, plants, animals, rocks, and other objects were imbued with "power," the capacity to instill strong feelings and to assist the person who befriended, ate, or wore them. According to Durkheim, ritual behavior preceded language, which only became necessary when communication with imaginary beings was mandatory[22].

More recently, neuropsychology has impacted explanations of these phenomena. A perspective that is especially useful in understanding shamanic epistemologies has been proposed by Newton (1996) who attempts to unravel certain entrenched philosophical puzzles concerning both consciousness and representational thought.

Taking exception to purely linguistic theories of cognition, Newton takes a parsimonious "postmodern" position on humanity's attempts to represent reality. For Newton, humanity's variegated experiences with reality demonstrate the vast range of specific sensorimotor images and sensations that constitute its direct, ongoing understanding of the environment. For Newton, thinking makes use of the same neurological (i.e., neurognostic) structures involved in sensorimotor activity, structures that take the form of analog models of reality; the resulting images ground humankind's concepts, constructs, and intentions.

To support this thesis Newton cites behavioral data, findings from neuroscience, and evolutionary evidence, that language was a tool for communication before it became the primary determinant of cognition. Taking issue with both the "reductionists" who explain sensory phenomena simply as brain properties and the "new mysterians" who see consciousness as something beyond the reach of physical theory, Newton constructs a sturdy framework that unifies not only body and mind but linguistic and nonlinguistic human activities as well.

Donald's (1991) model, compatible with that of Newton, gives mythmaking a key role in human evolution, and describes "scenario-building" as the primary function of human mental complexity (also see Alexander, 1979). When mythic worldviews were performed ritually, participants were confronted with representations of objects and events in addition to those items themselves.

Corballis (1991) posits a hypothetical "generative assembling device" in the human brain, and gives it credit for constructing these cognitive representations from "small vocabularies of primitive units" (p. 219). Jerison (1990) describes language as a "sensory-perceptual development" and states that its role in communication first evolved as a side effect to its role in reality construction; thus, "we need language more to tell stories than to direct actions."

In the telling we create mental images in our listeners that might normally be produced only by the memory of events as recorded and integrated by the sensory and perceptual systems of the brain" (pp. 15-16). This capacity required an enormous amount of neural tissue, and the convolutions of the human brain were associated with the development of language and related capacities for mental imagery (p. 16).

Some of these mental images are termed "images of achievement" by Vandervert (1996) because they reflect a learned imaging process in the cerebral-motor cortex. This process extends into the extrapolated anticipatory future by means of fast time computations of the cerebellum, and these images continually predict the outcomes of the next steps of human action or achievement. These images are often symbolic in nature, allowing for a condensation of considerable information and meaning.

Since the time of Goethe, many scholars have proposed that the epistemology of primordial people began with their sensorimotor experiences (Flaherty, 1992, p. 168). According to these scholars, mythmaking, a basic propensity of humankind, has its referents in bodily functions as well as in observable nature.

Sansonese (1994) notes, "The more ancient the myth, the more often do parts of the human body play an explicit role in the myth" (p. 7), for example, Adam's Rib and the Egyptian myth of Set and Isis. It will be recalled that one of the possible derivations for the term "shaman" is "one who is excited, moved, or raised" while another is "inner heat"; both refer to bodily processes and the appreciation of the sensory world. In addition, they both are examples of politicized talents (along with fire mastery, symbolic death, and entering "trance") that privatize shamanism and restrict its membership.

In his account of the evolution of the human mind, Mithen (1996) describes the emergence of general intelligence as well as of four specialized "cognitive domains," namely technical intelligence, social intelligence, natural history intelligence, and language. It is likely that these "domains" share information in what Baars (1997) refers to as a "global workspace."

Consistent with Newton's (1996) emphasis on language as a tool for communication (and contrary to Durkheim's position), Mithen (1996) holds that language was originally social. Once the capacity for language was present it was highly adaptive, eventually providing early humans with the ability to reflect on their own and other people's mental states (p. 140).

In this way, it began to interact with social intelligence and, still later; early humans were able to talk about tool-making (technical intelligence) as well as hunting and plant gathering (natural history intelligence). Such capacities were advantageous because they could construct more accurate, hence more adaptable, models and descriptions of external events (Povinelli, 1993, p.507).

Once these intelligences became linked across their respective domains, the resulting "linkage" enabled the production of symbolic artifacts and images as a means of communication. It also led to the essentially human tendency to attribute personality and social relationships to plants and animals, a result of the integration of social intelligence and natural history intelligence.

Artifacts indicating human body decoration (e.g., pieces of ocher) date back 80,000 years or more (Gore, 1997, p. 98); other artifacts demonstrating the capacity for visual decoration (e.g., beads, pendants) date back 40,000 years (Mithen, 1996, p. 155) to the time after the Cro-Magnon people emerged. A human-shaped ivory statuette from Hohlenstein-Stadel in southern Germany is the earliest existing statuette and has been dated at 30,000 to 33,000 years

(Mithen, 1996, pp. 162). The origins of shamanism are often traced back at least 30,000 years (Eliade, 1972, pp. 503).

In western Europe, the Upper Paleolithic era began some 35,000 years ago, and is best known for its remarkable efflorescence of image-making (Clottes & Lewis-Williams, 1998/1996).

For example, the paintings in the Lascaux caves of southern France date back 17,000 years. The prone figure depicted on one of the walls is often regarded as a shaman experiencing an altered state of consciousness (e.g., Eliade, 1972/1951, p. 504), but Berman (2000) asks, if shamanism was so important in Paleolithic times why do such figures occur so rarely? (p. 25). No matter what these images represent, it is possible that symbolic image-making had been accomplished earlier but was executed on materials that did not survive.

During my visit to Lascaux in 1997, our group was allowed only 35 minutes to tour the cave and appreciate its images; even so, it would take the cave's atmosphere several hours to recuperate from our intrusion. We were overwhelmed by the raw power of the colorful wild horses, antlered reindeer, and massive bison we encountered. Negative space, a technique not used again in Europe until the 16th century, was utilized to create perspective. The cave's surface brings a three-dimensionality to the paintings —a naturally-formed hole provides the eye for one animal, and a bulging rock becomes the shoulder of a bison.

There are a plethora of geometric forms thought by some to be signatures of the artists; if so, this convention was not revived until the Renaissance. Some animals have been cleverly painted so that they share body parts, while other figures are superimposed on each other and are distinguished by color shading (Societe Prehistorique Francaise, 1990; Vanaria, 1997). And, for some observers, the most exceptional feature of the drawings is their narrative form; they appear to tell a story (Delluc, Delluc, & Delvert, 1990, p. 57).

I agree with Tattersall's (1998) comment that upon leaving Lascaux one is overawed by the magnificence of what these remote ancestors wrought many millennia ago. However, Hughes (2000) notes that the rock paintings in the sacred cave sites scattered across northwestern Australia, "are as impressive as anything in the caves of Lascaux or Altamira, and tens of thousands of years older. As far as we know, The Australian Aborigines stood at the very dawn of human image-making" (pp. 110-111).

In the European caves, "a small nodule becomes an animal's eye; sometimes a natural swell of the rock face was taken to delineate the chest or shoulder of an animal; sometimes the edge of a shelf became the back of an animal. To these natural features, the artists added lines, thereby transforming the given into the created. Frequently these images appear to be coming out of the rock wall. At Rouffignac, for instance, a horse's head is painted on the side of a protruding flint nodule. The rest of the horse is apparently behind the rock face" (Lewis-Williams &

Clottes & Lewis-Williams, 1998/1996, p. 16). To some, these features suggest a search for spirit animals that could become "allies" if they could be drawn by shamans through a permeable "membrane" that separated the ordinary and the non-ordinary worlds (*ibid.*). In the Niaux cave, for example, the shadows cast across the rock can represent, to the expectant eye, the outline of a bison; then only a few deft strokes were needed to add the rest of the body. If the light is moved, the animal disappears back through the "membrane."

The person has thus mastered the spirit animal; he or she can make it come and go at will (p. 17). Once more, Berman (2000) cautions that there are other explanations for the profusion of animal images, one of them a simple desire to execute a naturalistic portrayal. Sometimes, grazing deer are simply grazing deer (p. 31).

Symbolic or not, Winkelman (2000) points out that neuropsychology provides a basis for these rock art motifs; hardwired neurologically structured perceptual constants are the structural basis of these motifs, reflecting perceptions obtained through shamanic states of consciousness. The animal images reflect "the importance of neurognostic perspectives in understanding shamanism" (p. 6).

Clottes and Lewis-Williams (1998/1996) take a somewhat extreme position, stating that "all shamanic activity and experience necessarily take place within a particular kind of universe, or cosmos. [But] the ways in which this shamanic cosmos is conceived are generated by the human nervous system rather than by intellectual speculation or detached observation of the environment" (p. 19). For me, neurognostic potentials and social construction operate in tandem, and the ensuing dance produces a phenomenon that needs to be examined from the vantage point of both perspectives.

Commenting on the paintings themselves, Mithen (1996) deduces, "There is nothing gradual about the evolution of the capacity for art: the very first pieces that we find can be compared in quality with those produced by the great artists of the Renaissance.... All that was needed was a connection between these cognitive processes which had evolved for other tasks to create the wonderful paintings in Chauvet Cave" which date back some 30,000 years (pp. 162-163).

Also predating Lascaux was the extraction of decorative red and black pigment from Bomvu Ridge in South Africa, some 40,000 years ago (Boshier & Costello, 1975).

The magnificent distinctiveness of these works is noteworthy in view of Ludwig's (1992) proposition that "the visionary or magic function of these media...was more important than esthetics" (p. 459).

"The shaman artist...employed carved masks, music and art for the purposes of healing, negotiation with unseen spirits, exerting magical influences on creatures, and depicting his [or her] adventures in the spirit world" (*ibid.*). Again, neurognostic structures can be hypothesized to have formed the basis for these creative products; Clottes (in Gore, 2000) asserts "People can no longer say art evolved from crude beginnings" (p. 108).

The sepia, black, and red ocher Chauvet, Altamira, and Lascaux paintings might be symbolic. However, Berman (2000) offers an alternative: the experience of these early humans was direct and immediate (p. 81). This epistemology runs through many postmodern writings; for example, Globus (1995) remarks, "We do not know reality, according to postmodernism, by means of any representations of reality. We know reality directly and immediately; there is nothing that gets between us and the reality we always and already find ourselves in" (p. 127).

Modernity, in contrast, relies on representations of reality—mental and neural representations that mediate between humanity and the world. In other words, modern epistemologies assume that an investigator can provide a near-identical match between words and the phenomena they attempt to describe. Postmodern epistemologies assume that this type of representation is impossible, and that symbolism, metaphor, and allegory provide better descriptions of outer and inner experience and several descriptions, some of them paradoxical, frequently are used to "deconstruct" a phenomenon in an attempt to creatively fathom it.

reflecting new connections rather than new processing power" (Mithen, 1996, p. 209).

To this discussion of signal systems, I would add that role-playing, as well as language, be considered a likely contender as the mechanism for cognitive fluidity. Pretending and role-playing enable people to represent the internal state of others, a skill that enables cognitive cross-referencing to take place.

Clottes and Lewis-Williams (1998/1996) have proposed three stages of shamanic consciousness. In Stage One, people move from alert consciousness to a "light" alteration, beginning to experience geometric forms, meandering lines, and other "phosphenes" or "form constants," so named because they are wired into the nervous system. For example, the Tukano of South America use undulating lines of dots to represent the Milky Way, the goal of shamanic journeying.

cules into which only a few people could congregate (p. 20).

From an epistemological perspective, the shaman gained knowledge from his or her journeys into other realms of existence, and communicated the results to members of the community (Flaherty, 1992, p. 185). Shamans provided information from a database consisting of their dreams, visions, intuitions, as well as their keen observations of the natural and social world. Sansonese (1994) suggests that there was "a degree of genetic predisposition for falling into trance" and that this ability made a significant contribution to social evolution (p. 30). For example, there was a succession of Indo-European shamans whose traditions included parent-to-child transmissions of shamanic lore that, in turn, institutionalized extended-family shamanic groups (*ibid.*).

The ability to manipulate symbols was essential in the interpretation of dreams and visions as well as in the creation of myths. For Sansonese (1994), "a myth is an esoteric description of a heightened proprioception" (p. 36). "Myth describes a systematic exploration of the human body by privileged members of archaic cultures. Myth springs from an age of universal narcissism, rooted, one must suppose, in the elemental struggle for survival." (p. 37). Explanations were needed for birth, death, illness, procreation, and other bodily phenomena, as well as for cyclones, forest fires, floods, sunsets, eclipses, and the changes of seasons.

> Shamanic epistemology also attempts to explain "reality," employs repeated observations, and makes statements about general principles. However, credence is given to revelation and inspiration from the "spirit world," from plant and animal "allies," and from "journeys" associated with changed states of consciousness.

Shamanic Epistemology

For the shaman, everything provided knowledge about everything else, and the whole of being was "fundamentally an immense signal system" (Kalweit, 1992, p. 77). Shamanic states of consciousness were the first steps toward deciphering (or deconstructing) the signal system, and this was made possible once humanity's symbolic capacity matured.

At that point "language shifted from a social to a general-purpose function, consciousness from a means to predict other individuals' behavior to managing a mental database of information relating to all domains of behavior. A cognitive fluidity arose within the mind,

In Stage Two, people begin to attribute complex meanings to these "constants," and in Stage Three, these constants are combined with images of people, animals, and mythical beings. Experients began to interact with these images, often feeling themselves to be transformed into animals, either completely or partially (e.g., the celebrated Les Trois Freres animal/human); shamanic journeys are generally felt to be more feasible in this form (p. 19). Various chambers of Upper Paleolithic caves seem to have been restricted to advanced practitioners; some caves have spacious chambers embellished with large, imposing images while elsewhere there are often small, sparsely decorated diverti-

There were many contenders for survival millennia ago. However, Mithen (1996) proposes that *homo sapiens*, who date from about 250,000 years ago (Jerison, 1990, p. 10), had an evolutionary advantage over other early humans. *Homo sapiens sapiens* were able to use symbolism in image-making and storytelling, both of which were adaptive because they helped to make sense of one's body, one's peers, and one's environment.

Neanderthals were powerfully built, large brained people who seemed to display an equivalent sophistication to modern humans in their manufacture of stone tools, and had the vocal mechanisms needed for rudimentary speech. But Neanderthals lived in inclement climates

(Mithen, 1996, p. 125), were prone to degenerate diseases (p. 126), and lacked the technology to sew garments and—most curiously—the ability to produce elegant pictorial images. There are a few pieces of pierced bone attributed to Neanderthals, but even these artifacts are in doubt (p. 135).

There is no conclusive evidence that ritual was a part of Neanderthal burials, or that human-made objects were placed within the graves (p. 136). In any event, the Neanderthals disappeared less than 30,000 years ago (Tattersall, 1998). In the meantime, with specialized intelligences that could effectively communicate with each other, *homo sapiens sapiens* were probably unique among early humans in their ability to symbolize, mythologize, and, eventually, to shamanize.

Taussig (1987) describes the "inscription of a mythology in the Indian body" where "power is invested" (p. 27), while Sansonese (1994) remarks, "Something is being described in myth, something about the human body, something essential to its workings but also truly technical and beyond mere fetish" (p. 38). He also notes that "the development of myth parallels the esoteric impulse in storytelling" (p. 38). The domination of *homo sapiens sapiens* may have been due to their ability to take sensory and motor activity, using it as a bridge to produce stories that assured their survival (Boaz, 1997; Cavalli-Sforza & Cavalli-Sforza, 1995; Fagan, 1990; Kingdon, 1993; Ruhlen, 1994; Stringer & McKie, 1996).

The way people come to report the feeling states that arise within their own bodies is incompletely understood (Lubinski & Thompson, 1993). Nevertheless, these private events have been a prime source for the creation of myths by the shaman and the community (Devereux, 1997). Lubinski and Thompson (1993) have underscored the role of pharmacological agents in bringing internal feeling states into awareness, citing animal research to buttress their argument. Merkur's (1998) description of "psychedelic ecstasies" includes categories in which internal dialogues reflect feeling states invoked by LSD-type drugs, while Nesse and Berridge (1997) have identified the associated neural mechanisms, noting their evolutionary origins.

To the impact of external pharmacological agents, one might add the contribution of the body's own biochemistry, especially during rapid eye movement (REM) sleep, often characterized by dreaming. Ullman (1987) claims that REM sleep reflects a genetic imperative that often orients the dreamer's "felt connections to others" in the interest of species survival; research with other organisms suggests that REM sleep or a precursor is the earliest form of mammalian sleep (Siegel, 1997).

Hobson (1988), operating from a different paradigm, adds that dreaming is a "behavioral state" that reflects an evolutionary specialization (pp. 112-113). He continues, "in dreams, problems are not only posed but sometimes even solved" (p. 16) and somatic stimuli are one source of the images that the brain converts into dream narratives (p. 46). I would suggest that shamans were especially adroit in using dream and psychedelic imagery to address and find solutions to the conundrums periodically faced by members of their community and the group as a whole.

Shamanism and "Higher" States

Wilber (1981) notes that shamans were the first practitioners to systematically access "higher" states of consciousness. He categorizes these "higher" states as the "subtle" (those leading to enhanced mental imagery both with form, e.g., angels, spirits; and without form, e.g., "white light," "music of the spheres"); the "causal" (those states in which there are no longer any forms in one's awareness, e.g., "pure awareness," "the void"); and the "absolute" (the state in which consciousness has experienced its "true nature" and in which a "ground of being" is experienced). According to Wilber the shamans' focus has been on "subtle" states because their technology was directed toward assisting other people with the images obtained in their shamanic journeys.

Wilber (1981) has taken the position that consciousness not only unfolds during the life-span of an individual, but during the evolution of humanity in general, with some individuals representing the "farthest reaches" of that development (p. 142). In his hierarchy of "higher" states of consciousness, shamans are placed at the "subtle" level because their technology, described as "crude" (p. 142), was directed toward assisting others with the images and knowledge that was produced in shamanic journeys. Wilber grants that an occasional shaman broke into the "causal" realm, but insists that it was not until the emergence of the meditative and contemplative traditions that "causal" and "absolute" states could be systematically attained.

> Shamanic epistemology also attempts to explain "reality," employs repeated observations, and makes statements about general principles. However, credence is given to revelation and inspiration from the "spirit world," from plant and animal "allies," and from "journeys" associated with changed states of consciousness.

This evolution of consciousness, according to Wilber, was not part of a biological process but due to the development of such elements of spiritual practice as "rigorous systems of ethics," "emotional transformation," the "training of attention and concentration," and the "cultivation of wisdom."

However, Eliade (1972/1951) found comparative examples of the oldest types of Christian and Hindu mystical experience in Alaskan Eskimo shamanism. Walsh (1990) found "rigorous systems of ethics" in those North American shamanic traditions emphasizing compassion. He discovered "emotional transformation" among Australian aboriginal shamanic initiation programs, and "training of attention and concentration" among Eskimo initiates who were subjected to a 30-day period of isolation where they were directed to "think only of the Great Spirit."

Furthermore, Walsh found "cultivation of wisdom" in Ainu, Cuna, and Zuni shamanic traditions where entire mythologies, pharmacopoeia, and song cycles had to be memorized and understood. After surveying the cross-cultural research, Coan (1987) warns, "It would be a mistake to assume that shamanism represents just one stage either in the evolution of human society or in the evolution of human consciousness" (p. 62).

Brown and Engler (1986) administered Rorschach Inkblot Test to practitioners of "mindfulness meditation," discovering that their responses illustrated their stages of meditative development, reflecting "the perceptual changes that occur with intense meditation" (p. 193). One Rorschach was unique in that the "advanced master" integrated all 10 inkblots into a single associative theme (p.191).

However, Klopfer and Boyer (1961) had obtained a similar protocol from an Apache shaman. This shaman used the inkblots to teach the examiner about his lived worldview and his ecstatic flights through the universe. Brown and Engler (1986) suggested that this may be a response that, regardless of the spiritual tradition, points "a way for others to 'see' reality more clearly in such a way that it alleviates their suffering" (p. 214).

Moreover, a careful reading of Wilber (1983) suggests a limited familiarity with the literature on shamanism. He refers to Eliade's (1972/1951) *Shamanism: Archaic Techniques of Ecstasy* as "the definitive study of the subject" (p. 70). Yet, it takes nothing away from the importance of this pioneering work to suggest that Eliade "did not address the subject matter in the appropriate cultural context" (Ripinsky-Naxon, 1993, p. 11). For example, Eliade displayed "personal bias" in using the term "degenerate" to describe the use of mind-altering substances by shamans, failing to "recognize the critical role of hallucinogens" in many forms of shamanism (p. 103).

In addition, Wilber (1981) makes such sweeping generalizations that it is hard to believe that he recognizes the varieties of shamanic experience. He calls the bird "the classic symbolism of shamanism" (p. 70), although in some shamanic societies, the deer or the bear is the central totem (e.g., Ripinsky-Naxon, 1993). Wilber claims that the "true" shamanic experience involves "a severe crisis" (pp. 73-74) although there are accounts of shamanic callings that do not involve physical, emotional, or spiritual catastrophes (e.g., Krippner & Welch, 1992). Indeed, the shamanic "crisis" could well be a political strategy that limits the number of contenders for the shamanic role in those societies that demand it.

Wilber describes shamanism as a "religion," albeit one that is "extremely crude, very unrefined, and not highly evolved" (p. 75), placing it at the fifth level of an eight-level spectrum (p. 253). But most writers on shamanism focus on its technologies, its worldviews, and its ways of knowing rather than on its resemblance to institutionalized religions (Harner, 1980; Krippner & Welch, 1992).

Indeed, there are Buddhist shamans, Islamic shamans, Christian shamans, and neo-pagan shamans. At most, shamanic practices have led to religious syncreticism (Ripinsky-Naxon, 1993, p. 207), e.g., Tibetan Buddhism and Taoism reflect earlier shamanic practices. By writing about "the true shaman" (p. 76) rather than of shamans and shamanic experiences (Heinze, 1991; Walsh, 1990), Wilber focuses on a hypothetical figure and that has been socially constructed over the ages. He could have served his purposes better by spreading his net more widely, catching and evaluating an assortment of practitioners and social groups who have manifested so-called "subtle" states over the millennia.

Wilber probably would consider María Sabina's *veladas* typical "subtle" state imagery, but what could María Sabina have chanted that would have been more meaningful to her clients and more descriptive of her work?

These are my children,
These are my babies,
These are my offshoots,
My buds,
I am only asking, examining,
About His business as well,
I begin in the depth of the water,
I begin where the primordial sounds forth,
Where the sacred sounds forth.
I am a little woman who goes through the water,
I am a little woman who goes through the stream,
I bring my light,
Ah, Jesus Christ,
Medicinal herbs and sacred herbs of Christ,
I'm going to thunder,
I'm going to play music,
I'm going to shout,
I'm going to whistle,
It's a matter of tenderness, a matter of clarity,
There is no resentment,
There is no rancor,
There is no argument,
There is no anger,
It is life and well-being.
      (Estrada, 1981, abridged, pp. 136, 150-151, 165, 175)

In these brief excerpts from María Sabina's *veladas*, we find a woman who goes into the primordial waters of oceanic consciousness. However, she does not stay there because her orientation is toward service, toward healing, toward her community, and toward the children and babies to whom she strives to bring life and well-being.

Obviously, there is no way of knowing if María Sabina had reached the "causal" or "absolute" realm of Wilber's hierarchy. If so, what knowledge would she have obtained that would have been more useful to her in her mission than the symbolic images and metaphors that emanated in her *veladas*? Nor is Coan (1987) impressed by Wilber's "sharp dichotomy" (p. 143); the shaman can use many dimensions of consciousness at different times for different purposes. No shamanic performance is ever exactly the same!

These *veladas* demonstrate María Sabina's shamanic ways of knowing by means of the "sacred herbs" that facilitate her journey through the "heart" and through the "water," bringing her "light" and "tenderness" in the service of "life and well-being." Here we have an example of the shamanic images "that are directed at reestablishing and maintaining a balanced relationship between nature and the community and at caring for the spiritual and physical welfare of its members" (Ripinsky-Naxon, 1993, p. 207).

The *veladas* also provide examples of ritual as social performance (V. Turner, 1968) and of symbols that seem to "trigger" healing (E. Turner, 1992). From a postmodern perspective, it is merely an intellectual exercise to arrange such manifestations of consciousness on a scale of "lower" to "higher" without considering the demands of a local situation at a particular moment in time.

Discussion

Western science is characterized by a search for satisfactory explanations of "reality." This search is achieved by statements of general principles; these can be tested experimentally or through repeated observations (Goldstein & Goldstein, 1978). Shamanic epistemology also attempts to explain "reality," employs repeated observations, and makes statements about general principles.

However, credence is given to revelation and inspiration from the "spirit world," from plant and animal "allies," and from "journeys" associated with changed states of consciousness. A provocative example is the complex brew *ayahuasca*, which goes by many other names, depending on the part of the Amazon where it is used. Shamans have imbibed *ayahuasca* for hundreds of years, but its origin remains a mystery to Western investigators. Some tribes attribute this knowledge to spiritual beings from subaquatic realms, others to the intervention of giant serpents (Luna & White, 2000).

Narby (1998) comments, "Here are people without electron microscopes who choose, among 80,000 Amazonian plant species, the leaves of a bush containing a...brain hormone, which they combine with a vine containing substances that inactivate an enzyme of the digestive tract, which would otherwise block the effect. And they do this to modify their consciousness. It is as if they knew about the molecular properties of plants and the art of combining them, and when one asks them how they knew these things, they say their knowledge comes directly from [the] plants" (p. 11). For three decades, I worked with an intertribal medicine man and shamanic healer, Rolling Thunder.

When I asked him how he was able to identify the curative power of plants he had never used previously, he told me, "I ask the plant what it is good for. Some plants are only meant to be beautiful. Other plants are meant for food. Still others are to be used as medicine. Once a healing plant has spoken to me, I ask its permission to take it with me and add it to my medicine pouch." Rolling Thunder's epistemology was remarkably similar to that of the Amazonian shamans who work with *ayahuasca*.

In a world beset by quandaries and crises, survival no longer depends upon the process of natural selection or chance mutations, but rather on intentional deliberations and conscientious decision-making. Western modernity has failed to build a universal human culture upon a foundation of abstract rational thought.

Humanity can not repeat the past, but postmodernity would do well to reconsider the personal, metaphorical language that the Royal Society of London deliberately scuttled in its attempt to produce a universal language of objective and unequivocal symbols (Mahoney & Albert, 1997, p. 23). The failure of this project ignored one of the points permeating this essay: language makes use of the same structures as those involved in sensorimotor activity; these structures take the form of analog models of reality, and the resulting images ground humankind's concepts, constructs, and intentions.

Vandervert's model (1996) provides a "neuro-epistemological" framework for this proposition; he writes that "the neuro-algorithmic organization of the phylogenetic brain is that which evolved originally as the algorithms for perception, learning-memory, cognition, and emotion-motivation involved in the struggle for survival" (p. 82). These representations are reflected in shamanic technologies which, first and foremost, were devoted to finding game animals, locating and using medicinal plants, determining the best time to plant and harvest crops, and other matters of daily survival. Shamanic technologies also had spiritual uses, but contemporary Westerners often emphasize the transcendental side of shamanism to the neglect of its practical aspects.

Vandervert (1997) proposes that "image-schemas" (see Mandler, 1988) are not tantamount to the organism's storehouse of images, but the space-time representations that co-exist with perceptual processes, both of which precede mental imagery. These space-time simulation structures are genetic in origin and are responsible for the state-estimating functions that are connected to the cerebrum's mapping systems. The resulting image-schemas are whetted by experience as well as by developmental processes.

Vandervert's proposal that image-schemas represent "foundational meanings" (p. 111) is reminiscent of Jung's description of "archetypes," the struc-

> "It is as if they knew about the molecular properties of plants and the art of combining them, and when one asks them how they knew these things, they say their knowledge comes directly from [the] plants."

tural predispositions that allegedly provide the organizing principles for consciousness and behavior.

These image-schemas collectively represent what Vandervert considers to be a "calculus" of archetypal processing. Such image-schematic processing, although a process of natural selection, had the immanent potential to lead to emergent future state estimates (i.e., nonlinear simulations) that extended beyond purely naturally selected states. This combination of image-schematic elements extended beyond the selective mechanism that evoked them. In this way, image-schematic simulations imparted a freedom beyond natural selection that provided a world of potentially new paths for human intention.

The nervous system evolved in ways that enabled it to foresee many future events, and rapid simulation was the basic approach to survival-conducive prediction (Fox, 1988, pp. 160-161). The nervous system's ability to produce such simulation structures as image-schemas permitted anticipatory, feedforward processing (see Pribram, 1991, chap. 6). For Vandervert, image-schemas represent the foundational structures needed "for modeling/mapping functions conducive for survival." Without this ability to make estimates of future conditions, vertebrate organisms could not have survived to reproduce (pp. 114-155). According to Vandervert, these processes originated in the cerebellum but eventually involved "the entire mapping machinery of the brain" (p. 118); the auditory-vocal sharing of image-schematics eventually led to language (p. 120).

I would propose that the image-schemas of those men and women who a community held to be shamanic practitioners were especially adept when prediction was demanded. Game needed to be located, weather patterns needed to be forecast, enemy movements needed to be anticipated, and flight paths needed to be discovered.

These tasks required feedforward processing, and the shamanic fine-tuning of image-schemas through heightened perception and/or changed states of consciousness may have assisted this assignment. Such neurognostic frameworks are needed to coalesce human neurophysiology with human epistemology, and to explore what Chalmers (1996) refers to as "the hard problem": how consciousness arises from physical systems.

"While evolution can be very useful in explaining why particular physical systems have evolved, it is irrelevant to the explanation of the bridging principles in virtue of which some of these systems are conscious" (p. 121).

One final example from the life of María Sabina demonstrates these image-schemas. When she was called to shamanize, doña María received the image of an open book that grew until it reached the size of a person. She was told that "This is the Book of Wisdom. It is the Book of Language. Everything that is written in it is for you. The Book is yours, take it so that you can work." In accepting this call, doña María became a "woman of language" and what Rothenberg (1981) calls a "great oral poet" (p. 10).

Now may be the time to reconsider the ways of knowing exemplified by doña María, and their sources in imagination, intuition, visions, dreams, the senses, and the body.[33] Perhaps these ways of knowing can enter into tandem with intellect and reason to construct cooperative and collaborative lifestyles for the pluralistic world in which we live, a world which shamanic epistemology would appreciate and enjoy.

Endnotes

[1] In this essay, the term "consciousness" is used to describe an organism's pattern of perceiving, thinking, and feeling at a given point in time. "Awareness" is used to denote "conscious awareness," hence is a more limited and specific term than "consciousness." Some writers (e.g., Goldman, 2000, p. 3) use the terms "conscious" and "aware" interchangeably, but there are values in making a differentiation, especially when discussing epistemology and consciousness.

[2] Durkheim's work has been unjustly ignored by many contemporary writers. His suggestion that language is associated with "displaced reference" (i.e., to communicate what is imagined or imaginary) is worthy of consideration when discussing shamanic states of consciousness.

[3] Reports reminiscent of shamanic epistemology and technologies appear from time to time in first-person reports regarding technical and creative accomplishments. Robert Louis Stevenson wrote that ideas for some of his short stories came from the "little people" who influenced his dreams; Giuseppe Tartini dreamed that a devil composed a piece of violin music for him which he later transcribed; Sriniwasa Ramanujan noted that the Hindu goddess Namakkal provided him with original mathematical insights while he dreamed; Herman Hilprecht attributed an archeological discovery to a Babylonian priest who visited him in a dream; Francisco Candido Xavier's prodigious literary output was supposedly made posible by discarnate "spirits" who dictated his poety, plays, and best-selling novels; Johannes Brahms confided that his best symphonic work was divinely inspired (e.g., Krippner & Dillard, 1998).

References

Barber, T.X. (1999). A comprehensive three-dimen Alexander, R.D. (1979). *Darwinism and human affairs*. Seattle: University of Washington Press.

Anisimov, A.F. (1963). The shaman's tent of the Evenks and the origin of the shamanistic rite (E. Dunn & S. Dunn, Trans.). In H.N. Michael (Ed.), *Studies in Siberian shamanism* (pp. 84-207). Toronto: Arctic Institute of North America, University of Toronto.

Baars, B.J. (1997). *In the theater of consciousness: The workspace of the mind*. New York: Oxford University Press.

Berman, M. (2000). *Wandering god: A study in nomadic spirituality*. Albany: State University of New York Press.

Boaz, N.T. (1997). *Eco homo: How the human being emerged from the cataclysmic history of the earth*. New York: Basic Books.

Boshier, A., & Costello, D. (1975). *Witchdoctor*. Johannesburg: Museum of Man and Science.

Bourgignon, E. (1976). *Possession*. San Francisco: Chandler and Sharp.

Brown, D.P., & Engler, J. (1986). The stages of mindfulness meditation: A validation study. Parts I & II. In K. Wilber, J. Engler, & D.P. Brown, *Transformations of consciousness* (pp. 161-218). Boston: Shambhala/New Science Library.

Casanowicz, I.M. (1924). *Shamanism of the natives of Siberia*. Washington, DC: Annual Report to the Smithsonian Institution.

Cavalli-Sforza, L.L., & Cavalli-Sforza, F. (1995). *The great human diasporas: The history of diversity and evolution* (S. Thorne, Trans.). New York: Addison-Wesley.

Chalmers, D.J. (1996). *The conscious mind: In search of a fundamental theory*. New York: Oxford University Press.

Clottes, J., & Lewis-Williams, D. (1998). *The shamans of prehistory: Trance and magic in the painted caves* (S. Hawkes, Trans.). New York: Harry N. Abrams. (Original work published 1996)

Coan, R.W. (1987). *Human consciousness and its evolution: A multidimensional view*. New York: Greenwood Press.

Corballis, M.C. (1991). *The lopsided ape: Evolution of the generative mind*. New York: Oxford University Press.

deMause, L. (1998). The history of child abuse. *Journal of Psychohistory, 25*, 216-236.

deRios, M. D. (1984). *Hallucinogens: Cross-cultural perspectives*. Albuquerque: University of New Mexico Press.

Delluc, B., Delluc, G., & Delvert, R. (1990). *Discovering Lascaux*. Lucon: Sud Ouest.

Devereux, P. (1997). *The long trip: A prehistory of psychedelia*. New York: Penguin/Arkana.

Diamond, J. (1997). *Guns, germs, and steel: The fates of human societies*. New York: Norton.

Donald, M. (1991). *Origins of the modern mind: Three stages in the evolution of culture and cognition*. Cambridge, MA: Harvard University Press.

Durkheim, E. (1995). *The elementary forms of religious life*. (K.E. Fields, Trans.). New York: Free Press. (Original work published 1912)

Eliade, M. (1972). *Shamanism: Archaic techniques of ecstasy* (W. R. Trask, Trans.). Princeton, NJ: Princeton University Press. (Original work published 1951)

Estrada, A. (Ed.). (1981). *María Sabina: Her life and chants.* Santa Barbara, CA: Ross-Erickson.

Fagan, B.M. (1990). *The journey from Eden: The peopling of our world.* London: Thames & Hudson.

Flaherty, G. (1992). *Shamanism and the eighteenth century.* Princeton, NJ: Princeton University Press.

Fox, R. (1988). *Energy and the evolution of life.* New York: Freeman.

Gazzaniga, M.S. (1994). *Nature's mind.* New York: Basic Books.

Globus, G. (1995). *The postmodern brain.* Philadelphia: John Benjamins.

Goldman, A.I. (2000). Can science know when you're conscious? Epistemological foundations of consciousness research. *Journal of Consciousness Studies, 7,* 3-22.

Goldstein, M., & Goldstein, I.E. (1978). *How we know: An exploration of the scientific process.* New York: Plenum Press.

Gore, R. (1997, September). The dawn of humans. *National Geographic,* pp. 92-99.

Gore, R. (2000, January). People like us. *National Geographic,* pp. 90-117.

Grim, J.A. (1983). *The shaman: Patterns of Siberian and Ojibway healing.* Norman: University of Oklahoma Press.

Guryev, D. (1990). *The riddle of the origin of consciousness* (A. Lehto, Trans.). Moscow: Progress Publishers.

Harner, M. (1980). *The way of the shaman.* New York: Harper and Row.

Harner, M. (1988). Shamanic counseling. In G. Doore (Ed.), *Shaman's path* (pp. 179-187). Boston: Shambhala.

Heinze, R.-I. (1991). *Shamans of the 20th century.* New York: Irvington.

Hobson, J.A. (1988). *The dreaming brain.* New York: Basic Books.

Hoppal, M. (1987). Shamanism: An archaic and/or recent belief system. In S. Nicholson (Ed.), *Shamanism: An expanded view of reality* (pp. 76-100). Wheaton, IL: Quest.

Hughes, R. (2000, September 11). The real Australia. *TIME,* pp. 99-100, 102, 104, 106-107, 110-111.

Jerison, H. (1990). Paleoneurology and the evolution of mind. In R.R. Llinas (Ed.), *The workings of the brain: Development, memory, and perception* (pp. 3-16). New York: W.H. Freeman.

Kalweit, H. (1992). *Shamans, healers, and medicine men.* Boston: Shambhala. (Original work published 1987)

Katz, R. (1982). *Boiling energy: Community healing among the Kalahari Kung.* Cambridge, MA: Harvard University Press.

Kingdon, J. (1993). *Self-made man: Human evolution from Eden to extinction.* New York: John Wiley & Sons.

Klopfer, B., & Boyer, L.B. (1961). Notes on the personality structure of a North American Indian shaman: Rorschach interpretation. *Projective Techniques and Personality Assessment, 25,* 170-178.

Krippner, S. (1993). Cross-cultural perspectives on hypnotic-like procedures used by native healing practitioners. In J.W. Rhue, S.J. Lynn, & I. Kirsch (Eds.), *Handbook of clinical hypnosis* (pp. 691-717). Washington, DC: American Psychological Association.

Krippner, S. (1995). Psychical research in the postmodern world. *Journal of the American Society for Psychical Research, 89,* 1-18.

Krippner, S., & Dillard, J. (1988). *Dreamworking.* Buffalo, NY: Bearly.

Krippner, S., & Welch, P. (1992). *Spiritual dimensions of healing: From tribal shamanism to contemporary health care.* New York: Irvington.

Laughlin, C., McManus, J., & d'Aquili, E. (1990). *Brain, symbol, and experience: Toward a neurophenomenology of consciousness.* Boston: Shambhala.

Lerche, P. (2000, September). Quest for the lost tombs of the Peruvian cloud people. *National Geographic,* pp. 64-81.

Lewis, I. (1990). Shamanism: Ethnopsychiatry. *Self and Society, 18,* 10-21.

Lewis-Williams, D.J. (1998). The mind in the cave -- the cave in the mind: Altered consciousness in the Upper Paleolithic. *Anthropology of Consciousness, 9,* 13-21.

Lubinski, D., & Thompson, T. (1993). Species and individual differences in communication based on private states. *Behavior and Brain Sciences, 16,* 627-680.

Ludwig, A.M. (1992). Culture and creativity. *American Journal of Psychotherapy, 46,* 454-469.

Luna, L.E., & White, S.F. (2000). Introduction. In L.E. Luna & S.F. White (Eds.), *Ayahuasca reader: Encounters with the Amazon's sacred vine* (pp. 1-17). Santa Fe, NM: Synergetic Press.

Mahoney, M., & Albert, C.J. (1997). Worlds of words. *Constructivism in the Human Sciences, 1*(3/4), 22-26.

Mandell, A. (1980). Toward a psychobiology of transcendence: God in the brain. In J.M. Davidson & R.J. Davidson (Eds.), *The psychobiology of consciousness* (pp. 379-464). New York: Plenum.

Mandler, H. (1988). How to build a baby: On the development of an accessible representational system. *Cognitive Development, 8,* 141-149.

McClenon, J. (1997). Shamanic healing, human evolution, and the origin of religion. *Journal for the Scientific Study of Religion, 36,* 345-354.

Merkur, D. (1998). *The ecstatic imagination: Psychedelic experiences and the psychoanalysis of self-actualization.* Albany: State University of New York Press.

Mithen, S. (1996). *The prehistory of the mind.* New York: Thames and Hudson.

Narby, J. (1998). *The cosmic serpent: DNA and the origins of knowledge.* New York: Jeremy P. Tarcher/Putnam.

Nesse, R.N., & Berridge, K.C. (1997). Psychoactive drug use in evolutionary perspective. *Science, 278,* 63-66.

Newton, N. (1996). *Foundations of understanding.* Philadelphia: John Benjamins.

Peters, L.G., & Price-Williams, D. (1980). Towards an experiential analysis of shamanism. *American Ethnologist, 7,* 397-418.

Pinker, S. (1997). *How the mind works.* New York: W.W. Norton.

Povinelli, D.J. (1993). Reconstructing the evolution of mind. *American Psychologist, 48,* 493-509.

Pribram, K.H. (1991). *Brain and perception.* Hillsdale, NJ: Lawrence Erlbaum.

Quartz, S.R., & Sejnowski, T.J. (1997). The neural basis of cognitive development: A constructivist manifesto. *Behavioral and Brain Sciences, 20,* 537-596.

Ripinsky-Naxon, M. (1993). *The nature of shamanism.* Albany: State University of New York Press.

Rogers, S.L. (1982). *The shaman: His symbols and his healing power.* Springfield, IL: Charles Thomas.

Rothenberg, J. (1981). Preface. In A. Estrada (Ed.), *María Sabina: Her life and chants* (pp. 13-20). Santa Barbara, CA: Ross-Erikson.

Ruhlen, M. (1994). *The origin of language: Tracing the evolution of the mother tongue.* New York: John Wiley & Sons.

Rychlak, J.F. (1997). *In defense of human consciousness.* Washington, DC: American Psychological Association.

Sandner, D. (1979). *Navaho symbols of healing.* New York: Harcourt Brace Jovanovich.

Sansonese, J.N. (1994). *The body of myth: Mythology, shamanic trance, and the sacred geography of the body.* Rochester, VT: Inner Traditions International.

Shweder, R.A. (1979). Aspects of cognition in Zinacanteco shamans: Experimental Results. In W.A. Lessa & E.Z. Vogt (Eds.), *Reader in comparative religion: An anthropological approach* (4th ed., pp. 327-331). New York: Harper & Row.

Siegel, J.M. (1997). Monotremes and the evolution of REM sleep. *Sleep Research Society Bulletin, 4,* 31-32.

Societe Prehistorique Francaise. (1990). *La vie prehistorique* [Prehistoric life]. Dijon: Fantan.

Stevens, A. (1982). *Archetypes.* New York: William Morrow.

Stringer, C., & McKie, R. (1996). *African exodus: The origins of modern humanity.* New York: Henry Holt.

Tattersall, I. (1998). *Becoming human: Evolution and human uniqueness.* New York: Harcourt Brace.

Taussig, M. (1987). *Shamanism, colonialism, and the wild man: A study in terror and healing.* Chicago: University of Chicago Press.

Turner, E., with Blodgett, W., Kahuna, S., & Benura, F. (1992). *Experiencing ritual: A new interpretation of African healing.* Philadelphia: University of Pennsylvania Press.

Turner, V. (1968). *The drums of affliction: A study of religious processes among the Ndembu of Zambia.* Oxford: Clarendon.

Ullman, M. (1987). Dreams and society. In M. Ullman & C. Limmer (Eds.), *The variety of dream experience* (pp. 279-294). New York: Continuum.

Vanaria, T. (1997, March). Creation theory. *Ambassador,* pp. 20-25, 40.

Vandervert, L.R. (1996). From *idiots-savants* to Albert Einstein: A brain-algorithmic explanation of savant and everyday performance. *New Ideas in Psychology, 14,* 81-92.

Vandervert, L.R. (1997). The evolution of Mandler's conceptual primitives (image-schemas) as neural mechanisms for space-time simulation structures. *New Ideas in Psychology, 15,* 105-123.

Wade, J. (1996). *Changes of mind: A holonomic theory of the evolution of consciousness.* Albany: State University of New York Press.

Walsh, R. (1990). *The spirit of shamanism.* Los Angeles: Jeremy P. Tarcher.

Wasson, R.G. (1981). A retrospective essay. In A. Estrada (Ed.), *María Sabina: Her life and chants* (pp. 7-11). Santa Barbara, CA: Ross-Erikson.

Whitley, D.S. (1998). Cognitive neuroscience, shamanism and the rock art of native California. *Anthropology of Consciousness, 9,* 22-37.

Wiercinski, A. (1989). On the origin of shamanism. In M. Hoppal & O.J. von Sadovszky (Eds.), *Shamanism: Past and present* (pp. 19-23). Los Angeles: International Society for Trans-Oceanic Research.

Wilson, E.O. (1998). *Consilience: The unity of knowledge.* New York: A.A. Knopf.

Wilber, K. (1981). *Up from Eden: A transpersonal view of human evolution.* Garden City, NY: Doubleday.

Wilson, S.C., & Barber, T.X. (1983). The fantasy-prone personality: Implications for understanding imagery, hypnosis, and parapsychological phenomena. In A.A. Sheikh (Ed.), *Imagery: Current theory, research, and application* (pp. 340-387). New York: John Wiley & Sons.

Winkelman, M. (1992). *Shamans, priests and witches: A cross-cultural study of magic-religious practitioners.* Tempe: Anthropological Research Papers, Arizona State University.

Winkelman, M. (2000). *Shamanism: The neural ecology of consciousness and healing.* Westport, CT: Bergin & Garvey.

Winkelman, M. (1997). Altered states of consciousness and religious behavior. In S. Glazier (Ed.), *Anthropology of religion: A handbook of method and theory* (pp. 393-428). Westport, CT: Greenwood.

Carlos Castaneda and Richard deMille:

Differentiating Experiences from Events, and Validity from Authenticity in the Anthropology of Consciousness

Stanley Krippner

Part I [1]

Carlos Castaneda in 1962

Anthropology can be defined as the scientific study of human beings, past and present, their cultures (including social structures, languages, etc.) and their physical and social evolution. The anthropology of consciousness focuses on alternations in consciousness (e.g., perception, cognition, emotions), as well as indigenous healing systems and their practitioners (including shamans), and the neuroscience underlying performed mythologies such as rites, rituals, and ceremonies.

Whether anthropologists engage in fieldwork, participant-observation, or archival studies, they attempt to distinguish between event and experience, and between authenticity and validity. Epictetus, the ancient philosopher, famously wrote that what happens to us is not as important as our reactions to what happens to us. Marcus Aurelius wrote much the same thing as did, centuries later, Alfred Korzybski and Albert Ellis. They knew the difference between event and experience.[1]

When don José Rios, the celebrated Huichol shaman, was a young man he lost his right hand while operating farm machinery. He reframed the accident as

Photo: Wikipedia

a call to become a shaman. He conducted a lengthy apprenticeship and became a folk legend both in Mexico and abroad.

When another iconic Mexican shaman, doña María Sabina, lost two husbands in her younger years, she reframed the losses as a call to shamanize, because married women could not become sabias, "those who know" (Estrada, 1981; Villoldo & Krippner, pp. 155-159). Both don José and doña María knew the difference between event and experience.

In my work with medicine men, medicine women, and shamans, I have paid special attention to the difference between event and experience. When the inter-tribal medicine man Rolling Thunder told me that he often shape-shifted himself into an eagle and flew through the skies, I felt the most parsimonious way to deal with this report was to consider it an experience. I did not negate the possibility of it also being an event, but there is no way of providing enough evidence to decide the matter. Further, for the purposes of my investigation, it was Rolling Thunder's experience that was paramount (Jones & Krippner, 2012).

The same could be said of shamanic out-of-body experiences, near-death experiences, and past life experiences. There may be sophisticated, complex, and labor-intensive ways of determining the veridicality of these reports, but—for the anthropology of consciousness—veridicality is not as important as the careful recording of the experiential accounts.

In contrast, parapsychology is profoundly interested in events and their veridicality. Parapsychologists place considerable value on experiential reports but chiefly as a step toward constructing a controlled observation or experiment that can determine if an experiential report corresponds to an event.

My 1980 visit to the Zulu shaman, Credo Mutwa, included a ritualistic "throwing of the bones" for the new decade. Credo Mutwa made several predictions, based on the arrangement of the fallen bones, one of which was that Nelson Mandela would become South Africa's prime minister during the forthcoming decade. This experiential report corresponded to an event (Krippner, 1991).

The anthropologist Richard DeMille (1976) has differentiated between authenticity and validity. This differentiation can be illustrated in regard to the controversy surrounding Margaret Mead's interviews of young Samoan women. Her 1928 book Coming of Age in Samoa reflected an authentic venture in that she actually went to Samoa and recorded the reports about their romantic lives. However, another anthropologist, Derek Freeman (1983) claimed that the participants in Mead's study did not provide entirely accurate information. Therefore, in Freeman's opinion, Mead's reports were authentic but of dubious validity. But subsequent investigations have questioned Freeman's conclusions (e.g., Orans, 1996) and the ensuing controversy is an excellent example of the interplay between authenticity and validity.

> Parapsychologists place considerable value on experiential reports but chiefly as a step toward constructing a controlled observation or experiment that can determine if an experiential report corresponds to an event.

An Indian parapsychologist asked a shaman, Yashoda Devi, to hold a group of seeds while chanting, and her experiences were duly recorded. But the seeds she held produced plants that were significantly taller than a control group of seeds planted and nurtured under identical conditions. The significant plant growth qualifies as an event, even though the issue of causation is open to several interpretations (Rock & Krippner, 2011, p. 118).

Kilton Stewart's field work among the Senoi tribe of the Malay Peninsula provided reports connecting the extensive use of family dreams to the tribes peaceful and collaborative nature (Stewart, 1977). However, an overseas visitor was murdered by the Senoi not long after Stewart had written up his accounts. Furthermore, later investigators found no evidence that Senoi families shared dreams at breakfast, despite Stewart's claims. Once again, an anthropological account was authentic but not valid.

DeMille conducted a thorough investigation of archival records of the Yaqui Indians who Carlos Castaneda claimed to have visited. He found no evidence of consciousness-altering plants being used in ways that Castaneda had described. Nor could he verify Casteneda's descriptions of several other Yaqui customs or the existence of don Juan Matus, Castaneda's purported mentor. However, many of Castaneda's anecdotes inspired countless readers of his books. His ritual for inducing lucid dreams has worked for several dreamers. Even though Castaneda never produced field notes from his alleged excursions, DeMille concluded that much of what Castaneda wrote was valid, even though of doubtful authenticity. (The works of DeMille and Castaneda will be explored in greater detail below in Parts II and III of this article.)

Sometimes accounts of tribal customs are neither authentic nor valid. Lobsong Rampa wrote a series of bestselling books concerning ancient Tibetan practices, accounts supposedly dictated by the spirit of a Tibetan lama (e.g., Rampa, 1956). The practices did not match scholarly accounts, and Rampa's sincerity was also questioned. The same can be said of many writers who claim to have obtained wisdom from visits to other planets or to parallel universes. For the most part, these accounts are not authentic and also lack validity.

In 1925 an adventurous anthropologist, William McGovern, ventured into the Amazon, later writing up his exploits in a book, Jungle Paths and Incan Ruins. His accounts of initiations and rituals raised doubts at the time. For example, McGovern described a shaman who drank a substance called "kaapi" and gave a detailed description of a funeral service being held nearly 200 miles away by another tribe. A few weeks later, McGovern had the opportunity to visit that tribe and reported that the shaman's account was completely accurate.

Similar reports have been given by anthropologists who have gone to Brazil and Peru, imbibing "kaapi," "yage," "hoasca," or "ayahuasca." It appears that McGovern was ahead of his time and that his report was both authentic and valid. Once again, the correspondence between the experience and the event is open to several interpretations, but it is more than likely that McGovern reported it accurately.

In conclusion, anthropologists of consciousness deal with material in which it is important to distinguish between experiences and events. In addition, anthropologists of consciousness need to insure that their reports are both authentic and valid. These emphases will bring scientific rigor to the anthropology of consciousness.

Part II [2]

A Review of Richard de Mille's
The Don Juan Papers

Carlos Castaneda's five books have sold millions of copies around the world. His accounts of don Juan Matus' teachings about a separate reality involving a-journey to Ixtlan which yielded tales of a second ring of power, will soon be followed by a sixth book, The Art of Stalking—according to Richard de Mille. Dr. de Mille should know. His efforts to stalk Castaneda were first revealed in his 1976 book, Castaneda's Journey (revised in 1978). He has now edited The Don Juan Papers, authoring or co-authoring nearly half of its 43 chapters (The Don Juan Papers: Further Castaneda Controversies, edited by Richard de Mille. Ross-Erikson Publishers, Santa Barbara, California, 1980. 519 pages. $8.95.)

De Mille claims that Castaneda's work is best understood if viewed as a gigantic hoax. He presents three varieties of proof for this assertion. First, Castaneda's reports from the field contradict each other; "Carlos meets a certain witch named La Catalina for the first time in 1962 and again for the first time in 1965. Though he learns a lot about seeing in 1962, unaccountably he has never heard of it in 1965" (p. 18). The anthropologist Barbara Myerhoff told de Mille that she first was told about don Genaro's leap across the waterfall in 1966 but Castaneda's narrative cites 1968 as his first meeting with Genaro.

A second kind of proof arises from absence of convincing detail and the presence of implausible detail. No specimen of don Juan's hallucinogenic mushroom was brought back for verification, although Gordon Wasson—the famed mycologist—had challenged its identification in 1968. In addition, Castaneda presents no Indian name for any of the plants or animals that he and don Juan allegedly collected and hunted for nearly a decade.

Third, de Mille notes "When don Juan opens his mouth, the words of particular writers come out" (p. 19). The Don Juan Paper's contain an "Alleglossy" which lists some 200 excerpts which suggest literary influence of earlier publications on Castaneda's work. Some of the correspondences appear farfetched (e.g., a suggestion that the subtitle Further Conversations with Don Juan was suggested by Marcel Griaule's proposed sequel to his book Conversations with Ogotem-mi).

Others of Castaneda's passages, however, are remarkably similar to statements in books by Eliade, Furst, Lama Govinda, Myerhoff, Sapir, Suzuki, Wasson, Wittgenstein, and others. Joseph Chilton Pearce praised Castaneda. in his 1971 book, The Crack in the Cosmic Egg. De Mille presents evidence that Castaneda returned the compliment, adapting several of Pearce's ideas for his 1972 book, Journey to Ixtlan.

De Mille could have stopped stalking after puncturing Castaneda's cosmic bubble. However, he has proceeded to explore the implications of what he has discovered with scholarship and humor, exposing what he considers to be hypocrisy in publishing, in Academia, and in science itself.

He asks why the University of California Press tolerated the subtitle A Yaqui Way of Knowledge for Castaneda's first book when Castaneda himself disclaimed any intent to suggest that don Juan's teachings were typically Yaqui in nature. De Mille asks why the U.S. Library of Congress classifies most of the books as Yaqui history despite objections by knowledgeable scholars. He questions the procedure by which Castaneda was awarded the Ph.D. by UCLA despite the lack of appropriate documentation (e.g., field notes) for a dissertation which was essentially the same as Journey to Ixtlan.

De Mille que-ries the judgment of well-credentialed reviewers who hailed Castaneda's books as scientific breakthroughs. Few of Castaneda's early supporters have admitted that they made a mistake; the defensive replies of those who have answered de Mille's inquiries, by and large, are evasive and embarrassing.

> De Mille claims that Castaneda's work is best understood if viewed as a gigantic hoax.

The lessons of Castaneda are teased out of the fiasco by de Mille and his contributors in a number of chapters which are both provocative and valuable. De Mille distinguishes between validity (the correspondence between the content of a scientific report and some established background of theory and recorded observation) and authenticity (whether or not the report arises from the persons; places, and procedures it describes).

In a tour de force, de Mille contrasts books which are both valid but authentic (e.g., Myerhoff's Peyote Hunt) with those which are largely valid but inauthentic (e.g., Castaneda's A Separate Reality), invalid but authentic (e.g., Turnbull's The Mountain People), and those which are in-valid and inauthentic (e.g., von Daniken's Gold of the Gods). Honest errors in reports can result from misperception of events or misinterpretations of events correctly perceived; neither of these bear on authenticity but both bear on validity.

However, Castaneda stands accused of being inauthentic because of his contradictions and his cribbing. Although some instances of invalidity can be spotted in Castaneda's work (e.g., lizards' eyes cannot be sewed shut with agave fiber and cholla thorn, hallucinogenic mushrooms have no effect if they are smoked), Castaneda's first three books are "surprisingly valid" (p. 57).

The teachings of don Juan have inspired many readers to change their lives in positive ways; even though don Juan is seen by de Mille as a figment of Castaneda's imagination, his statements about clarity, fear, old age, and death make sense. De Mille concludes that "by forcing us to look anew into the subtle relationships between validity and authenticity, Castaneda bas made a substantial contribution to the social sciences" (p. 67).

Kenneth Minogue deals with the argument that it is not important whether don Juan actually existed. Minogue notes that if Castaneda's books represent a reworking of themes familiar in the occultist tradition, they only need to be understood in those terms. If Castaneda is correctly reporting the magic of another culture, "then the perceptions and cognitive variations that mark off its assumptions from ours would pose a genuine cultural and sociological problem" (p. 196). Stephen J. Reno adds that if Castaneda had admitted trying to produce a modern myth, "most of the complaints against him would never have seen print" (p. 257). He admits that the don Juan saga still appeals to him "notwithstanding my rejection of its literal truth" (p. 258).

Paul Riesman contributes a splendid discussion of how science and art go in opposite directions. An artist tries to communicate something that is personal, whether or not he or she is aware of how much is fabrication, while a scientist "is trying to communicate something that is the case regardless of his perceiving, recording, or analyzing" (p. 212). Neither, of course, can escape the fact that in some sense we all create what we see.

Richard McDermott examines the progressive entry of Castaneda into don Juan's world, finding that "the first four books stand as a remarkable introduction to a serious philosophical concern" (p. 293). McDermott notes that Castaneda eventually discards his reliance on the notion of "an external, co-experienceable world as the sole criterion of what is real; admitting the reality itself depends on what counts as real in a particular social setting" (p. 293).

This motif runs through many of The Don Juan Papers and forces readers to re-evaluate and re-think their own concepts of reality. De Mille's point of view is clearly stated; there is a "boss reality" that will "knock you flat" if you ignore it (p. 52). Other writers are not so sure, and the different approaches to this basic issue is one of the book's salient features.

One's approach to the nature of reality will affect one's verdict on Castaneda. Is he a misunderstood poet of the human condition? A careless researcher who confused his dates but who actually did meet don Juan or someone(s) like him? Is Castaneda a raving psychotic? An amoral psychopath? A clever trickster?

Personally, I tend to agree with Castaneda's ex-wife Margaret when she describes the books as "conversations he is holding with himself" (p. 369). Even so, there are lessons to be learned here and de Mille is to be congratulated for bringing them to our attention.

Where does de Mille go from here? Castaneda and I have a mutual friend who has asked Castaneda his opinion on de Mille. Castaneda is said to have replied, " I am pleased that I have provided de Mille with the reason for his existence." But de Mille's talents, now revealed, need not depend on Castaneda's future books for their manifestation.

With Castaneda's Journey and The Don Juan Papers, de Mille has established himself as an impressive scholar who is willing to face disturbing truths—one who is capable of taking on worthier opponents than this particular trickster-teacher.

Part III [3]
Experiment with Carlos Castaneda

Carlos Castaneda, as a graduate student in anthropology, wrote four books concerning the teachings of "don Juan Matus," a name given by Castaneda to a Yaqui Indian brujo supposedly living in Mexico. Castaneda claimed to have studied with "don Juan," ingesting mind-altering substances, confronting "spirits" and "allies," having "out-of-body" experiences, and eventually becoming a brujo, or sorcerer, himself. Three pilot studies were carried out with Castaneda by Douglass Price-Williams, an anthropologist at the University of California, Los Angeles.

The most complex of these studies was initiated in 1975 and resembled the experiments in ESP and dreams conducted by one of the authors (S. K.) at Maimonides Medical Center. However, Castaneda's task was more difficult as he was not given the names of the seven subjects. Nor were the subjects told that they were participating in the study. Price-Williams had selected seven individuals he knew personally, and recorded their names in the presence

> An artist tries to communicate something that is personal, whether or not he or she is aware of how much is fabrication, while a scientist "is trying to communicate something that is the case regardless of his perceiving, recording, or analyzing."

of his wife, who served as a witness to the events.

During the following week, Price-Williams contacted the subjects and asked them if they had recalled any interesting dreams. The responses are summarized below:

Subject 1, a research psychologist, dreamed about Castaneda and a "swarm of fish" flying in the sky. He stated, "The fish resembled the kind of carp one sees in Hawaii."

Subject 2, a graduate student dreamed of a chimpanzee which was eating "a bunch of tiny light colored monkey babies—the size of tiny mice." On the following night, the student dreamed that he was to meet a mutual friend of himself and Castaneda. Instead, a pack of dogs attacked him.

One of the dogs was the "size of a small rat or mouse."

Subject 3, was an anthropologist. He dreamed that Price-Williams had acquired a "carp farm in Hawaii" and was looking for someone to manage it.

Subject 4, an architect, dreamed of insects, bumblebees, and rodents. The creatures were not perceived as threatening but were "coming to see me" and buzzed around his head. The dream was so out of character for the architect that he told his wife about it as well as a friend.

Subject 5, was a physical scientist. He had a dream or waking reverie about a strange animal, "larger than a cat, slightly repulsive." It was gray and "could have been a rat with long legs."

Subject 6, a parapsychologist, dreamed about a toilet bowl "in which there are two rodent-like fish, or fish-like rodents." Although not aggressive, "there is something disgusting about them. They look half cartoon-like, with pink bodies, black ears, and long black tails."

Subject 7, was another graduate student. His dream was of a small cat "that had the breasts of a woman." The creature rubbed against the dreamer's leg.

It is surprising that all seven people remembered dreams without being told they were part of a dream experiment. It is also remarkable that the dreams centered around animals, principally cats, fish, and rodents. What had Castaneda been doing? He had been going through a ritual by which images of several of his "allies" would appear in the dreams of the seven subjects—individuals of whose identities he was unaware. Price-Williams has not claimed his studies are conclusive, and there are certain methodological shortcomings that need to be tightened up in future experiments.

Nevertheless, his work shows how science can investigate even the most unusual phenomena if the sorcerer, shaman, or "healer" is cooperative.

Endnotes

[1] Krippner, S., & Schroll, M. (2014). Differentiating experiences from events, and validity from authenticity in the anthropology of consciousness. *Paranthropology: Journal of Anthropological Approaches to the Paranormal*, 5(4), 5-14.

[2] Krippner, S. (1981, September/October). Review of *The Don Juan papers: Further Castaneda controversies*, edited by Richard de Mille. *Association for Humanistic Psychology Newsletter*.

[3] Adapted from Krippner, S., & Villoldo, A. (1976). *The realms of healing*. Celestial Arts.

Bibliography

DeMille, R. (1976). Castaneda's journey: The power and the allegory. Santa Barbara, CA: Capra Press.

DeMille, R. (Ed.). (1980). The Don Juan Papers: Further Castaneda Controversies. Santa Barbara, CA: Ross-Erikson.

Estrada, A. (1981). María Sabina: Her life and chants. Santa Barbara, CA: Ross-Erickson.

Freeman, D. (1983). Margaret Mead and Samoa: The making and unmaking of an anthropological myth. Cambridge, MA: Harvard University Press.

Jones, S. M. S., & Krippner, S. (2012). The voice of Rolling Thunder: A medicine man's wisdom for walking the red road. Rochester, VT: Bear & Company.

Krippner, S. (1991). Vusamazulu Credo Mutwa: A Zulu sangoma. In R. I. Heinze (Ed.), Shamans of the 20th century (pp. 33-41). New York, NY: Irvington.

Krippner, S. & Villoldo, A. (1976). The realms of healing. Millbrae, CA: Celestial Arts.

Mead, M. (1928). Coming of age in Samoa. New York, NY: William Morrow.

Orans, M. (1996). Not even wrong: Margaret Mead, Derek Freeman, and the Samoans. Novato, CA: Chandler and Sharp.

Rampa, T.L. (1956). The third eye. New York, NY: Ballantine.

Rock, A.J., & Krippner, S. (2011). Demystifying shamans and their world. Exeter, England: Imprint Academic.

Stewart, K. (1977). Dream exploration among the Senoi. In H-M. Chiang & A. H. Maslow (Eds.), The healthy personality: Readings, 2nd ed. (pp. 127-137). New York, NY: D. Van Nostrand.

Villoldo, A., & Krippner, S. (1987). Healing states. New York, NY: Simon & Schuster.

---

the eye of leaf (36)
jim perkinson 10/26/98

. . . they hang there in the late october canopy of
stolen sunlight
against the growing grey haze which envelopes like
memory
of having once been bark outside the pith of spirit

. . . they hang 30 yards down the path
    like tiny african masks
suspended confetti of small faces
hallucenogenic ecstasy
    caught and held and staring now
yellow rain in another world
    on different time drifting
    groundward in a fall imperceptible
    in this one
and they rain in the eye like brain dance
    like laughter of the nose
    like cerebellum visions climbing up from the
reptilian cord
    like an open cranial dream
    like prayer descending
    like god's cry to human being begging a body
        for the germ of a bone in motion

they are silent
    these gold mirrors
    these suspended animations
        from the elsewhere of elm
they shout no message
they bear no hermes fruit
they alone stop in no known context,
oblong signs of the release of evil
spirit fetish eyes . . .

. . . before dropping under our feet
like so many crushed leaves.

eternity is the slight invisible crack at the edge
of every sun-touched object shimmering for one
eyeblink
before disappearing into   everything.

Anyone Who Dreams Partakes in Shamanism

Stanley Krippner

The Wisconsin farm where I spent my youth was located near an Indian path known as the Black Hawk Trail. In 1832, Henry Atkinson's forces attacked Indian envoys that were sent by Chief Black Hawk to discuss a peaceful settlement of their differences. The resulting conflict raged for five months and was known as the Black Hawk War. The noble Sauk leader was defeated at the Battle of Bad Ax River. General Atkinson proceeded to punish the tribes that had supported Black Hawk's cause.

I spent many hours looking for Indian arrowheads after my father had plowed the land. I found a few, and developed an interest in Native Americans, especially the Pottawatomie tribe that had lived on the land many centuries earlier. In 1950, I graduated from Fort Atkinson High School and later attended the University of Wisconsin and Northwestern University. Whenever I had the opportunity, I continued to read about Native Americans, their history and their mythology.

I have kept dream diaries since my days in high school, and on the night of September 18th 1958, while engaged in my graduate studies, I dreamed that I was back in Wisconsin, camping near Lake Ripley—a popular vacation spot near our farm. However, the dream took place before Europeans had arrived in the area; there were lush woods and wild animals in my dream, as well as a Native American who was painting a remarkable design on a piece of leather. The design portrayed deer, cougars, and snakes, all co-habiting in the forest. He beckoned me to take a closer look at the painting, and then I woke up.

In my extra-curricular readings, I had run across the term "shamans," those socially designated practitioners who obtain information from their dreams and visions, sharing this knowledge with members of their community. I was con-

---

Krippner, S. (2009). Anyone who dreams partakes in shamanism. *Journal of Shamanic Practice, 2* (2), 33-40.

Painting: Hao Li

vinced that this dream character was a shaman and hoped that I would meet one someday.

I had to wait until 1967, when I met Grandmother Twyla Hurd Nitsch at a conference during my tenure as the director of a dream laboratory at Maimonides Medical Center in Brooklyn, New York. Grandmother Nitsch's grandfather, Moses Shongo, was the last of the great Seneca medicine men, and was the custodian of spiritual traditions dating back to the days of the Iroquois Confederacy that also consisted of the Mohawks, Oneidas, Onondagas, Cayugas, and Tuscaroras.

Because Grandmother Nitsch and I were both speakers at the conference, I was able to converse with her, learning about the "power objects" and "power animals" that served as allies when Seneca medicine men and women conducted healing ceremonies. I suspected that the Native American in my dream was painting a canvas that included my own "power animals."

At the same time, I was aware that dreamers tend to interpret their dreams in accord with their own pre-existing beliefs (Morewedge & Norton, 2009) or what David Feinstein (2008) and I have referred to as "personal mythology." When meaning is attributed to dreams, an interpretation is made through the lens of one's religious beliefs, secular desires, and world views. A dream about falling from the sky can be interpreted as succumbing to sexual desire, failing in a business venture, or as a warning not to book an airplane ticket.

There is evidence that dreams may make a greater impact on behavior than waking thoughts because of their dramatic nature and their openness to a motivated interpretation (Morewedge & Norton, 2009). Over the years, I have seen how my own dreams often reflect "doctrinal compliance," my eagerness to dream in imagery that conforms to my personal myths.

Caveats in Cross-Cultural Research

Cross-cultural psychologists suggest that psychological generalizations cannot be made on the basis of research conducted in one cultural context, but rather must be demonstrated through cross-cultural research. This position is especially pertinent when applied to educational, counseling, and psychotherapeutic interventions; a particular approach might be successful in one society, e.g., a Western culture, but inappropriate in another, e.g., a non-Western culture. On the other hand, a comparison of interventions from non-Western cultural settings may yield information that can enhance Western practices. A "culture" is a particular group's shared way of life; such practices as healing,

> When meaning is attributed to dreams, an interpretation is made through the lens of one's religious beliefs, secular desires, and world views.

teaching, and dreaming are an important component of many cultures, both past and present.

I have compared models of several native healing traditions with those of allopathic medicine, finding both similarities and differences (Krippner, 1995a). Intending to do the same for dreamworking systems, I located an 8-facet model proposed by Ullman and Zimmerman (1979) that compared three Western systems, those of Sigmund Freud, Carl Jung, and Montague Ullman. I added two facets to the model, and revised several others to provide a better basis for cross- cultural comparison (Krippner, 1994; Krippner & Thompson, 1996).

In 1993, I met Lonko Kilapan during a speaking engagement in Santiago, Chile. He was introduced to me as a shaman, although he made no such claim. At the time, Kilapan was president of the Araucanian Confederation and ran a small museum that displayed Araucanian artifacts. In addition, he had written several books about Araucanian lore (Kilapan, 1974, 1987). In an interview and subsequent letter, Kilapan told me that the Araucanos (also known as the Mapuche, who Kilapan considers the ancestors of the Araucanos) divide dreams into four categories: dreams from the unconscious (e.g., wishes, memories, symbols), dreams evoked by outside stimuli (e.g., food, alcohol), telepathic and clairvoyant dreams, and precognitive dreams.

According to Kilapan, dreams from the unconscious reflect memories of life experiences, especially those making the most profound impressions. Instead of dreaming about a tree we saw, we might dream about its branches or flowers; instead of dreaming about an entire journey, one might dream about an animal that crossed one's path during the trip. Elements from past experiences can become symbols; the initials engraved on a tree trunk may symbolize love, while a shining knife may symbolize terror.

Sometimes only the emotions associated with the event are recalled: happiness, embarrassment, wishes, aspiration, deception, pain. During this type of dream, pieces of memories may occur in random order, without logic. The dream entwines them all, turning them into some type of story.

Sometimes dreams are evoked by outside stimuli and foreign agents. If the sleeping person hears a loud noise, the unconscious incorporates it into the dream. Other examples would be screams, strange sounds, and earthquake tremors. At times indigestible food or an excess of alcohol can evoke this type of dream. It can also occur if the dreamer falls out of bed. The resulting dream can reveal the way in which that person would behave if confronted with such an event while awake. Within an instant, the dreamer's life history releases a dream scenario.

According to Kilapan, in telepathic and clairvoyant dreams, this extraordinary capacity is able to operate more easily when one is asleep than during the day when there are so many other distractions. He told me that couples who have lived together for several years report this type of dream, as do people who live at a distance and have some need to communicate with each other. In Kilapan's opinion, spirits of the dead can communicate with the living in this way as well.

Precognitive dreams have been reported for millennia. Just as telepathy and clairvoyance supposedly demonstrate the permeable nature of space, precognition is said to demonstrate the arbitrary nature of time. In some dreams, the dreamer claims to step through a door into the future. It is not uncommon for people to report precognitive dreams that issue warnings, describing a place they should not travel or a person they should avoid. Other dreams are said to predict positive events. Kilapan observed that these abilities were used more frequently in former days by the Araucanos and their ancestors, the Mapuche.

Jungle Buccaneers

In April, 1998, I gave a seminar at the International Holistic University in Brasilia as part of a celebration of indigenous knowledge. During that same week, *pajés* from some 40 tribal nations met at the university to plan strategies for fighting "ecopiratism," the theft by outsiders of their resources. This meeting was sponsored by the National Foundation of Indians, and I was able to interact with several of the shamans at mealtimes, and paid several visits to their encampment, which was located by a beautiful waterfall.

At the end of the week, Citambe Pataxo, a *pajé* from the Pataxo nation, and I were invited to ring the "peace bell," a gift from a Japanese foundation to the university in honor of its work on behalf of conflict resolution.

Citambe and other *pajés* told me that in 1996 a corporation based in the United States had sent representatives to the rainforest, where they had obtained permission from the National Foundation of Indians to study animals indigenous to the rainforest. Instead, they drew blood samples from members of the Karitania and Surui tribes. A member of the team had lured the tribal shamans into the rainforest, purportedly to locate wild animals, while other members of the team were drawing blood claiming it needed to be studied to protect them against tropical diseases.

Later, the corporation offered the DNA from these blood samples for sale on its website; it was purchased by military and business groups who were stationing their representatives in tropical areas, hoping it would yield clues as to how the Brazilian Indians could resist diseases and fatigue despite the intense heat. Earlier, a group of "researchers" had queried Brazilian shamans about their herbal knowledge, later publishing articles on the topic with no compensation to the tribes (Veloso, 1998).

The shamans who met in Brasilia drafted a Charter of the Principles of Indigenous Knowledge; I promised Citambe Pataxo and the other *pajés* that I would publicize their resolution and, on my return to the United States, was successful in having it published in several periodicals (e.g., Krippner, 1999a, 1999b). The Charter states, in part:

> We know that various plants, animals, insects and even our own blood samples are exported from Brazil to other countries....The invader's greed has resulted in the transformation of our national resources into money. This greed has brought sickness, starvation, and death to our people....Our Great Mother Earth has been mortally wounded, and if she dies, we will die as well....We are from the Earth and we will stay here. We can help all humanity, and we want to help them. But we need help as well. At the same time, we cannot condone the theft and the destruction. It is time for this to stop. This is our word. (1999b, p. 11)

Many of the shamans I spoke to during the week underscored the importance of dreams in their traditions. One of them remarked, *"Qualquer pessoa que sonha pratica um pouco de xamanismo."* Anyone who dreams partakes in a bit of shamanism. My experiences with shamans and their communities in South America, and from other countries of the world as well, reinforce this statement (e.g., Descola, 1996).

A similar sentiment was voiced by Thomas (2006) who observed that the shaman represents the attentiveness and the introspection needed to reconcile alienated men and women with what they have lost through family and social prohibitions. Reflecting on his own experience, Thomas remarked, "It seems remarkable to me that the initiatory guidance I had been lacking from family and

> This tattered world has never needed knowledge and direction from both the world of dreams and the world of Nature, from both intuition and reason, and from both imagination and common sense, as much as it needs it now.

culture was provided to me in the form of dream after dream that kept waking me up to my predicament and the prospect of transformation" (p. 4).

I have used the metaphor of working with the "inner shaman" in my seminars on personal mythology (Feinstein & Krippner, 2008). Thomas remarked that this "inner shaman" shows us that by relating receptively to our wounds, they will begin to heal. There is a sense of relief that accompanies the penetration of the wound to our psychological defenses. This is especially evident when we try to disown our shadow or our wounded self in an infantile relationship with someone else, our dreams will often prod us into embarking on a more rewarding relationship that we need to have with ourselves.

Perhaps my 1958 dream represented my own "inner shaman," a resource that I have drawn upon over the years. And in 1967, Grandmother Nitsch told me that the Earth is one of humanity's most important teachers; indeed, I think she would agree that this tattered world has never needed knowledge and direction from both the world of dreams and the world of Nature, from both intuition and reason, and from both imagination and common sense, as much as it needs it now.

Preparation of this chapter was supported by the Chair for the Study of Consciousness, Saybrook Graduate School and Research Center, San Francisco, California. It was presented as a keynote address at the annual convention of the International Association for the Study of Dreams, Chicago, June, 2009.

References

Assunção, A., & Jecupé, K.W. (2006). *Words of a moon-man: An interview with Kaká Werá Jecupé*. Retrieved October 18, 2006, from http://people.mills.edu/jspahr/chain/assuncao-jecupe.htm

Bernstein, D. M., Belicki, K., & Gonzalez, D. (1995). Trait personality and its relationship to two different measures of dream content. *Sleep Research, 24*, 139.

Degarrod, L. N. (1989). *Dream interpretation among the Mapuche Indians of Chile*. Unpublished doctoral dissertation, University of California, Los Angeles.

Descola, P. (1996). *The spears of twilight: Life and death in the Amazon jungle*. New York: New Press.

Faron, L. (1968). *The Mapuche of Chile*. New York: Holt, Rinehart and Winston.

Feinstein, D., & Krippner, S. (2008). *Personal mythology: Using ritual, dreams, and imagination to discover your inner story* (3rd ed.). Santa Rosa, CA: Energy Psychology Press/Elite Books.

Graham, L.R. (1995). *Performing dreams: Discourse of immortality among the Xavante of Central Brazil*. Austin: University of Texas Press.

Jecupé, K.W. (1998). *A terra dos mil povos* [The land of a thousand people]. São Paulo, Brazil: Editora Petrópolis.

Jokić, Z. (2006). Cosmo-genesis or transformation of the human body into a cosmic body in Yanomami shamanistic initiation. *Shaman, 14*, 19-39.

Kilapan, L. (1974). *El origen griego de los araucanos* [The Greek origin of the Araucanians]. Santiago, Chile: Editorial Universitaria.

Kilapan, L. (1987). *Sistema numeral araucano* [Araucanian numerology]. Santiago, Chile: Editorial Universitaria.

Kracke, W. H. (1987). "Everyone who dreams has a bit of shaman": Cultural and personal meanings of dreams -- evidence from the Amazon. *Psychiatric Journal of the University of Ottawa, 12*, 65 - 71.

Krippner, S. (1994). 10-facet model of dreaming for use in cross-cultural studies. *Dream Network Journal, 13* (1), 9 – 11.

Krippner, S. (1995a). A cross-cultural comparison of four healing models. *Alternative Therapies in Health and Medicine, 1*, 21 - 29.

Krippner, S. (1995b). A model of dreaming derived from the Mapuche tradition in Chile. In R. I. Heinze (Ed.), *Proceedings of the 12th International Conference on the Study of Shamanism and Alternate Modes of Healing* (pp. 97-106). Berkeley: Independent Scholars of Asia.

Krippner, S. (1999a, June). Jungle buccaneers. *Brazil*, pp. 54-58.

Krippner, S. (1999b). Protecting indigenous knowledge from ecopiratism. *Shaman's Drum, 52*, pp. 8, 10-11.

Krippner, S., & Thompson, A. (1996). A 10-facet model of dreaming applied to dream practices of sixteen Native American cultural groups. *Dreaming, 6*, 1–96.

Morewedge, C.K., & Norton, M.I. (2009). When dreaming is believing: The (motivated) interpretation of dreams. *Journal of Personality and Social Psychology, 96*, 249-264.

Shepard, Jr., G.H. (2004). Central and South American shamanism. In M.N. Walter & E.J.N. Fridman (Eds.), *Shamanism: An encyclopedia of world beliefs, practices, and cultures* (Vol. 1, pp. 382-393). Santa Barbara, CA: ABC-CLIO

Tedlock, B. (1991). The new anthropology of dreaming. *Dreaming, 1*, 161-174.

Thomas, J.W. (2006). *The shaman in the disco and other dreams of masculinity*. Bloomington, IN: iUniverse.

Ullman, M., & Zimmerman, N. (1979). *Working with dreams*. Los Angeles: Tarcher.

Veloso, B. (1998, April 21). Pajés se unem contra biopirataria [Shamans unite against biopiratism]. *Correio Brasiliense*, p. 18.

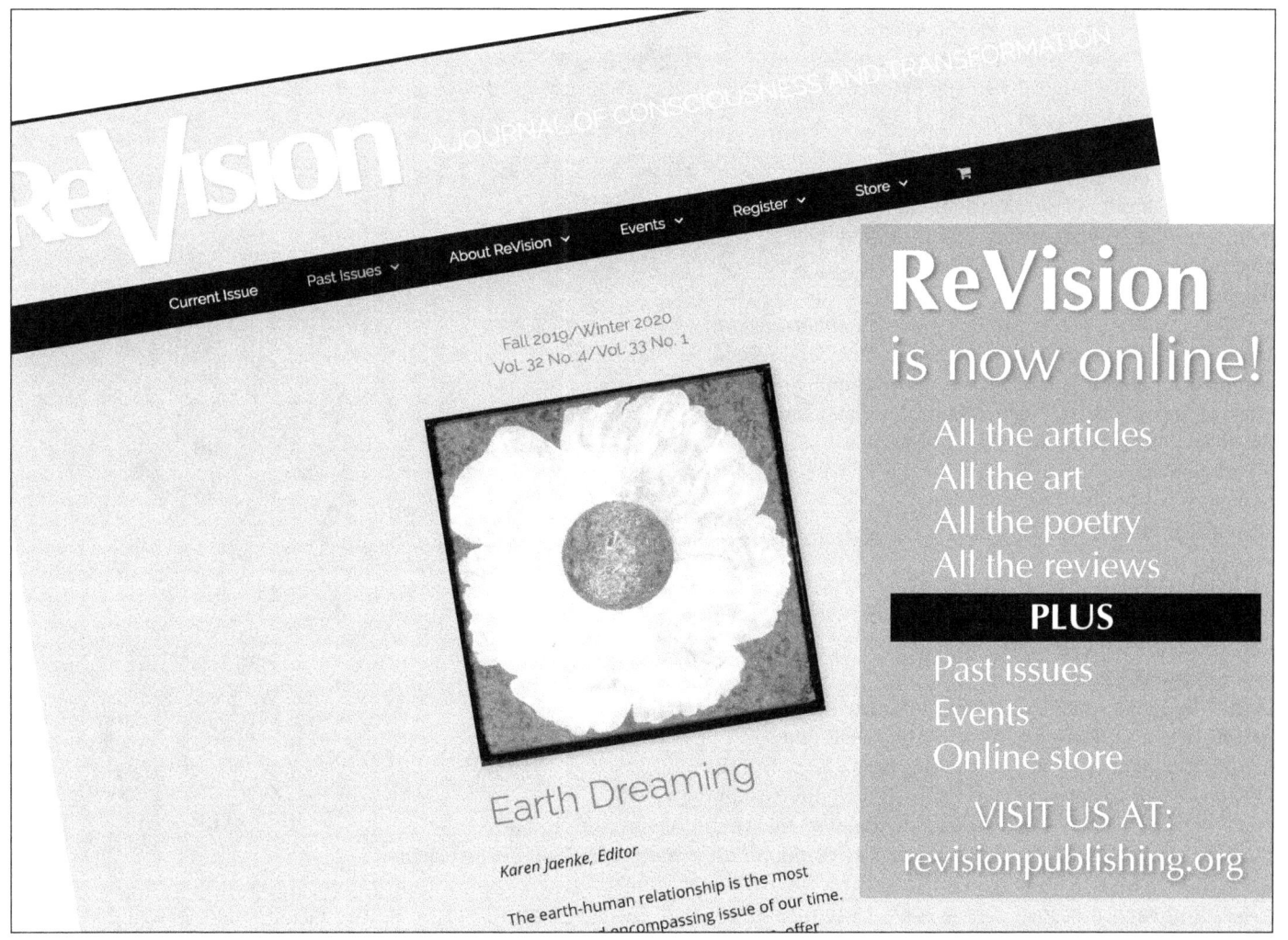

Indigenous Dream Models in South American Shamanic Cultures

Stanley Krippner

Over the years, I have met several dozen shamans from the world's six inhabited continents, often at conferences that focused on cross-cultural healing practices or environmental activism. In May, 1992, I was invited to speak on shamanism at an ecology conference in Brasilia, the capital of Brazil. Paulo Xavante, a shaman from the Xavante tribe, began the day with an outdoor ritual. Much to my surprise, he attended my lecture that afternoon.

After I had described the link between shamanic practices and environmental issues, I paused for questions and comments. Paulo was the first to raise his hand. Somewhat in apprehension, I called upon him, and (in excellent Portuguese) he said, "I hope that all of you have been listening to the doctor. What he just told you about shamans is absolutely accurate." It was one of the finest compliments I have ever received.

The Xavante Indians of the Mato Grosso plateau of central Brazil live in a mosaic of ecosystems, sharing the land with jaguar, puma, anteaters, termites, parrots, and a variety of other wildlife. Their land has been threatened by an encroaching agricultural frontier as well as the construction of dams on their life-sustaining rivers. Nevertheless, the Xavante have tried to maintain their traditional way of life in the face of military incursions, agribusiness corporations, missionaries, and homesteaders.

Krippner, S. (2013). Indigenous dream models in South American shamanic cultures. *Indie Shaman*, 17, 29-35. **Art:** Pen and ink by Gary Newman

Known as fierce warriors and excellent hunters, the Xavante also are skilled in fishing and land management. The dream world is an essential element of Xavante life because dreams allow them to maintain contact with their ancestors. When Xavante elders dream about the "immortals," they share the dream with the entire village, which begins preparing a reenactment of the dream with the elders playing the roles of the ancestors. These dream ceremonies help to align the present with the past, providing cultural continuity. On other occasions, tribal members will sing and dance each other's dreams thus developing a sense of trust among tribal members (Graham, 1995).

At that same 1992 conference, I met Peter Yanomami, another Brazilian shaman. With Paulo Xavante, he led one of the closing ceremonies after giving an impassioned speech about endangered species—which included Brazil's native people. The Yanomami live in Amazonas State and surrounding areas extending into Venezuela. The invasion of their land by some 40,000 settlers and gold miners in the 1980s cost the lives of thousands of Yanomami, mainly to Western diseases against which they had no protective antibodies.

The Yanomami are very protective of their environment; Peter Yanomami told me that his ancestors buried their trash instead of burning it. They feared that the latter practice would sear a hole through the heavens, and that the direct rays of the sun would injure humans and other life forms. The Yanomami believe that they can travel to the heavens in their dreams, as well as to the "underground world." The Yanomami cosmos is multi-layered and is enclosed within the abdomen of a giant boa constrictor (Jokić, 2006). Yanomami shamans also encounter the spirit world by ingesting *epena* or "the semen of the sun," a snuff made from Virola, a member of the nutmeg family (Shepard, 2004, p. 389).

The Guaraní Indians in the southeast part of Brazil also have a venerable dream tradition. The tribal legends hold that in primordial times native people divided themselves into three groups, the People of the Sun, the People of the Moon, and the People of Dreams. The Xavante and the Guaraní are members of this latter group; some communities hold Dream Circles, or morning dream-sharing sessions. Often, a dream is shared that begins to give direction to the daily life of the village and it is not necessarily the dream of a *pajé* or shaman. Indeed, a child can have a dream that indicates a new direction for a community (Jecupé, 1998).

In April, 2004, I met João Guaraní, a *pajé* for the Aty Guaraní tribe, when I was attending a conference in Curitiba. He invited a few of us to a temple for a lengthy ceremony. His stately female assistants sang traditional songs, taking a break while a variety of mind-altering substances were passed around the circle—three smoking mixtures and three beverages. I expected to hallucinate or to experience intense visual imagery; instead, the effect of the substances was to induce clarity of thought that lasted for several days. I only wish I had been given the recipe for those concoctions!

The time came for each of us to make a closing statement. In the best Portuguese I could muster, I wished the Aty Guaraní well in their fight against encroachment on their lands, a battle that has driven some young people in a neighboring tribe, the Guaraní-Cayowá in the state of Mato Grosso do Sul, to hang themselves in protest. I urged them to consult their dreams instead, reminding the group that the Guaraní are "People of the Dream." João Guaraní was profoundly moved; he had no idea that I knew about the rash of suicides that have taken the lives of many young men and women.

On my return to California, I was told about the work of Kaká Werá Jecupé, a member of the Tupy-Guaraní tribe, and author of *The Land of a Thousand People* (1998). He has written about how the *pajé* is known to speak "beautiful words" (*neeng-porã*) that come from the heart. Dreams are important because they are moments when humans are stripped of *nander-ekó* or rational thought. Dreamers are in a spiritual state where the *awá* or "integral being" can emerge, connecting them with a deeper reality. For example, some people can direct their dreams to someone who is several hundred miles distant; others can foretell both positive and negative events that will affect the community (Assunção & Jecupé, 2006).

> Dreams are important because they are moments when humans are stripped of nandereká or rational thought.

Caveats in Cross-Cultural Research

Cross-cultural psychologists suggest that psychological generalizations cannot be made on the basis of research conducted in one cultural context, but rather must be demonstrated through cross-cultural research. This position is especially pertinent when applied to educational, counseling, and psychotherapeutic interventions; a particular approach might be successful in one society, e.g., a Western culture, but inappropriate in another, e.g., a non-Western culture.

On the other hand, a comparison of interventions from non-Western cultural settings may yield information that can enhance Western practices. A "culture" is a particular group's shared way of life; such practices as healing, teaching, and dreaming are an important component of many cultures, both past and present.

A close examination of North and South American shamanic dream systems reveals a remarkable sophistication and complexity that exceeded the simplistic systems brought to the Americas by European conquerors. More often than not, European dreamers were urged to ignore their dreams, since the dreamer would not know which ones were divinely inspired and which betrayed "demonic" influence (Rock & Krippner, 2011, p. 113).

Shamans from both of the Americas faced no such dilemmas as they had centuries of traditional dreamwork to fall back upon allowing them to determine the structure and function of a dream report. In most of these traditions, individuals and family members were encouraged to work with their own dreams. For unusual dreams, the tribe's shaman or other dreamworker could be consulted (Degarrod, 2004).

I have compared models of several native healing traditions with those of allopathic medicine, finding both similarities and differences (Krippner, 1995a). Intending to do the same for dreamworking systems, I located an 8-facet model proposed by Ullman and Zimmerman (1979) that compared three Western systems, those of Sigmund Freud, Carl Jung, and Montague Ullman. I added two facets to the model, and revised several others to provide a better basis for cross-cultural comparison (Krippner, 1994a).

The Mapuche Dream Model

Kilipan's mention of the Mapuche piqued my interest and I was able to locate a doctoral dissertation by Degarrod (1989), "Dream Interpretation among the Mapuche Indians of Chile." The author of this study collected 380 dreams and their interpretations over a period of 17 months in the field. As an example of how the modified Ullman-Zimmerman model can be used cross-culturally, I applied it to Degarrod's data (Krippner, 1995b).

Degarrod identified four levels of analysis in the dream: (1) the intratextual level that focuses on specific dream imagery; (2) the contextual level that deals with the social and personal life of the dreamer, as well as the dreamer's reactions to his or her dreams; (3) the intertextual level that relates a particular dream to other dream texts of the same individual or that of others; (4) the retrospective level where the dreamer examines the events following the dream for the purpose of understanding its meaning. Within this framework, I applied my modification of the Ullman-Zimmerman model and its 10 questions.

1. What is the function of dreaming? A dream (i.e., *peuma*) provides the Mapuche with information about present or future actions of others on the dreamer, guides decision-making and provides a rationale for one's actions, and/or serves as a channel of communication between the dreamer and other people, and between the dreamer and the spirit world. Hence, dreams can be divided into present-oriented and future-oriented dreams.

2. What motivates people to recall their dreams? Dreams are extremely important to the Mapuche. They can validate knowledge and the assumption of traditional roles and careers. For ordinary dreamers, prestige is obtained if the meaning of a dream is presented in a way that seems effortless. They can be used to diagnose illness, especially alleged "sexual possession." Dreams are often sought by the Mapuche, especially in times of stress. Especially valuable are the dreams of shamans (*machi*, who traditionally are women), diviners (*pelon*), chiefs (*lonco*), ritual leaders (i.e., *niempin*), and the "official" tribal dreamers (i.e., *peumafe*). These dreams often express the traditional codes of Mapuche society, as dictated by the spirits (i.e., the "supernaturals"). In addition, the diviners would often locate lost objects in dreams by sleeping with an object that once was in physical contact with what had been lost.

3. What is the source of dreams? Among the Mapuche, dreaming is an activity of the soul (i.e., the *poulli*) that leaves the body at night, wandering about encountering other souls. The soul's nighttime experiences are recalled at dawn when the soul reunites with the body. In the case of ordinary persons, the soul wanders without volition and is a mere receiver of its experiences. Through dreams, the soul encounters benign spirits who may give good advice, or malevolent spirits who may do it harm. Through these encounters, the dreamer learns about the present or the future, and--upon recalling and interpreting the dreams--takes the appropriate action.

4. How do dreams convey their meanings? Dreams can convey their meanings either literally or symbolically. A dead relative coming to take the dreamer on a journey can symbolize death. Sometime the decision is made by default; dreams narrated to public audiences are accompanied by literal interpretations while those narrated in the privacy of the home often undergo symbolic interpretation.

5. Are the meanings of dreams universal? The Mapuche are very flexible in

> The soul's nighttime experiences are recalled at dawn when the soul reunites with the body.

their interpretation process. They examine dreams in relationship to the circumstances of the people around them. The intervention of others in the interpretation process permits the dream's meaning to be modified and manipulated. The contextual waking reality is taken into account during interpretation. Mapuche dream interpretation is an open system; dreamers can modify and maneuver the meanings of the dreams according to their specific social context.

6. What is the role of one's current life situation in dreams? Dreams guide Mapuche actions and decisions because dreaming, imagining, and thinking are on the same continuum. In imagining and thinking, the soul also leaves the body but with volition, embarking on a much shorter journey. (Death is the longest journey of them all; night terrors and visions are visits to the dreamer by spirits). Waking reality is balanced with dreaming reality during the interpretation process.

7. What techniques are used to work with dreams? Dream interpretation among the Mapuche uses several perspectives. Through various modes of interpretation dreamers can relate to different levels of time, to different aspects of their culture, to other members of their tribe as well as to outsiders, and to the world of the spirits.

   a. For example, through intratextual analysis, the dreamer connects his or her dream imagery with common cultural and personal symbols. Contextual analysis integrates the dream with his or her social and individual life situation. Intertextual analysis integrates the dream with the dreamer's previous dreams and sometimes with the dreams of other family members. Retrospective analysis permits the full meaning of dreams to be found and new symbols to be created. Any of these types of analysis may permit conversions from a metaphoric reversal to a literal system of analysis.

b. Dreams considered to be negative (i.e., *wesa peuma*) are shared as soon as possible, and the interpretation is usually communal, within the family. This allows dreamers to intervene in each other's problems, and may facilitate healing. The interpretation of positive (i.e., *kume peuma*) dreams is more likely to be a private matter. The classifications are made on the basis of the prophecies in the dream. If the dream is ambiguous, the dreamer may wait for future events to assist in the interpretation.

c. There are informal gatherings at which these dream reports are narrated as part of four different types of oratory: ritualized speech, improvised emotionally-toned songs, accounts of heroic deeds, and narratives of folk tales.

8. What is the role of the dreamworker? Most Mapuche dream interpretation is conducted within the family each morning and before important events. Difficult and troublesome dreams are taken to the shaman or other knowledgeable person. Each family and individual participating in the process brings to it their own idiosyncrasies and belief system. A Mapuche shaman can determine the direction of his or her dreams, bringing volition to the process in order to visit the spirit realm and communicate with his or her spirit advisors. Shamans sometimes use mind-altering substances to heal through dreams, to obtain specific information about the future, or to contact the spirits. Contextual analysis can determine who has the prerequisite characteristics for becoming a shaman, and legitimize shamanic initiation through dreams. However, in Mapuche society, everyone is considered to be a potentially important dreamer.

9. What role does dreaming play in the dreamer's culture? Dreams are fully intertwined with all aspects of Mapuche culture. Dream interpretation is not an isolated event; it is integrated into all aspects of the dreamer's life through the multilevel analysis. Through intertextual and contextual analysis, the dreamer establishes communication with other people. This sharing and interpretation of dreams effects different types of communication between the narrators and the participants of the event. The dreamer's social position and the nature of the dream influence the rendition of the dream report, where the dream report is discussed, and the type of interpretation used. Dreams also are used to validate various aspects of the culture such as myths, songs, and social rankings.

10. How are anomalous and visionary dreams viewed? Through the dream experience itself and various means of analysis, the Mapuche can link and integrate different people and time periods. Retrospective analysis, by providing information about the future, links the dreamer's present activity to future events. Inter-textual analysis links past dreams to those of the present. Because of these inter-temporal links, the interpretation system helps to shape and influence the Mapuche views of the past, the present, and the future.

It is customary for dreams about the "supernaturals" to be interpreted literally. It is typical for positive dream reports to be communicated only after their prophecy has been fulfilled. This retrospective analysis permits the verification of premonitions received in dreams and perpetuates, thereby, the use of dreams as forecasting devices. It also establishes the dreamer as a competent channel of communication with the spirit world.

As an example of Mapuche dreamwork, Degarrod (1989) cites a puzzling dream that was reported by "Julio" during her fieldwork:

> They dressed me with white clothing like a Catholic priest. The clothing fit me very nicely. It wasn't loose like priests usually wear, but a little tighter. It felt very good on my body as if it belonged to me. (p. 94)

Julio was confused because to dream of clothes is a negative sign, but white is positive. However, he felt good in the dream and enjoyed its imagery, so he decided to postpone labeling the dream. Two weeks later, a ceremony was held among people from two Mapuche reservations. The Roman Catholic Church was organizing the event, and planned to have both chiefs and priests lead the ceremony.

To Julio's delight, he was one of the persons chosen to lead prayers. He felt proud because of his position in the ritual, being surrounded by important people. Retrospective analysis had enabled him to interpret the dream. It had announced that he would act like someone of importance in front of the community. In addition, he had found a new symbol; henceforth, for him to dream of white clothing would be a positive sign.

The Mapuche often change their dream reports over time, following the contributions of family and community members. This phenomenon is reminiscent of research between dream content and personality. When dream content analysis scores were compared with personality test scores for a sample of university students in Canada, no significant relationships were found.

However, when the students filled out questionnaires which asked them about dream content, significant relationships were found in such areas as extraversion, agreeableness, conscientiousness, and openness. The authors of this study concluded that "one's personality may tell us little about what a person actually dreams, but it can tell us a great deal about what a person thinks she/he dreams" (Bernstein, Belicki, & Gonzalez, 1995, p.139).

These research data and the Mapuche proclivity to relate dreams in ways that reinforce their status correspond with postmodern distinctions between "fixed texts" and "fluid texts", the latter term being more descriptive of dream reports.

It is apparent that the Mapuche dream legacy is a complete model of dreaming and dreamworking, even in Western terms. Unlike Westerners, the Mapuche integrate their dreams into every major facet of their waking life (Faron, 1968). For them, there is no rigid division between dream life and waking life. The same can be said for many Native American dream models, especially those practiced before the arrival of the Europeans (Krippner & Thompson, 1996). Among most North and South American Indian tribes, the shaman was the focal dreamworker, but it was acknowledged that "everyone who dreams has a bit of shaman" within them (Kracke, 1987).

This presentation of the Mapuche dream model is in keeping with Tedlock's (1991) well-grounded perception that social scientists can learn more from native people's dreams by "studying dream theories and interpretation systems as complex psychodynamic communicative events" than by making typological or statistical comparisons between so-called "Western" and "non-Western" dreams (p.174).

If contemporary dreamworkers are motivated to learn from native people, the Mapuche culture is still accessible, and the cooperation that Degarrod attained in her dissertation research serves as testimony to what can be ascertained by contemporary scholars.

Or could it be that prejudice against the indigenous people of the Americas propels the general public, the popular media, and perhaps the academic community itself toward the "mysterious East"? If so, the field of dream studies in general and Western dreamworkers in particular will lose a splendid opportunity to explore the deeper dimensions of the human psyche from a unique perspective.

An African-Brazilian Model of Dreaming

In September 1994, Pai Ely, a *pai do santos* ("father of the spirits") of an African-Brazilian Candomblé temple in Recife, was an invited speaker at the Eleventh International Conference on the Study of Shamanism and Alternate Modes of Healing, held in San Rafael, California (Krippner, 1994b). I had met Pai Ely in 1990, and arranged his invitation to San Rafael.

Following his presentation, he was interviewed by April Thompson and Andrea Hartmann, addressing the interface of his version of Candomblé mythology and his clients' dreams. Thompson and Hartmann used a semi-structured interview format based on the 10-facet model of dreaming. Pai Ely articulated his perspectives on each of the 10 facets of the model.

1. What is the function of dreaming? "For a medium, dreams are valid for learning about the future and for determining acts of charity. But otherwise, they are the fantasy of one's mind. If you do not have special abilities, dreams have no useful function."

2. What motivates people to recall their dreams? "If people have a reason to remember their dreams, it becomes a part of their nature."

3. What is the source of dreams? "Premonitions in dreams come from God; other dreams come from one's earthly experiences."

4. What is the source of dreams? "When dreams come from God, their language is spiritual. If the dreams do not come from God, their language is simple."

5. Are the meanings of dreams universal? "Dreams that come from a spiritual level have a universal language. Other dreams do not."

6. What is the role of one's current life situation in dreams? "If you have compassion for others, dreams will help you determine how to direct your acts of charity. Then your life situation is important. Otherwise, it does not matter."

7. What techniques are used to work with dreams? "If you relax before you go to sleep, you will remember your dreams better and will be able to understand them more easily."

8. What is the role of the dreamworker? "The dreamworker helps the dreamer determine how to do something for humanity, something that is indicated in the spiritual dreams."

9. What role does dreaming play in the dreamer's culture? "There is not a great deal of discussion about dreams in my part of Brazil."

10. How are anomalous and visionary dreams viewed? "A person's spiritual guides direct dreams about the future and dreams about charitable acts. If people are out of touch with their spiritual guides, dreams may be dangerous and signify they must return to a spiritual life."

In summary, Pai Ely's perspective on dreams resembles those of dreamworkers in many native cultures whose mythic perspective differentiates between spiritual dreams and ordinary dreams (Krippner & Thompson, 1996). Like these practitioners, Pai Ely entertains the possibility that dreams can be used for purposes of healing and to guide one toward a more compassionate, spiritual life. However, his dream model is not as fully developed as those found in many indigenous cultures of the Amazon, social groups whose daily existence depends to a greater extent on the accuracy of the counsel obtained through their own dreams or those of their shamans (e.g., Descola, 1996).

Many of the shamans I spoke to in Brazil and elsewhere underscored the importance of dreams in their traditions. One of the Brazilian shamans remarked, *"Qualquer pessoa que sonha pratica um pouco de xamanismo."* Anyone who dreams partakes in a bit of shamanism.

> "For a medium, dreams are valid for learning about the future and for determining acts of charity. But otherwise, they are the fantasy of one's mind."

References

Assunção, A., & Jecupé, K.W. (2006). *Words of a Assunção, A., & Jecupé, K.W. (2006). Words of a moon-man: An interview with Kaká Werá Jecupé.* Retrieved October 18, 2006, from http://people.mills.edu/jspahr/chain/assuncaojecupe.htm

Bernstein, D. M., Belicki, K., & Gonzalez, D. (1995). Trait personality and its relationship to two different measures of dream content. *Sleep Research*, 24, 139.

Degarrod, L. N. (1989). *Dream interpretation among the Mapuche Indians of Chile.* Unpublished doctoral dissertation, University of California, Los Angeles.

Degarrod, L.N. (1994). Dreams and visions. In M.N. Walter & E.N.J. Fridman (Eds.). *Shamanism: An encyclopedia of beliefs, practices, and cultures* (pp. 89-95). Santa Barbara, CA: ABC-CLIO.

Descola, P. (1996). *The spears of twilight: Life and death in the Amazon jungle.* New York: New Press.

Faron, L. (1968). *The Mapuche of Chile.* New York: Holt, Rinehart and Winston.

Graham, L.R. (1995). *Performing dreams: Discourse of immortality among the Xavante of Central Brazil.* Austin: University of Texas Press.

Jecupé, K.W. (1998). *A terra dos mil povos* [The land of a thousand people]. São Paulo, Brazil: Editora Petrópolis.

Jokić, Z. (2006). Cosmo-genesis or transformation of the human body into a cosmic body in Yanomami shamanistic initiation. *Shaman*, 14, 19-39.

Jones, S.M.S., & Krippner, S. (2012). *The voice of Rolling Thunder: A medicine man's wisdom for walking the Red Road.* Rochester, VT: Bear/Inner Traditions.

Kilapan, L. (1974). *El origen griego de los araucanos* [The Greek origin of the Araucanians]. Santiago, Chile: Editorial Universitaria.

Kilapan, L. (1987). *Sistema numeral araucano* [Araucanian numerology]. Santiago, Chile: Editorial Universitaria.

Kracke, W. H. (1987). "Everyone who dreams has a bit of shaman": Cultural and personal meanings of dreams—evidence from the Amazon. *Psychiatric Journal of the University of Ottawa*, 12, 65 - 71.

Krippner, S. (1994a). 10-facet model of dreaming for use in cross-cultural studies. *Dream Network Journal*, 13 (1), 9 – 11.

Krippner, S. (1994b). Visiting a "pai do santos" in Recife, Brazil. In R. I. Heinze (Ed.), *Proceedings of the 11th International Conference on the Study of Shamanism and Alternate Modes of Healing* (pp. 234-245). Berkeley, CA: Independent Scholars of Asia.

Krippner, S. (1995a). A cross-cultural comparison of four healing models. *Alternative Therapies in Health and Medicine*, 1, 21 - 29.

Krippner, S. (1995b). A model of dreaming derived from the Mapuche tradition in Chile. In R. I. Heinze (Ed.), *Proceedings of the 12th International Conference on the Study of Shamanism and Alternate Modes of Healing* (pp. 97-106). Berkeley: Independent Scholars of Asia.

Krippner, S. (1999a, June). Jungle buccaneers. *Brazil*, pp. 54-58.

Krippner, S. (1999b). Protecting indigenous knowledge from Ecopiratism. *Shaman's Drum*, No. 52, pp. 8, 10-11.

Krippner, S., & Thompson, A. (1996). A 10-facet model of dreaming applied to dream practices of sixteen Native American cultural groups. *Dreaming*, 6, 1–96.

Rock, A.J., & Krippner, S. (2011). *Demystifying shamans and their world.* Exeter, UK: Imprint Academic.

Shepard, Jr., G.H. (2004). Central and South American shamanism. In M.N. Walter & E.J.N. Fridman (Eds.), *Shamanism: An encyclopedia of world beliefs, practices, and cultures* (Vol. 1, pp. 382-393).

Tedlock, B. (1991). The new anthropology of dreaming. *Dreaming*, 1, 161-174.

Ullman, M., & Zimmerman, N. (1979). *Working with dreams.* Los Angeles: Tarcher.

Veloso, B. (1998, April 21). Pajés se unem contra biopirataria [Shamans unite against biopiratism]. *Correio Brasiliense*, p. 18.

---

blessing (34)
jim perkinson 10/4/98

be blessing of bone—supple as tree in the purity of storm
be storm—raining ripped roofs over the pride of brick
be stone as whiskey in the belly--like hot truth
be the wing of sun-seeking geese crying over the hurt of tomorrow
be in each other's eye
be like the smoke of time-shrouded sorrow
be between the bullets of teeth
be over all the fingers of lost, seeking cheeks of understanding
be like jazz in hand, like blues in heart, like song of nowhere
       bursting now into a thousand possibilities
be the rap of revelation, the interruption of assimilation, the stove of cooked isness—
       burning black recipes
be amen of street-corner at midnight, the coffee of nose at dawn
be without the end of narrative in the middle of your neighbor's tongue
be the joint of metaphor blowing white up the vein of community
be the bond of syncopation
be the cut across the body of same
be the note between the lines
be calabash of ancestor eyes
be the now of nirvana on the thigh of desire
be tomorrow today
    like a trope rioting truth
    like instinct
    like a verb from the third eye
    like blood in heat
    like a word over the void
    like the groan of knowledge inside the groin of despair
be that
be it
be all
be where   the one shouts many
beware   being unaware
be be be be
bop.

Research Perspectives in Parapsychology and Shamanism

Stanley Krippner

Stanley Krippner and Grey Wolf, Grand Falls OR

Shamans can be defined as socially-designated practitioners who purport to obtain information or exert influence useful to their social group, and in ways not ordinarily available to their peers. The term "shaman" is a social construct and, as such, is applied to men and women whose communities have their own terms for describing these practitioners. Dating back at least

Krippner, S. (2015). Research perspectives in parapsychology and shamanism. *Paranthropology: Journal of Anthropological Approaches to the Paranormal*, 6, 2-53.

Photo: Stanley Krippner

30,000 years, shamans report experiences that parapsychologists would conceptualize as putative psi phenomena—reported interactions between organisms and their environment (including other organisms) in which information and influence have taken place that can not be explained through conventional science's understanding of sensory-motor channels. In other words, these reports are anomalous because they appear to preclude the constraints of time, space, and energy as understood by Western science. This first-hand report is typical of many such reports:

It is 1972, and we are standing in a parking lot in gathering twilight. Maybe there are 20 of us, including half a dozen physicians. Standing there, leaning in, we are watching a Shoshone shaman, Rolling Thunder, attempt to heal the wound of a teenager boy lying on a massage table. It is a painful wound, torn into the muscle of his leg, and the boy is clearly in discomfort, and just as obviously medicated. He got this wound through some kind of accident. And it is not healing properly, which is what has brought him to this Virginia Beach parking lot at the back of Edgar Cayce's old hospital, now the headquarters of the Association for Research an Enlightenment (A.R.E.), the organization founded in 1931 to preserve Cayce' readings, discourses given while Cayce lay seemingly asleep but actually in a state of non-local awareness, in which time and space took on different meanings. It seems fitting to be standing here, a generation later, watching for signs of another non-local phenomenon, namely therapeutic intent expressed as physical healing.

For many reasons Edgar Cayce should be acknowledged as the father of complementary and alternative medicine. His observations about health and his therapeutics are today as fully integrated and general as no longer to be associated with him. They are part of the contemporary paradigm. But the therapeutic intent, about which Cayce spoke, the idea that the consciousness of one person can therapeutically affect the well-being of another is still very controversial. If this works I will see something, we all will, that shouldn't be possible—if the world is strictly physical.

A small log fire that I had built earlier at Rolling Thunder's request, flickers on the ground, and is just below the boy's head. I am here as a journalist. This ceremony is taking place as a part of my interview with Rolling Thunder. Some of my income comes from writing for the Virginian-Pilot about unusual people who come to Virginia Beach, which typically means coming to the A.R.E.

Hugh Lynn Cayce, the A.R.E.'s Executive Director, called late on Monday afternoon to say a shaman, a medicine man, as he explained it, was coming. If I wanted to interview him I could pick him up at the Greyhound station and talk to him that afternoon. Saturday he would be doing a traditional Native American healing ritual, which I was welcome to attend. That's how I first heard about Rolling Thunder. Of course I accept, and he gives me the time. Four o'clock. I have to check the location; it seems so improbable, "The Greyhound bus station in Norfolk?" "The same," Hugh Lynn replies.

I had done a number of these interviews, and was thinking of doing a book comprised of them. Although I had interviewed some other journalists, and a few scientists, many of the people I had met through Hugh Lynn put themselves forward as spiritual teachers and were accepted, by at least some people, as being the genuine article. Having spent hours talking to these men and women, listening to their stories, their answers to my questions, their affect, how they dressed, how they stood, their eyes, what I can only call their beingness, I have begun to develop some discernment. It is clear to me that authenticity is in part a measure of the continuity between the public persona and private personality. To the degree they are not one and the same that person seems diminished.

About a month before, Hugh Lynn had alerted me to the arrival of an Indian of another type, a Hindu priest from India. He arrived in a Cadillac accompanied by an entourage. In the trunk of the car was the food he would eat, as well as the pans it would be prepared in, and the dishes upon which it would be served. "The master is so evolved, he is barely in touch with the physical plane anymore," an acolyte, a senyasin once explained to me as he brought out the boxes.

"Wow," I thought. "This man must

> He thanks me, asks me to build a small fire where he is to work, and turns and walks down the bank and into the woods. "Don't forget the steaks," he says as he strolls away.

be in a truly exalted state of consciousness." I looked forward to hearing him speak later that night. During the event, however, he was quite disappointing. He had beautiful diction, but spoke almost nothing but platitudes and slogans. By the time he was through I realized I was dealing with shtick, whether consciously contrived or not I couldn't tell. But it taught me a lesson I never forgot: If an expert is someone from more than 100 miles away with a briefcase, a holy man may be only someone from a distant land, practicing an unfamiliar faith, with a different set of altar ornaments.

This is still very much in my mind on a hot summer afternoon as I drive down to the Greyhound station. The Norfolk iteration of this cultural institution comes complete with the usual crowd: Sailors are joshing one another. Marines are playing a game of blackjack; old black ladies are sitting cooling themselves with paper church fans. And leaning up against the snack counter I spot a middle-aged Indian, with an unblocked cowboy hat, an old tweed jacket, and a bolo tie with a turquoise slide. He is eating some cheddar cheese Nabs, and drinking a coke. He smokes a pipe, I can tell, because it is sticking out of the breast pocket of his jacket.

We introduce ourselves, and he picks up a small bag and we walk out to the car. Twenty minutes later we are driving down Shore Drive, which parallels the coast, and he asks me to stop at a supermarket. Would I go in and buy two steaks? Sure. In those days I was a vegetarian, really a vegan, and buying steaks for a powerful shaman seems very odd. But hospitality demands his request be honored, so I go into the market and buy him two of the best Porterhouse cuts they have. A mile further and Shore Drive cuts through a state park, and suddenly we are in beach wilderness such as the 16th century colonists would have seen, and it runs on for several miles. We are about midway through when Rolling Thunder asks me to pull over. Reaching for his bag, he opens the door and gets out of the car, asking me when he is supposed to be at the A.R.E.

I think he wants to take a leak. But no; he clearly intends to leave me. About seven p.m., I say, he thanks me, asks me to build a small fire where he is to work, and turns and walks down the bank and into the woods. "Don't forget the steaks," he says as he strolls away. He is completely natural in all of this. It is not being done for effect and, as it is happening, it seems the most obvious and appropriate thing for him to be doing. Only, as I watch him vanish into the trees, does it become clear how unusual this is. Presumably he is going to sleep in the woods.

Rolling Thunder reminds me of a Polish sergeant I once met. He was so thoroughly secure in his esoteric skill set that what seemed improbable he did with effortless competence. I realize they are just different kinds of warriors.

The next afternoon I go up to the A.R.E. with the steaks in a cooler. Someone has moved a massage table out into the parking lot. Not quite sure where the fire should be I gather wood from the forest that borders the back of the parking lot, and set it up near the table, then leave for an early dinner. When I get back, just before seven, a crowd has gathered. I get the cooler out of the car, and go over and light the fire.

Hugh Lynn comes over, wearing an ironed white shirt without a tie, and a windbreaker. He always reminds me of a prosperous small town banker. In fact he has the mind of a Medici, and is the most interesting person I have met doing these interviews. He introduces me to two of the doctors, then goes over to the vans parked nearby, and talks with two women. They are the mothers who have accompanied their sons. Inside each van one of the boys to be healed lies quietly in the back. It is twilight now and I can see them framed in the overhead light in the vans. Another physician almost in silhouette moves between them.

Precisely at seven Rolling Thunder, looking exactly as he had the prior day walks out of the woods holding his small bag. He goes up to Hugh Lynn who, seeing him coming, calls everyone together. He says a few words of introduction, and while he does this Rolling Thunder kneels down and pulls out from the bag what I can see, from maybe three feet away, is the breast and extended wing of a crow or raven. The pinion feathers are spread. Seeing me, he thanks me for the fire, and asks if I have brought the steaks. I go to the cooler and bring them over. He takes one, and tears off the plastic wrap, and the paper tray, handing this back to me. He walks the few feet back to the fire and drops the steak into the gravel and dirt, next to the little fire ring of stones I have made. It is the strangest thing he has done yet, but like walking into the woods, it just seems the thing to do.

He gestures to Hugh Lynn, who goes over to one of the vans, and the boy within is brought out on a stretcher, and placed on the massage table. As Rolling Thunder talks quietly to the boy, he seems to be having trouble at first focusing on what is being said, probably because the move has caused him additional pain. But gradually he calms down and lays still, his eyes closed. His mother comes over and stands to one side. While this is going on, by unspoken consensus we observers have been slowly shuffling forward until we reach an acceptable compromise between intruding and being able to closely observe. It turns out that this is an arc about eight feet away from the boy on the table.

Rolling Thunder begins a soft slow chant. I cannot make out the words, just the rhythm of the rising and falling sound. He begins making slow passes over the boy's form using the wing and breast of a raven, moving it just an inch or two above his body. I can see the feathers spread slightly against the air pressure as his arm sweeps along. They are long graceful strokes. Every second or third stroke he flicks the wing tip down towards the steak on the ground. As it grows darker the fire becomes more prominent, and the boy and the man drift into shadow.

It goes on monotonously. Everything else is silent. Suddenly, I notice that there is a white mist-like form taking shape around and in front of Rolling Thunder's body. Sometimes I can see it, sometimes not. But it becomes stronger, steadier, until it is continuously present. It is almost dark now, but the fire gives enough light to see. Then it takes form, slowly at first, but as if gathering energy into itself it takes form. I can clearly see that the smoke-like figure is a wolf. Rolling Thunder moves as rhythmically as a clock. Sweep. Sweep. Flick. Sweep. Sweep. Flick.

After about 30 minutes the form begins to fade, first losing shape, then becoming increasingly insubstantial. Finally, it is nothing more than a chimera, there and not there. Then it is gone. Rolling Thunder straightens up, and stops. He makes a kind of gesture, and somehow we are released and come forward. The boy is very peaceful. His mother also has come forward, and she leans over him, kissing his forehead. The wound is completely healed. It looks like your skin does when a scab falls off leaving smooth unlined pink skin, shiny in its newness. I am

> The wound is completely healed. It looks like your skin does when a scab falls off leaving smooth unlined pink skin, shiny in its newness. I am astonished.

astonished. Clearly so is everyone else. I go over to Hugh Lynn. Hugh Lynn asks me, "What did you see?" I tell him, and when I say the mist took form, he says, "Was it a wolf?"

There is a kind of break. People go to the bathroom or get a drink of water. About 30 minutes later we gather again. The second boy is brought out. I cannot see anything wrong with him. His mother, however, is very attentive, so something is wrong. Hugh Lynn says it is a broken bone that will not heal. Rolling Thunder asks for the second steak, and I go back to the cooler to get it. This one he also drops to the ground. He says nothing to me, and I know better than to say anything to him.

The chanting begins, and all appears to be headed towards what it once was. The mist, about two inches thick, begins to form. It grows stronger, stops flickering, but, just as it begins to take form, it stalls. It happens once, a second time, a third. This time I look around and my eyes are drawn to the mother. I have no idea how I know this, but I know the boy's mother is blocking this from happening.

As Rolling Thunder is beginning a fourth attempt he suddenly stops. He straightens up, turns and walks over to Hugh Lynn. He says, "I cannot do this. The mother will not permit it. She has a possessive mother's love, and it is very powerful." "Yes. I noticed. I'll talk to them."

Hugh Lynn goes over and talks to the doctor for a while, then the mother and the son. I can't hear them. Then he comes over to where I am standing, and says, "He was drifting away from her, now he is dependent once again. She is conflicted about giving that up."

People are departing. I can hear cars starting and, in the glare of their headlights, I go over and kick out the fire. Rolling Thunder is there before me. He reaches down and I can see the steaks. Both are withered and gray. One of them hardly looks like meat at all. "You put whatever is wrong into the steak?" "That's right. The fire will purify and release it."

He throws them into the hot coals. The fat crackles and catches fire. The two of us stand there in silence. It doesn't take long, and they are gone. During those minutes I don't know what Rolling Thunder is thinking. But I am trying to reconsider how the world works. (Adapted from Jones & Krippner, 2012, pp. 41-48)

KEY QUESTIONS AND ISSUES

Ever since shamans have reflected on their experiences, they have described reveries that appeared to transmit thoughts of another person, dreams in which they seemed to become aware of faraway events, rituals in which future happenings supposedly were predicted, and mental procedures that were said to produce direct effects on distant physical objects or living organisms (Rogo, 1987).

Are these occurrences instances of what parapsychologists now refer to as "telepathy", "clairvoyance", "precognition" (e.g., "non-local information"), and "psychokinesis" (i.e., "non-local perturbation")? Or are there conventional ways to explain these reports? It is one matter to report an experience, and these reported experiences are worth studying because they yield valuable information about the shaman's inner world (Rock & Krippner, 2011).

However, an event differs from an experience (Krippner, Pitchford, & Davies, 2012), and few scholars would take the position that shamanic experiences refer to a verified, veridical event (Laughlin, 2011: 376).

Parapsychologists who study shamanism suggest that when shamans attempt to locate lost objects, they may be demonstrating clairvoyance. When they seek to communicate with someone at a distance, they could be manifesting telepathy. When they try to divine the future, they might be displaying precognition. When they attempt to heal someone at a distance, they could be practicing psychokinesis.

Purported psi phenomena are the most dramatic of the special powers that provide shamans with their authority, prestige, and stature. Can these alleged capacities be demonstrated under so-called "psi-task conditions" that would rule out such conventional explanations as logical inference, perceptual cues, subliminal perception, deception, and coincidence? This is the challenge that would establish some shamanic experiences as shamanic events.

From a philosophical standpoint, presumptive parapsychological phenomena in shamanic practices differ from "supernatural" or "miraculous" phenomena. The latter, if they exist, stand apart from nature and may even suspend or contradict natural laws and principles. Parapsychologists assume that the phenomena they investigate are lawful, natural, and—at some point—will "fit" into

> Parapsychologists assume that the phenomena they investigate are lawful, natural, and—at some point—will "fit" into the scientific body of knowledge, either with or without a revision of the current scientific worldview.

the scientific body of knowledge, either with or without a revision of the current scientific worldview.

RESEARCH FINDINGS

Weiant, in a paper delivered at an American Anthropological Association convention in 1960, reviewed some ethnographic accounts of possible parapsychological phenomena, remarking: "I feel very strongly that every anthropologist, whether believer or unbeliever, should acquaint himself with the techniques of parapsychological research and make use of these, as well as any other means at his disposal, to establish what is real and what is illusion in the so-called paranormal. If it should turn out that the believers are right, there will certainly be exciting implications for parapsychology" (in Van de Castle, 1977:668).

The literature in scientific parapsychology presents a varied picture of research directions, ranging from second-hand reports and interviews, to first-person informal observations, to controlled observations, to controlled experiments, as well as phenomenological accounts. This essay, in giving examples (and evaluations) of each category, does not provide a comprehensive review; however, representative studies (almost all of them from the anthropological literature) have been cited that illustrate the problems and the prospects inherent to this field of study. Each research category is followed by a critique including suggestions for future investigators.

Interviews and Second-Hand Reports: When Halifax (1979:134-135) interviewed the Mazatec shaman Maria Sabina in 1977, precognition was one topic they discussed. Sabina remarked, "And you see our past and our future which are there together as a single thing already achieved, already happened. So I saw the entire life of my son Aurelio and his death and the face and the name of the man that was to kill him and the dagger with which he was going to kill him because everything had already been accomplished."

Carpenter and Krippner (1989) interviewed Rohanna Ler, an Indonesian shaman, who told them of her "call" to heal. One of Ler's sons began to lose his sight and did not respond to conventional medical treatment. When the boy's eyes began to bleed, Ler was close to utter despair.

One night, Ler had a powerful dream in which an elderly man appeared and told her that it was her fate to become a healer. Her son was the first person she would heal; but if she turned down the call he would go blind and never recover his sight. The dream visitor gave Ler a stone; upon awakening she found a stone in her bed, placed it on her son's eyes, and he recovered completely. Subsequent dream visitors purportedly gave Ler a ring that she used as a "power object" in her healing sessions.

Murphy (1964:60) wrote of a St. Lawrence Island Eskimo informant who recalled a shaman producing sounds as though spirits were walking underneath and around the floor of his house, until "the house seemed to shake and rattle as though it were made of tissue paper and everything seemed to be up in the air, flying about the room." Another shaman was noted for his "fox spirit" that allegedly could be seen running around the rim of the drum while the shaman conducted a ceremony.

Murphy attributed these feats to conjuring, claiming that "some shamans were more imaginative or better ventriloquists than others, while some were more dexterous at sleight of hand" (Ibid.). Murphy gave no specific explanations of the alleged techniques of legerdemain, a common omission from anthropological accounts that take a dismissive perspective toward what they have observed.

Critique: Interview material and second-hand reports can be valuable reflections on the life and beliefs of native people. However, interviewers need to be well trained so that they do not give inadvertent cues signaling the interviewee what is "expected" or what the interviewer "wants to hear."

Many anthropological reports have been accepted as valid, but several decades later have fallen into disrepute as other investigators, conducting research in a more rigorous manner, have provided quite different descriptions and reports.

On the other hand, an investigator who concludes that conjuring was at work needs to provide at least one plausible scenario for readers to consider. The Parapsychological Association has urged its members to consult with magicians when conducting research in which sleight of hand may surreptitiously have been utilized or, better yet, to add a magician to the investigative team.

First-Person Eyewitness Observations: Eyewitness observations date back to Bogoras (1904-1909) who made an intensive study of the Chuckchee Eskimos at the turn of the century. He related sitting in a tent as tribal members placed a walrus skin over the shaman's shoulders.

As the shaman invoked the spirits, the walrus skin seemed to take on a life of its own. The portion draped over the shaman's back began elevating and shifting, although it never left the shaman's back. Bogoras grabbed the skin to discover how the trick was being done, but could not pull it off the shaman's back. Moreover, Bogoras claimed that he had been thrown about the tent by the skin's contortions, as the shaman sat quietly. Bogoras watched another shaman produce an incision into the skin of a client. Later, the shaman closed the opening and no trace of the incision remained.

A 1914 report by a Father Trilles concerned a Yabakou practitioner who told the priest he was about to have an out-of-the-body journey to a magicians' palaver in a distant village. The missionary expressed skepticism, and asked the practitioner to tell a student, who lived along the way, that he should come to see him at once, bringing shotgun cartridges.

"After gesticulation, words, chants, and having rubbed himself all over with a reddish liquid smelling like garlic, he fell into a lethargic sleep. His body was perfectly rigid." The priest passed the night in the shaman's hut to be sure that there was no subterfuge. Three days later, the missionary's student arrived with the cartridges (Van de Castle, 1974, pp. 276-277).

Erdoes (1972) related attending a *yuwipi* (i.e., sweat) ceremony in a converted railroad car with members of his family and about 40 local Sioux residents. Once the kerosene lamp had been extinguished and the drumming commenced, Erdoes claims that tiny lights began to appear throughout the room, the shaman's rattles flew through the air, and Erdoes' electronic flash unit began flashing of its own accord (pp. 280 - 281).

Hallowell (1971) worked with the Salteaux Indians in Manitoba, Canada, and described a shamanic session held for a woman whose son had been missing for a week. Shortly after the ceremony began, the voice of a young man seemed to manifest through the shaman explaining that he was in good health and gave the location where he was camping. Two days later, the son arrived home; he confirmed that during the night of the session he had been asleep at the very location indicated through the shaman (p. 68).

Adrian Boshier, an amateur South African anthropologist who refused to take medication for his epileptic seizures, found that these seizures attracted the attention of the local natives who saw them as "signs" that he should become an apprentice for extensive shamanic training. Telling a parapsychological conference about his apprenticeship in 1973, Boshier (1974) reported that he had visited one shaman who "threw the bones" during a shamanic ritual and told Boshier details about his past and future "that were absolutely correct."

Turner (1994) contributed a first-person observation of a "spirit" who appeared to take visible form during a shamanic ceremony in Zambia. Lyons (2012) has collected dozens of firsthand observations from North American tribal members, many of which involve shamans. One of these, the "shaking tent" ceremony can only be conducted by a shaman, was initially reported by a Father LeJeune in 1634, making it not only the first in-depth report of this ceremony but the first record of what was then referred to as Indian "conjuring" (Lyon, 2012, p. 225). Both male and female shamans have officiated when the designated tent begins to "shake," followed by reports of "spirit voices" and flying objects. The shaman is tightly bound or wrapped in a blanket before the ceremony begins but appears unbound at its cessation.

Critique: These observations are provocative and suggest directions that future research can take. By themselves, they are barely evidential because the reader does not know how to assess their veracity. An observer requires a background not only in conjuring but in critical analysis. Could the shamanic practitioner be eliciting information from the observer that was later used in making a prediction or a statement about the observer's personal life?

Nor does the reader know how many sessions observed by the writer produced material that was not accurate, how many dreams provided incorrect data? How many clients of the shaman did not obtain useful details about their lives and problems? Hyman (1977) has demonstrated how a performer can give a "cold reading" by using vague statements and sensory cues to construct a seemingly accurate description of a client. In many cases, the "hits" so impress the client he or she forgets or ignores the "misses".

The account of the "mist wolf" at the beginning of this essay was an observation attested to by a number of people and written up by one of them, Stephen Schwartz, years later. It is a fascinating report but would have been more impressive had it been recorded immediately after the ceremony ended. Also,

> "Again she began singing softly, and within five minutes of this she tore off one of her necklaces, and holding it in front of her as if it were a divining rod, she walked around the Landrover, climbed into the back and took out the skin."

it lacks follow-up material in regard to the outcome of Rolling Thunder's ministrations to on behalf of the two boys. Many remarkable recoveries last for a few days following which the participant, regrettably, returns to his or her original condition.

Controlled Observations: Perhaps the first attempt to obtain controlled data regarding the anomalous abilities of shamans was initiated by Bogoras (1904-1909). Bogoras was an ethnologist who had heard many reports about "spirit voices" that whistle and speak during Chuckchee ceremonies in Siberia. Bogoras attributed these phenomena to ventriloquism; he decided to record a session and obtained permission to observe a shaman famous for his ability to evoke "voices" from the spirits.

Bogoras placed a recording funnel some distance from the shaman who sat in a stationary position during the demonstration, and who conducted the ceremony in almost total darkness. Several supposed spirit voices were heard. Soon Bogoras realized that the voices came from various points in the tent and not only from the area where the shaman was sitting.

The distance effect also was apparent to people who heard the recording of the session, and Bogoras admitted that there was a marked difference between the voice of the shaman himself, who seemed to be speaking away from the funnel, and the spirit voices that seemed to be talking directly into the funnel.

However, Bogoras never admitted that anything he had witnessed could have been anomalous; in his final report, published by the Museum of National History, he concluded that everything he observed was due to trickery, although he never explained how the voices could have been produced and manipulated.

Laubscher (1938), a South African psychiatrist, attempted to test the claims of Solomon Baba, a Tembu diviner. Unseen by anyone, Laubscher buried a small purse wrapped in brown paper, covered it with a flat stone, and placed a gray stone on the brown one. He then drove to the home of Baba who lived 60 miles away. Shortly after Laubscher's arrival, Baba began to dance. He then accurately described the purse, the wrapping paper, and the stones. On another occasion, Baba described the appearance of some missing cattle from a distant region, and even predicted the exact day of Laubscher's forthcoming trip to England although the specified date was several months after the time for which the original passage had been booked.

When Boshier (1974:27) was working with a museum in Swaziland, he had an opportunity to test a local "witchdoctor" named Ndaleniin the company of another native practitioner and Boshier's friend, a "Miss Costello." The "target" item to be identified was the skin of a gemsbok, a South African antelope.

Boshier recalls (paraphrased): "Leaving her in my office with the other witchdoctor and Miss Costello, I went to a neighboring building and took out the skin of a gemsbok. This I hid beneath a canvas sail on the back of my Landrover. Then I called her outside and told her I had hidden something that she must find. With the aid of the other witchdoctor, she knelt down and began to sing softly. Then, in a trance state, she informed me that I had hidden something across on the other side of that building over there. She told me that it had more than one color, that it came from an animal, and that it was raised up off the ground.

Suddenly she got up, ran around the building, out into the front where the Landrover stood and knelt down beside it. Again she began singing softly, and within five minutes of this she tore off one of her necklaces, and holding it in front of her as if it were a divining rod, she walked around the Landrover, climbed into the back and took out the skin."

Critique: Boshier's study was impressive but flawed; because he knew the identity of the "target" item, he may have passed nonverbal cues to Ndaleni who picked them up, consciously or unconsciously, just as a stage magician will locate an object hidden in the audience by observing the gestures and eye movements of the crowd.

As for Laubscher's work, another person should have interviewed Solomon Baba. Laubscher knew the identity of the hidden object, and the reader of his report has no guarantee that Solomon Baba did not elicit clues from Laubscher during interactions that might have occurred before, during, or after the trance dance.

As for Bogoras, his account is presumptive in concluding that ventriloquism was at work and in not providing an explanatory mechanism for the differences that he and others purportedly observed on the recording. Investigators who claim that fraud has occurred need to present a plausible scenario. They, too, should have a background in conjuring if they are to write knowledgeably about unusual phenomena. Chari (1960) has provided a guide to sleight-of-hand effects that one must be on guard for, basing his report on his investigations of fakirs in India, while Wiseman and Morris (1995) have compiled an excellent set of guidelines for testing psychic claimants.

> As the term is usually employed, human beings perform "magic" while so-called "supernatural" agencies (e.g., spirits, deities) perform "miracles." "Magical" practices and phenomena would be amenable to scientific study because, unlike "miracles," they follow "natural laws."

Rose (1956) conducted a series of telepathy and psychokinesis tests with Australian aborigines using specially designed cards and plastic dice, which were placed in a shaker and tossed on a table with the goal of having certain die faces appear uppermost. He obtained statistically significant results in several of his telepathy experiments; at above chance levels, subjects were able to guess the design on which Rose's wife was focusing, out of the subject's sight.

Psychokinesis tests yielded chance results; Rose reported that the aborigines did not believe they could influence psychokinetic phenomena since that was a prerogative of the tribe's "clever men" (i.e., shamans). Two of these "clever men" were given telepathy tests but their scores were not significant; however, they were not tested for psychokinesis, their alleged forte.

Giesler (1986) conducted several studies, each carried out with a different group of Afro-Brazilian "shamanic cultists." In one study the participant was asked to describe the location where someone (an "out bounder") had been taken—one which was had been determined after the shaman and the "out bounder" had parted company. In another task, a glass of water, a white candle, and a spirit figure (taken from the Afro-Brazilian pantheon of deities) were displayed and the participant was asked to guess the order in which the three objects appeared in a hidden list. The results were suggestive but not conclusive.

In Garhwal, India, Saklani (1988) screened a number of shamans who claimed to incorporate various deities (e.g., "Muslim Pir", "Goddess Dhari"). One shaman, Yashoda Devi, was selected for parapsychological studies. Tests in which Devi attempted to match "token objects" with their "owners" yielded non-significant results as did an examination for psychokinetic effects on methanol.

However, the height of plants from seeds was significantly greater in the group "treated" by being held by Devi, while she chanted, than in the control group which had not been held by her. A significant effect in the absorption of saline solution "treated" by the shaman was observed over a control concoction containing no saline. The growth of seeds sown in the field and "treated" by flasks of water previously held by Devi was somewhat more rapid on certain days of the study than that of control seeds given ordinary water. Saklani did not make it clear as to whether the person making the measurements was "blind" to the "treated" and control materials; even a fair-minded experimenter can inadvertently "tilt" the results if he or she knows which group represents the experimental condition and which group represents the control.

Critique: Giesler's and Saklani's work are among the few experimental parapsychological investigations to have been made of native practitioners who claim to have anomalous abilities. The results are neither compelling nor conclusive, but there were a few provocative results.

In addition, their experimental designs, as well as their suggestions for improvements, might pave the way for future studies. Giesler (1984:315), for example, has called for a "multi-method" approach that would (1) focus more attention on the psi-relevant contexts in native cultures; (2) combine ethnographic and experimental methodologies so that the strengths of one offset the weaknesses of the other; (3) incorporate a "psi-in-process" method into the field research design. Giesler proposed that with this approach, the researcher may study ostensible psi processes and their relationship with other variables in the contexts of shamanic rituals and practices such as divination, trance mediumship, and healing. This would allow for control of the conditions of a "psi task," and the results could be evaluated with a minimum of interference or disturbance of the psi-related activity.

Phenomenological Accounts: For the shaman, there are no rigid boundaries between "waking life" and "dream life"; both are regarded as "real" but full admission to the latter "reality" usually depends on training and discipline. Malidoma Patrice Somé (1994:233), an African Dagara shaman, remarked, "Nothing can be imagined that is not already there in the inner or outer worlds."

Somé's autobiography is a phenomenological account of his preparation, initiation, and apprenticeship, often marked by presumptive psi phenomena. For example, Somé (1994:244) recalled that at a crucial period in his initiation, he was told to enter a cave. He recalled (paraphrased):

> "I went that way, jumping from rock to rock until I reached the entrance to the magical cave. The floor was sandy and dusty; I noticed with surprise that the walls were perfectly carved out of red granite. My fire went out. I closed my eyes in an effort to blot out images of what would happen if I had to back out. When I opened them again, I could see a light a little distance ahead of me. It grew bigger and bigger, and soon I realized that I had reached the other side of the mountain.
>
> Writing about what came next is an extremely difficult task. I saw a tree that distinguished itself from the others by its unusual size. Under the roots of the tree was a bluish-violet stone that glowed as I looked at it. It had a very bright center whose light increased and decreased, making the stone seem as if it were breathing. My hand had taken on a violet color as if the irradiation of the stone were infectious. The violet was so powerful that I could clearly see it shining through the back of the hand stuck on top of it.
>
> Soon I felt as if I were in the middle of a huge violet egg that had no shell. Inside this egg there was a whole world, and I was in it. In that moment of awareness, I had an epiphany; the light we encounter on the road to death is where we belong. I could remember the entire experience I had just lived through, but it bore the aftertaste of a fantastic dream. Actually, I felt more like myself than I had ever felt before.
>
> Suddenly, out of nowhere, I saw a girl and found myself asking her for directions. She said, pointing west, 'You see those mountains over there? Go to the one in the middle, and cross to the other side of it.

> They realized the value of drama, of shock, and of surprise in mobilizing a client's self-healing capacities, and provided these elements through theatrical means.

> There is a cave there. That is your way home.' I found the cave the girl had told me about and ran in. It became dark as soon as I reached its interior. I could see the stony ceiling two or three feet above me. I had crossed back through the mountain almost instantaneously. Something bit me inside my hand. It was the blue stone, my only proof that what had happened had been real.

Critique: A phenomenological account is not evidential because it lacks the controls necessary to rule out prevarication, memory distortion, self-deception, and the like. However, there are very few accounts as graphic and as detailed as that offered by Somé. Obtaining a shaman's "inner" view of a potentially parapsychological experience is a unique opportunity that should be encouraged by future investigators.

Implications

"Magic" is a term used to describe a body of applied technology used to influence domains that a society believes are incalculable, uncertain, or unaccountable (Malinowski, 1954:139-140); if "magic" represents "natural" principles (e.g., conjuring, attribution, anomalous occurrences that—in principle—are lawful), it is amenable to parapsychological investigation (Winkelman, 1982). As the term is usually employed, human beings perform "magic" while so-called "supernatural" agencies (e.g., spirits, deities) perform "miracles." "Magical" practices and phenomena would be amenable to scientific study because, unlike "miracles," they follow "natural laws."

EXPLANATIONS FOR THE PHENOMENA

In his anthropological survey of unusual experiences among tribal people, Jensen (1963:230) remarked, "there can be no doubt that man actually possesses such abilities," and left it open as to whether these capacities are parapsychological or not.

There are many alternative explanations such as suggestion, imagination, exaggerated reporting, or a temporary extension of one's sensory and motor skills under unusual circumstances (e.g., physical and emotional arousal, ingestion of mind-altering substances, high levels of motivation). Nonetheless, the literature demonstrates that anomalous phenomena may be linked to shamanic calling, to shamanic training, and to shamanic practice.

It is likely that many if not most accounts of shamans' anomalous behaviors and experiences have ordinary explanations. One's reputation becomes enhanced as tales are told and retold over the years, becoming embellished in the process. In addition, coincidence can be magnified by practitioners who point out the significance of an unexpected rainstorm, the sudden appearance of a "power animal," or an event that seems to conform to someone's dream of the previous night.

It also must be recalled that in the shamanic worldview, one's imagination and dreams are as "real" as public events, and those who listen to a shaman's stories might not be able to separate the two.

In addition, shamans were the first magicians as well as the first healers. They realized the value of drama, of shock, and of surprise in mobilizing a client's self-healing capacities, and provided these elements through theatrical means. Murphy (1964), in her work among Eskimo shamans on Canada's St. Lawrence Island, discovered that instructions in ventriloquism and legerdemain were part of shamanic training.

Reichbart (1978) suggested that deliberate sleight-of-hand can be used by shamans to create a psychological environment conducive to the manifestation of genuine parapsychological phenomena.

Kelly and Locke (1982) suspected that parapsychological investigations in shamanic settings will become more fruitful to the degree that investigators succeed in penetrating sympathetically and in detail the interior of individual settings. A promising example was the work of Boshier among shamans in southern Africa, but his untimely death cut short these contributions.

However, Van de Castle (1974:281) was able to break through some of the customary reserve of Cuna Indian practitioners in Panama by bringing along a British sensitive who was so successful in demonstrating his skills in diagnosis and healing, that villagers began requesting his services.

In regard to the scientific status of parapsychology, Irwin (1999:319) has taken a position that is frequently heard among contemporary parapsychologists: "In the final analysis, what fairly can be said of parapsychology?

As far as spontaneous cases are concerned it seems likely that there are numerous instances of self-deception, delusion, and even fraud. Some of the empirical literature likewise might be attributable to shoddy experimental procedures and to fraudulent manipulation of data.

Be this as it may, there is sound phenomenological evidence of parapsychological experiences and possibly even experimental evidence of anomalous events too, and behavioral scientists ethically are obliged to encourage the investigation of these phenomena rather than dismissing them out of hand. If all of the phenomena do prove to be explicable within conventional principles of mainstream psychology surely that is something worth knowing, especially in relation to counseling practice; and if just one of the phenomena should be found to demand a revision or an expansion of contemporary psychological principles, how enriched behavioral science would be."

The study of shamanism by behavioral and social scientists affords a unique opportunity to meet these goals. This opportunity has been bypassed for many decades, but the current interest in shamanism affords a chance for parapsychologists, with their unique training and perspective, to enlist anthropologists, psychologists, and other scientists to join the investigation.

References:

Bogoras, V. (1904 - 1909) The Chuckchee: The Jessup North Pacific Expedition New York: American Museum of Natural History.

Boshier, A. (1974) African apprenticeship In A. Angoff & D. Barth (Eds.) Parapsychology and Anthropology (273 - 284) New York: Parapsychology Foundation.

Carpenter, B. & Krippner, S. (1989) Spice island shaman: A Torajan healer in Sulawesi Shaman's Drum, Fall: 47 - 52.

Chari, C.T.K. (1960) Parapsychological studies and literature in India International Journal of Parapsychology 2:24 - 36.

Erdoes, R. (1972) Lame Deer, Seeker of Visions New York: Simon & Schuster.

Giesler, P.V. (1984) Parapsychological anthropology: Multi-method approaches to the study of psi in the field setting Journal of the American Society of Psychical Research, 78:289 - 330.

Giesler, P.V. (1986) GESP testing of shamanic cultists: Three studies and an evaluation of dramatic upsets during testing Journal of Parapsychology 50:123 - 153.

Halifax, J. (1979) Shamanic voices New York: E.P.Dutton.

Hallowell, A.I. (1971) The Role of Conjuring in Salteaux Society New York: Octagon Books.

Hyman, R. (1977) "Cold reading": How to convince strangers that you know all about them Skeptical Inquirer 2:18 - 37.

Irwin, H.J. (1999) An Introduction to Parapsychology (3rd edition) Jefferson NC: McFarland.

Jensen, A.E. (1963) Myth and Cult among Primitive People. Chicago: University of Chicago Press.

Kelly, E.F., & Locke, R.G. (1982) Pre - literate societies Parapsychology Review May - June: 1 - 7.

Laubscher, B. (1938) Sex, Custom and Psychopathology: A Study of South African Pagan Natives New York: McBride.

Malinowski, M. (1954) Magic, Science and Religion, and Other Essays Garden City NY: Anchor Books.

Murphy, J.M. (1964) Psychotherapeutic aspects of shamanism on St. Lawrence Island, Alaska. In A. Kiev (Ed.) Magic, Faith, and Healing (pp. 53 – 83). New York: Free Press.

Reichbart, R. (1978) Magic and psi: Some speculations on their relationship Journal of the American Society for Psychical Research 72:153 - 175.

Rose R. (1956) Living Magic: The Realities Underlying the Psychical Practices and Beliefs of Australian Aborigines Chicago: Rand McNally.

Rogo, D.S. (1987) Shamanism, ESP, and the paranormal In S. Nicholson (Ed.) Shamanism: An Expanded View of Reality 133 - 144 Wheaton IL: Theosophical Publishing House.

Saklani, A. (1988) Preliminary tests for psi - ability in shamans of Garhwal Himalaya Journal of the Society for Psychical Research 55:60 - 70.

Some', M.P. (1994) Of Water and the Spirit: Ritual, Magic, and Initiation in the Life of an African Shaman. New York: Tarcher / Putnam.

Turner, E. B. (1994). A visible spirit form in Zambia. In D.E. Young & J.-G. Goulet (Eds.), Being changes by cross-cultural encounters. (pp. 71-95). Peterborough, Ontario, CA: Broadview Press.

Parapsychology and Postmodern Psychology

Stanley Krippner

"The universe is not an idea of mine. It is my idea of the universe that is an idea of mine." (Pessoa, 1917/1971, p. 178)

What philosophers refer to as the "modern" worldview is responsible for impressive advances in technology, industry, and scientific discovery. However, it has not prevented (and may even have been partially responsible for) unprecedented fragmentation, nihilism, and devastation. As Morris Berman (1984) states: "Western life seems to be drifting toward increasing entropy, economic and technological chaos, ecological disaster, and ultimately, psychic dismemberment and disintegration" (p. 1).

However, the epoch of "modernity" is now being supplanted by the era of "postmodernity." Some psychologists (e.g., Gergen, 1994) see "postmodernism" as a welcome corrective to the excesses of "modernism," replacing its mechanistic and reductionistic assump-

Krippner, S. (2008). Parapsychology and postmodern psychology. In F.E. da Silva (Ed.), *Fourth Psi Meeting: Parapsychology and Psychology* (pp. 189-196). Curitiba, Brazil: Instituto Nacional de Pesquisas.

Photo: Stanley Krippner, 1971

tions and activities with those that are more organic and holistic in nature. Other writers (Held, 1995; Matthews, 1998), however, are alarmed at the nihilism and "anti-realism" that the "postmodern" movement has left in its wake.

Worldviews

This essay acknowledges that postmodernity has arrived—more quickly in some parts of the world and at some levels of society than others—and explores the implications of the postmodern condition for science in general and for psi research specifically. Prigogine and Stengers (1984) comment, "Today the balance is strongly shifting toward a revival of mysticism..., especially among cosmologists. It has even been suggested by certain physicists and popularizers of science that mysterious relationships exist between parapsychology and quantum physics" (p. 34).

In addition, this essay admittedly gives a "privileged" position to rational, scientific inquiry, especially as informed by the issues raised in an era of postmodernity. This scientific perspective probably is the best process to help humanity (in general) and psi research (in particular) avoid self-deception, as well as helping both making wise decisions, locally and globally. Scientific inquiry may produce data that are interpretive, situated, and specific (Sampson, 1978), but the information so yielded can still be of value if its context is appreciated and if such forms of inquiry as qualitative methods, participatory research, and case studies are honored rather than marginalized (e.g., Braude, 2007).

This essay also draws upon the psychological contributions of both social constructionists (e.g., Gergen, 1994) and cognitive constructionists (e.g., Mahoney, 1990). Critics of the concept of selfhood (e.g., Sampson, 1978) attack the type of individualism that ignores the collective aspects of human existence; however, there are unique sensibilities and capacities that people develop during the life span. The interplay between individual and society are responsible for learning, creativity, and human change (Martin & Sugerman, 1996, p. 315). Further, this interplay is evident when the data produced by parapsychologists is examined (e.g., Radin, 1997).

Parapsychology and Anomalous Reports

Parapsychology, perhaps because many of its leaders were trained as psychologists, has evidenced a strong tendency to model itself after experimental psychology. In this paradigm, the experimental approach is the method of choice and repeatability of experimental results is considered to be a primary aim (Broughton, 1991), although this proposition is not unanimous (e.g., White, 1990). Nevertheless, quantitative psi research is firmly enmeshed in the methods advocated by modern science. Even so, its implications--at least to some parapsychologists--diverge from the modern worldview and demonstrate an affinity to aspects of postmodernity (Krippner, 1995).

The book, *Foundations of Parapsychology* (Edge, Morris, Palmer, & Rush, 1986) concludes by suggesting that psi research may contribute to "a greater respect for the potentials of consciousness" (p. 377). This purview is berated by the psychologist James Alcock (1986) who refers to this line of thought as "the new millennialism," an attitude perhaps incited by "growing disillusionment with the ability of science and technology to alleviate human social problems and suffering" (p. 560). In this provocative statement, Alcock seems to agree with the postmodernists that the goals of the Enlightenment project have not been met.

An example of anomalies studied by psi researchers is the work my colleagues and I conducted at the Maimonides Medical Center in Brooklyn, New York (Ullman & Krippner, with Vaughan, 1989). These studies paired a volunteer subject with a "telepathic sender"; the pair interacted briefly, then separated and spent the night in distant rooms. An experimenter randomly selected an art print (from a collection or "pool") and gave it to the sender in an opaque sealed envelope, to be opened only when the sender was in the distant room. The experimenter awakened the subject when electroencephalographic monitoring equipment indicated he or she was dreaming and requested a dream report.

These reports were transcribed and sent to outside judges who, working independently, matched them against the pool of potential art prints from which the actual print had been randomly selected.

> All too often, mainstream science has ignored or misrepresented our research ... one "human and social value" of psi research has been the depathologizing of many people's unusual beliefs and experiences.

Statistical evaluation was based on the average of these matchings, as well as by self-judgings of the subjects following the conclusion of the experiment.

As far as we could determine, there was no way in which sensory cues or fraudulent subject/sender collaboration could have influenced the dream reports and statistical results, having had three magicians visit our laboratory and check our research. Our results showed an overall pattern of statistical significance supporting the telepathy hypothesis. We also conducted experiments, using a similar procedure, to explore precognitive dreams, again obtaining robust data.

Were these experiments of "human and social value"? Before our results were published, reports of telepathic or precognitive dreams were often pathologized, and were considered a symptom of mental illness (e.g., American Psychiatric Association, 1980).

Our studies, published in virtually every major psychiatric journal in the United States, played a significant role in countering this allegation. Although reports of anomalous dreams are still included as a symptom of schizophreniform conditions in the 1994 edition of the American Psychiatric Association's *Diagnostic and Statistical Manual*, these symptoms are properly contextualized and are not given the emphasis they received in earlier editions of the manual.

All too often, mainstream science has ignored or misrepresented our research (Child, 1985), but the case can be made that our data helped to deconstruct stereotypes about people with purported psi experiences. Indeed, another body of data argues against automatically linking anomalous experiences with psychopathology (Krippner & Winkler, 1996). Hence, one "human and social value" of psi research has been the depathologizing of many people's unusual beliefs and experiences.

Human Values in Inquiry

Postmodernists would agree that inquiry holds the potential of contributing to the quality of life, even though that "quality" is defined differently in various times and places. But some would go one step further: Toulmin (1982) notes that scientists need to set aside the "value-free" conception of *scientific objectivity as detachment* in favor of a "value-laden" concept of *scientific objectivity as justice*, finding ways of treating "other persons, objects, and processes of nature in a fair and equitable manner" (p. 107). Other postmodern writers, given their rejection of "universal truths," would deny that there is an objective code of morality and ethics that should prevail opting, instead, for studying the social context of an idea, the speaker's point of view, or the biased interests lying behind a proposed moral code.

In concordance with modern science, our research program at Maimonides can be construed to have been of "intrinsic human value" in that it suggests a "connectedness" among members of the human species, one that provides imagery that links people together at deep levels, and that supplies an agency that works against social fragmentation (Ullman, 1996, p. 257).

So-called "grass roots dream-appreciation groups" that work with dreams, including those with anomalous elements, hold that dreamers themselves can appreciate the significance of their dream reports without having to rely on the interpretive guidance of "experts" (Hillman, 1990, p. 19). But this questioning of the power of "experts" has a distinctly postmodern tenor, especially in a field where, not so long ago, psychotherapists' interpretations of their clients' dreams were only challenged by those renegades who were "in denial" or who had problems "relating to authority figures" despite Sigmund Freud's (1914/1975) insistence that his technique "imposes the task of interpretation upon the dreamer himself" (p. 96).

There are psi researchers who have presented possible applications of psi research to medicine, technology, military intelligence, business, and politics (e.g., Radin, 1997). To many psi researchers, "applied parapsychology" may be premature, but the fact remains that governmental intelligence agencies, corporate executives, respected physicians, and even a number of politicians have overtly or covertly consulted "remote viewers," mediums, healers, and seers for assistance and advice. This possibility of technological, strategic, and military applications once resulted in an unparalleled amount of funding for psi research by various branches of the U.S. government, especially at Stanford Research Institute, SRI International, and Science Applications International Corporation.

When some of the data were declassified, there were various opinions regarding the evidence for psi they yielded (e.g., Hyman, 1996; Utts, 1996). Nevertheless, the fact remains that the U.S. Central Intelligence Agency felt that the project was of sufficient potential value to invest millions of dollars in its operation for three decades.

Psychological science is continually constructed from the perspectives of different communities. Psi research, even at its most rigorous, is the most controversial aspect of the consciousness studies domain (Krippner, 1988). The fact that its serious full-time practitioners include, at most, only a few dozen workers (worldwide) with extremely limited funding sources, the harassment of parapsychologists seems out of proportion to their perceived threat.

But from a postmodern perspective, all research methods can be viewed as inherently political, and intertwined with issues of power and legitimacy. The most widely used research methods are permeated with a powerful group's assumptions about researchers, what is to be researched, and the relationship between them (Lather, 1990).

Psychological science and rational positivist thought are built upon the canon of refutability, but many postmodernists would deconstruct this principle in favor of what "pragmatic implications for society" a conclusion provides (Gergen, 1985, p. 273). Psi researchers, on the contrary, would point out that mainstream science has not been sufficiently empirical. For the psychologist William James (1902/1985), *radical empiricism*, "the act of respecting experience itself" (p. xxiv) encompassed every human activity, even the most controversial and idiosyncratic—telepathy, clairvoyance, precognition, etc., included.

Is Inquiry Always "Rational"?

Standard empiricism and the philosophy of knowledge adhere to rational standards of inquiry, but only within the context of justification. For the modern world, science has become a "privileged" way of acquiring knowledge; it is more likely to yield justified beliefs than any other approach (Schick, 1997). The modern philosophy of knowledge forces a sharp distinction between how a new discovery is made (which can be intuitive rather than rational-empirical) and how it is justified (which must be rational-empirical).

But the role of intuition and mysticism in disciplined inquiry is not discounted by postmodernists who, with a sense of irony, often place them at the same level as rational, positivist thought, even in the justification phase of knowledge. These postmodernists insist that each style or genre of inquiry operates according to local rules or conventions, and these conventions will largely determine the way we understand the putative objects of representation. Scientific writing, at times, may furnish no more accurate a picture of reality than fiction (Gergen & Kaye, 1992, p. 173). The philosopher Jean Baudrillard (in Poster, 1988) takes the position that insights from the aesthetic domain of imaginary representations can be applied to every claim of "truth" including those of modern science. In other words, aesthetic inquiry can supplement or even take priority over rational inquiry.

I have had several opportunities to observe departures from modern science's highly touted "rational standards of inquiry" firsthand in regard to inaccurate criticisms of the dream ESP experiments my colleagues and I conducted at Maimonides. For example, E.G. Romm (1977), a debunker of psi research, cited a study in which she alleged a "telepathic sender" had been installed in a room draped in white fabric and had ice cubes poured down his back. The alleged "dream receiver" reported "white" was judged to have made a "hit" by an independent panel. Yet, she observed, words such as "miserable", "wet", or "icy" would have been better hits.

In actuality, no telepathic sender had been involved. This had been a *precognition* experiment (Krippner, Ullman, & Honorton, 1971). The multi-sensory experience arranged for the research participant the next morning (by someone who had not heard his dream reports) involved placing him in a room in which all the furniture had been draped with white sheets, then surprising him by dropping two ice cubes down his back.

The research participant's exact words, from a dream reported *before* the multi-sensory experience took place, were: "I was just standing in a room, surrounded by white...Predominant colors were pale and ice blues and whites." His mention of "ice" fulfills Romm's request for a word such as "icy."

An additional example of a curious interpretation of our material is that taken by the psychologist C.E.M. Hansel (1980, pp. 246, 253) who states that "precautions were taken to exclude the possibility of information being transmitted by normal means, but the original precautions did not appear to be adequate." As an example, he cites one of our articles that states that the agent was encouraged to write down his or her associations.

Hansel *infers* that this encouragement came from an experimenter who "appears to have been with the agent when he opened his target envelope," and that this interaction could have become the source of sensory cues to the research participant during the post-sleep interview. After investigating this charge by reading the reports (published and unpublished) of the particular experiment in question, the psychologist Charles Akers (1984) concluded, "It is clear that the experimenter had no contact with the agent, after the agent had selected the target envelope. How then did the agent receive instructions for the night? (This was Hansel's question.) It turns out that the instructions were on a written form, enclosed in the envelope" (p. 129).

Several other examples of misrepresentation can be found in a psychology book written by Leonard Zusne and W. H. Jones (1982, pp. 260-261). First, it is implied that one of the experimenters had a chance to know the identity of the target. The author's state, "After the subject falls asleep, an art reproduction is selected from a large collection randomly, placed in an envelope, and given to the agent."

In fact, the target was already in the envelope at the time the session began, usually having been placed there by a person who was not present during the night. Second, it is noted that "three... judges rate their confidence that the dream content matches the target picture," implying that the judges knew the identity of the target while making their evaluations. In reality, a judge was presented with a dream transcript and a pool of potential targets and was asked to evaluate the degree of similarity between the transcript and each target in the pool.

These misrepresentations pale by comparison with Zusne and Jones' assertion that research participants were "primed prior to going to sleep" so that they could better incorporate the target material in their dreams. It was claimed that they were "primed" through the experimenter's "preparing the receiver through experiences that were related to the content of the picture to be telepathically transmitted during the night.

> These misrepresentations pale by comparison with Zusne and Jones' assertion that research participants were "primed prior to going to sleep" so that they could better incorporate the target material in their dreams.

Thus, when the picture was Van Gogh's Corridor of the St. Paul Hospital, which depicts a lonely figure in the hallways of a mental hospital, the receiver: (1) heard [Miklos Rosza's music for the film] *Spellbound* played on a phonograph; (2) heard the monitor laugh hysterically in the room; (3) was addressed as "Mr. Van Gogh" by the monitor; (4) was shown paintings done by mental patients; (5) was given a pill and a glass of water; and (6) was daubed with a piece of cotton dipped in acetone. The receiver was an English "sensitive," but it is obvious that no psychic sensitivity was required to figure out the general content of the picture and to produce an appropriate report, whether any dreams were actually seen or not" [pp. 260-261].

In actuality, this description is of another *precognitive* dream session. *Following* the research participant's night at Maimonides, an envelope containing a target picture, accompanied by a packet containing multi-sensory experiences, was randomly selected. The English "sensitive" in question was put through the series of experiences noted by an experimenter who had not overheard the "sensitive" reporting his dreams.

Among the dream reports that night were such statements as "I saw a large concrete building..., a patient escaping from upstairs....She had a white coat on, like a doctor's coat....Medical people..., white cups on a tray." When the "sensitive" was shown the Van Gogh painting, he exclaimed, "My God—that's my dream!" (Krippner, Ullman, & Honorton, 1971).

There is another important aspect of these experiments that the debunkers failed to report; not only did the dream reports of the "sensitive" match the multi-sensory experiences at statistically significant levels, but a replication study with the same "sensitive" produced data that attained an even higher level of significance (Krippner, Ullman, & Honorton, 1972).

What can be said about such gross misrepresentation of our experiments as those given by such otherwise competent professionals as Romm, Hansel, Zusne, and Jones? The psychologist J.V. Bradley (1984) reported similar misrepresentations of fact on a controversial statistical topic.

Another psychologist, L.J. Ravitz (1968) produced several instances where his work on electrodermal activity during hypnosis had been incorrectly described. Both authors hypothesized that unconscious bias had interfered with correct reporting.

The Modesty of Parapsychologists

Most parapsychologists "privilege" rational, scientific assessment, but many take a conservative position as to the "factual character" of psi phenomena. Douglas Stokes' (1986) appraisal is not unique among his colleagues in psi research: "A fair and objective examination of spontaneous case material raises at least a reasonable suspicion that psi phenomena exist. There are hints from the experimental literature that it may be possible to bring such phenomena under experimental control.

Because the reported effects are not as yet repeatable by the majority of investigators, it cannot be claimed that psi phenomena have been scientifically demonstrated to exist. It would however be premature to close the book on the issue; psi phenomena are worthy of further study" (p. 418). In *Foundations in Parapsychology*, the authors (Edge et al., 1986) frankly state, "The bottom line is that the apparent ESP demonstrated so far in controlled environments is simply not strong enough or reliable enough to *compel* acceptance of ESP as a fact of nature" (p. 182).

The modesty of parapsychologists in regard to their data, coupled with the facts that its serious full-time practitioners include, at most, only a few dozen workers worldwide, and that these investigators have extremely limited funding sources, the harassment of parapsychologists and the misrepresentation of their work seems out of proportion to their perceived threat. It also casts doubt upon modern science's claim to make a "rational assessment" of "ideas" and "facts."

I take the position that parapsychological data *per se* have not attained the potency to justify a paradigm shift. As many critics put it, extraordinary claims require extraordinary evidence. However, psi research is one of several data sources indicating that the modern worldview is incomplete at best and flawed at worst. For example, its data proffer a view of "mind" that depends upon connection with, rather than isolation from, other "minds" (Williams, 1997, p. 342).

At the same time, I would admit that postmodernism often devalues reason, repudiates all universals, and abandons the search for values. The gullibility of some postmodernists was exposed by a hoax in which a non-sensical essay by Alan Sokal (1996) was submitted to a journal specializing in postmodernist theorizing and was accepted (Pinsker, 1996)!

In addition, there is an inbuilt paradox with the postmodern position that the language used in systematic discourse relies on context and social constructions for its meaning and purpose. But postmodernists themselves use language, hence undermining their own utility in providing a potent critique. At its most salutary, however, postmodernism proposes strategies for preserving the very pluralism that monolithic social, political, and academic orders put at risk. Critics of postmodernism often underestimate the diversity of thinkers who operate under this label.

Parapsychology and a Postmodern Worldview

White (1993) has expressed the opinion that contemporary psi research, operating under a modernist paradigm, has not been able to achieve its mandate. From a postmodern perspective, there are several steps that psi research could take to redress this imbalance.

(1) Perhaps parapsychology could attain salience more rapidly if it attempted to forge alliances with some of the movements that are suggestive of an emerging paradigm. For example, many physicists do not see psi phenomena as inconsistent with quantum theory (e.g., Bohm 1980).

Holonomic theory suggests that psi phenomena simply reflect the presence (to some extent) of all information at all levels of reality (e.g., Pribram, 1986). General systems theory could subsume psi at one or more levels of a living system. In biological synergy and human ecology, psi may play an important role in mediating mind/body and organism/environment interactions. Moving into closer collaboration with these, and other, perspectives would increase the power necessary for psi research to be more influential, to become a formidable contender in the scientific scene.

(2) The role available to psi research is unique. Parapsychology has developed methods and techniques of investigating anomalous events that, by and large, are more sophisticated than those to be found in any other field. These

> ... psi research is one of several data sources indicating that the modern worldview is incomplete at best and flawed at worst.

approaches were derived from modern science but in combination with the forthcoming contributions of postmodern science could yield disciplined, rigorous means of research eminently suitable for the tasks ahead. Purported psi phenomena are not the only anomaly that need to be taken seriously, but parapsychologists could lend their expertise to researchers of near-death experiences, out-of-body experiences, alien abduction experiences, and a host of other reports that have been too long ignored.

(3) In the postmodern worldview, the conceptions and applications of psi might take on forms radically different than those that characterize it at the present time. This is not surprising because the current models of psi are the results of the modern worldview. Psi in the postmodern

age might be simpler, more elegant, and more parsimonious than can be imagined today. The current dichotomies between "brain" and "mind," between "body" and "psyche," and between "matter" and "spirit" may be resolved in favor of a systems-oriented interactionist model of consciousness. What today is considered "extra-sensory" may tomorrow be conceptualized as "super-sensory"; current conceptions of "psychokinesis" may be subsumed by discoveries of the organism's "biological fields" and their distant influences (e.g., Laszlo, 1996).

(4) Postmodern psi research can present a dual approach. On the one hand, laboratory work and controlled observations should continue, but with the recognition that this task reflects a complex interlocking of research participant, researcher, time, and place—any one of which can skew the results in a way that may underline "local truth" rather than "universal truth." At the same time, the investigation of "texts" of people's exceptional experiences can adhere to William James' (1907/1978) call for "methodological pluralism," using heuristic, hermeneutic, and phenomenological methods that may yield insights into psi phenomena that are more profound than anything captured in a laboratory.

> Parapsychology has developed methods and techniques of investigating anomalous events that, by and large, are more sophisticated than those to be found in any other field.

Other Voices

Modern psychology typically excludes what postmodernists refer to as "the other," including women and minority groups (Sampson, 1993), members of "other" cultures (Taussig, 1987), the natural environment (Roszak, 1992), and what the parapsychologist Rhea White (1991, 1997) refers to as "exceptional human experiences". These experiences of "other" genders (e.g., cross-dressing), lifestyles (e.g., gay and lesbian behavior), cultures (e.g., Native American ceremonies), and "realities" (e.g., "leaving the body," recalling a "past life," seeing a "nature spirit") have been dismissed, ignored, ridiculed, and pathologized by modern psychologists. Nevertheless, narratives of lucid dreams, shamanic journeying, sexual "merging", firewalking, peak sports performance, etc., demand attention and respect if the totality of human activity is to be appreciated.

Names are not designed to refer to substantial things or to independent entities that exist by themselves. They are determined rather by human interests and human purposes, but neither of these are fixed and invariable. Foucault (1980) points out that language is midway between nature and discourse, and that science needs to shift from paradigm to discourse. With these injunctions in mind, one recalls the claim that exceptional human experience can not be verbally communicated. This assertion has not been welcomed by modern psychology, but from a postmodern viewpoint it is reasonable, considering that language is conceptual and can be applied to nonconceptual experience only with great difficulty.

Postmodernity does not speak with a single voice on these topics. What might be called "constructive postmodernists" believe that the constant reexamining of one's beliefs, and learning about one's socially constructed reality are the most important learning tasks needed for survival at this time in history. Yes, there is an objective cosmos that humans can seek to understand, although all such attempts are to some extent subjective because no human endeavor can be purely objective (Anderson, 1990, pp. 269-270).

"Constructive postmodernism," exemplified by the writings of such philosophers as Hoyt Edge (1994) and David Griffin (1997), deconstruct longstanding "modernist" trends in parapsychology, but then reconstruct them into postmodern perspectives. Edge asserts that the glorification of reason, the determination to dominate nature, and the attempts to reduce knowledge to universal "laws" and "essences" have resulted in a worldview incapable of meeting contemporary challenges. Instead, Edge posits a metaphorical "cosmic web" that is intrinsically moving, dynamic, and challenging--and psi-friendly in its implications. Ryzl (2007) has described these connections as a "voyage to the rainbow," a worldview that easily encompasses science, philosophy, art, and religion.

Griffin subscribes to Albert North Whitehead's proposal that each event is a product of its whole past world, with its allowance for "action at a distance" as a psi-friendly philosophical framework. Whitehead's paradigm contrasts with the two forces Griffin identifies as dominant in Western cultures: (1) conservative and fundamentalist religion (which some would say is premodern), and (2) reductionist materialism. Ferre' (1994) also has found Whitehead's philosophy to provide an alternative worldview in which parapsychology may play a constructive role.

Perhaps because of its mercurial nature, metaphors abound in psi research (Williams, 1996, 1997); psi has been described as an "elusive quarry" (Hyman, 1989) which rests at the "margins of reality" (Jahn & Dunne, 1987), often in vain. In 1975, I used the metaphor of a siren's song to describe the lure of psi research (Krippner, 1975), describing parapsychologists as the "outcasts of science" (p. 290), i.e., what postmodernists would call "the other."

I observed that instead of fame, fortune, promotions, awards, and honorary degrees, parapsychologists typically find themselves involved in controversy, debts, job insecurity, and the admonition that they are wasting their time studying ESP and PK. The parapsychologist George Hansen (Hansen, 2001) has observed that parapsychologists' marriages frequently dissolve, parapsychologists' laboratories often close, and parapsychologists' professional reputations are repeatedly impaired.

In other words, psi research itself may be inherently deconstructive (Hansen, 2001). Well-meaning friends tell psi researchers that there are pressing world problems to which they should be devoting their efforts. Instead, they follow the song of the siren, their relationships and careers often ending up a broken pile of broken debris on the rocks and shoals of their hapless odyssey. An antidote for the Scylla of ESP and the Charybdis of PK is to enter psi research with a sense of play, entertaining different views and perspectives while maintaining one's balance (Edge, 1994; Williams, 1997).

Toulmin (1982) writes that "postmodern science puts us in a position to reverse the cosmological destruction wrought by modern science, from A.D. 1600 on. The world view of contemporary, postmodern science is one in which practical and theoretical issues, contemplation and action, can no longer be separated; and it is one that gives us back the very unity order and sense of proportion...that the philosophers of antiquity insisted on" (p. 264). This reunification of the worlds of humanity and nature is not a task for psi research alone, but parapsychology has a unique opportunity to play a vital role in this mission.

References

Barber, T.X. (1999). A comprehensive three-dimen

Akers, C. (1984). Methodological criticisms of parapsychology. In S. Krippner (Ed.), *Advances in parapsychological research*, (Vol. 4, pp. 112-164). Jefferson, NC: McFarland Publishers.

Alcock, J. (1986). Parapsychology as a "spiritual science." In P. Kurtz (Ed.), *A skeptic's handbook of parapsychology* (pp. 537-565). Buffalo, NY: Prometheus.

American Psychiatric Association. (1980). *Diagnostic and statistical manual on mental disorders* (3rd ed.). Washington, DC: Author.

American Psychiatric Association. (1994). *Diagnostic and statistical manual on mental disorders* (4th ed.). Washington, DC: Author.

Anderson, W.T. (1990). *Reality isn't what it used to be*. San Francisco: Harper and Row.

Berman, M. (1984). *The reenchantment of the world*. New York: Bantam.

Bohm, D. (1980). *Wholeness and the implicate order*. London: Routledge and Kegan Paul.

Bradley, J.V. (1984). Antinonrobustness: A case study in the sociology of science. *Bulletin of the Psychonomic Society, 22*, 463-466.

Braud, S. (2007). *The gold leaf lady and other parapsychological investigations*. Chicago: University of Chicago Press.

Broughton, R. (1991). *Parapsychology: The controversial science*. New York: Ballantine.

Child, I.L. (1985). Psychology and anomalous observations: The question of ESP in dreams. *American Psychologist, 40*, 1219-1230.

Edge, H.L. (1994). *A constructive postmodern perspective on self and community*. Lampeter, Wales: Edwin Mellen Press.

Edge, H.L., Morris, R.L., Palmer, J., & Rush, J.H. (1986). *Foundations of parapsychology: Exploring the boundaries of human capacity*. Boston: Routledge & Kegan Paul.

Foucault, M. (1980). *Power/knowledge: Selected interviews and other writings, 1972-1977* (C. Gordon, Ed. & Trans.). New York: Pantheon.

Freud, S. (1975). *The interpretation of dreams* (rev. ed.) (J. Strachey, Ed. & Trans.). London: Hogarth. (Original work published 1914)

Gergen, K.J. (1985). The social constructionist movement in modern psychology. *American Psychologist, 40*, 266-275.

Gergen, K.J. (1994). *Toward transformation in social knowledge* (2nd ed.). Thousand Oaks, CA: Sage.

Gergen, K.J., & Kaye, J. (1992). Beyond narrative in the negotiation of therapeutic meaning. In S. McNamee & K.J. Gergen (Eds.), *Therapy as social construction* (pp. 166-185). Newbury Park, CA: Sage.

Griffin, D.R. (1997). *Parapsychology, philosophy, and spirituality: A postmodern exploration*. Albany: State University of New York Press.

Hansel, C.E.M. (1980). *ESP and parapsychology: A critical re-evaluation*. Buffalo, NY: Prometheus Books.

Hansen, G. (2001). *The trickster and the paranormal*. New York: Xlibris.

Held, B.S. (1995). *Back to reality: A critique of postmodern theory in psychotherapy*. New York: W.W. Norton.

Hillman, D.J. (1990). The emergence of the grassroots dream movement. In S. Krippner (Ed.), *Dreamtime and dreamwork: Decoding the language of the night* (pp. 13-20). Los Angeles: Tarcher.

Hyman, R. (1989). *The elusive quarry: A scientific appraisal of psychical research*. Buffalo, NY: Prometheus Books.

Hyman, R. (1996). Evaluation of a program on anomalous mental functioning. *Journal for Scientific Exploration, 10*, 31-58.

Jahn, R.G., & Dunne, B.J. (1987). *Margins of reality: The role of consciousness in the physical world*. New York: Harcourt Brace Jovanovich.

James, W. (1978). *Pragmatism: A new name for some old ways of thinking*. Cambridge, MA: Harvard University Press. (Original work published 1907)

James, W. (1985). *The varieties of religious experience: A study in human nature*. New York: Penguin Books. (Original work published 1902)

Krippner, S. (1975). *Song of the siren*. New York: Harper and Row.

Krippner, S. (1988). Parapsychology and postmodern science. In D.R. Griffin (Ed.), *The reenchantment of science: Postmodern proposals* (pp. 129-140). Albany: State University of New York Press.

Krippner, S., & Winkler, M. (1996). The "need to believe." In G. Stein (Ed.), *The encyclopedia of the paranormal* (pp. 441-454). Amherst, NY: Prometheus Books.

Krippner, S., Ullman, M., & Honorton, C. (1971). A precognitive dream study with a single subject. *Journal of the American Society for Psychical Research, 65*, 192-203.

Krippner, S., Ullman, M., & Honorton, C. (1972). A second precognitive dream study with Malcolm Bessent. *Journal of the American Society for Psychical Research, 66*, 269-279.

Laszlo, E. (1996). *The whispering pond*. London: Element Books.

Lather, P. (1990). Postmodernism and the human sciences. *The Humanistic Psychologist, 18*, 64-84.

Mahoney, M. (1990). *Human change processes*. New York: Basic Books.

Martin, J., & Sugarman, J. (1996). Bridging social constructionism and cognitive constructivism: A psychology of human possibility and constraint. *Journal of Mind and Behavior, 17*, 291-319.

Matthews, W.J. (1998). Let's get real: The fallacy of post-modernism. *Journal of Theoretical and Philosophical Psychology, 18*, 16-32.

Pessoa, F. (1971). *Selecao poetica*. Rio de Janeiro: Jose Aguilar Editora. (original work written 1917)

Pinsker, S. (1996, June 24). Hoax unveils the arrogance of academia. *Insight*, p. 30.

Poster, M. (Ed.). (1988). *Jean Baudrillard: Selected writings*. Cambridge, MA: Polity Press.

Pribram, K.H. (1986). Behaviorism, phenomenology and holism in psychology: A scientific analysis. *Journal of Social and Biological Structure, 2*, 65-72.

Prigogine, I., & Stengers. (1984). *Order out of chaos: Man's new dialogue with nature*. New York: Bantam.

Radin, D.I. (1997). *The conscious universe: The scientific truth of psychic phenomena*. San Francisco: HarperSanFrancisco.

Ravitz, L.J. (1968). The danger of scientific prejudice. *American Journal of Clinical Hypnosis, 10*, 282-3O3.

Romm, E.G. (1977). When you give a closet occultist a Ph.D., what kind of research can you expect? *The Humanist, 37*(3), 12-15.

Roszak, T. (1992). *The voice of the earth*. New York: Simon & Schuster.

Ryzl, M. (2007). *Voyage to the rainbow*. Victoria, BC: Trafford.

Sampson, E.E. (1993). *Celebrating the other: A dialogic account of human nature*. Boulder, CO: Westview Press.

Schick, T., Jr. (1997, March/April). The end of science? *Skeptical Inquirer*, pp. 36-39.

Sokal, A. (1996). Transgressing the boundaries: Toward a transformative hermeneutics of quantum gravity. *Social Text, 217*, 46-47.

Stokes, D. (1986). Parapsychology and its critics. In P. Kurtz (Ed.), *A skeptic's handbook of parapsychology* (pp. 379-423). Buffalo, NY: Prometheus Books.

Taussig, M. (1987). *Shamanism, colonialism, and the wild man: A study in terror and healing*. Chicago: University of Chicago Press.

Toulmin, S. (1982). The emergence of post-modern science. In M.J. Adler (Ed.), *The great ideas today, 1981* (pp. 68-114). Chicago: Encyclopedia Britannica.

Ullman, M. (1996). *Appreciating dreams: A group approach*. Thousand Oaks, CA: Sage.

Ullman, M., & Krippner, S., with Vaughan, A. (1989). *Dream telepathy: Experiments in nocturnal ESP* (2nd ed.). Jefferson, NC: McFarland.

Utts, J. (1996). As assessment of the evidence for psychic functioning. *Journal of Scientific Exploration, 10*, 3-30.

White, R.A. (1990). An experience-centered approach to parapsychology. *Exceptional Human Experience, 8*, 7-36.

White, R.A. (1991). Feminist science, postmodern views, and exceptional human experience. *Exceptional Human Experience, 9*, 2-10.

White, R.A. (1993). Parapsychology and transpersonal psychology. *Exceptional Human Experience, 11*, 2-14.

Williams, C. (1996). Metaphor, parapsychology and psi: An examination of metaphors related to paranormal research. *Journal of the American Society for Psychical Research, 90*, 174-201.

Williams, C. (1997). Hoyt Edge's "postmodern perspective" and its application to parapsychology. *Journal of the American Society for Psychical Research, 91*, 333-346.

Zusne, L., & Jones, W.H. (1982). *Anomalistic psychology: A study of extraordinary phenomena of behavior and experience*. Hillsdale, NJ: Erlbaum.

How "Healing" Happens

Stanley Krippner

Science aims not merely to classify and describe phenomena but also to explain and predict them. Thus science organizes its phenomena in such a way that it will assist explanation of past events and prediction of future events. However, phenomena in the psychological world change more quickly than phenomena in the physical world, thus they are not as amenable to prediction and control. This is one factor which has prevented many scientists from adopting a psychophysiological model of reality. One can imagine the resistance that will be met if a psychic dimension is proposed; even those investigators who accept the reality of psi processes admit their unpredictability and rapid rate of fluctuation.

A number of directions could be taken by workers in parapsychology who are eager to see the psychic model of reality accepted and integrated with psychophysiology. Some researchers have proposed bold ideas that, if accepted, would unite the psychic and the psychophysiological, leading to the "paradigm shift" that Thomas Kuhn wrote about in his book on scientific revolutions.

Adapted from **Krippner, S., & Villoldo, A.** (1976). *The realms of healing.* Celestial Arts.

Photo: Stuart Fischer

Inyushin's "biological plasma" —the proposed new state of matter—would be an example of a new paradigm. Another would be Andrade's "biological organizing model." Other writers are more cautious, saying we are not yet ready for this step.

In the Journal of Parapsychology, R. H. Thouless has commented:

> It would .... be a misunderstanding ... of Kuhn's ideas to infer that our task now is to think out a new paradigm. It is not thus that scientific revolutions have taken place in the past. The call is rather to more detailed and more precise research.

As we know more about the psi phenomena and as our knowledge becomes more exact, the shape of the future paradigm will gradually become clear.

And in an article in the *Journal of the American Society for Psychical Research*, J. G. Pratt noted that "No theory has yet been adequately confirmed in the field because of its logical consistency and strength." Pratt argues for further research that will ultimately provide material for a paradigm constructed by "the future Einstein of parapsychology."

While some parapsychologists continue to search for a "repeatable experiment" that would lead to prediction and control of psi, others say this is only necessary *after* the need for a new paradigm is obvious. Charles T. Tart has reflected, "Replication is more important in a science when it is in a paradigmatic stage. At the present level in parapsychology, we might just as well stumble along hoping we'll run into something with a greater yield."

Those who have begun to speculate on how psi processes would interface with psychophysiology typically turn their attention to human consciousness. In so doing, their efforts run counter to those scientists who object to using the term "consciousness" because it cannot easily be measured or defined in terms of external activity or behavior. This extreme position has been ridiculed by Irving L. Child in his book *Humanistic Psychology and the Research Tradition*:

> ... The purist might have wished to dispense with the concept of a star, since at most only the radiant energy reaching the earth could be known—and for most stars only the marks produced on a photographic plate through lengthy exposure to very weak energy.

The eminent philosopher Karl Popper has met this problem head on by speaking of three worlds." One "world" represents the total of all matter and energy in the cosmos, the second "world" represents the total of all consciousness, and Popper's third "world" represents humanity's models, ideas, concepts, and theories about matter, energy, and consciousness. It is one of the tasks of the third "world" to propose how the first two interact. At least three points of view have been proposed by those who have studied this issue:

1. Consciousness is a property of the brain and other forms of matter, just as hardness is a property of metal and warmth is a property of fire. Without matter there can be no such thing as consciousness.

2. Consciousness and matter are separate. Sometimes their functions overlap, but it is quite easy for them to exist independently of each other. Thus it is possible for "spirits" to exist without a physical body.

3. Consciousness and matter can exist separately but typically they interact. For science to study consciousness properly, this interaction must be understood.

While in Copenhagen, one of the authors (A. V.) had the opportunity to discuss with the Danish physicist R. D. Mattuck the quantum mechanical theories of Evan Harris Walker, a noted physicist and mathematician. Dr. Walker has presented a concept of consciousness which many people believe allows it to be studied from an interactionist point of view. Quantum theory lies at the foundation of modern physics. Quite in distinction from the older, classical physics based on the laws of motion set down by Isaac Newton, quantum theory, is based on two totally distinct equations.

The first equation describes not only what is going to happen but all the infinity of events that can happen, all the events that are possible in literally any situation. But that first equation does not tell what *will* happen. Of course, when one checks up, or observes, what is going on, one will always find that one event is happening. The other possibilities, then, did not occur.

> In quantum theory, the question is whether the tree has fallen or if it is still standing. Both are possible. Thus the first equation of quantum theory says something that seems like nonsense: the tree is standing and the tree has fallen.

The second equation simply makes formal this statement that when an investigator looks, that person finds that only one event happened. In addition, the second equation outlines a procedure for determining the likelihood that one possibility will occur rather than another possibility.

This concept may be difficult for a person to conceive at first because most events occur on an atomic level. In addition, Western culture is accustomed to very simple notions of cause and effect. The idea of cause and effect tells us that a given cause leads to a result, a single effect. If one drops a ball, it falls. If one hits a baseball in a particular way, it flies away in a given direction. All understanding of physics before the turn of the century was based on this concept. But the new physics—quantum mechanics—points out that this picture is too simple.

This new picture can be illustrated by a common, if artificial, example—the example of a dead tree that falls far from anyone who can see or hear it. People used to ask the question that if no one heard the tree fall, was there any sound. But this is merely a semantic question. In quantum theory, the question is whether the tree has fallen or if it is still standing. Both are possible. Thus the first equation of quantum theory says something that seems like nonsense: the tree is standing *and* the tree has fallen. The second equation states that if investigators go and look they will only observe one of these two possibilities—and that possibility will become the reality.

The statement that both conditions exist is not just due to a lack of knowledge as to whether or not the tree has fallen. This is one of the remarkable aspects of quantum theory. There are many experiments that can be carried out to show that both must really be considered to have a kind of partial reality, a potentiality. There are cases that can be tested in which the possibility of the existence of one case actually affects the character of the other case. These instances exist in almost every problem studied in quantum mechanics.

The first of these two basic equations of physics is called the "Schrodinger equation."[1] It is actually deterministic and describes the—objective—world, but as an overview of all the possible things that can happen. The second equation that formalizes and embodies the so—called "Copenhagen interpretation" is not deterministic but probabilistic. It describes what happens when we observe the physical world and thus incorporates processes that are more than simply part of the objective world. This process is probabilistic. The equation does not say what will be observed but simply that only one event will be observed. What happens appears to be kind of a game of chance!

Such unreliable behavior in nature was found abhorrent by many of the great physicists. Albert Einstein, for example, insisted that God did not play dice with the universe. One thing happened—the tree fell or it did not fall, whether anyone knew it or not. This discontent in physics arose from a desire on the part of physicists to return to an earlier day of certainty—the certainty of classical physics, the cause and effect of Newtonian mechanics. But in that earlier mechanics, there was no place for the concept of consciousness, and no conception of the human being as other than a mechanism just like any other mechanism.

The discontent with quantum theory gave rise in the 1950s to the proposal by David Bohm of "hidden variables." Bohm originally thought these "hidden variables" were some subatomic machinery that would soon be discovered to show that cause and effect held ironclad even on the atomic level. It has now come to be realized that these variables must go undetected escaping observation in any ordinary experiment. These variables, which were discussed by such innovative theorists in physics as Werner Heisenberg, link the deterministic and indeterministic worlds together but in a way quite unsuspected until recently.

Heisenberg formulated the "uncertainty principle" in which he demonstrated that if the position of a particle (such as an electron) was very precisely known,

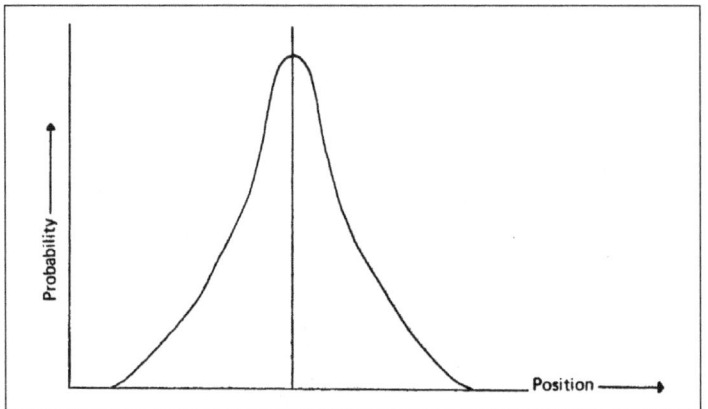

Probability distribution for the position of the particle (wave-packet).

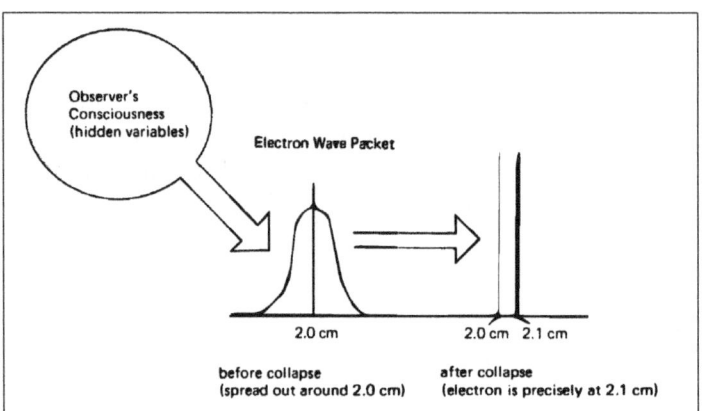

Interaction between the consciousness of the observer and the electron determine the exact location of the particle through collapse of the electron wave packet.

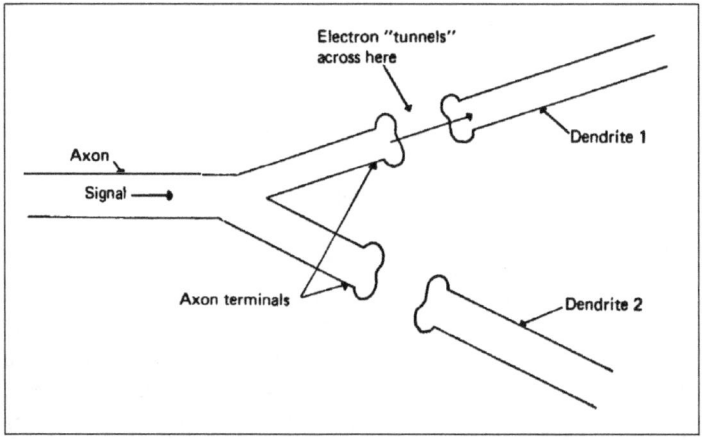

Diagram of "healer" interacting with healee causing "healer" to rise to a higher degree of order.

an observer could know its velocity only very imprecisely. On the other hand, if the observer had a very precise knowledge of the particle's velocity, its position would become very imprecise. In other words, one of the variables would always remain "uncertain."

Because there is this "uncertainty" or "fuzziness" about a particle's position and velocity, when a particle of known velocity is drawn, it can only be depicted as being more or less near a particular place. That is, one can only specify the *probability* of the particle being at a particular position. This "fuzzy" picture of the particle is referred to as a "wave packet." For example, one can only say that it is most probable that the particle is at a position of 2.0 centimeter (cm.)—but it could also be at 1.9 or 2.2 cm. (In reality, of course, the position of subatomic particles would be even smaller—one ten-millionth of a centimeter or less.)

Imagine that someone measures the position of a particle and finds that the first measurement yields 2.1 cm. Yet the next time it is measured, with all other factors remaining the same, one finds it is at 1.9 cm., and the third time at 2.0 cm. This fact that the "fuzzy" particle acquires a *precise* position in each *individual* measurement is called the "collapse of the wave packet."

There is a tendency when first encountering these facts about the fuzzy nature of position to ascribe this imprecision simply to errors that occur in measuring the particle's position. Heisenberg's uncertainty relations do derive from simply calculating the magnitude of errors produced as an effect during measurement. But if this were all there was to it, quantum mechanics would be reduced to just a few rules on accuracy in physical calculations.

It is not that way, however. The Heisenberg formulations describe not a limit on our knowledge as much as a limit on the reality of position as something exact. The idea that a body is located in one place at a given time moving with an exact speed is false. The position of a body and its motion must be represented in a much more complex fashion.

Feeling that there must be some undetected influence acting upon this particle which would cause its position to differ from one measurement to the next, a few physicists have elaborated on the notion of "hidden variables." In other words, the particle, aside from having the qualities of position and velocity, would have something else accompanying it—a "hidden variable." This cannot be detected directly, but the effects of it can be measured. When the particle is measured to be located at 2.0 cm., it is because there is a "hidden variable" associated with the particle which caused the wave packet to "collapse" at 2.0 cm.

If the experiment is conducted again, and a measurement of 2.1 is obtained, it is because the "hidden variable" had another value associated with it on that occasion. So while the effect of these "hidden variables" can be observed, the "variables" themselves have yet to be identified.

Perhaps, thought Walker, "hidden variables" are the mechanisms through which consciousness interacts with the particles in the physical world. Walker went on to describe consciousness in terms of "hidden variables" which can have different values, and which determine the exact position of a particle at any moment of time.

The interactions between the consciousness of the observer and the physical world, by means of the "hidden variables," do not occur in the form of a force or energy field, but through what might be called an "information field." The "hidden variables" supply information to the systems, so that the "collapse" of the electron wave packet occurs at a specific point in space. Then, to move the electron to the right—for example—by PK, one causes the wave packet to "collapse" to the right of its original position. In other words, it produces an ordering of the brain's information processing, selecting one stream of consciousness from the myriad of possibilities permitted for quantum mechanical processes in the brain.

The situation is similar to that of expecting a visit from a friend on either Sunday, Monday, or Tuesday; the probability of the friend's coming is 0.33 for each of those days. But when the friend telephones and pinpoints Tuesday as the day of arrival, the probability distribution is suddenly narrowed to 1.0 for Tuesday and 0.0 for Sunday and Monday. The probability distribution—or wave packet—of the friend's arrival has "collapsed" to the value of Tuesday.

Or other friends could announce their arrival on Tuesday at either the bus station, railroad station, or airport. When

> In other words, the particle, aside from having the qualities of position and velocity, would have something else accompanying it—a "hidden variable."

they call again and say they are flying in, the probability distribution has "collapsed" to the value of the airport. In one instance the "collapse" is in time, in the other it is in space. In both, the wave packet "collapses" to a specific point as new information is supplied.

Walker's first application of this theory was in constructing a quantum mechanical model of the brain. He attempted to explain how electrical impulses in the form of electrons which would otherwise move in a largely random fashion in the brain, were made to move coherently from one nerve cell to another along a particular brain pathway. The process by which an electron moves from one nerve cell to another was referred to as "quantum mechanical tunnelling" by Walker.

The act of standing up, for example, would involve transmitting the information "I want to stand up" by means of "hidden variables" to cause the electron wave packets to "collapse" at precise points so that the electrical nerve impulses would travel along the correct "pathway" in the brain. Eventually, appropriate information is received by the motor center corresponding to the muscles used in standing up.

The brain contains billions of nerve cells, each having a transmitting fiber, or axon, and at least one receiving fiber or dendrite. The "hidden variables," acting in the form of an "information field," have to regulate the exact timing of the "collapse" of electron wave packets, so that the nerve signal that is leaving one axon makes the "jump" to the correct dendrite in its prescribed pathway.

As the nerve impulse "tunnels" in this way, its "pathway" is prescribed by consciousness. Walker has estimated that if only chance were operating in the path and a nerve impulse were to go through ten nerve cells, the odds that a person could—for example—pick up a pencil would be nearly one out of ten million. Something is operating in "tunnelling" and the "hidden variables" appear to be consciousness.

In this way, Walker accounts for information "directed outward" from the brain in such acts as picking up a pencil or standing upright. However, consciousness also processes information entering the brain. Thus, the "hidden variables" must also adjust themselves to the positions of electrons in the brain. When we "see" the image of a tree several feet high, the "hidden variables" adjust themselves to the pattern of electron movements in the brain which "correspond" to the image of the tree. Thus consciousness is continuously aware of "information fields" and electron movements in the brain.

Walker has described consciousness in terms of its information content. He has estimated the rate at which information is processed by what he has called the "will" function of the brain—as when people "will" to stand up, choose one piece of food over another, etc. Walker has estimated that the "will" can supply information to the brain at the rate of 10^4 "bits" per second,[2] a "bit" being a measure of information equal to one unit of data, one "yes-or-no" choice. This would suggest that consciousness can be associated with an output of 10^4 "bits" of data per second, "tunnelling" through the proper collapse of wave packets in the brain.

In addition, the brain is constantly being bombarded with information from the external world, as well as from the organism itself. Visual impressions, sounds, and other external sensory data as well as metabolism, respiration, and other internal functions flood the brain. This input material is processed by the brain's unconscious computer-like functions, according to Walker, at a rate of approximately 10^8 "bits" of information per second. He refers to this as the total "conscious data rate." Walker estimates the "unconscious data rate" as 10^{12} "bits" per second.

Ordinarily, the data rate of the "will" is smaller than the total "conscious data rate." However, according to Walker, under certain conditions—such as altered states of consciousness—this rate can increase 10,000 times to the total "conscious data rate" of 10^8 "bits" per second. In this case, one's total conscious activity would involve the faculty of "will."

If Walker's theory is correct, a PK process occurs constantly in the brain. Consciousness influences the physical through the brain. Consciousness moves an electron from one nerve cell to another via the continuous flow of information contained by the "hidden variables" which "determine the collapse" of the electron wave packets.

If PK can affect one electron, why can it not affect several electrons? If it can affect electrons inside the brain why can it not affect electrons outside the brain? Quantum physicists claim to have demonstrated that "hidden variables" have a property referred to as "non-locality"; they have no fixed position in space or in time. They coordinate events through-

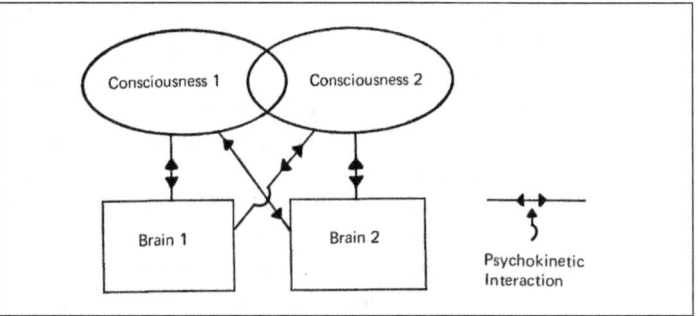

Diagram of consciousness interacting with its own and with another brain. (Note that because of non-locality, consciousnesses must overlap each other to some extent.)

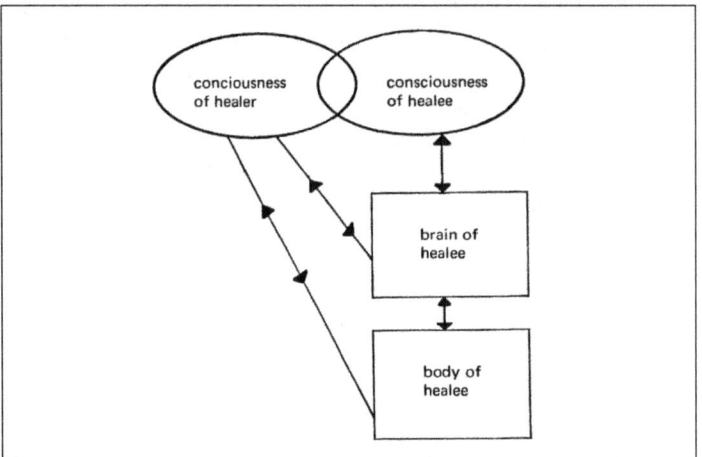

Diagram of "healer" interacting with healee causing "healer" to rise to a higher degree of order.

out space and time regardless of where these events are to be found or when they occur. If this is so, consciousness, as Walker sees it, would have the quality of being non-local in space and time yet to be connected to the events in one brain; the consciousness of others, and to the events influencing other people. For this reason; consciousness may well extend beyond the limits of the body and the brain, although it is only in certain instances and with certain people that PK on a noticeable scale is easily observed.

For example, Walker has calculated that Nina Kulagina's[3] reported ability to psychokinetically move a small object across a table would require 10^4 "bits" of information per second—a feat within the range of what is possible by the "will." Walker has further conjectured that the distance an object can be moved by PK is not as dependent on the object's weight as it is on the degree that the subject can focus his or her "will."

It should be recalled that many "psy-

chic healers" operate in altered states of consciousness, temporarily inactivating their ordinary personality roles. Many of them claim to be turning their own "wills" over to a "will" higher than their own—to El Hermanito or Saint Michael or the Old Black Ones. The "healers" then become "vehicles" for a benevolent "spirit" who purportedly works through them to "heal" afflicted persons.

If Walker is right, it would be possible, in certain altered states of consciousness, for a "healer" to employ the full "conscious data rate" of 10^8 "bits" of information per second. If a rate of 10^4 could move a small object across a table, what act of "healing" could not be carried out by a rate of 10^8?

Even the form of "psychic surgery" which purportedly involves "pulling apart" and "rejoining" skin and tissue would be theoretically possible. It would, of course, be infinitely complicated to alter molecular bonds and, later, restructure them. There would have to be a successive "collapse" of wave packets by the billions in the skin and tissue.

Complicated though this may seem, there are analogs for it. When a person "sees" a tree or an animal or a building, considerable "tunnelling" is going on. In "psychic photography," an image is purportedly produced on photographic film through PK if legitimate, this effect represents an effect in the same order of complexity as "psychic surgery."

What of the other types of purported "psychic surgery"—the alteration of the "bioplasmic body" of a healee, the "teleportation" of distant objects to the healee's skin, the "materialization" of objects from free-floating atoms in the cosmos? Human "will," according to Walker's theory, may be able to account for all of these phenomena, but by using explanations which, are quite amenable to investigation.

In an interview and exchange of letters with one of the authors (A. V.), Dr. Walker discussed the implications of his theory for people investigating "psychic healing":

> There is the important question of how the consciousness knows how to rearrange the atoms, etc., to achieve "healing." The answer to this question is so simple that it is hard to understand. It is simply that the consciousness does not need to know the "path" from the sick condition to the healthy condition. All that is required is that (1) there exists an allowed or possible "path" from the sick to the healthy condition no matter how improbable—including the possibility that the atoms suddenly "tunnel" to the proper positions; (2) that the consciousness can recognize the healthy (and of course the sick) condition so that the proper state, if allowed by quantum mechanics, can be selected, and (3) that the psychic's channel capacity (which I have designated $W\Psi$) be sufficiently high so that the selection of the desired state can be carried out—in other words, that the state can be found. [/Indent]

The difficulty many people have in understanding this process is that one is too accustomed to the customary mode of thought in which the observer stands outside the physical process looking in—describing the "path" from one state, some initial condition, to a subsequent state. But the consciousness (including the "will") is the mechanism that selects states! And in this *action* on the physical system of selecting from the quantum mechanically allowed states, there is a "reaction" (to borrow Isaac Newton's term) which is the conscious experience in which state selection is felt.

Although most of one's conscious experience is tied to the present state of one's brain at any instant, the $W\Psi$ (psychic's capacity) channel is the link with the overall quantum mechanical system that extends beyond the body and beyond the present moment. We usually do not realize this because the $W\Psi$ channel is so much less in magnitude than the consciousness data rate.

But because the $W\Psi$ channel transcends time and space, it is intimately tied to the future state to be selected. Thus the psychic *feels*, at the moment he attempts to "heal," the "healed condition" as though he were there in the future to see it—and to some extent he is. There is really no paradox here nor much real difficulty in understanding how this happens. The consciousness simply selects the appropriate state. The unwanted states are stuffed off as dead skin that does not feel good.

The reason all this appears as a paradox comes from the development of scientific thought. In Newton's day this explanation would have seemed simpler than the explanation that Newton gave. Newton did not explain "why" but described "how." Indeed, "why" has no meaning when applied to the inanimate. The physicist does not explain "why" one magnet attracts another, but describes the fundamental properties of matter that give properties of matter that give rise to the phenomenon. But such a description of "free will" in terms of mechanics would equally be an inappropriate mode of explanation, for there is no outside machinery that dictates the selection of the "will."

This is easier to understand for simpler selected states of consciousness. Suppose you want to call the toss of a coin. If your call is correct, you will be very happy. The toss is made and while the coin is in the air a small part of your consciousness is already linked to the experience of the fall of the coin and the choice of your call being heads. If that channel were perfect, your feeling now would tie in the correct call linking together the call of heads with the fall of heads. But only one part in ten thousand of your consciousness is linked. The feelings will be mixed, your choice will come from some clue in the present and your call will probably be by chance. However, the psychic has simply learned to feel more precisely.

The importance of understanding these processes is practical as well as theoretical. Recently, I was visited by a 41-year-old man who underwent brain surgery as an adolescent. The operation was performed because he had had three epileptic attacks. To cure this minor dysfunction, the man was robbed of nearly half the capacity of his brain. Here we see all the absurd gall of a plumber working on a computer with a fire ax. Many surgeons, psychologists, and psychiatrists with no knowledge whatever of what the mind is have become the pillars of our medical world.

In contrast, the "psychic healer" does not always succeed, but does begin by asking "Is the plug in? Is the power on?" Walker's theory is not accepted by all physicists or parapsychologists. When he presented it at the Twenty-Third International Conference of the Parapsychology Foundation, some of the participants referred to it as "nonsense." Even many of those who are impressed with Walker's theory would feel that it cannot be extended to explain some of the incredible stories involved in "psychic healing." For example, how could a "healer" diagnose an illness without knowing a great deal about anatomy and physiology? However, this information is present at some level, such as in an altered state of consciousness where a data rate of 10^8 is possible.

Perhaps the "healer" in an altered state focuses on his or her knowledge of one's own molecular structure, projects this onto the healee, and compares it with the more familiar data of one's own anatomy and physiology, until the disease is diagnosed. If the "will" can diagnose, the "will" could also "heal. " It is only one step from understanding the healee's psychological and physiological states to being able to alter them—or to influence the "will" of a healee so that "self—healing can take place

Many psychotherapists emphasize the "will" as well, most notably the practitioners of psychosynthesis. Roberto Assagioli, the founder of psychosynthesis, wrote, in *Act of Will*, that psychotherapy involves movement toward a goal (the patient's recovery) that is facilitated by a genuine volitional act—willed, decided, and executed in active volition between the patient and therapist, in which each participates in a specific manner. Precisely the same type of interaction appears to occur in "psychic healing" and Walker may have given science a clue as to the underlying subatomic mechanisms which allow "healing" to happen.

In applying Walker's ideas to illness, one could say that an organism in ill health has a high degree of bodily disorder. There are an unlimited number of ways of being unhealthy but relatively few ways of being healthy. So if we consider the organism, in a figurative way, as a wave function with a high probability of unhealthy states, one of the effects of a "healer" may be to supply information to the sick person's system.

This causes the "collapse" of the wave function to occur at another point—namely, that of health. This point would be characterized by a high degree of order. In effect, the consciousness of the "healer" may be providing information through its "hidden variables" to the healee. At the same time, the healee responds by stimulating the body's natural self-repair mechanisms.

In other words, Walker has used quantum theory to explain psi phenomena. And the authors of this book have demonstrated how Walker's theory can explain "psychic healing" phenomena without resorting either to "spirits" or to undiscovered forms of "energy."

Walker attempted to summarize his theory for Willis Kinnear in a book of readings on psychical research. Walker wrote:

Consciousness refers to the immediate inner experience—sensory, emotional, intellectual .... Despite the fundamental reality of ... our own conscious reality, it has not been incorporated into prior physical concepts ...

A new tack has been taken in which consciousness has been treated as something having innate reality with its own characteristics distinct from those of purely material bodies ... In this new understanding, consciousness exists as a distinct entity associated with certain physical processes occurring in the brain of our body ...

At the same time that the brain is processing sensory data, a separate process is going on interconnecting a small part of the brain's competing functions. About one ten-thousandth of all this computing is tied directly together by means of a process called quantum mechanical tunnelling ...

... This mechanism is not entirely physical and is not deterministic. But how can one talk about something like that and call it science? ... The remarkable fact is that not only can it be done, it has turned out to be necessary to introduce such ideas into physics ... We can show that arising from our conscious experience there exists a distinct entity identifiable with the concept of will ... that determines from moment to moment the state of our consciousness-brain association.

This flow amounts to only one ten-thousandth of our total conscious experience, one part in a hundred million of all the data processing carried out by the brain subconsciously, but it is exceptional in that it is at the same time linked to other conscious entities in the universe. This connecting link provides the basis for understanding in detail paranormal phenomena, including an understanding of psychokinesis ...

J. Z. Young, in *An Introduction to the Study of Man*, has written that the attempt to find general schemes to include particular things or events is evidently a rather common human tendency. Every human society has its ways of "understanding" particular natural events as "caused by" some member of a "spirit world."

Attempts of this sort usually fail for lack of economy and efficiency rather than of consistency or generality. The Walker theory is economic and efficient as well as consistent and general. Time will tell if this theory will explain the unusual events of "psychic healing."

Endnotes

[1] Even though the "Heisenberg formulation" was developed about the same time, the "Schrodinger formulation" is closer to the more fundamental character of the phenomenon.

[2] 10^4 is a monumental amount of "bits"; it stands for 10 multiplied times itself four times.

[3] Examples of images allegedly produced psychokinetically on film by Nina Kulagina appear in *The Energies of Consciousness*, edited by Stanley Krippner and Daniel Rubin.

www.ingramcontent.com/pod-product-compliance
Lightning Source LLC
Chambersburg PA
CBHW080552230426
43663CB00015B/2810